METROPOLITAN ANXIETIES

T0346588

This book is dedicated to the forgotten Irish who found rest but not dignity in the paupers' graves of Scotland

Metropolitan Anxieties
On the Meaning of the Irish Catholic Adventure in Scotland

MARK BOYLE
National University of Ireland, Maynooth

Routledge
Taylor & Francis Group

LONDON AND NEW YORK

First published 2011 by Ashgate Publishing

2 Park Square, Milton Park, Abingdon, Oxon OX14 4RN
711 Third Avenue, New York, NY 10017, USA

Routledge is an imprint of the Taylor & Francis Group, an informa business

First issued in paperback 2016

Copyright © 2011 Mark Boyle

Mark Boyle has asserted his right under the Copyright, Designs and Patents Act, 1988, to be identified as the author of this work.

All rights reserved. No part of this book may be reprinted or reproduced or utilised in any form or by any electronic, mechanical, or other means, now known or hereafter invented, including photocopying and recording, or in any information storage or retrieval system, without permission in writing from the publishers.

Notice:
Product or corporate names may be trademarks or registered trademarks, and are used only for identification and explanation without intent to infringe.

British Library Cataloguing in Publication Data
Boyle, Mark.
  Metropolitan anxieties : on the meaning of the Irish Catholic adventure in Scotland.
  1. Irish--Scotland--Ethnic identity. 2. Irish--Scotland--Religion. 3. Irish--Scotland--
  Social conditions. 4. Catholics--Scotland--Biography.
  I. Title II. Series
  305.8'91620411-dc22

Library of Congress Cataloging-in-Publication Data
Boyle, Mark.
  Metropolitan anxieties : on the meaning of the Irish Catholic adventure in Scotland / by
Mark Boyle.
      p. cm.
  Includes bibliographical references and index.
  ISBN 978-0-7546-3379-2 (hbk. : alk. paper) 1. Irish--Scotland--History. 2. Irish--
Scotland--Social conditions. 3. Immigrants--Scotland--History. 4. Catholics--Scotland--
History. 5. Families--Scotland--History. 6. Oral history--Scotland. 7. Collective
memory--Scotland. 8. Anti-Catholicism--Scotland--History. 9. Scotland--Ethnic relations.
10. Irish--Migrations--History. I. Title.
  DA774.4.I72B698 2011
  941.1'0049162--dc22

                                                                          2011009330

ISBN 13: 978-0-7546-3379-2 (hbk)
ISBN 13: 978-1-138-25170-0 (pbk)

Contents

**PART III   CARTOGRAPHICAL REFLECTION: METHOD AND
            DIALOGUE UNDER SCRUTINY**

List of Tables and Figures

Tables

Figures

Acknowledgements

Many times I was forced to conclude that this book would never see the light of day. Oral history testimonies were collected from members of the Irish Catholic community in Scotland in the period 2000–2002. The final manuscript was not completed until May 2011. The scale of the transcription processes and the volume of analyses undertaken was part contributor to the delay. A personal relocation from the University of Strathclyde in Glasgow to the National University of Ireland Maynooth in County Kildare in 2007 was also a factor. The quest to understand the complexities and nuances of the works of French philosopher, novelist and political activist Jean-Paul Sartre also undoubtedly frustrated speedy completion. In truth however, the delay in completing the work bears witness to the awesome sense of responsibility I have felt in being entrusted with people's life stories and serving as a guardian of precious fragments of knowledge and insights. To ask seriously the question of the meaning and intelligibility of the Irish Catholic adventure in Scotland is to make a most fundamental intervention in the story of this community. Eventually however, lest the sense of responsibility breed complete paralyses, there comes a time when it is essential to declare a reading of the archive. And in any event, in due course written transcripts and oral recordings will be made available which in themselves will serve as an important research resource. Through further scrutiny of this archive it will be possible to debate and correct the necessarily partial interpretations furnished here.

The work clearly could not be completed without the tremendous generosity of the 76 members of the Irish Catholic community in (the west of) Scotland who gave more than their time. Words cannot express the warmth, support, comradeship, and solidarity participants afforded the author in the period 2000–2002 in particular. Participants invited me with open arms into their homes, offered meals, tea and coffee, Tunnoch's tea cakes, blessings, holy water, and lucky charms, and shared intimate details of their lives which I had no right to be privileged to hear. It is no exaggeration to say that stories so moved me that on leaving participants' houses I was often deeply touched and on occasions emotionally exhausted. Above all else then, tribute needs to be paid to 'the cast', a towering community with enough collective wisdom to fill a dozen libraries over. Undoubtedly my efforts to capture their stories have fallen woefully short. And many will disagree with the sense I have made of particular biographies. But I hope this manuscript does sufficient justice to those who gave of their time and support that they feel the outcome on balance worthwhile and valuable.

Acknowledgements also go to the academic support apparatus I have drawn upon throughout the work. Previous colleagues at the University of Strathclyde in Glasgow, in particular Robert Rogerson, Graham Hollier, Michael Pacione, Guy

Baeten, Arthur McIvor and David Miller deserve particular mention for creating a convivial and encouraging mileu in which to work. Current colleagues at the National University of Ireland, Maynooth have also provided the spur which has allowed the work to be completed. In particular I am indebted to Rob Kitchin who besides being an inspirational colleague has proven to be a wonderful personal comrade, fellow traveller and confidant. Acknowledgements also go to Mary Gilmartin, Jim Walsh, Ronan Foley, Conor Murphy, John Sweeney, Dennis Pringle, Patrick Duffy, Gerry Kearns, Karen Till, Sean O'Rain, Chris Morash, Proinnsias Breathnach, and Brendan Gleeson, who have all helped along the way both directly and indirectly. Thanks also go to Mary Weld, Gay Murphy and Neasa Hogan for their administrative support, to Jim Keenan and Michael Bolger for cartographic and technical support, and to Interns David Martin and Gráinne Corrigan for updating the oral archive using digital technology. A raft of other colleagues from Ireland and beyond have encouraged various aspects of the work, at various stages, including Denis Linehan, Willie Jenkins, Breda Gray, Joe Bradley, Audrey Kobayashi, Tom Devine, and Christine Milligan. In particular I am indebted to Audrey Kobayashi (Kingston, Ontario) for serving as a 'guiding light' in the search for the merits of Jean Paul Sartre today.

Chapters in the book have not been published in any form save Chapter 2, 'Metropolitan anxieties: a critical appraisal of Sartre's theory of colonialism' which was co-written with Audrey Kobayashi and published in the *Transactions of the Institute of British Geographers* (TIBG) NS in 2011. I wish to thank Audrey Kobayashi, and the editor of TIBG NS Alison Blunt, for agreeing to allow the paper to be republished as a chapter in this book. Early outputs of the work have been presented orally and useful feedback obtained at the University of Lund (Sweden), University of Ulster (Magee College, Derry), York University (Toronto Canada), University of St Andrews (Scotland), and the University of Dundee (Scotland), at the Annual Meetings of American Geographers in New York, Los Angeles, New Orleans, and Chicago, at the Annual Conferences of the Royal Geographical Society (with the Institute of British Geographers) in London, at the Conference of Critical Geographers in Mexico City, and at the Anglo-French conference for Political Geographers in Reims, France. In addition, funding provided by the British Academy and University of Strathclyde Research and Development Fund facilitated transcription of the tapes, funding provided by ScotEcon, the Gebbie Legacy, and the National Institute of Regional and Spatial Analyses (NIRSA) assisted in the undertaking of analyses, and above all else, the awarding by the Levehulme Trust of a Leverhulme Research Fellowship created the space to substantially progress the writing up of the book. Finally, especial thanks go to Val Rose at Ashgate for her extraordinary patience and willingness to extend deadlines even though the excuses grew increasingly lame and for her advice on the title and the introduction.

Of course in the end, it is the immediate family supports that matter most. To my mother, thanks for inculcating a love of Donegal and its people and for keeping it light and breezy. In regard to my late father, I wish to pay tribute to his formidable and unclassifiable intellect, an intellect that I have failed to encounter in any academic setting. Expect the unexpected! To Anne-Marie thanks for forcing me to keep it real. To my brothers: Bryan; credit is due for teaching me to survive the vicissitudes of following Celtic FC in good times and bad, and Brendan the voyager; thanks for providing the global vista. To Mary and Eric, thanks for introducing me to the world of the Gallowgate and the Irish pubs of the East End of Glasgow. I also pay tribute to the luminous life and colourful personality of Stephen O'Brien, a friend who sadly passed away whilst this project was in maturation. And finally, and above all else, my deepest and most sincere thanks and love go to my wife Deborah and sons Patrick and Joseph who have suffered much to allow this book to be completed. They can scarcely believe how slow I write and why I agonise over sentences for hours if not days, especially so when they read them! I hope I do not live to regret the days I missed with you all to bring this study to fruition.

Here it is then, but do not stop praying to St Martha on a Tuesday night.

Maynooth, July 2011

Empire Exhibition, amusement park, Bellahouston Park, 1938. Glasgow is crowned second city of the British Empire (Courtesy of Glasgow City Archives and Special Collections)

Preface
Liberating Nausea

Something has happened to me: I can't doubt that anymore. It came as an illness does, not like an ordinary certainty, not like anything obvious. It installed itself cunningly, little by little: I felt a little strange, a little awkward, and that was all. Once it was established, it didn't move anymore, it lay low and I was able to persuade myself that there was nothing wrong with me, that it was a false alarm. And now it has started blossoming. I don't think the profession of historian fits a man for psychological analyses. In our work, we have to deal with simple feelings to which we give generic names such as Ambition and Interest. Yet if I had an iota of self knowledge, now is the time when I ought to use it. (Antoine Roquentin in *Nausea*, Sartre 1938: 13)

In many ways Jean-Paul Sartre's first novel *Nausea*, published in 1938, serves as an inspiration for this book. Regarded as a literary exposition of the philosophy of existentialism, *Nausea* charts the psychological dramas experienced by Antoine Roquentin in the fictional seaport of Bouville (taken to be Le Havre), as he comes to terms with the realisation that his existence precedes his essence, his freedom comes before his being. Roquentin struggles to put a name on his condition referring to it as radical vertigo, anguish, and dread of the absurdity and contingency of human existence, before finally apprehending it as *nausea*. Nausea derives from the profound recognition that people have a fundamental responsibility to determine how they exist in the world. I am thrown into the world in a random and meaningless way. Hell is other people: I come to know myself only through the look of others, the meaning of which I know because I too look. Nausea engulfs me when I come to grasp that it is 'I' and only 'I' who has responsibility for internalising or contesting the stultifying effects of oppressive objectifications, stereotypes, stigmatisations, and inscriptions. Whilst nausea most frequently energises a flight into bad faith, it is most productive when it is courted, embraced, and lived. Although 'man(sic) is a useless passion' he is condemned to be free and makes his true being by deciding and choosing.

This book takes nausea to be an important existential condition experienced by many who enter the public sphere in Scotland, and in particular in the city of Glasgow, as an Irish Catholic or a person of Irish Catholic heritage. Undoubtedly in the past, the public realm in Scotland has rarely been radically and equally open to the Irish Catholic community and disclosure of one's Irish Catholic heritage has often excited unwanted attention, elevated suspicion, and unwarranted scrutiny. This 'sensation of being seen' has its origins in Britain's long colonisation of Ireland and in manifestations, echoes, and mutations of a colonial gaze in the present within Scotland. Whilst being Irish Catholic in the public realm is to exercise the full authority of one's freedom, it is also to court a dizzying nausea and radical vertigo. Nausea motivates a ubiquitous desire to put one's head down and micro-manage exposure of one's heritage and culture. Lives are led in bad faith in order not to rock the boat. But in so far as it is a critical point of departure for action, bad faith is also the origin of a liberating quest to restore human dignity for those cowed by metropolitan fantasies of superiority. It is paralysing and generative in equal measure.

But crucially, the title 'Liberating Nausea' is also appropriated here in quite an alternative sense to pose a question of vital importance. Alterity has secreted a potent cultural category 'Irish Catholic in Scotland', a construct which demands continual attention and critical scrutiny. Newness has entered the world through this category and the many properties it conceals but has this category also bred a sense of cultural stases and perhaps even cultural myopia and narcissus? For some, the extraordinary persistence and virulence of the category Irish Catholic in Scotland has rendered it itself something of a problem. Critics, usually those seeking to deny that Scotland has proven a challenging environment for the Irish Catholic community to settle into, allege that an unhealthy obsession with the category has led to a self imposed estrangement from Scottish society and a wholly disproportionate sense of grievance. Those who invest in the category fail to realise that anti-Irish Catholic sentiment in Scotland was never that institutionalised, systematic or virulent and in any case such sentiment has waned through time to the point of irrelevance today. Nausea needs to courted once more to liberate migrants and descendants from the very cultural formations which they initially birthed, cultural formations which now threaten to become oppressive and stunting in themselves. Nausea needs to be liberated from the fruits of its own labours.

Of course in the politically volatile Paris of the 1950s and 1960s, an ageing Sartre was to discover Marx and to take more seriously the social and economic origins of bad faith, nausea, and personal projects. Any theory of human freedom needed to be a social theory of human freedom and human freedom now could only be achieved though collective action and not existential meditation, introspection or psychoanalysis. But Sartre's turn from existentialism to Existential Marxism led him not to a Marxist theory of human freedom which was based upon universal class struggle but instead to a search for historically grounded insights on potential pathways to revolutionary praxis. He chose to reject dogmatic and prefabricated social movements which ultimately imprisoned freedom and focused instead on species of socialism which foregrounded the freedom of the human person and not the tyrannical encrustations of a fossilised 'Party' or ethnic tribe or visceral nation-building project. Progressive movements risked lapsing into crippling monstrosities if they did not continually choose their futures. This search led him to valorise the work of so called groups in fusion; novel, hybridised, historically contingent, and endlessly original collectives which emerge from positions of subordination, marginalisation, and alterity.

This book argues that the Irish Catholic community in Scotland has practised a form of progressive tribalism and has existed for nearly two centuries in some ways as a Sartrean Group in Fusion. But its history has also included lapses into bad faith and metastases into regressive tribalism. Looking forward, I assert that the Irish Catholic community in Scotland is *condemned* to take *responsibility* for its adventure in Scotland. It cannot complain about estrangement from Scottish society because it alone is responsible for this estrangement. It has a chronic duty to police its cultural secretions and the social, political, economic, and cultural movements it has birthed to ensure that its tribalism remains cosmopolitan and progressive and not insular and regressive. Sartre's principal message to the Irish Catholic community in Scotland would be that nausea needs to liberate and be liberated. For Antoine Roquentin to court nausea in any meaningful sense was to radicalise a perpetual search for new beginnings. Perhaps Roquentin's discovery that real beginnings lie at the root of an authentic existence is one which ought to capture our attention more today:

> First of all the beginnings would have to be real beginnings. Alas! Now I can see so clearly what I wanted. Real beginnings, appearing like a fanfare of trumpets, like the first notes of a jazz tune, abruptly, cutting boredom short, strengthening duration; evenings among those evenings of which you say: 'I was out walking, it was an evening in May.' You are walking along, the moon has just risen, you feel idle, vacant, a little empty. And then all of a sudden you think: 'Something has happened.' It might be anything: a slight crackling sound in the shadows, a fleeting silhouette crossing the street. But this slight event isn't like the others: straight away you see that it is the predecessor of a great form whose outlines are lost in the midst and you tell yourself too: 'Something is beginning.' (Antoine Roquentin in *Nausea*, Sartre 1938: 59)

Chapter 1

Provincialising the Scotland's Secret Shame Debate: An Enquiry into the Meaning of the Irish Catholic Adventure in Scotland

I came to Scotland from County Mayo in 1936. I was a young girl of 20, full of life. We made our way through Ayrshire and up to Fife. I met my husband who was a Ganger, he was in charge of a group of Potato diggers, when I was working in the fields too. We got married in 1942. We worked on the Potatoes. I loved it. It took me a few days to get used to it. The worst thing was getting up awful early in the morning. You got up at about two or three o'clock in the morning. I thought I was hardly in bed sleeping. But you never said a word. You got up and got on with it. Once you were on your feet, you know first thing in the morning in the countryside on a sunny day in the summer, it was lovely. Some days you had it good, other days you didn't. But it was lovely. I enjoyed every minute of it. I loved it. I think Scotland is a lovely country. It's a beautiful country. But England I have no time for at all. (Interviewee 7)

My mother came here in 1946 just after the war. So there was still all those things about 'No Irish Need Apply' at that point. She worked as a District Nurse in the Health Service in Kinning Park. She was just telling me the other day about how ignorant and prejudiced the doctors could be and they were supposed to be the educated ones. The area was becoming quite mixed with Asian and Irish families staying there. The doctors would always pick out the Irish kids as they went through and would comment on how dirty they were and would tell the Nurses to watch themselves in inspection rooms in case they caught anything. It was all done innocently but that shows you how ingrained attitudes were. The Irish had nits in their heads as rule so watch yourself in there. (Interviewee 13)

My husband put his finger on it. We were just coming up to Derry when we were coming back from Ireland one weekend, and he said; 'I think I know why you all want to be back here. You have freedom. You're with your own people. There's no strain on you. You can be yourselves'. He said, 'I can see you physically relaxing. You don't need to think about what the next man is thinking about you'. And I think it is the opposite here. It's very frustrating for the kids as I think they feel we're forever saying 'oh don't do that', 'don't wear that', 'don't show anybody that'. (Interviewee 14)

I think in the long run my grandparents made the right choice in coming to Scotland. They certainly had a very hard life coming to a strange country with an entirely different culture and where they weren't really liked or well treated and only got the most menial of jobs. But as time went on things got better for them. They proved their worth and were fortunate to get better jobs and settle in one place. Their families certainly had better and more comfortable lives. And with each generation things have improved right down to my own family. Although I worked in the mill from when I was 14 years old, I was 26 when I got married and my husband had a good job as an engineering foreman in Babcocks. So we were comfortably well off and were fortunate to see our three sons graduate. I don't think we would have been any better off if my grandparents had gone to the United States. So I think it was a blessing for us that my grandparents came to Scotland. (Interviewee 27)

I would say what I've said rather frequently in the past, which is that we should say our morning and evening prayers to almighty God that he so ordained our lives that we moved to a country that subscribes to the Protestant ethic. And by an application of not dissimilar criteria we prospered. Do you feel you benefited from exposure to Scottish culture? Yes. In the same way you benefit from having a cold shower. It's not always pleasant. (Interviewee 44)

The mining village I was brought up in didn't have the same nonsense as they have here [in Glasgow]. The women next door was President of the *Eastern Star*, Mrs McKiddie, she actually made my sisters First Holy Communion dress. And we as kids used to get up early on a Saturday morning to watch the neighbours doing their little Orange parade in the village before the main parade. There was this sort of tolerance and of course they would be working in the same pit and everything. In the shipyards and the big factories bigotry I think was worse as people didn't necessarily know each other outside of work. But in any event for me it's not the guy from the housing estate who wears his 1690 tattoo that's the problem. I see the ones in the suits who have real influence as the ones who are deep down bitter. (Interviewee 53)

It was very hard for the Irish in Glasgow when the troubles broke out. I remember being in the Western Infirmary in the Day Unit having tests done and when I went in there were two women talking about the troubles. The nurse drew the curtain back and I could see them and they could see me and I said 'hello'. But they just ignored me and started talking about Southern Ireland and how bad the Irish were. I felt like sitting up and shouting. But it was when the troubles were really bad in 1969. Things were harder for the Irish in Scotland then and really you couldn't blame people. There were soldiers killed in Northern Ireland and you would hear how the IRA were involved. They didn't realise what effect their comments were having on people, the majority of folks, who were just as frightened as to where it was all going to end up as they were. (Interviewee 61b)

This book presents findings from a new oral history archive which the author collected between 2000 and 2002. This archive consists of 67 interviews with 76 members of the Irish Catholic community in Scotland, comprising first generation settlers through to fourth generation descendants. These interviews recount the multiple and complex journeys the Irish Catholic community took and continues to take, both to and within Scotland, and help to excavate this community's various and contradictory encounters with social, economic, political, and cultural alterity and belonging. Each interview was fully transcribed and has now been digitally enhanced for sound quality. It is intended that in time both the oral and the written archive will be deposited in a central location and will become an important research resource for those interested in studying the social and collective memories which have been produced and disseminated by the Irish Catholic community in Scotland. This book represents the first attempt to mine the archive and digest its significance but it is hoped that it will not be the last.

This archive was collected, collated, and analysed against the backdrop of a decade of heated public debate over the status of sectarianism and bigotry in contemporary Scotland. Controversy has fastened on the degree to which anti-Irish and anti-Catholic sentiment continues to wound, debilitate, and impede the lives of Irish Catholics and Scots with an Irish Catholic lineage, living particularly in the west of Scotland. The debate has been characterised by vigorous claims and counter claims over the enduring scale and impact of sectarianism and bigotry, whether anti-Irish and anti-Catholic sentiment continues to result in social, economic, cultural, and political discrimination and disadvantage, and the extent to which the Scottish Government ought to be doing something to combat remaining instances of intolerance. Some view allegations of discrimination and estrangement as paranoia or worse politically loaded; others regard lingering mentalities and residual attitudes as little more than a hangover from the past which will steadily peter out with time; whilst others again insist that the persistence of hostile assumptions and prejudices needs to be taken seriously.

To be clear, this book harbours no desire to make a contribution to the resolution of what has been labelled the 'Scotland's secret shame' debate. I take up no position on how sectarian or bigoted or discriminatory Scottish society has been to Irish Catholic immigrants and their descendants, past or present. Instead I approach the debate with an altogether different ambition. In fact, the existence of bitter dispute over the extent to which people with Irish Catholic heritage belong or do not belong in modern Scotland presents a remarkable, geographical, anthropological, sociological, and political puzzle. That such different claims as to the importance and virulence of sectarianism and bigotry exist in the first place is itself a crucial object of enquiry. It immediately suggests that the community under discussion is not easily captured. Is this a product of a deficiency in the scale of social scientific surveys of this community? Will a piling up of additional research findings resolve the matter? Or is debate being frustrated by a more profound limit to knowledge? Arguably, the most interesting question which the Scotland's secret shame debate has provoked, a question which thus far has failed to generate a worthy answer, is the following: *is the Irish Catholic encounter with Scotland intelligible and if so what is the nature of this intelligibility?*

Broadly speaking, two principal explanations of Irish Catholic alterity from Scotland have been presented: one which might be said to be a product of professional and institutional social scientific enquiry and which has sought to defend establishment Scotland; the other which might be appropriately described as derivative of radical and critical social scientific enquiry and which has sought to place a spotlight on institutional sectarianism and bigotry in mainstream Scottish society.

According to commentators from the first camp attention has to be given to the exaggerated sense of paranoia which exists within the Irish Catholic community. The Irish Catholic community has contrived to conjure up a debate about its marginalised position within Scottish society as a buffer against the growing authority of the Scottish Parliament in Edinburgh. Fearing that further devolution from Westminster might lead to the formation of a 'New Stormont' in Edinburgh, the Irish Catholic community has begun the process of staking its territory and defending its interests. Specifically, anxiety about the potential loss of public funding for Catholic schools is what has animated claims of discrimination and bigotry. Social scientific surveys of occupation, income, health, crime, educational attainment, etc, prove that there exists no systematic bias or inequality in opportunity. The debate over Scotland's secret shame then has no rooting in objective conditions but reflects one community's exaggerated fear of the implications of the new political dispensation for Scotland.

According to commentators from the second camp, Scotland needs to be thought of as a location where a number of indigenous and establishment constituencies have enjoyed, and to some extent still do enjoy, a certain vista on the Irish Catholic community; a privilege of seeing without being seen. The debate over Scotland's shame has very real origins in objective conditions. Irish Catholics have been treated as indigestible because of their race, nationality, class, politics and religion. The troubles which flared up in Northern Ireland from the late 1960s undoubtedly contributed to a stirring of latent passions. But more importantly, a series of locally specific conditions have conspired to reproduce tensions and consolidate a bizarre longevity to a cultural politics which has long ceased to be important in other British cities. What manifests itself as an anachronistic residue elsewhere continues to excite tensions in a very live way in Scotland. Those who deny the pervasive and lingering presence of anti-Irish and anti-Catholic sentiment in Scottish society are living in denial.

The chief purpose of the book is to develop and apply a novel theoretical framework through which the question of the intelligibility of the Irish Catholic encounter with Scotland might be best handled. I submit that to understand public disputation over sectarianism, bigotry, and discrimination in contemporary Scotland it is first necessary to recognise the seminal and pivotal importance of Britain's long and troublesome colonisation of Ireland. The British Empire and the Irish diaspora share a complex history of intersection and co-constitution.

The British imperial project and the Irish diaspora have persistently met in the most unlikely of locations around the globe, including in Ireland, the United States, the United Kingdom, Canada, Australia, New Zealand, and Argentina, and have constituted Anglo-Irish relations anew in each case. Points of confluence are most clearly evidenced in the case of Irish migration to the United Kingdom and in my case Scotland, where former colons now dwell as diasporeans in a former metropolitan heartland (Delaney 2007).

When framed in this way it becomes possible to bring the Scotland's shame debate into conversation with recent thinking in Postcolonial Studies regarding the very possibility of searching for the intelligibility or meaning in history of subaltern or colonised populations. To enquire seriously into the sense which is to be made of the ongoing claims of Irish Catholic alterity and estrangement from Scotland is to enquire seriously into the status of theoretical practices and modes of sociological knowing which are deposits of British colonial history and its historical and cultural legacies, mutations and contemporary manifestations. I take cognisance of the pervasive and debilitating effects in the Scotland's secret shame debate of what might termed *metrocentricism*, a practice which is predicated upon an insufficiently reflexive commitment to the superiority of particularly metropolitan forms of social scientific practice and universal theorising. I offer the claim there is a need to provincialise all bodies of scholarship which assert proprietorial control and authority over the correct interpretation of the Irish Catholic encounter with Scotland. I cast suspicion on all voices in the debate who claim to know the truth about the experiences and biographies of a community which bears the stamp of a complex colonial history and which as a consequence defies easy apprehension and capture. I question the wisdom of those who display a certain confidence that the meaning and telos of such a community can be painted in a few broad brush strokes.

I hypothesise that those who refuse to recognise the importance of alterity, and its ugly manifestations in sectarianism and bigotry, in the making of the Irish Catholic community in Scotland, and many do so in good faith, in all sincerity, and with the utmost integrity, are so embedded in the intellectual residues and social scientific practices stamped with the legacy of British colonial history that they are incapable of denaturalising and decentring these residues and practices. Across the past decade, in the worst moments the instrumental social scientific traditions of the metropole have arguably served more to mystify and obfuscate than to reveal and explain. But crucially I insist that metrocentricism is equally problematic for critical and radical social enquiry and not just establishment or professional social science. Even within critical literature, there is a growing awareness of the colonising tendencies of apparently radical and progressive theory. Critiques of metrocentrism, it turns out, may themselves be deeply metrocentric. Those who assert that the cultural history of the Irish Catholic community in Scotland is in important ways a product of institutional sectarianism and bigotry also need to reflect upon the reifications of metrocentric ontology they reproduce when making this kind of claim.

One of the most disappointing features of the Scotland's secret shame debate for instance, has been the scramble to claim legitimate sovereignty over what knowledge counts and what does not. For some academics in particular, the fact that many who are most vocal within the Irish Catholic community are not social scientists but instead artists, musicians, football commentators, and literary critics, has been taken as evidence of their lack of qualification to enter the debate. This defence of the supremacy of certain forms of social scientific knowledge is potentially very misleading and unhelpful. Recently, Michael Burawoy (2005) has offered a sociological reading of the production, circulation, legitimation, and consumption of four kinds of social scientific knowledge, which he terms, 'professional', 'policy', 'public', and 'critical' sociology respectively (Figure 1.1). For Burawoy the key is not to assert the supremacy of any one type of sociological enquiry but instead to appreciate that each method produces knowledge and grasps at the world differently so as to furnish distinctive insights; insights which are worthy and legitimate within, but limited and defined by, their own terms of reference. Perhaps those who argue that anti-Irish Catholic sentiment is institutionalised in Scotland base their truth claims on forms of critical and public sociological reasoning whilst those who deny the existence of pervasive sectarianism and bigotry base their truth claims on forms of professional and policy sociological reasoning. Either way it would seem unnecessarily self limiting to fail to appreciate the virtues and vices of different ways of capturing and apprehending the elusive history of this most complex community.

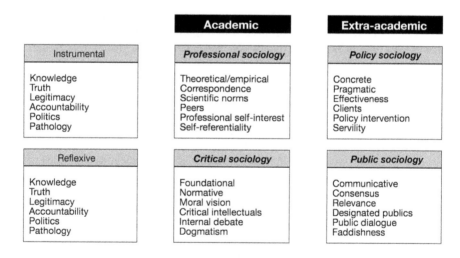

Academic		Extra-academic
Instrumental	***Professional sociology***	***Policy sociology***
Knowledge Truth Legitimacy Accountability Politics Pathology	Theoretical/empirical Correspondence Scientific norms Peers Professional self-interest Self-referentiality	Concrete Pragmatic Effectiveness Clients Policy intervention Servility
Reflexive	***Critical sociology***	***Public sociology***
Knowledge Truth Legitimacy Accountability Politics Pathology	Foundational Normative Moral vision Critical intellectuals Internal debate Dogmatism	Communicative Consensus Relevance Designated publics Public dialogue Faddishness

Figure 1.1   Division of sociological labour

I propose that to date the problem with the Scotland's secret shame debate has been with the ways in which the problem of alterity and estrangement has been framed. I call attention to the situated production of all academic, activist, policy, and public vistas on the Irish Catholic adventure in Scotland and offer an approach to the interrogation of this community which is alert to the challenges which the act of framing *per se* presents. Any search for a definitive theoretical and/or empirical resolution to this debate, critical or revisionist, might justifiably attract the criticism of metrocentricism. Importantly again, attributions of metrocentricism must be levelled *equally* at those constituencies who deny there is a problem in Scotland *and* those constituencies who argue that sectarianism and bigotry are institutionalised in Scottish life. Both believe in a fundamental sense that they are better and indeed best qualified to decipher the legibility of the Irish Catholic encounter with Scotland. The challenge is to recognise the value of different modes of sociological enquiry and sociological knowledge whilst resisting the tendency to claim sovereign supremacy for any one.

How are we to progress? It is the view of this author that it is impossible to even approach the question of the meaning of the Irish Catholic adventure in Scotland without developing a framework that is alert to five basic fundamentals:

- The central importance of the history of asymmetric and colonial Anglo-Irish relations in the mediation of the Irish Catholic encounter with Scotland.
- The recognition that Irish Catholics have experienced alterity and belonging from and to Scottish society in wide variety of ways, mediated in part by date of migration, place of origin, location of destination, generation, age, gender, class, and sexuality.
- The awareness that Irish Catholics have chosen to create and bear responsbility for creating a particular type of Irish Catholic community which is distinctive from Irish Catholic communities in Ireland and in other parts of the diaspora.
- The registering that many of the most impressive cultural practices (from everyday events to social and political movements) which the Irish Catholic community has deposited have been those which have been co-authored with progressive communities in Scotland,
- The importance of monitoring and critiquing anti-racist racism within the Irish Catholic community itself and of holding in tension the workings of anti-colonial and Irish nationalist impulses.

With these as guiding precepts, the purpose of this book is to harness the complex and rich theory of colonialism which French philosopher, political activist, and novelist Jean Paul Sartre developed and struggled over, to venture a qualified and partial interpretation of the Irish Catholic experience of Scotland. In unexpected ways, Sartrean Existentialism, and laterally Sartrean Existential Marxism, continues to animate and influence theorists and activists interested in imperialism, colonialism, anti-colonialism, decolonisation, postcolonialism and neo-colonialism. It is time his work was dusted down and considered anew. According to Anne Buttimer (1993) the dramas of western humanism are best captured in Promethean mythology in which the liberation cry of humankind unfolds in a trilogy, beginning with *Phoenix*, when new life emerges with vitality promising a new beginning, progressing through *Faust* when such life ossifies into a stifling and rigid organised institution, and ending with *Narcissus* the moment when self perpetuating bureaucracies generate internal self-critique and a context is created for Phoenix to reassert its presence. In developing a theory of colonialism, Sartre's existential roots draw him back to Prometheus but mediated by his turn for inspiration to Marxism, his Phoenix, Faust, and Narcissus bear the titles 'seriality', 'fusion', and 'metastases', or 'masses', 'spontaneity', and 'Party'. I will modify Sartre's trilogy slightly and attempt to characterise the history of the Irish Catholic encounter with Scotland in terms of a circular mutation between groupings or collectives which I will title masses, spontaneity, and tribe.

But the charge of metrocentricism is one that any application of Sartre's theory of colonialism to particular and concrete colonialisms needs to wrestle with. Histories of capitalism and colonialism will only ever be partially captured by Sartrean theoretical constructs, formulations and postulations. Moreover, arguably the limits to Sartrean thought manifests its visibility most clearly when his theoretical artillery is brought to bear on the question of the dramatic lives and times of (once) colonised populations who now live in diaspora in a (former) metropole. In these instances it is especially clear that something more is required if local, contextually specific, idiographic and contingent cultural responses to territorial annexation and resistance are to be properly grasped. The entanglement of a multiplicity of biographies in diaspora spaces like Scotland is arguably best conceptualised as simultaneously mediated by what Brah (1996) refers to as multiple modalities of power. Brah (1996) invokes the concept of multi-axial power to refer to the manner in which different modalities of power (principally, class, race, gender, ethnicity, nationalism, generation and sexuality) intersect in diasporic spaces. Diasporic communities are organised around different modalities of power which in the course of settlement are inserted into prevailing modalities of power in indigenous communities. Complex patterns of 'insiderness' and 'outsiderness', belonging and estrangement, have emerged. This thesis has found its way into literature on the Irish diaspora in the work of a number of feminist scholars and scholars interested in the gendered nature of the migration experience (Walter 2001; Gray 2000, 2004; Hickman 1999, 2000; Hickman et al. 2005; Mac An Ghaill 2001; and Nash 2004, 2008). It is time now to widen its contribution.

Chakrabarty (2007) offers a theory of two histories as a way of addressing metrocentricism within Postcolonial Studies. History 1 is based upon a particular universal telos, for instance Marx's reading of capitalism, whilst History 2 is constitutive of numerous other tendencies in history that do not necessarily follow the eschatology of Marx's capital. Chakrabarty (2007) proposes that postcolonial theorists should resist the temptation to prioritise History 2 over History 1, by say avoiding the abstract theories of western social science in favour of recovering pristine subaltern histories. Instead the critical agenda is to explore the productive tensions which exist between History 1 and History 2. History 2 has the potential to arrest the thrust of capitalism's universal history and help it to find local ground whilst History 1 has the ability to assist History 2 to render its wider location meaningful. The preferred method then is to run both histories concurrently, understanding them to be distinctive but mutually enriched through dialogue.

Chakrabarty's two histories approach goes some way to grasping and resolving the problem which disputation over Scotland's secret shame presents. But this framework is rooted ultimately in Indian contributions to Postcolonial Studies. Of course there can be no denying the ability of Indian scholarship to capture thinking within Postcolonial Studies more generally. But there are limits to its wider application. The Irish Catholic community in Scotland occupies a unique postcolonial location in at least four distinctive senses: a) The British empire, not least as it has interfaced with Ireland, provides a specific moment in the history of colonisation; b) dwelling in diaspora, concern is with the grating together of the coloniser and the colonised in the metropolitan heartland itself rather than in the colonial field; c) unlike other colonised populations who now reside in diaspora in metropolitan cores, anti-Irish racism serves as a form of racism between two white populations and skin colour is less important, and; d) whilst the conflict in the North of Ireland which erupted in the late 1960s has served to keep the story of British control over Ireland live and current, the cultural politics of colonialism which plays out in Scotland is best seen as an anachronistic and mutant derivative of a past history. It would be foolish to approach the Irish Catholic community in Scotland as a subaltern population, equivalent to anything which might be found in India, whose logic and telos is fundamentally and incommensurably other.

My chosen path is to harness insights which might be gleaned from the geographical lexicon and to promote the idea of writing two different histories of the Irish Catholic adventure in Scotland, on this occasion *topological* and *topographical* rather than History 1 and History 2, whilst paying attention to the *cartographical* tools which allow these histories to be brought into dialogue. These three terms, topology, topography, and cartography have a specific meaning in the context of geographical representation and spatial mapping. But they are portable and have pertinence when thinking through the historical geographies of Irish migration to and settlement into Scotland. In this context they can be taken to mean the following:

> *Topological historiography*: historiography which searches for the anatomical structure, rules of behaviour, inner logic, and intelligibility of the Irish Catholic community in Scotland. Beneath the cacophony resides a symphony which can be captured using the methods posited by mathematical calculus. Topological framings take refuge in the muscular arms of strong and organised analytical frameworks, nomothetic pattern seeking, theoretical inscription, and conceptual schemas.
>
> *Topographical historiography*: historiography which abandons itself to a detailed description of the unique contours, idiosyncratic turns and twists, nooks and crannies, knolls and depressions, and happenstance anarchy and

busy chaos which mark the Irish Catholic adventure in Scotland. The rich local, unique, detailed, and contingent facets of this community can only be explored through embodied practices which make full use of the five senses.

Cartographical reflection; the moment when the different mapping techniques which have been used to represent topological and topographical histories are placed under heightened critical scrutiny. Cartographic reflection considers the contributions which different representational meshes or coordinate system or legends or symbolic taxonomies make to the brokering of dialogue between topological and topographical historiography.

The purpose of this book then is to bring Sartre's theory of colonialism (Topology) into productive tension with the rich and complex historical geography of the Irish Catholic adventure in Scotland (topography), using the methodological techniques provided by Sartre's own progressive-regressive method and the oral history method (cartography) to broker the dialogue. These three geographical metaphors constitute my chosen means of holding in tension a desire to render intelligible the complex experiences of the Irish Catholic community in Scotland whilst resisting the seduction of metrocentric over-determinations of this intelligibility. In putting these ideas to work I am explicitly claiming that metrocentric theories share similar strengths and weaknesses to topological abstractions, that the Irish Catholic encounter with Scotland has similar complexity and detail as topographic landscapes, that the challenge of using metropolitan theory to render intelligible the Irish Catholic experience in Scotland is akin to the challenge of facilitating dialogue between topological and topographical representations, and that 'cartography' is a useful metaphor to foreground when thinking through how topology and topography can be brought into different kinds of conversations through different mediators or translators or brokers. Such a framework would appear to be more attuned to the specific colonial encounter I am studying here and I offer it as a potential supplement to scholarship within subaltern studies more generally which is seeking new ways to cast and apprehend relations between European modernity and its continuing theoretical contributions and colonial others with stories which demand radically alternative modes of narration.

It will be apparent by now that this book does not seek to capture the experiences of all Irish migrants settling into Scotland. Between a quarter and a third of the estimated 500,000 Irish migrants who settled in Scotland in the period from the late 1840s to the late 1920s were of the Protestant faith (Walker 1991, more generally see Akenson 1992, 1993). Insofar as they occupy a structurally different relationship with Irishness and Britishness, and identify themselves as Irish only in a qualified and specific way, this community did not form part of the present study. This exclusion is not an oversight or yet another selective claiming of Irishness. Instead, it is a recognition of the fact that 'Irish/Ulster Protestants' living in Scotland have had a different experience of the country than 'Irish Catholics'. I submit that the search for the meaning of the Irish/Ulster Protestant encounter with Scotland in history is incommensurable with the search for the meaning of the Irish Catholic encounter with Scotland in history. There are laudable reasons to draw more inclusive boundaries around the Irish community, but there are also vital analytical reasons for recognising the different experiences of both communities too.

But even this is vague and it is important to clarify how the category 'Irish Catholic community' in Scotland is used in this book. For ease of narration this complex construct is cited without persistent qualification and defence. It is true that few people living in Scotland with an Irish Catholic ancestry continue to define themselves as essentially 'Irish' or Catholic, at least in any simple way. Critics therefore point to the futility of the concept, lamenting it as a referent without a clear object. But surely these critics cannot be serious in expecting the idea to be taken literally. The category Irish Catholic in Scotland cannot adequately be mapped onto Irish-born residents who now live in Scotland or people with an Irish heritage who now live in Scotland. It is not a category with an essential referent or clearly defined object but instead a 'hyper-real' construct; a flag around which people gravitate, albeit to different degrees. It has the same status as concepts such as 'orientalism' or 'the west' or 'whiteness', it does not map neatly on to any empirically defineable empirical population; but like these categories it does not lack tremendous power because it is ambiguous and chaotic. It will be a central role of the book to try to figure out who the Irish Catholic community in Scotland are and who they have become. It is for this reason that I begin the substantive section of the book (Chapter 4) with an explicit reflection on the journey the category Irish Catholic in Scotland has taken as it has become transplanted into Scotland and germinated in new directions.

It should also be understood that the archive was collected before the spectacular property crash and associated banking crises, fiscal meltdown, and deep economic recession, which has been visited upon Ireland from 2007. The oral testimonies were in fact generated in the midst of the preceding roar of the Celtic Tiger economy which boomed from 1993 to 2007. The archive and by implication this book cannot therefore comment on the present crises and its implications for the story of the Irish Catholic community in Scotland and for diasporic engagements with Ireland. Moreover it is clear that emigration, the historic barometer of the health of the Irish economy, has once again commenced and once again threatens to blight the country's demographic profile. It is unlikely that Scotland will be a chosen destination for many migrants who seem to be casting their aspirations more towards Australia and Canada. But Irish migration to Scotland will certainly increase in the next two or three years and will create a new Irish Catholic community in Scotland with a new and fresh story. This is clearly a group that future additions and extensions of the archive might productively focus upon.

The remainder of the book is organised around three sections containing eight chapters. In section 1, the virtues and vices of topological readings of the cultural politics of colonialism are examined. In Chapter 2 Sartre's theory of colonialism is outlined and considered. In Chapter 3, a provincialisation of positions and counter positions in the Scotland's secret shame debate is then ventured. In section 2, attention then turns to the stories the Irish Catholic community tells itself about its travails in Scotland – this will form the basis of my topographical historiography. A methodological prologue first introduces the progressive regressive method and the oral history archive. Chapters 4 to 8 then focus upon five central stories which circulate within Irish Catholic families, addressing respectively: *nationality* – senses of belonging and attachments to Ireland and Scotland, *disaporic imaginings of home* – including the romaticisation of Ireland as a wonderland; *politics* – the virtues and vices of Irish nationalism and anti-imperialist struggles; *culture* – Scottish hostility towards Irish cultural traditions, including and in particular Roman Catholicism; and *class* – socio-economic discrimination and comparative disadvantage. Finally, in Chapter 9 the benefit and disbenefits of bringing Sartre's theory of colonialism into conversation with the Irish Catholic encounter with Scotland will be critically scrutinised. Here the progressive regressive method and the oral history method, will be placed under scrutiny with respect to their capacities to broker fruitful dialogue between topological and topographical mappings

PART I
Topological Mappings
and their Limits

Chapter 2

Metropolitan Anxieties: A Critical Appraisal of Sartre's Theory of Colonialism[1]

Introduction

Since the publication of Said's *Orientalism* in 1978, Geography and Postcolonial Studies have combined to excavate the geopolitical imaginaries and global projections which 'Europe' ('the West') mobilised and continues to mobilise to legitimate colonial adventures, build hegemonic projects and manufacture consent (Said 1978). Moreover Postcolonial Studies has stimulated Anglo-American Geography itself to reflect upon its own emergence in and through empire and by encouraging a historicising and relativising of geographical imaginations spawned from within professional and institutional wings of the discipline has sought to raise awareness of the complex ways in which Anglo-American Geography has intermeshed with histories of colonialism and empire. Collectively, this body of work has effectively and critically deconstructed European ways of imagining, demonising, and belittling other, non-European, and past and present colonised societies.

Nevertheless, as revealed in the proliferation of such mantras as 'unthinking Eurocentrism', 'history without a centre', and 'provincialising Europe', within Postcolonial Studies, there is now a well established wariness that in spite of its professed critical and radical ambitions postcolonial theory itself might be open to the charge that it too is guilty of interpreting the history and culture of non European societies principally through European frames of reference. Whilst aspiring to a decentring of the sovereign supremacy assumed by the European geographical imagination, postcolonial theory, it seems, continues to fall prey to a certain kind of *Eurocentrism* or *metrocentrism*, defined here as a set of theoretical practices predicated upon an insufficiently reflexive commitment to the superiority of particularly European ways of rendering the world intelligible. Postcolonial theory, it is feared, remains dogged by a certain Eurocentric and colonial mentality.

One limit of postcolonial theory stems from its reification of conceptual frameworks which betray specifically European treatments of time and space. Chakrabarty labels these treatments 'historicism', defined as a 'mode of thinking about history in which one assumed that any object under investigation retains a degree of unity of conception throughout its existence and attains a full expression

1   This chapter has been co-authored by Audrey Kobayashi (see Acknowledgements).

through a process of development in secular historical time' (Chakrabarty 2007: 11). Postcolonial theory asserts proprietorial control and authority over the right to apprehend the meaning of all concrete colonialisms and anti-colonialisms. Postcolonial theory gathers together a variety of different territorial annexations, labels them collectively as 'colonialism', 'imperialism', and 'neo-colonialism', frames them as instances of a singular universal process, and explains them with reference to an overarching master narrative. In so doing it sabotages its capacity to render legible the trajectory of territorial dispossessions and acquisitions, resistances and counter insurgencies which might in reality be unique, particular, and specific.

How to handle the colonising tendencies of postcolonial theory has emerged as a central concern for postcolonial scholars, especially within Indian contributions to postcolonial scholarship where the charge of metrocentricism has been particularly and forceably articulated. Spivak (1981, 1988) of course has commented upon the incommensurability of *Western theory* and *non-Western subalterns* and questioned whether radically marginalised and disenfranchised (Indian) women in particular might ever speak to or more accurately be heard by Western audiences. More recently Chakrabarty (2007) has proposed a two theories of colonialism approach which explores productive tensions between History 1 and History 2; where History 1 is based upon universal historical logic for instance Marx's reading of capitalism, whilst History 2, is constitutive of numerous other tendencies in history that do not necessarily follow the telos of capital. Meanwhile and with specific respect to South America, Mignola (1995) has placed the 'grammar of decoloniality' under scrutiny and championed the importance of social movements which emerge from forms of 'border thinking' which refuse both European coloniality and European modernity. Meanwhile Cooper (2005) has advocated a celebration of a 'politics of difference' which foregrounds colonialism's variety of cultures, the diversity of colonial and imperial strategies, the material geographies of annexation and control that result, variations in the form and strategies of anti-colonial movements and resistances, and geographically differentiated experiences of decolonisation and independence.

A key weakness of projects which seek to identify, critique, and respond to metrocentricism within postcolonial theory is the assumption that to a meaningful degree European ways of apprehending the world are largely coherent and monolithic. In historicising and relativising Eurocentric scholarship critical scholars often gloss over important spatial and temporal variations in European theoretical framings and practices (Withers 2007). In fact the counter claim that different manifestations of European modernity have given birth to different traditions of postcolonial theory provides both Geography and Postcolonial Studies with a new impetus for dialogue (for a review of dialogue to date see Sidaway 2000, Blunt and McEwan 2002, Minca 2003, Nash 2004, Pickles 2005, McEwan 2008, Kearns 2009, and Pollard et al. 2009). There is a pressing need to write historical geographies of theories of colonialism which at once interrogate, critique, and provincialise Eurocentric framings of the world, whilst at the same time take seriously the range of different and complex theoretical projects and practices which have emerged in different metropolitan locations and at different times.

More specifically, now is an opportune moment to better understand the situated production of treatments of time and space, especially as these treatments bear on theories of colonialism, at different times and in different places in Europe's emergence, mutation, and decline. Of course this project has occupied the attention of Massey (2005) who has sought to excavate from European modernity, alongside dominant species of historicism, treatments of time and space which approach space as a progenitor of history rather than an instantaneous freeze frame or simple slice through temporal processes. There is an urgent need to further develop Massey's archaeology of formulations of space and time within European modernity whilst at the same time critically evaluating how these formulations have both underpinned and in turn have been constituted by metropolitan apprehensions of the colonial problem. The objective is not to make the case for a revalorising of theories of colonialism produced and circulated from a European vista but instead to scrutinise, qualify, specify, and ruminate on the circumstances, conditions, terms, and bases under which such theories might offer insights which are meaningful, useful, and progressive.

Postcolonial Studies is customarily traced to the foundational works of Fanon, Memmi, Du Bois, Gramsci, and Said, translated and amplified by among others Bhabha, bell hooks, Spivak, Gilroy, and Young. In contrast, the seminal role played by French philosopher, novelist, and political activist Jean-Paul Sartre (1905–80) has been largely overlooked and obfuscated (Majumdar 2007). This neglect has proven fatal as for some the charge that postcolonial theory remains wedded to metrocentric theoretical constructs must ultimately be traced to Sartre. According to Werhs for instance, 'the dominant conceptual frameworks of postcolonial theory remain tethered to assumptions embedded in the first form of anti-colonial theory to assume a major role in western intellectual history, that of Jean-Paul Sartre and his associates' (Werhs 2003: 763). Likewise for Young (2001: VII), 'while postcolonial theory customarily traces its overt intellectual and political origins through more recent theoretical developments back to Fanon, Memmi, Du Bois, Gramsci, and Marx, the historical as well as the theoretical significance of Sartre's role and influence remains undervalued and unexamined'.

The purpose of this chapter is to rescue Sartre from critics who are too quick to indict his shadow as a significant point of origin of postcolonial theory's general inability to make sense of the histories of societies which dwell beyond the core. I seek to frame Sartre's theory of colonialism against the backdrop of a particular brand of twentieth-century French and in particular Parisian intellectual and political life, consumed with the future of Marxism. I contend that Sartre's imbrication in fierce struggles over the status of Marxism led him to a theory of colonialism which contested and rethought rather than submitted to and sealed metrocentric fetishisations of historicism. I contend that Sartre's philosophical commitment to a historicised phenomenology of existence as spatial lies at the root of his departure from historicism. For Sartre, conceptions of space and time vary as colonial projects unfold and these conceptions play a central role in the rise and fall of such projects My mission is to use Sartre, struggles within the Parisian academy, and twentieth-century French colonial politics, to clarify the case for and against criticising Sartrean thought as metrocentric and therein to build an argument in favour of heightening awareness of the variegated forms of European modernity and the variegated theoretical enterprises these forms have secreted.

  This chapter is divided into four sections. Sections one to three sequentially build, illustrate, and question the claim that Sartre's postcolonial theory serves in important ways as a debilitating *entrée* for postcolonial studies. Throughout, my intention is to locate and situate Sartre's thinking on colonialism against the backdrop of an intellectually, politically, and militarily turbulent twentieth-century Paris. In section one I argue that Sartre's interest in colonialism was motivated by a concern to rescue what he viewed as an authentic Marxism from its deviant, tyrannical, fossilised, and crystalline secretion in Stalinist Russia and to find a new basis for Marxist historical teleology. In the second section, I examine Sartre's political writings and activism and identify themes that have come to be recognised as Sartrean universals. In the third section I argue that at a key moment in his intellectual journey Sartre rejected historicism and recast the theory of colonialism to be a theory of 'totalising without totalisation'. In the final section I argue that Sartre's theory of colonialism constitutes and is constitutive of a particular theory of spatiality, which permits him to approach time as radically open to newness.

The purpose of Sartre's theory of colonialism: Sartre's intellectual journey from Existentialism to Existential Marxism

Sartre's two principal philosophical works were *Being and nothingness* (first published in 1943) and the *Critique of dialectical reason* – hereinafter to be referred to as the '*Critique*'). *Being and nothingness*, of course, continues to stand as the definitive outline of existentialism; the *Critique of dialectical reason*, Sartre's Marxist work, by contrast, is only now getting the recognition it deserves. Although comprising one single project, the *Critique* in fact encompasses three different 'books' and two different 'volumes'. *The Problem of method* was first published in 1957 (first translated into English in 1964) and subsequently reappeared as an introduction to Volume 1 of the Critique. The theory of practical ensembles, which made up the body of Volume 1, was first published in 1960 (first translated into English in 1976). Volume 2 of the critique, titled *The intelligibility of history*, was first published posthumously by Arlette Elkaïm-Sartre in 1985 (first translated into English in 1991). The entire project remained unfinished and it has to be remembered that Volume 1, and especially Volume 2, had to be heavily edited before publication.

  In one of his most celebrated passages in *Being and nothingness*, Sartre (1943: 59) ponders the performance of a waiter in a café. What, Sartre muses, is this waiter 'playing at': 'We need not watch long before we can explain it; he is playing at being a waiter in a café. There are indeed many precautions to imprison a man (sic) in what he is, as if he lives in perpetual fear that he might escape from it, that he might break away and suddenly elude his condition' (Sartre 1943: 59). From this apparently banal example Sartre comes to frame alienation in terms of the twin concepts of nausea and bad faith, the pillars of his existentialist philosophy. By nausea Sartre means the profound sense of anguish, vertigo, and terror that people feel when they come to glimpse the contingency and absurdity of their existence and the awesome responsibility they have by dint of their absolute freedom. Unable to bear this burden, human beings forsake 'being for themselves' and become 'beings for others', and shelter in the safer waters of bad faith.

By the time he came to write the *Critique*, Sartre had undergone a transition; from a philosopher of human freedom to an activist intellectual concerned with social and political critique and action. *Being and nothingness* had established the conditions under which human beings initiate relations of alienation and projects searching for freedom. But freedom now needed to be more firmly founded in the social; it could never be realised at the level of the individual through existential psychoanalysis, deep individual meditation, or self mastery and could only be addressed by social and political movements capable of changing underlying social and economic structures; in our age capitalism. Recognising the importance of his internment in a prisoner of war camp in France under German occupation, Ronald Aronson dates Sartre's conversion to the early 1940s and characterises it as a somewhat drawn out affair:

> In slow, definitive stages, between 1940 and 1957, Sartre first became committed to political activism, to socialism, to developing an integration of thought, writing and action, to building a non communist democratic social movement, to close relations with the communist party and the Soviet Union, to using Marxism as a tool of analyses, and then in *Search for a method* and the *Critique*, to Marxism as a Philosophy. (Aronson 1987: 236)

Sartre himself identified his 1947 book on *Humanism and terror* as the critical moment of transition. It was during this period that he also published *Materialism and revolution* (1946) and *What is literature?* (1947), two key texts announcing a radical departure from (although not a repudiation of) *Being and nothingness*. By 1952, and prompted by the decision of the French government to suppress the French Communist Party in the wake of anti-NATO riots in Paris, Sartre wrote *The Communists and peace*, in which he 'swore to the bourgeoisie a hatred which would only die with me.' (Sartre 1969: 128). These works were the precursor to *The problem of method* and finally, in the late 1950s, *The Critique of dialectical reason* itself (for an extended mapping of Sartre's transition see Fatouros 1965, Poster 1975, Chiodi 1976, Craib 1976, Lawler 1976, McBride 1981, Catalano 1986, Gerassi 1989, Flynn 1997, Fox 2003).

Sartre's thinking evolved against the wider backdrop of the emergence of a new tradition of Western Marxism, that which might loosely be termed French Existential Marxism (Poster 1975). French Existential Marxism came to prominence during the period 1956 (the date of the Soviet invasion of Hungary) to say May 1968 (the student uprising in Paris). Alongside Edgar Morin, Pierre Fougeyrollas, Jean Duvigand, and Henri Lefebvre, Sartre emerged as a key thinker within the tradition. French Existential Marxism arose in part as a reaction to the degeneration of the Communist Party in Stalinist Russia into a crippling bureaucracy and imperial oppressor. The French Existential Marxists were free thinkers within the Marxist tradition, critics of dogmatic French and Soviet communism, non-conformist Communists, and eventually non-Communist Marxists. French Existential Marxists sought to rescue Marxism from its growing critics by offering an alternative to Soviet Communism. Scholarship and debate centred upon alienation and its transcendence; the challenge of freeing the mystified consciousness of fetishisms, reifications, and obfuscations through social and political practice. They believed that Marx's historical teleology was correct but that the transition to a socialist society was not hard-wired into capitalism's contradictions and would occur only through active struggles around alienation.

In the search for a rejuvenated Marxism, French Existential Marxists turned to the sociology of modern western society, and in particular focused upon the one dimensionality of existence in the age of technology, commodification, and bureaucratisation. By contrast, Sartre was drawn to the problem of colonialism, convinced that colonisation, rebellion, and resistance heralded a profoundly significant moment in the unfolding of history. For Sartre anti-colonial struggles were the only true heirs of authentic Marxism; only in the colonies might the genuine historical potential of Marxism be fulfilled. Anti-colonial movements then were not to be approached as local and specific but always as part of a universal global transition from capitalism to socialism. It is little surprise then that towards the end of Volume 1 of the *Critique*, Sartre dedicates a section to 'Racism and colonialism as praxis and process', which specifically uses the case of colonialism to support the theses he was developing. Racism and colonialism were the social forms of modern human oppression.

Sartre's conversion to Marxism and his desire to put existentialism to the service of rescuing Marxism was mediated in particular ways by his disputations and solidarities with Maurice Merleau Ponty (1908–61) (Aronson 2004, Stewart 1998, Kelly 1999). Sartre had become friends with Merleau Ponty as early as 1927 when they studied in Paris at the École Normale Supérieure and together they had co-founded the journal *Temps Modernes*. Merleau Ponty was at this point more politically aware and engaged and Sartre attributed to him 'the push needed to release me from my immobility'. But their relationship was to sour. In 1953, following a disagreement over editorial policy, Merleau Ponty resigned as co-editor of *Temps Modernes*. This fallout was to intensify into a deep-seated philosophical antagonism and from 1953 to 1956 Merleau-Ponty began a bitter critique of Sartre's supposed fanatical Marxism.

From 1940, Merleau-Ponty had begun to view the Soviet Union as a distortion or detour or perversion of the real Marxist course of history and had adopted what was referred to as a 'wait and see' approach to Soviet Marxism. By 1955 he saw no reason to continue to wait. Appalled by the brutal oppression of the Stalinist regime and by Soviet imperialism in Eastern Europe, Merleau Ponty announced his rejection of Marxism and Communism in his famous *Adventures of the dialectic* (Merleau Ponty: 1955). The Soviet Union was not an aberrant instance; it held the truth about the inability of communism to deliver emancipation. Merleau-Ponty dedicated an entire chapter to Sartre's thought and taunted him for his 'ultra-bolshevism'. Sartre he alleged, was at sea philosophically and politically. Philosophically, he continued to defend the sovereignty of individual consciousness and freedom while at the same time supporting the idea that history has meaning and that capitalism is hard-wired from the outset to metamorphose into communism. Moreover, politically, Sartre was trying to find freedom in the social world precisely where it was being corroded.

Curiously, Sartre was never to respond to Merleau Ponty's attack, although Simone de Beauvoir did, accusing Merleau Ponty of presenting, in bad faith, a 'pseudo Sartreanism'. Sartre's only official response came in his moving eulogy *Merleau Ponty vivant* following Merleau Ponty's sudden death in 1961, in which it became clear that the pain of losing his erstwhile friendship had contributed to his silence. Nevertheless, while not offered as such, it is clear that the *Critique of dialectical reason* was Sartre's reply. That he undertook this momentous project reveals the depth to which Merleau Ponty's attacks had shaken his confidence. Writing at a furious pace and recklessly medicating himself on Corydrane (a combination of aspirin and amphetamine which was popular among students and intellectuals at the time) to counter fatigue, Sartre dedicated his energies to putting existentialism to work to solve some of the core weaknesses of historical materialism. His mission was to establish a basis for the claim that there could be 'totalisation' (an end to history) even if there was no 'totaliser' (an inner mechanism determining the transition). History could be rendered intelligible even if it was always only an aggregate outcome of molecular struggles.

Sartre's theory of colonialism then was motivated principally by his concern to develop a Marxist theory of colonialism and imperialism that would be capable of rescuing Marxism from its tyrannical, fossilised, and crystalline degeneration under Stalin in the Soviet Union. Sartre's Marxism remained committed to historical teleology and the inevitability of the defeat of capitalism, and to the establishment of a global socialist society. Anti-colonial movements throughout the world were to be interpreted as staging posts in this transition. All particulars were part of a universal process. All struggles were in the end struggles over capitalism and freedom for the colonised was freedom for the labourer. Defeat of colonialism was in crucial ways defeat of capitalism. Colonialism was the battle ground in which history itself was being fought out. But Sartre's desire to account for the anthropology of the social and political movements which would change the world and his turn to existentialism as the key to a redeemed Marxism, when deliberated on and reasoned to completion, eventually led him to a different set of conclusions.

Sartrean universals and postcolonial lore: Sartre's political writings on colonialism and activism

France was present in Algeria for 124 years before the nationalist uprising of 1954 and in the ensuing eight-year War of Independence 250,000 Algerians and 25,000 French soldiers were killed (Cohen 2003). It is often presumed that Sartre's thinking on colonialism was most fundamentally shaped by the French colonial adventure in Algeria and undoubtedly Sartre's interests in racism, negritude, and 'tri-continentalism' bear the stamp of dramas of the Algerian War of Independence (French nationalists twice bombed his flat in Paris; he escaped injury on both occasions). But Sartre wrote and spoke prolifically, publicly, and polemically about imperialism and colonialism in a variety of different twentieth-century contexts. His interests extended in particular to the rise and fall of Nazi Germany (he had an interest in anti-semitism, enlisted for the French army, was held as a prisoner of war, and escaped to join the French resistance), the Cuban revolution (he visited Fidel Castro for a month in spring 1960 and was a keen student of the then youthful Cuban revolution), the Maoist revolution in China (from 1949 Sartre searched in Maoism for an alternative to Stalinism), and Vietnam (in Stockholm in May 1967 Sartre served as Executive President of the Russell International War Crimes Tribunal and charged the US with war crimes in Vietnam and Cambodia).

Because Sartre insisted that colonialism and anti-colonialism had to be rendered intelligible as part of the wider meaning of history, his substantive writings and political activism are littered with programmatic statements asserting the universality of specific territorial sequestrations. Drawing upon a range of his more important substantive interventions, this section identifies Sartrean themes that have become *de facto* lore within Postcolonial Studies today. These include: the claim that colonialism is a political system designed to support particular capitalist practices; that this system is predicated upon a Manichean dependency between coloniser and colonised that alienates both; that colonialism creates conditions in which anti-colonial violence is inevitable and legitimate; and that anti-colonial movements need to renounce their ethnic consciousness and cultural heritage if they are to comprehend their wider role in the unfolding of history.

Sartre delivered 'Colonialism as a system' at a rally for peace in Algeria in Wagram in 1956 and published this speech in *Temps Modernes* in the same year. This paper set out starkly the claim that French annexation of Algeria was driven by a systematic political agenda designed in France in the first instance by Jules Ferry, the famous figure of the Third Republic, to support and defend French capitalism and its drive towards accumulation by dispossession. Rejecting those who obfuscate by speaking in terms of varieties of colonialisms, Sartre asserts;

The fact is that colonization is neither a series of chance occurrences nor the statistical result of thousands of individual undertakings. It is a system which was put in place around the middle of the nineteenth century, began to bear fruit in about 1880, started to decline after the First World War and is today turning against the colonizing nation. It is not true that there are some good colons and others who are wicked. There are colons and that is it. (Sartre 2001: 31, 32)

Sartre outlined the systematic and orchestrated ways in which French annexation of Algeria, by sequestration, confiscation, and unfair commercial transactions, was driven by a will to source cheap raw materials and to produce new and safeguarded markets for French goods. The French privatised property, erasing and replacing complex tribal claims to land ownership with a European mathematical calculus and set of cartographic metrics. French control over Algerian landed estates and the agro-industry then ensured that French capital could expand its investment in cash crops such as citrus fruits and viticulture beyond what was possible in France alone, and could penetrate new markets. The indigenous Algerian Muslim population, meanwhile, were driven either to form an immense agricultural proletariat or to eke livings off less productive soils in the interior of the country, beyond the reach of new irrigation systems.

Sartre recognised the central role that racism played in the legitimation of colonial endeavours. Metropolitan France reconciled any conscience about plundering Algeria by depicting the Algerian population as illiterate, uncivilised, primitive, and barbaric. There was a development lag between Europe and the rest of the world and it was a duty of Europe to spread the message of progress. A sub-human population did not require the protection of universal human rights, which extended only to the civilised world. The key assumptions of western liberal humanism did not extend to Africa. In his devastating 1961 Preface to Fanon's *Wretched of the earth*, Sartre undergirds the importance of European assumptions about the sub-humanity that existed beyond Europe:

> You know very well that we are exploiters. You know very well that we took the gold and the metals and then the oil of the 'new continents', and brought them back to the old mother countries. Not without excellent results: palaces cathedrals, industrial capitals; and then whenever crises threatened, the colonial markets were there to cushion or deflect it. Europe, stuffed with riches, granted de jure humanity to all its inhabitants. What empty chatter: liberty, equality, fraternity, love, honour, country, and who knows what else? That did not prevent us from holding forth at the same time in racist language: filthy nigger, filthy Jew, filthy North African. We saw in the human race an abstract principle of universality which served to conceal more realistic practices: there was on the other side of the seas, a race of sub humans who, thanks to us, in a thousand years would perhaps reach our status. (Sartre 2001: 151)

Sartre was especially interested in the wider production of culture that accompanied conquest. He recognised that colonial literature, poetry, theatre, music, drama, film, museums, archives, and photographs were central tools of oppression, perhaps every bit as oppressive as military violence and intimidation. Written as a 1954 Preface to Cartier-Bresson's *From one China*, Sartre considers the ways in which picturesque photographs of China and the Chinese were used to objectify and exoticise that country and its people, and thereby to legitimate certain kinds of Western interventions. This work reveals the deconstructive finesse and semiotic subtlety Sartre was capable of bringing to bear on the cultural products deposited by colonising and capitalist elites (Sartre 2001).

For Sartre, agitators and activists had a duty to wrestle control of cultural production back from their oppressors. In *What is literature* (1947) Sartre insisted that all literary writers had an obligation to be politically committed and that the central purpose of literature was to effect social and political change. Colonialism and anti-colonial struggles were at the heart of Sartre's monumental literary work *The roads to freedom* for which he was awarded but rejected the Nobel Prize for Literature in 1964. Constructed around three novels, *The age of reason* (1945), *The reprieve* (1945), and *Iron in the soul* (1949) (Sartre would never finish his fourth instalment, the novel *The Last Chance*, but two chapters were published in 1949 in *Temps Modernes* under the title *Drôle d'amitié*), the *Roads to freedom* is set within a Paris preparing for World War II (1938–40). From peace and false hope to war and defeat, and from Nazi occupation to the search for liberation, Sartre charts the changing structures of feeling experienced by a number of central characters, most notably Parisian Mathieu Delarue, but also major historical figures including Chamberlain, Daladier and Hitler. He depicts a steady movement from apathy, insularity, and private anguish, to a recognition of a shared plight and a public awareness of the dignity of communal resistance.

Sartre was one of the first critics to recognise that it was not only the colonised that existed in alienation. In his 1957 review of Albert Memmi's *The coloniser and colonised*, which became a Preface to the 1966 edition of this book, Sartre laments 'the pitiless reciprocity that binds the colonisers to the colonized … the impossible dehumanisation of the oppressed turns against the oppressors and becomes their alienation'. Reduced to violence, torture, and racism, to protect their new found riches, colonisers themselves had lost their humanity. For Sartre both the coloniser and colonised had become interlocked in a deadly Manichean tango that had rendered them inert; both had become casualties of colonialism and imperialism's insidious tendency to dehumanise. Ultimately, emancipation needed to be jointly authored.

Sartre's 1961 Preface to Fanon's *Wretched of the Earth* continues to stand as his most brutal and controversial statement on the necessity for anti-colonial movements to embrace violence as part of their struggle. But Sartre's views on violence were long in maturation (Aron 1975, Santoni 2003). His great fallout with fellow existentialist Albert Camus provided a significant moment in his advocacy of violence as a legitimate means to an end. Estranged from his native Algeria on account of the Second World War, Camus temporarily joined the Communist Party and agitated in diaspora against French colonial oppression of his homeland. But Camus was to become increasingly hostile to violent social and political upheaval and steadily adopted a socially conservative stance. In his philosophical essay *The rebel* (1951), Camus called for 'rebellion without revolution' and championed the many small victories that could be secured if utopian aspirations were to give way to more conservative and incremental challenges within capitalist societies and colonial systems.

Sartre rebuked Camus for his lack of political commitment, claiming that only those involved in struggle had the right to pass comment on the virtues and vices of those who struggle. Sartre collaborated with Francis Jeanson, whose 1952 *Temps Modernes* article attacked Camus as naïve. Later, when Jeanson's followers, known as the Jeanson Network, were put on trial in France for their support of the *Front de Libération Nationale* (FLN) Sartre wrote a support letter, again justifying the violence on the grounds that the FLN was a movement towards an end that represented not only the freedom of Algeria but also the freedom of France, which he viewed as having fallen under de Gaulle into a 'progressive diminution in liberties, the disappearance of political life, the generalization of torture, and the permanent insurrection of the military power against the civil power'. In 1958 in *L'express*, Sartre published 'A victory', a written response to Henri Alleg's *la question*, which was published in the same year and which drew on first-hand experience to reveal the extent of French use of torture in Algeria. For Sartre, Alleg's testimony was affirmation that violence was necessary as a redemptive recovery of the lost humanity of the oppressed.

In reaction to Nazi racialisations of the Jewish population, in 1946 Sartre wrote *Anti-Semite and Jew*, which offered the claim that it was the anti-semite who created the Jew rather than the Jew who had created the anti-semite. The objective of the Jew was to recover his or her authentic pre-racialised self. *Black Orpheus* (Orphée Noir) was written in 1948 as an introduction to the *Anthologie de la Nouvelle Poésie nègre et malgache de langue française* edited by Léopold Sédar Senghor, a future Senegalese President. It was Sartre's most significant engagement with the Negritude movement, a literary and ideological movement developed by francophone black intellectuals, writers, and politicians in France in the 1930s: a group that included, alongside Senghor, Martinican poet Aimé Césaire, Congolese independence leader Patrice Lumumba and the Guianan Léon Damas. In *Black Orpheus*, Sartre again claimed that it was the racist who had created the coloured person and not the coloured person who had created the racist. The task of the negritude movement was to recover the authentic experience of the Black person.

Although *Anti-Semite and Jew* and *Black Orpheus* appear at first sight to endorse an essentialising of Jewish and Black identity, it is immediately clear that Sartre approached both with a wider objective. For Sartre, independence movements aspiring to 'decolonise the mind', to purge the cultural influences of Europe from the 'periphery', and to restore pre-colonial cultural forms, risked lapsing into a misguided conception of human freedom. Sartre recognised that black experience of oppression was distinctive from that endured by the white proletariat. African poetry was incommensurable with European epistemology. But in spite of recognising the particularity of the case, Sartre wanted to force Negritude to universalise its vista and to metamporphose into the wider class struggle posited by Marxist eschatology. Negritude was in effect anti-racist racism, a negation of racism. The poets of the negritude movement were the only people capable of recovering the authenticity of human experience. Recognising the sensitivities of asking Black anti-colonial movements to renounce the particularities of their experiences, Sartre qualified that the 'colored man (sic) – and he alone – can be asked to renounce the pride of his color' (Sartre 1976b: 38).

Sartre's request that the negritude movement universalise its resistance led some to question his authority to serve as a spokesperson for 'third world' societies and to regard him as yet another well meaning but ultimately ignorant apologist from the metropolitan heartland (Haddour 2005). But, influenced hugely by the drift of Marxism in the Soviet Union into brutal and repressive Stalinism, Sartre refused to buckle and was keenly aware of the limitations of movements, organisations, and institutions claiming to stand at the vanguard of emancipation. He continued to advocate an abandonment of the category of race and nation, once racial and national consciousness had been achieved. The 'Party', Sartre argued, was structured to become an end in itself and not a means to an end. It was part of the problem. And arguably the prevalence of despotism, militarism, fascism, and dictatorship in many liberated colonies today suggests his caution was well founded.

Sartre wrote *Vietnam, imperialism, and genocide* in December 1967 in his capacity as Executive President of the Russell International War Crimes Tribunal. For Sartre Vietnam was the battle ground upon which history itself was being fought out. The United States was targeting Vietnam simply as a means of protecting capitalist interests everywhere. Meanwhile by default the Vietnamese were fighting on behalf of oppressed peoples everywhere.

> When a peasant falls in his rice field, mown down by a machine gun, we are all struck. In this way the Vietnamese are fighting for all men, and the Americans against all men ... the American government is well aware the present act of genocide – as a reply to a people's war – is conceived and perpetuated in Vietnam not only against the Vietnamese but against humanity ... in this sense imperial genocide can only become more radical – because the group aimed at, to be terrorized, through the Vietnamese nation, is the human group in its entirety. (Sartre 1974: 83)

In Istanbul in November 2005, and set within a wider critique of the neoconservative 'Project for the New American Century', a similar World Tribunal on Iraq was likewise conducted. Intriguingly, the World Tribunal on Iraq was inspired by and directly modelled on Sartre's fashioning of the Russell Tribunal.

'Masses', 'spontaneity', 'party': Sartre's theory of practical ensembles

It is possible that Sartre's theory of colonialism has been indicted as metrocentric simply because critics have focused upon what he was trying to do rather than on what he actually did. The objective of the *Critique of dialectical reason* was to establish a new basis for a Marxist theory of history and thereafter to cast the history of colonialism as a constituent moment in the general transition to Socialism. Sartre set out to establish that there could be a definitive totalisation (a socialist society) even though there was no overarching totaliser or hidden architect of history. But he failed in this task and as a consequence Volume 2 of the *Critique* was never completed. Sartre could only conclude that while there could exist totalising (a continual abstraction from the particular to the universal) there could never be totalisation (a final universal resting point).

In this section I argue that with hindsight Sartre's failure might be the source of his redemption. Ironically, what Sartre deposited as a set of intellectual ruins, incapable of solving a central theoretical problem of the day might by default form the basis of a theory of colonialism that dismantles the universalising tendencies of postcolonial theory. The focus is upon the theory of practical ensembles Sartre offers in Volume 1 of the *Critique*. Here Sartre's insinuation of existentialism into the Marxist canon leads him to the conclusion that the aggregate consequence of molecular struggles for freedom and against oppression and alienation is a series of unpredictable and historically novel social, cultural, and political collectives. Anti-colonial struggles cannot be reduced to constituent parts of a universal process, but rather emerge with their own history and along particular trajectories.

At the heart of Sartre's social theory of alienation is the concept of material scarcity. In spite of claims about a world of abundance, absolute and certainly relative scarcity remains an endemic feature of human existence. Scarcity in turn mediates social relationships and is the primary motive for and vehicle through which the objectification of others takes place. For Sartre, scarcity was never formally theorised by Marx because it was simply assumed to define the rules of the game; it was nowhere in *Capital* because it was everywhere in *Capital*. Typical of his mode of argumentation, Sartre deploys the everyday example of people waiting at a bus stop for a bus with limited spaces. This situation for Sartre represented a structured management of scarcity – everything from the technology of buses to the systems of creating timetables – set the constituent conditions under which human relations are constructed. Competition for scarce resources results in a loss of humanity; the other is objectified as a threat to my access to opportunities to appropriate and consume. The material world brings people, neighbourhoods, communities, cities, regions, nations, and continents into competition with one another and this competition is the source of the drive to dehumanise and objectify.

Sartre refers to those gatherings or 'masses' that shelter submissively under particular political and economic systems as *groups in series*. Groups in series are collectives rather than groups as such. Collectives fall prey to a particular existential condition that Sartre characterizes as an 'atomisation of the crowd', a 'passive unity', or a 'plurality of solitudes'. Groups in series consist of isolated individuals, frozen and rendered inert by their material needs, and ultimately living out a life of alienation from their full creative potential. To be part of a group in series is to live a 'mode of being that consists of serial behaviour, serial feelings and serial thoughts' (Sartre 1976a: 266). Deposited into fossilised landscapes, serial populations live in a space or location Sartre would refer to as a *practico-inert*.

However inert life may seem for groups in series, eventually it is alienation and its transcendence that triggers movement. For Sartre, newness enters the world, not only in conditions it did not choose, but precisely *because of* conditions it did not choose. In the theory of practical ensembles, Sartre sketches out a sequence of groupings he claims emerge from the depths of seriality in search of redemption. Occupying the premiere position in the emerging sequence is the cherished *group in fusion*, a kind of spontaneous and anarchic uprising and an effective movement for social change. The group in fusion both liquefies groups in series and then begins the task of reconstituting the now malleable collective into a more progressive form.

The processes through which groups in fusion emerge exercised Sartre enormously. He used the concept of the 'third party' as his central organising device. Consider two people attending to their gardens, he muses in typically Sartrean fashion, separated by a large opaque fence. Any union between these two activities is impossible until a third party, perhaps looking from an adjacent window, registers the situation and acts to effect synthesis. The continual expansion of third parties leads in turn to ever larger communions. The process is contingent and open, although also historically structured (a situation he also called 'rational'), and therefore it is indeed impossible to predict the form and trajectory of emerging groups in fusion. For Sartre then; a process totalising a multitude of acts of resistance can be accomplished without the help of any particular totaliser:

> Consider a regroupment behind some shelter after a flight. Some individuals will not take part in it: the action of the enemy will have cut them off completely from any synthetic community. For them, seriality itself, which began in panic, has culminated in molecular exteriority: the individual, alone, cut off from Others, continues his (sic, and thereafter) flight, loses his way, hides in a cellar, gives himself up etc. ... While I am on my way up to join with the central core of resisters who are sheltering behind some building, I happen to be in the practical field of another third party, who is coming out of another street and approaching the same group with the same purpose and the arrival of this third party at the group has real, objective links with my own approach: for me he increases the multiplicity of resisters, thereby increasing the chances of success and diminishing my personal risks. This is the joyful surprise which all the assembled demonstrators feel when, on the occasion of a demonstration which has been forbidden by the police, they see individuals and small groups converging from every direction, more numerous than they had expected, and

representing a hope to everyone. ... When I approach it to join it, I am already part of it. We have seen in what sense: as a limit of totalisation, as an impractical task which has to be done. And from this point of view the present multiplicity of the group constitutes me objectively as a member of a tiny group of desperate men who will get themselves killed on the spot, either as members of a huge invincible demonstration or as is more usual taking part in some intermediate formation. This internal synthetic constitution of me by the group is simply totalisation returning to me to give me my first common quality over the collapse of seriality. And it gives me this quality as power. Thus the third party comes to the group which already possesses him, as a constituent and constituted power; that is, he receives the power he gives, and he sees the other third party approaching him as his power. For in the group, the other third party, in so far as I totalise him with the others is not for me a third party object that is to say, a third party transcendent to me. As an individual he transcends me towards his projects in so far as I transcend him: this is simple reciprocity. ... In practice this means that I am integrated into the common action when the common practice of the third party poses itself as regulatory. I run with all the others; I shout: stop!; everybody stops. Someone else shouts lets go! Or to the left! To the right! To the Bastille! And everyone moves off, following the regulatory third party, surrounding him and sweeping past him. (Sartre 1976a: 374–80)

Seriality is perpetually on the brink of being liquefied but rarely succumbs to dissolution. The weight of the prevailing political and economic infrastructures which manage and mediate scarcity and the violence they promise for dissenters ensures that insurrection is stifled and suffocated. More often than not then, groups in fusion short circuit before they can grow to have any kind of impact. The result of their fleeting existence is the formation of mere islands of humanity in an inert series and only mini and partial guerrilla warfare on serial collectives.

For those groups that do survive, however, the central problem of scarcity resurfaces. The old system of resource distribution might have been toppled, but the group in fusion has to confront the reality that still there are not enough resource units and items of consumption to go around. Never solving the problem of scarcity – partly because historical conditions under capitalism actually work to create and re-imagine scarcity – those groups that do survive must crystallise and secrete new methodologies of resource allocation and rationing. Inequalities remain endemic and organisation of the administration of material goods is required lest disharmony lead to group implosion.

This process results in greater sophistication in the group's organisational structures. The group must organise or it will perish. The result is the formation of *groups in metastases*. Sartre spends considerable time looking at the ever more sophisticated degrees of structuredness of groups as they organise to secure their existence. There is no space here to review his sequence of groupings, nor the order he necessarily places them in, but it will suffice to note that they run from the fused group, through the sworn (or pledged) group, the statutory group, the organisation, the institution (state), and finally to social classes (see Hartmann 1981 for more detail). As structure becomes more imposing and forbidding and as freedom movements become formalised and bureaucratised, new types of groups in series emerge. The means of violence, hitherto directed at the oppressor, then become an instrument of self-discipline and internal group control. The group ossifies back into an inert collective and agency peters out.

For Sartre the metastases of the group in fusion into an ever yet more complex organism therefore unravels all the good that is initially done:

> The group reacts to this permanent danger [of collapse] with new practices: it produces itself as an institutionalised group; which means that 'organs', functions, and powers are transformed into institutions; that, in the framework of institutions, the community tries to acquire a new type of unity by institutionalising sovereignty, and that the common individual transforms himself (sic) into an institutional individual. [The result] is degraded forms of community. 'Degrade', here does not, of course have anything to do with a system of values: I merely mean that the group – whose origin and end reside in an effort by the individuals who are gathered to dissolve seriality in themselves – will, in the course of its struggle, actually reproduce alterity in itself and freeze into the inorganic so as to struggle against it within. ... In other words, our dialectical investigation makes a turning here and goes back towards the practico-inert, from which it removed itself a little earlier; it is beginning to appear that the movement of the investigation may possibly be circular. (Sartre 1976a: 591)

History unfolds in a circular process of regrouping and petrification and thus holds out no ultimate solution to human alienation. Sartre describes this double movement or dialectical circularity as a 'circular synthesis of disorder of order and order of disorder' (Sartre 1991: 272).

In the absence of any utopian exit, Sartre would seem to be advocating the group in fusion as the only revelatory moment of emancipation, however fleeting. Perhaps for Sartre the best that might be hoped for is a world which is perpetually liquefying inert serialities, with groups in fusion constantly forming and collapsing and never growing to a level of complexity that undermines their cathartic potential. If this is the principle source of hope in Sartre's dialectic, then perhaps Stephen Priest (2001: 1) may well be correct in his assessment of Sartre's career as best conceived of in terms of the motif 'liberty, equality, and fraternity'; referring respectively to his existentialist stage from the mid 1930s, his turn to Marxism in the 1950s, 1960s, and 1970s, and his drift to anarchism just before his death in 1980.

The theory of practical ensembles provides the basis of a theory of colonialism that refuses to conceive of anti-colonial movements as instances in a universal struggle destined to end with a transition to Socialism. Instead, it celebrates the local emergence of contingent, fluid, novel, hybrid, and creolised cultural and political forms. Sartre departs from historicism and is led to a circular history that approaches separate colonialisms as distinctive, unique and incommensurable with universal abstraction. Resistance is most liberating at that moment when unpredictable, volatile, historically unique, and often unnameable social, cultural, and political movements emerge; and most tyrannical when attempting to unify and aggregate these movements into organised, fossilised and crystalline bureaucracies and institutions. Freedom is to be found amidst struggle, not as an *après*.

Sartre's historicised phenomenology of existence as spatial

In this final section I argue that Sartre's departure from metrocentric universal theorising and in particular from metrocentric reifications of historicism derives from his novel and provocative recognition of the importance of spatiality. It is perhaps surprising that so few Anglo-American geographers have studied Sartre's thinking on space seriously. Samuels' (1978, 1981) pioneering work introduced Sartrean existentialism to the humanistic tradition which emerged in the 1970s. Kobayashi (1989) identified Sartre as a central figure around which humanistic geography and Marxism might be fused, and later highlighted the importance of Sartre's treatment of spatiality for geographies of racism (Kobayashi 2004). Jameson (1961) brought Sartre to the attention of Marxist geographers, particularly those interested in theorising capitalism and the postmodern condition (see for instance Soja 1989, Harvey 1989, Boyle 2005). Judith Butler has woven Sartrean thought into theories of performativity which have become important for non-representational geographies (for a useful summary of Butler's indebtedness to Sartre see Busch 1999). Davidson (2003) has located Sartre's existentialism at the heart of emerging geographies of emotion and affect. Doreen Massey has recognised the importance of Sartre in the historical geography of the emergence of modernity's discovery of the idea of 'space-time' (Massey 2005). These interventions notwithstanding, geographers have by and large failed to excavate and scrutinise Sartre's approach to spatiality. It is unsurprising then that only Peet (1998) and Blunt and Wills (2000) ascribe to Sartre any significant role in the history of the discipline and even then he attracts only subsidiary commentary in these texts.

A feature of Sartre's early work that has been largely overlooked is that his concept of being is fundamentally spatial and relative. That is, human existence occurs always in relation to others who are set at a distance from the self; that distance constitutes the recursive relationships that are the basis for both individual and social existence. As Martin Buber once put it, the fundamental human condition is established through the separation between human beings – distance, alterity, otherness – as a basis for human relationship. Engagement of the other, which Sartre describes as 'the look', involves objectification and placement of the other body, its setting at a distance from the self, as a mutually constitutive project which is fundamentally spatial, as well as the basis for relationships of power between human beings:

> My own look or my connection without distance to these people is stripped of its
> transcendence by the very fact that it is a look-looked-at. I am fixing the people
> whom I see into objects; I am in relation to them as the Other is in relation to me.
> In looking at them I measure my power ... My look simply manifests a relation
> in the midst of the world, a relation of myself-as-object to the object-looked
> at – something like the attraction which two masses exert over one another at a
> distance. ... In so far as I am looked at I do not unfold the distance, I am limited
> to clearing it. The Other's look confers spatiality on me. (Sartre 1943: 242)

Sartre's discussion of the look is key to understanding the ways in which distance
(measured in any number of ways but always – even in its metric form – as a
constructed quality of relationship), or the act of setting the other at a distance,
is the geographical basis for othering, through the construction of class, gender,
ethnicity, race, territory, sexuality, age, disability, and so on. Distance, or alterity,
ironically constitutes the human capacity for recognising both the self and the
other, and is the profound basis (in its objectification of the other) for oppression.
Spatiality is thus *the* form of human relationship. There is no abstract or objective
'space' to be filled, only the active filling of the world. To be human is to spatialise.
To engage with others is to spatialise the other in relationship. Perhaps Sartre's
most important contribution to the understanding of the importance of spatiality to
the human condition, always a recursive and discursive, or relational, condition,
is: 'To apprehend oneself as looked at is to apprehend oneself as spatializing-
spatialized' (Sartre 1943: 242). What more profound encapsulation of the
ontological significance of the concept of spatiality could geographers ask for?

Sartre's phenomenology of being as spatial is retained and developed in his
later writings, and not surprisingly underpins and infuses his writings on the
future of Marxism and the meaning of colonialism and anti-colonialism in history.
Sartre's phenomenology now becomes imbricated into his historical materialism
and a historicised phenomenology of spatial existence is developed. In *Being
and nothingness* Sartre had already insisted that consciousness is intentional
insofar as consciousness is always consciousness *of something*. The anatomy of
consciousness then is contaminated by and bears the imprint of the 'situation' in
which the human being dwells. In the *Critique* spatiality continues to be treated as
intentional, but greater concern was now registered with unpacking the rather crude
idea of the 'situation.' Deposited into particular social and historical contexts, the
'look' is put into play by different groups in different ways towards different ends
with different outcomes. In other words the human condition of spatiality becomes
concretised with different consequences depending upon prevailing social and
historical conditions.

The result is necessarily and profoundly a spatial, material landscape, in which
spatiality is defined not only as the recursive relationship between human beings,
spatialising spatialised, but also the relationship between human beings and
things. Things, or matter, are the product of human labour, produced historically,
and given meaning in a process that Sartre calls 'totalising totalised'. That is, the

mediation of the material world by human action both signifies and alienates the material products of history in a double dialectic. Praxis is a material act that gives meaning to the world, conditioned by the 'passive unity of prefabricated meanings' in which 'there are no material objects that do not communicate among themselves through the mediation of men [sic]; and there is no man who is not born into a world of humanised materialities' (Sartre 1976a 169). But praxis is also alienated as matter acts back upon the actor resulting in what Sartre calls the complex fact of 'accumulation outflow', or the creation of material conditions that turn praxis back upon itself, dissolving individual actions in their exteriority, in the process creating a landscape of uneven scarcity, and contested meanings.

Sartre's historicised phenomenology of spatial existence underpins his theory of colonialism. Ways of looking are both a product of and modality through which, particular formations of the colonial become possible, through particular forms of human relationship (spatialising-spatialised) and in particular landscapes (accumulation outflow). Sartre conceives of the different groups which form and dissolve at different stages in the process of colonialisation – namely groups in series, groups in fusion, and groups in metastases – as founded on, practising, and reproducing different ways of being spatial. I refer to these historicised phenomenologies as: spatiality as tyranny, spatiality as liberation, and spatiality as incarceration. I argue that the originality of Sartre's postcolonial geography rests upon his claim that different ways of looking (or objectifying the other) mediate and in turn are mediated by successive waves of colonial expansion, contestation, and retreat, and his assertion that because ways of looking are interrelated and organised in a particular causal sequence, colonial projects unfold in a circular way.

Sartre's concept of the group in series captures precisely the existential condition of the colonial subject. As colonial powers engage in territorial conquest and annexation, the 'look' performs as an act of tyranny, projecting poisonous hierarchies of civilisations, levels of humanity, and degrees of barbarism. Colonialism alienates both colonising and colonised populations and renders both inert. Out of the depths of this apparatus arises a new, dynamic, open, and turbulent spatiality. Fused groups or groups or groups in fusion depend upon and in turn reproduce new ways of looking – a restless, dynamic, fluid, and radical openness to transient coordinate systems, always being reconfigured, recalibrated, and rescaled. Third parties chronically and continually totalise strands of insurrection. Historically novel social, cultural, and political resistances emerge. Spatiality as liberation has a short life expectancy, however, and can only survive by ossifying into a new dispensation. Spatiality as incarceration then dominates, as freedom movements degenerate into crystalline forms, equally oppressive as the powers they were born to remove. The spontaneity of the group in fusion gives way to fratricidal imprisonment and incarceration. Groups in metastases work to incorporate, bureaucratise, count, regulate, discipline, and police internal threats. The dominant existential condition of this age is one of paranoia and the sense that one is under constant surveillance.

Conclusion

Very few scholars have taken literally and seriously the formal and specific theoretical architecture Jean-Paul Sartre erected in his efforts to make sense of and to resist colonialism. For a range of Left leaning anti-capitalist, anti-globalisation, environmental, anti-war, and anti-fascist social movements at least, Sartre is no antique, historical curiosity, or mere footnote in the history of thought. But even among these constituencies his influence is largely derivative, mediated and oblique, defined primarily by the tone and colour of his prose, and by his personality, reputation and aura. Within Anglo-American geography, interest in Sartrean Existentalism and Sartrean Existential Marxism largely waned with the rise of poststructuralism and the linguistic turn, the rejection of the possibility of searching in any meaningful way for a telos to History, and with the ascendancy of postmodernism and the marginalisation of grand theorising. In the stampede to claim new ground crude caricatures were drawn and Sartre steadily became branded as 'outdated', 'unfashionable', 'passé' and 'redundant'. In aggregate, Sartre casts a ghostly specter or looming shadow over Postcolonial Studies, formative of the collective consciousness and conscience, but in truth buried from public view and academic scrutiny.

It is therefore somewhat unfortunate that Sartre is now being indicted as a central point of origin of postcolonial theory's embroilment in a debilitating western historicism. This article has sought to clarify the case for and against framing Sartrean thought as Eurocentric or metrocentric in spite of itself. It has attempted to recover Sartre's theory of colonialism and to use Sartre, twentieth-century Paris, and the politics of the twentieth-century French colonial adventure, to make a case for a reinvigorated interest in the differentiated forms of European modernity and the complex and contradictory theoretical enterprises these forms have deposited. Here my project both consolidates Massey's (2005) clarion call for a historical-geographical excavation of formulations of time and space in European modernity and extends this project by foregrounding theories of colonisation as both constituted by and constitutive of such formulations. My objective is not to reassert the virtue of European modernity and its theoretical premises in any uncritical way but instead to hold open the possibility that within certain contexts we can still learn important, progressive, and useful lessons from certain theories of colonialism with European parentage.

I argue that caught up in the maelstrom of twentieth-century Parisian intellectual and political life, Sartre in fact displayed a complex relationship with metrocentric theoretical projects and practices. He provided a theory of practical ensembles which replaced Marxism's eschatology and linear teleology with a series of circular histories based upon the complex ways in which separate anti-colonial movements spiral off following their own contingent, creolised and anarchic trajectories. I identify his strong commitment to spatiality, developed into a historicised phenomenology of existence as spatial, as tempering and ultimately undermining his commitment to historicism. In the end Sartre could not establish a basis for a Marxian dialectic but instead did see the progressive political implications of recognising the workings of a socio-spatial dialectic which pivoted around such notions as happenstance juxtapositions, thrown-togetherness, perpetual fusion and the continuous search for new third parties.

In calling for a formal and serious investigation and comprehension of the nuances and intricacies of Sartre's scholarship and politics, in the final analysis I am not offering Sartre as a *solution* to historicism. Sartre's theory of colonialism ultimately begins with the assumption that the history of colonial populations has been 'jump started' in important ways by colonialism. Sartre does not provide a means of recovering subaltern historiographies so as to purge colonised populations of their European unconscious or to recover their 'authentic' pre-colonial identities. Sartre's approach falls well short of recognising that the entanglement of colonising and colonised biographies is mediated by multiple modalities of power; class, race and ethnicity for sure but also gender, age, and sexuality. Histories of capitalism and colonialism will only ever be partially captured by Sartrean theoretical constructs and we cannot deploy Sartre's theory of colonialism in any sense as a convincing overarching *explanatory framework*.

Nevertheless I conclude that it is simply wrong to designate the broad collection of scholars often categorised as 'structuralist', 'poststructuralist', or 'postmodernist' as fundamentally anti-Sartrean or post-Sartrean and complex genealogies, intellectual entanglements, and lines of continuity remain to be excavated and appreciated. Sartre's intellect was creative and nomadic and he proves fascinating in part as a result of his complexities, nuances, contradictions, quirks and ambivalences. I too insist upon preserving the unclassifiability and sheer strangeness of Sartre's approach. I find myself in sympathy with Fox (2003) who paints Sartre as schizophrenic thinker, traversing modernity and postmodernity, and offering simultaneously: a theory of the subject which walks a tightrope between the idea of the Cartesian, rational, unified, autonomous subject, and the socially and linguistically decentred, fragmented, and multiple subject; a theory of history which fluctuates between macro-theoretical, universalising, and totalising claims, and micro-theoretical contingent, indeterminate, and detotalised visions which challenge simple causality and linearity; and a politics which incorporates both universal struggles over political economy and the state and 'superstructural' concerns with locality, difference, culture, and identity.

How might one account for the seeming disjuncture between the nuanced interest in the local, the contextual, and the contingent in Sartre's more considered theoretical works and philosophical ruminations and the universal, bold, often crude, and sweeping claims advanced in Sartre's speeches, public proclamations and political activism? Of course it has to be remembered that many of Sartre's statements were designed to draw maximum publicity and his most crude and stark tendencies towards universal grand claims say more about his desire to access the public domain than about his thinking *per se*. Sartre, too, struggled to read all substantive colonialisms through a Marxist lens. His more considered statements reveal greater complexity in his analyses and a preparedness to treat aberrant cases as a problem for his theory and not just as rogue outliers. Paolucci (2007), for instance, presents a close reading of Sartre's writings on Cuba and his visit to the island in 1960. She concludes that Sartre saw in the youthful Cuban revolution a species of socialism that was centred on the freedom of the human person and not the tyrannical encrustations of a fossilised Communist Party. In fact Sartre could not reconcile the Cuban revolution with Marx's universal and abstract categories: to his own astonishment he declared; 'But this is not Marxism!' Sartre became interested in historically grounded insights on potential pathways to revolutionary praxis and came close to renouncing dogmatic, prefabricated models of social change, which ultimately imprisoned freedom. Once the complexities of Sartre's theoretical musings have been rediscovered and digested it will be necessary to re-read the corpus of his substantive writings and political activism and it is probable than an entirely more nuanced set of insights will be gleaned.

Chapter 3
The Scotland's Secret Shame Debate: Approach and Method

Introduction

Whilst alterity, or the sensation of being other, has been shown to figure large in accounts of the settlement experiences of Irish Catholics in many cities and regions across the world (Miller 1988; Boyle 2001a), the story of the Irish Catholic community in Scotland presents itself as an aberrant exception again; an anomaly in the wider experience of the Irish diaspora. Until recently it was assumed that questions of sectarianism and bigotry had by and large receded in Scotland and that the assimilation and integration of the Irish Catholic community into Scottish society, politics, economy and culture had run its course. It was widely believed that hostility towards Irish Catholics and Irish Catholic estrangement from the host population were now of mere historical curiosity. But across the past decade a vigorous debate has taken place over the continued virulence of anti-Irish and anti-Catholic sentiment in Scotland. This debate has vexed journalists, policy makers, academics, politicians, and community representatives alike. Debate over what has been labelled 'Scotland's secret shame' has forced a rethink of basic assumptions. This chapter offers an overview of public disputation over the degree of anti-Irish Catholic sentiment in Scotland, as it has played out across the past decade in public debate, confessional politics, academic study, and political life. Its purpose is to clarify the position this book takes on this debate. This position is predicated upon the claim that the most serious question the debate raises has yet to be sufficiently addressed, that is; *is the Irish Catholic adventure in Scotland intelligible and if so what is the nature of its meaning in history.*

Irish Catholic alterity from Scottish society: The public debate

A surprising debate?

Until recently the Irish Catholic encounter with Scotland was not thought to have been especially remarkable. Whilst refracted to take into account the specificities of the waxing and waning of anti-Irish Catholic sentiment locally, the story of Irish Catholics in Scotland had been extensively framed in terms of a reasonably conventional dominant narrative of initial indigenous hostility and migrant estrangement, a heightened sense of defensiveness as a redemptive buffer, a steady and largely linear process of assimilation and integration, and a gradual withering of anti-Irish Catholic sentiment to the point of irrelevance (Aspinwall 1996). Irish Catholics were at first distinguished by their class, religion, politics, and nationality, but steadily through time alterity waned and a new sense of belonging and attachment blossomed. This narrative of steady assimilation from an unpromising start, unfolding in a broadly unidirectional fashion, had been applied to the Scottish case in much the same way as it had been applied in any other location in which the Irish settled in numbers.

Irish migration to Scotland has a long heritage, traceable to the arrival of the Irish settlers in Argyll in the early fifth century (the 'Scots' who created the kingdom of Alba) and to the missionary work of the Irish Saint Columba who crossed from Derry to Iona to evangelise in 563AD. From this point migration from Scotland to Ireland and Ireland to Scotland, for military, religious, economic, trade, and family reasons spluttered and coughed, sometimes standing as a large movement, at other times appearing as a more sporadic, intermittent and short-term series of minor relocations. The surge in Irish migration to Scotland properly began in the 1840s at the time of the Irish Famine and peaked in the period from the late 1840s to the early 1920s, when somewhere in the region of 500,000 Irish, two thirds of them Irish Catholics, relocated across the Irish Sea. In 1851, a total of 207,000 Irish-born citizens lived in Scotland, some 7.2 per cent of the total population. As late as 1901, a total of 205,064 Irish-born lived in Scotland, constituting 4.6 per cent of the total population. By 1961 still some 80,533 Irish-born resided in Scotland, now comprising only 1.6 per cent of the national population. The majority of migrants derived from Ulster, including Donegal, and from County Mayo. Most settled in Glasgow, with Ayrshire, Argyle, Edinburgh, and Dundee also serving as important locations of reception.

Initially Scotland proved to be an arid and at times forbidding host. James E. Handley's classic and seminal *The Irish in Scotland 1798–1845* (Handley 1943) sought to track the early seasonal flows of agrarian labour from Ireland to Scotland, the movement of Irish labourers working in canals and on the railways, and the steady increase in the numbers of both opting to settle in Scotland on a more permanent basis. Whilst Handley's focus was not principally upon how the Irish community were treated by their new hosts, his work did include a section on the 'native attitude to the immigrant'. Handley concluded:

> In general, the attitude of the majority of lowland Scots towards the Irish immigrant was one of settled hostility. This hostility was due to economic, political, and religious reasons, one or other of which dominated according to the rank and training of the native, but all of which were to some extent present in the minds of those who objected to the settlement of Irish men and women on Scottish soil. (Handley 1943: 136)

Whilst Handley concluded his account in 1845, his thesis was taken to be relevant beyond this date. The Irish encountered anti-Irish sentiment as a consequence of their race, nationality, class, and politics. A profound and significant sense of alterity was to colorate their experience of settlement for most of the nineteenth century. As late as the 1930s, some factions within Scottish society were still warning of the economic, cultural, political, and social menace the Irish Catholic 'virus' presented to Scottish society and the need to repatriate Irish Catholics so as to cleanse Scotland of popery, strike breakers, and moral decadence.

Comparative research however suggests that over time Glasgow generated a less hostile environment for Irish Catholics than other destinations in the United Kingdom, and in particular Lancashire (Smith 1984; Neal 1988; Lowe 1989). In the 1840s, a time when many migrants arrived in Glasgow, the established Protestant churches were internally divided and paradoxically division contributed towards a less hostile reception. Moreover, Glasgow's heavy engineering base produced a less competitive labour market. Shared labour interests in the shipyards, the liberal political culture which gripped the city in the late nineteenth century and the rise of the Red Clydeside movement in the early twentieth century all provided important bonds, bridges and solidarities. The Irish Catholic community never formed into a ghetto, spatially or metaphorically. According to some, with the shared experience of the Second World War and certainly concomitant with the demise of shipbuilding and heavy engineering in Clydeside, the globalisation of the local economy, the massive post-war expansion of the welfare state and provision of collective consumption, growing secularism, and increases in interfaith marriages, divisions have receded, and for all intents and purposes Irish Catholics have economically, politically, socially, geographically, and perhaps even culturally integrated and assimilated with the host.

In *The Uneasy Peace: religious tension in modern Scotland,* Tom Gallagher (1987) traces this kind of story and presents a periodisation of the Irish experience which includes a meticulous account of the rise but also the fall of indigenous hostility to Irish Catholics in Glasgow, the principal city of settlement. According to Gallagher, Irish Catholics have substantially lost their status as an immigrant minority and in many senses have become one with the Scot:

> If sectarianism is still capable of a last hurrah in Scotland, the evidence presented in these pages suggests that it will not be on the scale witnessed in Northern Ireland. Scotland does not face an identity crisis as sharp as that encountered in Ulster .... Bilateral relations between groups like Catholics and Protestants in Ulster and the West of Scotland range along a continuum from a genocidal to a symbiotic one. In the 1970s, it became apparent that Scots were more to one side of this spectrum, whereas the peoples of divided Ulster were located perilously near the opposite edge .... Perhaps greater awareness of the progress Scots have made in healing their religious differences may inspire some of those in Northern Ireland who seek peace, by showing that their aspirations are not altogether beyond reach. (Gallagher 1987: 354)

For some time *The Uneasy Peace* has stood as the most authoritative and comprehensive account of the Irish Catholic encounter with Scotland and so Gallagher's portrayal of the general demise of Irish Catholic alterity through time, and certainly since the 1930s, has been taken as something of a truism.

To the extent that the major works which followed *The Uneasy Peace* were revisionist in spirit, the ambition if anything was to dispute whether anti-Irish Catholic sentiment ever was that bad in the past and to measure and empirically validate the claim that the Irish were now in any case 'out of the ghetto' (Devine 1991; Boyle and Lynch 1998; Mitchell 1998). Without question some of the most impressive revisionist contributions have focused upon the claim that historiographies of the Irish in Scotland rarely pay enough attention to political activism (both with respect to Irish nationalism and domestic Scottish politics) and therefore obscure the collective solidarity exhibited by Irish and Scottish workers (examples of work in this lively and emerging tradition are Kenefick 1997; Mitchell 1998; McFarland 2003; McBride 2006a, 2006b 2007, 2008, 2010; Ó Catháin 2007; and Foster et al. 2010). Martin Mitchell's (1998) justly acclaimed *The Irish in the west of Scotland, 1797–1848: Trade unions, strikes and political movements* provides a significant example of such positive revisionism. Mitchell's focus was upon the role of Irish migrants in: a) trade unions and militant striking, b) radical political movements including the United Scotsmen at the turn of the eighteenth century and the radical agitations of 1816–20; c) O'Connell's movement for Catholic Emancipation and the Reform Bills, and; d) Chartism and the campaign for the repeal of the Act of Union of 1800. Whilst the Catholic Irish were indeed used to divide the Scottish working classes, a strong counter current of collective empathy and praxis also existed. Mitchell's (2009) most recent edited collection *New Perspectives on the Irish in Scotland* provides a fresh updating of these more complex encounters which marked Irish settlement in Scotland.

Against this intellectual backdrop, the rise to prominence over the past decade of a public debate over the continued virulence of anti-Irish Catholic sentiment in Scotland has come as something of a shock. This debate raises questions, and for some doubts, about the adequacy of existing frameworks and forms of analyses. In a polemical lecture titled 'Scotland's Shame', delivered at the Edinburgh Festival in August 1999, Scotland's leading musical composer James MacMillan opened debate on the continuing pervasiveness of sectarianism and bigotry in contemporary Scotland in an explosive way. This lecture has proven to have had far reaching consequences. Delivered against the backdrop of the formation of the new Scottish Parliament in Edinburgh, MacMillan's tone was intemperate:

> If Scotland is to ever establish a genuinely pluralistic democracy where differences are not just recognised and respected but celebrated, nurtured, and absorbed for the greater good, we will first have to clear a seemingly insurmountable hurdle. In many walks of life, in the workplace, in the professions, in academia, in the media, in politics, and in sport, anti Catholicism, even when it is not particularly

malign, is as endemic as it is second nature. Scotland is guilty of sleep walking bigotry. (James MacMillan, Address to the Edinburgh Festival, August 1999)

A furore followed. MacMillan had touched a raw nerve. Was he in a time warp? Had he delivered a speech forty or fifty years out of date? Or had he let a genie out of a bottle that had for too long been plugged? In venting his anger was McMillan being inflammatory? Was he seeking to ensure that Catholic aspirations would not be eclipsed by the new Scottish Parliament? Was he merely laying the groundwork for a defence of Catholic schools under the new political dispensation? Or were critics culpable of gross negligence, overlooking the elephant that had for too long sat in the corner? In a country seeking to establish itself as a mature democracy, was MacMillan right to insist that sectarianism and bigotry stand as vital impediments to Scotland's aspiration to responsible statehood.

Reflecting upon his experience in 2006, MacMillan notes:

> Seven years ago this week I delivered a speech at the Edinburgh Festival entitled Scotland's Shame – Anti-Catholicism as a barrier to genuine pluralism. I was aware that the speech was potentially convulsive, but was unprepared for the full visceral shock of Scottish press vitriol. Before I even got home that day, a tabloid had burned a path to my door. Other redtops followed. It was clear they were in an awkward situation. No paper could claim that bigotry was a good thing, but I had included a critique of press attitudes and they wanted to fight back. My three kids were so terrified by the sequence of sullen visitors they were packed off with the childminder. The onslaught in the Scottish press was breathtakingly defensive. One commentator wrote a near-apoplectic and revealing rant in the *Herald* complaining about all the English coverage of the Edinburgh event. This washing was obviously too dirty for our Sassenach cousins to inspect. I have many friends in Scotland's media, some of whom were to give me fly-on-the wall reports of rattled discussions at the highest editorial levels. I was shocked to hear not just of the venom, but of the energy going in to stitching me up. The debate has ebbed and flowed since, developing in fascinating and fulfilling ways. The wounds of religious sectarianism are being cleansed. The Scottish executive has not fallen for the self-congratulatory and self-absolving narratives of the deniers. The Holyrood parliament is committed to tackling what Jack McConnell, the First Minister, refers to as 'Scotland's secret shame'. Official and unofficial initiatives point to a growing resolve to remove this blight from Scotland's reputation. The fearful, the squeamish and the defensive are gradually waking up and realising what has been going on these past few years. (James MacMillan, *The Guardian*, 7 August 2006)

Moreover, ten years after delivering the lecture MacMillan observed:

> Although the country's favoured experts frantically pronounce that sectarianism is a thing of the past, Scotland has given a fair impression of talking about

nothing else over the last few years. Reaction to my original lecture was 'breathtakingly defensive', 'incoherent' and 'unguarded'. Anti-Scottishness, mental derangement and even sedition were among the accusations being thrown about … It seemed imperative for some to assassinate my character. There is a sizeable element in our society that does not like this issue being discussed at all, and may think it is just the usual suspects up to no good, waging a mischievous and successful media campaign against the 'majority culture', or whatever. And the 'usual suspects' are ordinary Scottish Catholics, mostly of Irish origin who have been living with the consequences of these primal prejudices for generations. The chosen commentators spin a soothing message that we have nothing to worry about anymore. But perhaps we should be optimistic about the way the debate is blossoming. Peripherally puzzling though is the hectoring and bullying from the sidelines, attempting to stifle the emerging resolve to tackle this scar on Scotland. (James MacMillan, *The Times*, 8 December 2009)

The debate in the religious sphere

Cardinal Keith Patrick O'Brien, Scotland's foremost Catholic leader took MacMillan's rally cry to heart and has since campaigned vocally on issues such as crimes (including violent assaults) perpetrated against Catholics, the alleged socio-economic disadvantage suffered by Catholics, and unwarranted media attacks on the Catholic Church. He has complained that critics have sought to 'write off' anti Catholicism as an outcrop of football rivalries between Glasgow Celtic FC (notionally Catholic) and Glasgow Rangers FC (notionally Protestant) or as a result of alcohol fuelled brawls between youths exorcising their adolescent rites of passage, when in fact it has deeper structural roots in Scottish society. Arguably however, his chief concern has been with the institutional discrimination written into the Act of Settlement (1701) between Scotland and England, which denies Catholics the right of access to office of leader of the British Monarchy. Referring to Scotland's 'shadowy sectarian culture' O'Brien argues:

> Our constitution contains legislation which describes my faith as 'the popish religion' and defines me and my co-religionists as 'papists'. That this acranely offensive language enjoys legal sanction is outrageous. Sectarianism will continue to thrive until the British constitution is changed to amend the settlement act. Anyone who seriously believes that introducing legislation aimed at eradicating sectarian attacks, which are often verbal, while elements of the very lexicon of hate they seek to abolish remain on our statute books, is indulging in wilful ignorance. How can the state in the form of the Scottish Executive claim that religious discrimination is wrong when the state in the form of an Act of Parliament states that it is right? (Cardinal Keith O'Brien, *Scotland on Sunday*, 6 August 2006)

Protestant opinion has been divided. Moderate Protestant opinion has been conciliatory. In 2002, The Church of Scotland's Church and Nation Committee (Church of Scotland 2002) noted that the Kirk's record on sectarianism had not been particularly glorious and that 'sectarianism is not someone else's problem'. Recalling how the committee campaigned actively against Irish immigration to Scotland in the 1930s, the report noted: 'Our Church's record on this issue in times past is far from blameless. We may also be judged in hindsight to have turned a blind eye to sectarian attitudes which will still remain on and under the surface of the Church of Scotland today.' A working group was to be established to 'tackle the demon in society'. Moreover the report acknowledged that whilst the Orange Order 'clearly see themselves as a law-abiding group which promotes civil and religious liberty in Scotland it is widely perceived to be a sectarian organisation'. Accordingly, 'those within the Church of Scotland who associate themselves with the Order should reflect upon this and take this to heart'. The General Assembly was to debate the virtues of introducing an offence of 'sectarian aggravation' similar to law surrounding 'religiously aggravated crime'. The report called for a working group to be set up, if possible, in partnership with the Roman Catholic *Justice and Peace Commission*.

Meanwhile, Reverend John Miller, a former moderator of the General Assembly of the Church of Scotland, acknowledged:

> In 35 years in a Glasgow housing scheme I have learned a lot about these divisions and I have seen how they can affect every aspect of life. In more affluent areas of the city the divisions may not be so apparent, but they're still there, more subtly expressed but robust. To suggest that these attitudes are just found among drunken football fans or only in the west of Scotland is letting off society too lightly. They're found in business and in the professions, in local politics and in the golf club. And the divisions are still very deep .... In this locality the infants learn them very young. Children learn the power of a simple date written on the wall, or of three letters written on the road. The youth's all know their Ps and Qs (for Pope and Queen). And I've seen the havoc wrought when conflict, fuelled by religious division, has brought violent death. The work that is being done now in Glasgow schools and the bridges that are being built between faith's are crucial to change ... Being realistic, is it possible for centuries of religious conflict and bitterness to be put aside? Yes. I'll put my life on it. It isn't easy, it's taking time, but it's already happening. It will happen within my lifetime. We have the climate right now where people are willing to change. That's been a long time coming. (Revd John Miller, former Moderator of the General Assembly of the Church of Scotland, *The Tablet*, 22 July 2006)

In contrast militant Protestant opinion has dismissed MacMillan's claims as overblown, anachronistic, and little more than a stunt. There is no significant division with Scottish society and to the extent that old battles continue to rancour it is because faith-based schools continue to mark children out as different from early consciousness. Orange marches are a cultural tradition and legal right; they cannot be blamed for aggravating religious tensions. The Orange Order is more fearful of the establishment of a new Scottish Parliament than the Irish Catholic community and views Scottish nationalism as the single biggest threat to the future of the country. Putting aside all past grievances the Order is now prepared to actively support all pro-Unionist political parties including the Labour Party. If the Orange Order has any work to do it is in disciplining the unruly and unwelcome 'side show' which often accompanies marches even when not invited. The word 'sectarian' is much abused and inappropriately recycled in Scotland. Scotland cannot be compared to international cases where the label is more accurately applied. Within the Orange tradition in Scotland, there is a recognition that some degree of 'modernisation' is required. But the content of such internal debate and the pace of its progress reveals how far Orangeism in Scotland still has to travel. Reflecting upon the Orange Order's reading of the Scotland's shame debate, Grand Master Ian Wilson argues:

> It's gesture politics. You've got to ask how much it achieves. The Order has always advocated a single school structure. We ought not to go on pretending that this division in education is not making a contribution to sectarianism but our politicians are too scared to rock the boat. It irritates me when Jack McConnell talks about Scotland's shame. We are not at each others throats. If you want to see real sectarianism go to the Balkans or to Indonesia where people are killing each other and burning each other's houses down. (Ian Wilson, Grand Master of the Orange Order in Scotland, *The Tablet*, 22 July 2006)

The debate in the academic sphere

Meanwhile academics from many disciplinary backgrounds including Joseph Bradley, Gerry Finn, Patrick Reilly, Andrew O'Hagan, Rory Williams, Patricia Walls, Raymond Boyle, Bernard Aspinwall, Peter Lynch, Elinor Kelly, Graham Walker, David McMenemy, Alan Poulter, Patricia Walls, Rory Williams, Tom Devine, Michael Rosie, David McCrone, and Steve Bruce have joined forces to debate the question of Scotland's secret shame with an unusual degree of vigour and focus (for those seeking to gain a handle on the debate see McAspurren 2005, Kelly 2003, Bruce et al. 2004, Rosie 2004, and Flint 2008 for some of the broader and important statements and summaries). Some have taken their research out to new audiences and have become in important ways public intellectuals. The Scotland's secret shame debate has appeared to have galvanised and stimulated the academic community and has certainly fostered a productive dialogue between academy and public life.

For some academics, sectarianism remains firmly institutionalised in Scottish society. It is essential then to document the continued prevalence of anti-Irish and anti-Catholic attitudes and practices. Far from constituting a peripheral side show, football rivalry represents a powerful barometer of underlying social, cultural, economic, and political Protestant hegemony and Catholic powerlessness. Discrimination against the Irish Catholic community is evidenced in areas as diverse as politics (not least the legal restrictions on Catholics assuming the highest office in the state); employment, hiring practices and occupational earnings; the allocation of public sector resources; health inequalities; incidences of violent attacks and verbal abuse; biased and systematically negative media coverage; the routing of Orange marches through Catholic areas, and; approaches to the policing of civil society. To blame the sectarian divide in Scotland as a product of the presence of denominational schooling is simply disingenuous. Catholic schools exist in other societies which are not plagued by sectarianism and therefore cannot be blamed for causing the problem; if anything they promote integration, morality, and social cohesion.

This research tradition however has been met with fierce criticism. According to Patrick Reilly:

> The allegation of Scotland's shame by MacMillan invites three routine responses. The first is to deny that there is ever or has ever been any significant discrimination, to insist that the only enemies Catholics have ever had exist within their own fevered skulls, figments of their own morbid creating – paranoia is at once a clinical term that even football commentators now use with an easy familiarity. The second is to concede that once upon a time there was discrimination, although as in all good fairy tales, the ending is a happy one because discrimination no longer exists and need not concern us except as a historical curiosity. The third admits the continued existence of discrimination but warns against publicly discussing it, since this can do no good and may do harm, worsening the very situation to which it calls such injudicious attention. Let sleeping dogs die. The less we talk about anti Catholicism the sooner it will go away. (Reilly 2000: 30)

Critics round upon the definitional slippages that plague work on nationalism, diaspora, sectarianism and bigotry, the difficulties of assuming that simple relationships exist between sectarianism, bigotry, and discrimination, the weakness of the data sets which are being drawn upon to make the case, the fact that what data does exist points to greater assimilation than estrangement, and the competence of the research and researchers who claim otherwise (see in particular Bruce et al. 2004 and Rosie 2004). For Bruce et al. (2004):

> Scotland was never as sectarian as Northern Ireland and changes in the Scottish economy, polity, and society since the late 1930s have reduced the importance of religious and ethnic identity to a point of irrelevance .... It is surely no accident that the lists of those who think Scotland is still an endemically sectarian society are led by a musician, a novelist, and a professor of literature – all untouched by evidence beyond their personal experience. It is also significant that the few social scientists who insist that Catholics are still victims of considerable

discrimination support their argument with anecdotes drawn heavily from Scottish football. Claims about supposedly widespread social processes must be supported with society wide statistical data. Those cross tabulations, charts, and tests of significance may be hard to enjoy but they are unavoidable if this subject is to be treated seriously. (Bruce et al. 2004: 172–3, 153–4).

Critics contend that even in the 1930s, anti-Irish and anti-Catholic activism in Scotland never captured public life or public policy in any meaningful way. If the Irish Catholic community once occupied the lower rungs of the occupational strata this simply reflected their status as a poor immigrant community. The initial poverty displayed by the Irish Catholic community was true of any recent immigrant group. But immigrant socio-economic advancement has occurred and has created parity of occupational status. A wealth of careful historical analyses exists showing the ways in which Irish Catholics worked with Irish Protestants and indigenous Scots with equally low social, economic and political power to progressive ends. Moreover there are good sociological reasons to assume that anti-Irish Catholic prejudice has diminished. The changing economic base of the country has removed the stubborn sectarian practices which resided in the older industrial and factory workplaces. The new transnational companies have no truck with old habits. The rise of the Labour Party and the pre-, inter-, and post-war demolition of slum housing, the construction of social housing estates and the emergence of socialist inspired housing allocation policies, which were neither anti or pro Catholic, created new patterns of inter-religious mixing and coexistence.

Moreover wider trends towards secularism mean that the social conditions which might have aggravated sectarian conflict in the past have been removed (Aspinwall 2008). Whilst 49.21 per cent of the Scottish population call themselves Protestant (2.2 million people), and 15.9 per cent of the population identify with Roman Catholicism (803,700), 27.6 per cent of the Scottish population claim to have no religion (1.4 million) (Scottish Executive 2005a). The number who practise their faith is considerably lower again. Inter-faith marriage is now very common if not dominant. What passes off as sectarianism today (for instance, football rivalry between Glasgow Rangers FC and Glasgow Celtic FC or trouble at Orange and Republican marches and parades) is not sectarian as such; being little more than a cultural hangover from the past; nothing other than a 'boys game'; not the tip of an iceberg, but all that remains as the iceberg beneath the surface melts away. If sectarian divisions do persist they are not helped by the existence of denominational schools, discriminatory hiring practices within Catholic schools, and infringements on the public right to march.

Among the more sustained topics upon which academic debate has focused to date include:

• The role of Catholic schools as a source of division or a facility for building bridges (Finn 1999; Bruce 1999, 2003; Conroy 2001, 2003; McKinney 2007, 2008).

- Occupational, educational, and earnings discrimination, convergence and divergence between religious groupings (Walls and Williams 2003, 2005; Paterson 2000; Paterson and Iannelli 2006; Bruce et al. 2005; Battu 2005, Finn et al. 2009).
- The use of new information technologies to practice new forms of bigotry and the emergence of 'online sectarianism' (McMenemy, Poulter and O'Loan 2005; McMenemy and Poulter 2005).
- Sectarianism as a basis for youth conflict, assertions of masculinity, and gang organisation (Boyle 2001b, Holligan and Deuchar 2009; Deuchar and Holligan 2010).
- The role of housing strategy and policy in the promotion and/or taming of sectarian divisions (Paterson 2002).
- The status of football as a reflection of and/or cause of division and bitterness (Finn and Giulianotti 2000; Bradley 1996, 2004, 2006, 2008, 2009; Reid 2008; Burdsey and Chappell 2001; Esplin and Walker 2007, 2010).
- The importance of political and religious marches and the question of the uses and abuses of the rights to the city (Scottish Executive 2006d)
- The national identities claimed by Irish migrants and the extent of migrant and diasporic attachment to Scotland (Clayton 2002, 2005).
- Trends in inter-faith marriage and their potential social and political ramifications (Holligan and Raab 2010).
- Health inequalities, including differential mortality and morbidity rates (Mullen et al. 2000; Abbotts et al. 1997, 1998, 1999, 2001; Walls and Williams 2004).

Perhaps the wisest voice to have emerged in the debate remains that of Professor Tom Devine, Scotland's most acclaimed historian. In his edited collection titled *Scotland's shame: bigotry and sectarianism in modern Scotland*, Devine concludes with the observation that for two core reasons 'no final agreed position is yet possible on the question of anti-Catholicism in Scottish society' (Devine 2000: 261). First the protagonists in the debate would appear to be arguing about two different things. Some are concerned with 'social attitudes, the territory of the mind, the heart, and the spirit', where a 'culture of prejudice' is the object of analyses. Others are more interested in the effects of such a culture on actual life chances, positions in class and occupational hierarchies, rates of socio-economic advancement, political and electoral success, and equity in the distribution of items of collective consumption. Second, the data which would be required to address the question objectively simply do not exist. Disputes over data sets mean that claims and counter claims will continue to be made about what constitutes good evidence, good social science and indeed legitimate knowledge. It would appear that final resolution will come only when data of sufficient quantity and quality has been produced, disseminated, dissected, contested, and reconciled on the key issues.

The debate in the political sphere

Political leaders in Scotland responded to MacMillan's fears with serious intent. In June 2003 Section 74 of the Criminal Justice (Scotland) Act 2003 came into effect paving the way for stiffer sentences to be given to those found guilty of crimes aggravated by religious prejudice. In February 2005, Scotland's then First Minister Jack McConnell placed sectarianism at the forefront of his term of office by convening a national 'Summit on Sectarianism' (Scottish Executive 2005b and 2005c) and in January 2006 published an 'Action Plan on Tackling Sectarianism in Scotland' (Scottish Executive 2006a, 2006b). This Action Plan proposes 18 Action Points through which sectarianism might be tackled, focusing upon the role of education and schooling, sport and in particular football alliances, ecumenical worship and interfaith dialogue, marching and parades, and the importance of establishing a 'Task Force on Tackling Sectarianism'. According to McConnell;

> The bigoted and sectarian attitudes and behaviours of a minority have scarred Scottish life for too long. I have seen this bigotry throughout my life and I still see it today in some parts of Scotland. Manifestations of sectarian bigotry may change, but the divisions, anger and resentment that they cause remain firmly entrenched in Scottish life. It doesn't have to be like this ... The tide is turning against the bigoted few and we must let the bigots and bullies know that sectarian behaviour has no place in today's Scotland. I fully recognise that there are no quick fixes or easy solutions here, but I am certainly not pessimistic about our future. I truly believe that through positive action, we can put sectarian attitudes into the dustbin of history and build a better society. (Jack McConnell, Scotland's First Minister, Scottish Executive 2006a: 1)

A 'Second Summit on Sectarianism' was then held in December 2006 and a further 'Update on the Action Plan on tackling sectarianism in Scotland' was published in the same month (Scottish Executive 2006c).

Of course in May 2007, the Scottish National Party succeeded the Labour Party in Scottish elections and Alex Salmond replaced Jack McConnell as Scotland's First Minister and leader of the devolved Scottish Government. It remains an open question whether Salmond has pursued the anti-sectarian agenda with the same vigour but questions have already been posed about his commitment to this area of public policy. It is certainly the case that Salmond has tempered the heat and ferocity of the debate and for some it would seem accurate to say that the Scottish National Party have sought to quietly and diplomatically 'park' policy making in this area. The intensity of the debate is receding and the energy the Scottish Government has invested in addressing the topic has subsided. But it is interesting to note that in the run up to the election, Salmond was given public backing by Cardinal Keith O'Brien and himself made commitments to prioritise the repeal of the Act of Settlement:

I remember back in the 1980s when I worked for the Royal Bank of Scotland and in the banking sector at that time there were still some lingering, unspoken but real barriers for Catholics. There are bigots in all walks of life but today, within Scotland's highly successful financial community, discrimination on the grounds of religion would be stamped on vigorously. There is no doubt that a Catholic could rise to head any one of Scotland's top companies. Discrimination still does fester in some individuals and I'm sure it exists in some form in a small number of boardrooms and among a handful of decision makers, but we are light years on from where Scotland was half, even quarter a century ago. An independent Scottish government I lead will remove once and for all the institutionalised discrimination at the heart of the Act of Settlement – no ifs, no buts or maybes but decisive action. (Scotland's First Minister Alex Salmond, *Scottish Catholic Observer*, 30 November 2006)

Moreover, in early 2009 Salmond provided funding to keep the influential anti-sectarian lobby group *Nil by Mouth* alive. Nil by Mouth was founded by Cara Henderson following the sectarian murder of her friend and Celtic FC supporter Mark Scott in Bridgeton, a known Orange and Rangers FC neighbourhood in 1995. Nil by Mouth has been a leading campaigning and advocacy group ever since and has provided unrelenting critique of sectarian and bigoted practices in Scotland, to the discomfort of some.

Nevertheless in 2008 in the Scottish Parliament, former First Minister Jack McConnell accused Alex Salmond of failing to take forward the anti-sectarian agenda and not giving it the profile it deserved. Attacking Salmond for being 'weak' and 'complacent' in not hosting a 'Third Summit on Sectarianism'. McConnell asked the current First Minister 'to explain why he has not maintained the progress of recent years on sectarianism in Scotland'. He further demanded to know: 'Will he commit to reconvene in this coming year the sectarianism summit?' When Salmond attempted to defend the Scottish Nationalist Party's record on sectarianism McConnell countered: 'A sectarianism summit would take half a day from his diary in the next 12 months and he has refused to commit to any action to maintain the progress of recent years and end the appearance of complacency. I urge him to think seriously about leading Scotland on this matter and not be left behind.' McConnell alleged that sectarianism was like a cancer in society, it would grow back if not constantly subdued.

Meanwhile in 2009, in response to an article written by sports journalist Graham Spiers titled: 'Salmond accused of being soft on bigotry' Alex Salmond countered that he found headlines such as these 'personally very hurtful' and that he would fight bigotry in Scotland to the death:

I grew up in West Lothian, so sectarianism is not unknown to me from my youth. I've never hated anything quite as much as sectarianism. It is destructive, it is dreadful, it is a scar on our Scottish society. But I do think we deserve a legitimate debate on how to tackle it. I've got my own views on sectarianism in Scotland.

And just because I don't think that endless summits of high-heidyins is the best way to tackle it, does not mean that I diminish the problem. I think you've got to work at it at the grass roots, such as in the schools projects we've got going. Perhaps we should bring more humour into it, by presenting sectarianism as ridiculous, as absurd. It is something I would be quite interested in. I'm interested in the idea of depicting bigotry as old-fashioned, as something silly or stupid. But there is definitely a tragic side to it all, in terms of the casualties and the damage to our society. It is still a blight on Scotland and something we have to defeat. And it will be done by patiently working away to make it a ridiculous relic of the past. (Scotland's First Minister Alex Salmond, *The Times*, 18 March 2009)

In the same response Salmond referred to the formative importance of the infamous Monklands East by-election, called in 1994 after the death of John Smith, the then Leader of the Labour Party. In a heated and at times emotional campaign, politicians of all political hues became mired in local sectarian issues and the by-election degenerated into a conflict over the allocation and rationing of resources by and to different faith communities:

I was very affected by that by-election. Sectarianism was still a part of our politics well into the 1990s and that Monklands by-election was tousy and too often fought along sectarian lines. The nature of the whole campaign just made you feel dirty. I went to see Cardinal Tom Winning, a great cleric with a common touch, after Monklands and I said to him, 'Tom, what can we do about this'. He said two things to me. First, having been a parish priest in Lanarkshire in the 1950s, he said it was nothing like as bad as it was. And, two, he said: 'By your deeds are you known.' The point I'd like to make is, yes, we've got lots of things to do, and a distance still to travel, and we will nail bigotry. But let's get this in perspective. Scotland is not as sectarian a place as it was when I was growing up. In West Lothian and in parts of Lanarkshire it isn't even as sectarian as it was in the 1990s (Scotland's First Minister Alex Salmond, *The Times*, 18 March 2010)

Recent developments

For a period the debate displayed signs of abatement. It seemed that Alex Salmond's lower profile approach was producing results. But events in the past year have served to fan a new set of flames and sadly Scotland has become besmirched in the media, both at home and abroad, as a country with a sectarian problem. In tracking recent developments, attention might first be drawn to the furore which followed the singing of the so called 'Irish Famine Song' by fans of Rangers FC during a match with Celtic FC in August 2008. The singing of this song, targeted at migrants who fled to Scotland to avoid the Irish Potato famine in the late 1840s, was accompanied by the throwing of potatoes onto the field of play. The song is narrated as follows:

The Irish Famine song

I often wonder where they would have been
If we hadn't have taken them in
Fed them and washed them
Thousands in Glasgow alone
From Ireland they came
Brought us nothing but trouble and shame
Well the famine is over
Why don't they go home?

Now Athenry Mike was a thief
And Large John he was fully briefed
And that wee traitor from Castlemilk
Turned his back on his own
They've all their Papists in Rome
They have U2 and Bono
Well the famine is over
Why don't they go home?

Now they raped and fondled their kids
That's what those perverts from the dark side did
And they swept it under the carpet
and Large John he hid
Their evils seeds have been sown
Cause they're not of our own
Well the famine is over
Why don't you go home?

Now Timmy don't take it from me
Cause if you know your history
You've persecuted thousands of people
In Ireland alone
You turned on the lights
Fuelled U boats by night
That's how you repay us
It's time to go home.

Appalled at the ignorance of some Scots to the human tragedy that was the Irish potato famine, the Irish Consulate in Edinburgh submitted a formal complaint to the Scottish Government. Condemned by Rangers FC and threatened with arrest if caught singing the song, some Rangers FC fans protested that the reaction was exaggerated, that the song was merely a 'wind up' which was no worse than the republican rebel songs sung by Celtic FC supporters which glorified murders committed by Irish Republicans. The Irish, Catholic and Celtic community needed to take stock of its own sectarian spine before passing judgement on the problem of sectarian hate in Scotland. The Chairman of Celtic FC, former British Home Secretary Dr John Reid, joined the affray and in October 2008 commented:

> This song is vile, racist and sectarian. As both Rangers Football Club and Strathclyde Police have stated, the content of the song – which is directed against the community of Irish descent in Scotland – is in breach of Race Relations legislation and exposes its perpetrators to the risk of prosecution. The Irish Famine was a human tragedy of immense proportions. Few of those who sing this song will have stopped to think that famine is nonsectarian and the millions of people who died or were forced into mass emigration – some to Scotland – were from all faiths and traditions within Ireland. We should condemn racism and sectarianism without fear or favour wherever they arise. There is offensive chanting and singing going on and I encourage anyone who has not read the song, however distasteful it is, to read it so they can see that we are not over-reacting. (John Reid, Former British Home Secretary, Chairman of Celtic Football Club, 29 September 2008)

A recent test of the pervasiveness and virulence of anti-Catholicism in Scotland was prompted by the visit to Scotland by Pope Benedict XVI in September 2010. In preparation for the visit the Pope addressed Scotland's Catholic Bishops and observed that the country had for 450 years been troubled by religious division. He praised Catholic Schools for making a telling and critical contribution to the breaking down of sectarian barriers: 'You can be proud of the contribution made by Scotland's Catholic schools in overcoming sectarianism and building good relations between communities. Faith schools are a powerful force for social cohesion, and when the occasion arises, you do well to underline this point' (Pope Benedict XVI *The Times*, February 2010). But he also praised Scottish and British society for its reputation for tolerance also. Moreover, whilst the Free Presbyterian Church of Scotland led opposition to the visit on behalf of a number of smaller Protestant churches, secular and humanist opposition to the visit of the Pope were equally vehement and potent focusing upon financial, constitutional and moral grounds. In debate, the abuse of children by priests and alleged institutional covering up of such abuse, claims of an active participation of priests in IRA attacks in the 1970s, the insistence on segregated schooling, contraception, and sexuality, all emerged as key concerns. Meanwhile the Church of Scotland welcomed the visit and the Orange Order refused to condemn it. Notwithstanding the later revelation that Cardinal Keith O'Brien had received live ammunition and a death threat in the post in the run up to the papal visit, it appeared that progress was being made.

But still disputations rumbled on. In November 2010 and with reference to perceived unfair criticism of Category One Referees by some football clubs, including Celtic FC, the Scottish Senior Football Referees' Association called a one day strike. Celtic FC in particular had demanded that action be taken by the Scottish Football Association (SFA) against a referee who admitted to telling lies to Celtic FC manager Neil Lennon about a decision he made to rescind a penalty kick he had awarded to Celtic. More seriously amidst allegations that at the time of the papal visit to Scotland Head of Referee Development Hugh Dallas had distributed an offensive e-mail insinuating a connection between the Pope and Paedophilia, Director of Media in the Catholic Church in Scotland, Peter Kearney sought to question why the SFA had failed to disclose details of their investigation into the matter. Kearney demanded to know what the SFA were going to do with Dallas if he was found guilty of circulating messages which were 'totally unprofessional, gratuitously insulting to the Pope, deeply offensive to the Catholic community of Scotland, and an incitement to anti-Catholic sectarianism' (Peter Kearney, Director of Media, Catholic Church Scotland, *Daily Record*, 24 November 2010). Kearney demanded that the results of the SFA investigation be made public, that the SFA treat the matter with urgency, and that Dallas be sacked if findings against him were proved. Kearney defended the Church intervening in what was already a volatile milieu by adding: 'This is not a sport issue, it's much bigger than sport. It's an issue of religious respect, sectarianism and bigotry. If the person sent the email described, it is a personal attack on the leader of the Catholic Church and it's a bigoted and sectarian act.' According to Kearney, the incident proved that the Scottish nation remained plagued by a sectarian current which was 'deep, wide and vicious' (Peter Kearney, Director of Media, Catholic Church Scotland, *Daily Record*, 24 November 2010) On 27 November 2010 Hugh Dallas left his post as Head of Referee Development for 'family reasons'.

Meanwhile events surrounding Celtic FC manager Neil Lennon have served to generate much controversy and have reopened debate with renewed virulence. Lennon, who is both Irish and Catholic, was the subject of death threats in 2002 when he was a Celtic FC player and was forced to refuse captaincy of the Northern Irish football team and retire from international duty on police advice. He was assaulted in the West End of Glasgow in 2008 and was knocked unconscious. In January 2011 Lennon, who now served as manager of Celtic FC, and along with other Irish born Celtic FC football players, was sent live ammunition in the post. Throughout the Spring of 2011, packages containing nail bombs which were sent to Lennon as well as QC Paul McBride who was acting on behalf of Lennon and Labour MSP and Celtic FC supporter Trish Godman were intercepted by mail couriers. Finally (at least at the point at which this book is going to press), at an SPL match against Hearts FC in April 2011 Lennon was physically attacked by a football fan who managed to invade the pitch and access the coaching area during the match. The assailant was apprehended and charged with 'breach of the peace aggravated by religious prejudice and assault aggravated by religious prejudice'. This came just days after seven people were arrested outside Celtic FCs training ground for possession of an imitation weapon. The morning following the match with Hearts FC also witnessed the further interception of a package containing a bullet sent to Lennon and addressed to Celtic FC football stadium.

Against the backdrop of these events and prompted by a particularly fractious match between Celtic FC and Rangers FC, Scotland's First Minister Alex Salmond decided in favour of a more proactive and interventionist policy. Salmond convened a summit with representatives from both clubs, the Scottish Football Association (SFA) and Strathclyde Police in March 2011. The principal output from this summit was the production of a new six point action plan, consisting of:

- The creation of an autonomus pan-Scotland police football intelligence unit;
- Greater enforcement of existing legislation to deal with sectarianism and alcohol related offences;
- The institution of a task force consisting of senior police officers, government representatives and club security personnel, to deliver joined up policing of football matches across Scotland;
- The commissioning of a detailed academic study into the extent of the relationship of football to violent crime committed both in the domestic sphere and in the public spaces of the city;
- An agreement by Celtic FC and Rangers FC to commit to playing an enhanced role in a partnership approach to encourage responsible consumption of alcohol;
- A rebranded and re-enforced code of conduct for players and officials.

Speaking after Lennon was attacked in the coaching area of Hearts FC's ground, Salmond noted:

> Let's be absolutely clear as First Minister of Scotland, we are not going to tolerate sectarian displays of any kind in the terraces and stands of football matches; that will be driven from games in Scotland. Nor are we going to tolerate hate pedalled over the internet in anonymity: people think they've got some immunity as a result of that, that's not going to be tolerated either. There's no debate or discussion about this anymore in Scotland, that's just the way it's going to be. It's not going to be easy, it's going to be difficult, it won't happen in a match, perhaps it won't even happen in an entire season, but that's what's going to happen. We're going to eradicate it from our football game, and we're going to eradicate it from wider Scottish society. (Alex Salmond, Scotland's First Minister, Sky TV, 12 April 2011)

Meanwhile Peter Lawwell Chief Executive of Celtic FC lamented:

> We are the only Club to be the subject of such vile, sustained and relentless attacks. It is intolerable that any football club, or individual, going about their lawful business in the name of sport should be subjected to this ongoing campaign of hatred and intimidation. This is Scotland's shame and it is high time Scotland addressed it. Since moving here a decade ago, Neil Lennon has had to endure prejudice and violence both as a player and manager, having suffered no such problems elsewhere.

> In doing so, he has displayed a strength of character and resilience which deserves respect from all who oppose the campaign of intimidation against him … All right-minded people will surely condemn these actions but, as a society, we must also address the underlying factors that lead to such behaviour. (Peter Lawwell, Chief Executive, Celtic FC, Celtic FC press release, 12 April 2011)

Amidst the chaos of a public realm fearful of what might develop and concerned to stifle sectarian divisions lest they further escalate, academic Steve Bruce has continued to insist that the question of sectarianism in Scotland is a myth that needs to be finally laid to rest. According to Bruce, 'myths thrive on naivety, carelessness and exaggeration'. Social Scientific survey evidence needs to be foregrounded in debates that now suffer from bias and subjectivity. Most Scots do not follow Celtic FC or Rangers FC and most fans of both clubs are not bigots. There is no evidence of discrimination against Catholics in the labour market. As much as it is to be deplored, violence dubbed sectarianism is often nothing more than regular violence *per se*. Residential segregation never occurred in Glasgow like it did in Belfast. The labour movement galvanised the native Scot and Irish Catholic settler behind a common purpose. Interfaith marriage is on the ascendancy. According to Bruce, 'Scotland's disgrace is not religious bigotry. It is the unthinking way in which sectarianism is assumed, without evidence'. Bruce concludes:

> That some Rangers and Celtic fans wind each other up by falsely claiming to have strong religio-ethnic identities which are offended by the equally false religio-ethnic identities of the other side is not a reason for the rest of us to take such ritual posturing as the basis for judging the polity, society and culture of an entire country. (Professor Steve Bruce, the *Guardian*, 24 April 2011)

For right or wrong and whatever the outcome, as academic Tom Devine reminds us, Scotland remains the only place where Irish Catholics and Protestants settled in any great number over the past 200 years that still deems it necessary to have an anti-sectarian policy in the year 2011.

Approach and method: Transcending the will to topology

This book is based upon the interrogation of a new oral history archive the author collected between 2000 and 2002. This archive collects together stories which members of the Irish Catholic community tell about their migration to and settlement into Scotland. Those who take sectarianism and bigotry to be a problem in Scotland may search this book for accounts which foreground victimisation and discrimination, both in the past and the present. Appointing themselves guardians of Irish Catholic communal memory and oral history, they might smear this book as unnecessarily complicating histories of sectarianism and bigotry that are better conveyed using less obfuscatory data. Meanwhile, those who dismiss the significance of sectarianism and bigotry in Scotland may search this book for accounts which replace tales of intolerance, discrimination, bigotry, and sectarianism with positive stories which foreground kindness, acceptance, integration and assimilation, and which confirm the general belief that things are much better for the Irish Catholic community today than yesteryear. Appointing themselves guardians of the canons of social science research, they might smear this book as yet another piece of qualitative research that ought to be ignored as it fails the litmus test of good social science.

To be clear, the data collected for the purposes of writing this book are not and were never intended to serve as a contribution to resolving the 'two tribes' or 'one nation' debate in Scotland. I assume no especial position in this debate and offer no empirical evidence which is suitably equipped to come down on one side of the debate or the other. I do not seek to measure or scale or calibrate or survey or compute the objective status of anti-Irish sentiment and anti-Catholic discrimination and bigotry. For sure included in the book are tales of woe and bitter division, alongside of course stories of friendship and tolerance. But these testimonies can never be treated as anything other than illustrative. In no sense are claims to representativeness being made. The selection of particular biographies for scrutiny reflects an interest in shedding insights into particular processes. My choices in no way imply that some biographies are more important or more common or more typical than any others.

For this author, the most interesting question which the Scotland's secret shame debate has raised but which thus far has stimulated only an impoverished response is the following: *is the Irish Catholic encounter with Scotland intelligible and if it is what is the nature of this intelligibility?* My starting point is that the Irish Catholic community in Scotland occupies a unique cultural location; former colons now resident in a metropolitan heartland of former colonisers. I notice that this type of colonial encounter is unique in many ways; British and Scottish colonial relations with Ireland are distinctive; division and divide are being worked through in the metropolitan heartland and not the colonial periphery; both coloniser and colonised are white and racism on the basis of skin colour is less profound; and; the conflict in Northern Ireland notwithstanding both communities are coming into confrontation with one another out of the historical context in which relationships were historically cast. Nevertheless, even when framed in this way it is possible and useful to bring the Scotland's shame debate into dialogue with recent developments in the theorisation of concrete colonialisms which help us to critically interrogate the very foundations and assumptions upon which the debate is based.

Arguably, the Irish Catholic community in Scotland has become a victim of certain theoretical practices which need to be provincialised. These practices normalise culturally specific academic practices or ways of framing, researching, interrogating, and apprehending the Irish Catholic experience. In claiming to be able to theoretically and empirically establish the existence or non-existence of anti-Irish Catholic sentiment both camps in the Scotland's secret shame debate fall prey to what I will term *metrocentricism*, a practice which is predicated upon an unduly unreflexive commitment to the superiority of particularly western forms of social scientific practice and universal theorising in the search for the intelligibility of particular and concrete colonialisms. As observed in the previous chapter, the idea of metrocentricism has come to the fore recently in critical reflections on the status not only of professional and establishment social enquiry but also of critical and post-colonial theory itself. In seeking to comprehend the experiences, attitudes, practices, and politics of populations who have been colonised, past and present, arguably western social scientific research and radical and anti-colonial theory and praxis have assumed a certain sovereign supremacy over ways of knowing and apprehending the geopolitics of empire. Crucially, metrocetricism is equally a problem for critical, anti-establishment and radical sociological praxis as it is for professional, instrumental and/or establishment sociology. This idea has importance for the ways in which we think about the Scotland's shame debate. Here the difficulty is not so much that both camps base their claims to truth on different forms of sociological knowledge, but instead that both work under the assumption that they have a right and authority to make claims to truth in the first instance. Critiques of metrocentricism demand that renewed attention be paid to the situated production of readings of the Irish Catholic encounter with Scotland.

The purpose of this book is to build a case for borrowing three metaphors from the geographical lexicon to inform a search for the intelligibility of the Irish Catholic encounter with Scotland. Like Chakrabarty (2007) I too wish to offer a two histories approach but I replace History 1 and History 2 with the notions of topology and topography, and in addition give heightened attention to the cartographical tools or methods through which topology and topography might be brought into dialogue.

Topology. I search for the rules that allow the dots to be joined. I set five conditions on any topological account in this context: first the Irish Catholic experience of Scotland does not make sense without attention being given to the historical significance of British colonial rule in Ireland and the workings of a displaced, residual, and anachronistic colonial gaze in Scotland; second, any framework must provide an opportunity to vent and ventilate a wide diversity of stories about how this gaze is encountered, interiorised, and reacted to; third, attention must be given to the ways in which the Irish Catholic community in Scotland has chosen to craft an open and emerging social and cultural formation which is historically novel and different from the Irish Catholic communities which exist in Ireland and in other parts of the Irish diaspora; fourthly, any approach must allow an understanding of both processes of alterity and belonging and in particular how belonging often can be produced out of alterity, through relationships built upon a common sense of humanity between Irish Catholics and the native Scot; and finally, attention must be given to the risks inherent in anti-racist racism practised by Irish Catholics themselves and to the ongoing tension which exists between anti-colonialism and Irish Catholic nationalism. Without prejudicing the merits of different forms of sociological enquiry my theoretical framing then will draw inspiration in this instance from Jean-Paul Sartre's theory of colonialism.

Topographical. I paint the landscape in all its unruly complexity. The Irish Catholic encounter with Scotland has spawned a rich diversity of biographies and imbrications, intermeshings, and interweavings which cannot be reduced to interiorisation of or resistance to colonial objectification. There is a need to air and to share all stories, good, bad, and indifferent.

Cartographical. I reflect upon the mediating role of method in brokering dialogue between topology and topography. Topography always exceeds topology but it remains little more than anarchic driftwood and unintelligible morass without a topological vista. But how can topological and topographical historiographies be allowed to co-exist? What theoretical frameworks might both permit productive tensions to exist and better still harness these productive tensions so as to deepen and intensify insight? It is here that the work of cartography begins, providing a language to pro-actively mediate the dialogue and facilitating specific kinds of conversation.

The core problem with the Scotland's secret shame debate then is the debilitating will to topological historiography which undergirds the positions of both critics and apologists. In spite of their differences both share a common point of departure: that it is possible to figure out the meaning of the Irish Catholic encounter with Scotland. This community may have a complex trajectory and biography but it is capable of being apprehended and narrated. It has order, a pattern, a logic, and an intelligibility. The challenge is merely to search for the right cipher to unlock the secret and mysterious code. I question such faith in topological historiographies and perspectives. They are necessary but insufficient. The question of the meaning of the Irish Catholic encounter with Scotland demands more sophisticated handling. Although social scientific enquiry into Scotland's secret shame has revealed much of interest, it has failed to interrogate the metrocentric ontologies which have underpinned it. It is time to think more deeply about what the debate actually means, how it should be approached, and what is to be done if the debate is treated not as a policy debacle but more as a classic metrocentric anxiety.

My search for a method is predicated upon seven central propositions which can now be summarised in schematic form for direction:

1. British colonial rule over Ireland continues to reverberate culturally in Scotland, both directly and in mutant and derivative forms, and remains fundamental to some indigenous attitudes towards Ireland and the Irish. The echoes of empire continue to thunder in Scotland in definance of the historical passing of the British empire, in part as a result of the rebirth of conflict in Northern Ireland from the late 1960s. *I refer to this as the primary colonial look.* The Irish experience of Scotland is also fundamentally colorated by the fact that Irish migration to Scotland has placed former subjects of British colonial rule into a unique post-colonial

location. Underlying historical relations have heightened as well as been heightened by the existence of local tensions, struggles, and conflicts which have surrounded settlement and the planting of new roots. I refer to this as the *secondary colonial look*.

2. There is a Sartrean history to be written of the ways in which the Irish community interiorises and reacts to both primary and secondary colonial looks – *I refer to this as a topological history of the Irish Catholicic encounter with Scotland*. A Sartrean topological reading of the Irish Catholic community in Scotland would seek to frame the historical formation of this community in terms of a cyclical fluctuation between what he might term groups in series, groups in fusion, and groups in metastases or what I will term here masses, sponteneity and tribe. It would foreground the central importance of the problematic status of being Irish Catholic in the public realm and would draw attention to the critical importance of the toxic ways in which anti-Irish sentiment can be interiorised. It would express an interest in the local, contingent, novel, and unique cultural formations which result from groups in fusion and which give life to the emergent and fluid category 'Irish Catholic in Scotland'. But it would also be cautious of moves to essentialise this category and would be vigilant of the ways in which the category might become a source of enslavement rather than a vehicle for liberation. It would be attracted to the role which the category Irish Catholic in Scotland might play in the totalising of anti-colonial struggles more generally. It would ask if this role is being played to the full today.

3. There is a history to be written of the stories the Irish Catholic community tells itself about migration to and settlement into Scotland – *I refer to this as a topographic history of the Irish Catholic encounter with Scotland.* The Irish experience of primary and secondary colonial objectification has and continues to be mediated and usurped not only by date of migration, as most of the debate has focused upon thus far, but by generation, age, class, gender, sexuality, location of origin, location of destination, family composition, and so on. Diasporic communities and indigenous communities are organised around different modalities of power (principally, class, race, gender, ethnicity, nationalism, generation and sexuality) which intersect with each other in different ways. Diasporeans occupying a variety of social locations interlace with indigenous populations occupying a variety of social locations and the biography of each diasporean is therefore unique. There is no one encounter with the host, no one experience of estrangement or belonging, and no single experience of, common reaction to, or proactive engagement with alterity.

4. Topological historiography and topographical historiography need to be brought into a dialogue for mutual self enrichment. Topological mappings apprehend something of the Irish story in Scotland but are tempered and mediated by topography's insistence on recovering multiple, anarchic,

and complex biographical encounters. But topology helps topographical enquiry in so far as it recognises that in searching for complexity and messiness there is a danger that the permeation of many biographies with stories of alterity, and the workings of alterity on many life courses may be lost. The key is not to apply Sartre's theory of colonialism simplistically to the case of the Irish Catholic community in Scotland or to clumsily retrofit the experiences of this community within a Sartrean theoretical framework. Instead the task is to hold Sartre's universal theoretical constructs and an elevated interest in the local and the contingent in constant suspension, and to reflect upon the fruits which cross dialogue might bear. *I call this a moment of cartographical reflection.*

5. A set of cartographic tools are required to make this mapping possible. There needs to be a language through which dialogue might be mediated. Of course this language can never be thought of as a neutral bases for conversation and brokers what kind of conversation is possible. My cartographical tool box is based upon the *progressive-regressive* method and the method of *oral history*. Dialogue between topology and topography can usefully be undertaken by locating disaggregated molecular life stories into the broader sweep of history of which they are part. Sartre himself refers to this as a *progressive-regressive* method – his own method of choice. This method foregrounds the dialectical relations which exist between personal projects and the wider dramas of history; both context and charisma. The intention of this study then is to reveal how particular lives, personal projects, individual adventures, and unique family biographies have been lived out as the overarching drama has unfolded, intertwining with history whilst at the same time making that history. I use the *oral history* method here to mobilise Sartre's progressive-regressive method; that is to unravel the biographical threads through which history is constituted and in turn constitutes. Close study of the oral histories of migration and settlement produced, reproduced, negotiated, policed, circulated, and promoted by Irish Catholic families sheds unprecedented insights into how particular and unique biographies have been imbricated in and woven through the Irish encounter with this particular postcolonial space, and how these lives have played a role in shaping multiple and complex responses to and struggles over otherness. In many ways, the oral history method is *par excellence* a Sartrean method, capturing data which is capable of entering into dialogue with both Sartrean Existentialism and Sartrean Marxism.

6. There exist at least five types of stories around which it would seem important to explore productive tensions between topological and topographical mappings. These are respectively:

- Nationality – shifting senses of belonging and the emergence of complex national identities.
- Imagining Ireland – diasporic images of 'home' including the role of childhood holidays in producing a romanticised collection of images of Ireland.
- Political – the influences of anti-colonialism and Irish nationalism in diasporic attitudes to Irish and Scottish politics.
- Cultural – the ways of life at the life of ways which have marked Irish cultural life in Scotland, including the role of Roman Catholicism.
- Economic – experiences of poverty, discrimination in the workplace, and the quest for equality of opportunity and occupational status.

The approach adopted here is best represented through a particular type of textual strategy. This strategy is based upon the preservation of the integrity of topographical detail and the strict subordination of topology to topography through the empirical sections of this book. Topological mapping then becomes a force again in the concluding chapter of the book. Here, a formal interrogation of what my cartographic tools have been able to contribute to dialogue between topology and topography will be presented. As a consequence, the empirical chapters are heavily protected from the imposing narrative of topology and their structure is not formally stamped by the imperatives of topology. Whilst the presentation of oral testimonies is organised into definitive themes with their own logic and localised conclusions, no overall theoretical interpretation is forced onto the chapters and no formal analytical conclusions are incorporated at the end of each chapter. My choice of course is not to deposit a series of descriptive empirical chapters; the reader will note the tortuous analyses and active if subtle construction which underpins each chapter. But my goal is to avoid *metrocentric* over determinations of the meaning of particular family stories and to strive to allow these stories to speak for themselves and in all their complexity.

PART II
Topographical Mappings of the
Irish Catholic Adventure in Scotland

Prologue
The Oral History Archive

In selecting a set of cartographic tools which might be capable of mapping the topographical details of the Irish Catholic encounter with Scotland in a way that can facilitate later dialogue with Sartre's theory of colonialism, both Sartre's own progressive-regressive method and the oral history method presented themselves as worthy of deployment. The progressive-regressive method is taken by Sartre to refer to the value of studying biographies in their historical context; it is a variant of the Marxian maxim that men (sic) make history but not in conditions of their own choosing. Sartre introduces the method in the *Critique of dialectical reason* but puts it to work in his titanic biography of Gustave Flaubert which he completed in 1971 (Sartre 1987). Sartre asks; how is such a man like Gustav Flaubert possible? His search for an answer leads him to oscillate between individualised psychoanalytic and historical and societal interrogation.

Although not of this genre, this book takes oral history to be an archetypical Sartrean research method, a way of mobilising Sartre's own progressive-regressive method whereby individual and family biographies are placed in historical context whilst history is treated as a fabric woven together from a mass of different interacting biographies. Oral history can scale memory to finer levels of resolution, the trials and tribulations of everyday life can be excavated. Oral history has a role to play in prising open hidden pasts by recovering the unfolding of historical events from the vantage point of those normally excluded from the record. The collection of first-hand testimonies from those who lived through and experienced both dramatic and mundane pasts adds a richness to historiography which is often lacking. The passing down of memories to siblings provides for a retention of personal experiences which would otherwise be quite literally buried. Not only does oral history provide a 'history from below', it brings emotions, feelings, attitudes, ideology, and opinions to bear on otherwise dry and arid historical narratives.

Once doubted for its rigour and often thought of as a poor relation to professional historiographical methodology, undoubtedly oral history has now secured its status as a legitimate research method in the social sciences. In the United Kingdom, the journal *Oral History* produced by the *Oral History Society* has emerged as the standard outlet for research in the field. In the United States meanwhile *Oral History Review* published by the *Oral History Association* functions as a key reference point. More generally the *International Oral History Association*, formed to coordinate awareness of oral history research taking place around the world, publishes oral history research in its journal *Words and Silences*. Meanwhile, Thompson's (2000) *The Voice of the Past*, Perks and Thompson's

(2006) *The Oral History Reader*, Lummis' (1988) *Listening to history: The authenticity of oral evidence*, and Ritchie's (2003) *Doing Oral History: a practical guide* all provide useful starting points for those wishing to deploy the method.

Oral history as a social practice

Still the data generated through the oral history method struggles to gain the respect of some professional historians. For some the problem of 'faulty memory' gravely inhibits the ability of oral testimonies to shed insights into historical events. It is unrealistic for people to recount a faithful representation of what happened on a particular day or week or month or year, especially many years after the event took place. Retrospective accounts will be plagued by re-orderings of memory, lapses of memory, nostalgia, repression, and possibly even outright amnesia. Cognitive failure is inevitable, not least with age and time, and the truthfulness and therefore value of oral histories need to be severely questioned. Oral history interviews are simply not objective enough to be taken seriously by professional historiographers. They are useful only for populist local historiographies which are designed for public entertainment and amusement rather than rigorous scholarly exploration.

In response, oral history has become preoccupied with questions of objectivity, accuracy and representativeness. The practice of collecting, analysing and presenting oral histories has demanded that elevated rigour be applied when deciding upon sampling strategies, compiling interview schedules, recruiting and preparing respondents, conducting interviews, recording, transcribing and storing interviews, resolving ethical issues, and making use of the 'product'. But in fact the problem of 'faulty memory' deserves more philosophical and deeper investigation. Over the past decade, scholarship in a variety of disciplines has sought to critique orthodox conceptions of memory developed in mainstream Psychology. In contrast to what might be referred to as 'cognitivist' approaches to memory and memory failure, which privileges and indeed take for granted the concept of 'cartesian memory', recent work has sought to draw attention to the social structuring of memory.

The concept of social or 'collective memory' has been the subject of much debate in forums as divergent as the discourse-analytic turn within Social Psychology (Middleton and Edwards 1989), Sociology (Conway 2010), historical studies of memory (Samuel 1994 – see also the special issues of the journals *Representations* (Davis and Starn 1989) and *The Journal of American History* (Thelen 1989a)), Anthropology (see the special edition of *Oceania* (Lattas 1996)), and Theatre and Film Studies (see the special edition of *New Formations* (Carter and Hirschkop 1996)). In spite of its diversity, this literature is united in proposing that instead of enquiring into how accurate oral histories are or how faithful they recount past events, it is necessary to ask: a) through which semiotic media are memories produced stored, circulated, and consumed? and; b) what function the practice of oral history performs given the social context in which this practice takes place.

Firstly, recent developments in the conception of the social foundations of memory have pointed to the role of cultural repertoires, languages and more generally semiotic systems, in the appropriation of the past. Cultural repertoires furnish populations with a 'vocabulary' through which past events can be remembered and as such mediate between peoples and their past. Social memory in this context would refer to the ways in which populations, socialised into different cultures, possess different techniques of historical recovery. These techniques prove to be both enabling and constraining in so far as they furnish a competence to remember but only within certain conceptual schemas. From routine everyday accounting practices to more organised commemorative practices such as theatre, museums, folklore, music, poetry, literature, photography, marching and parades, cultural repertoires present populations with a grid through which temporality can be tamed and understood. Oral history represents one type of commemorative practice and imposes its own distinctive filter on what is to be remembered and how.

Secondly, according to Halbwachs (1992), one of the earliest theorists of social memory, memory is best conceived as being structured by inter-subjective relations. Halbwachs invites readers to log the number of memories recalled during a day which are the product of questions put by others or preparations made by readers in anticipation of requests from others. In response to this rhetorical question, he argues that it is indeed primarily through negotiation with others that memories are affirmed (remembered), rejected (forgotten), or reshaped. Furthermore, and crucially, the shaping of memory through conversation needs, he argues, to be situated within its proper social context. In Halbwachs' study for instance, memories are seen to be incited principally in relation to participation in certain social groups (those of kin, religion, and class). Since the bulk of memory work is of this sort, what he calls remembering together, Halbwachs argues that it is meaningless to think of memory as being the possession of an individual as such. Instead, it is better conceived as being a *social practice*.

Beyond Halbwachs' pioneering work, the concept of memory as a social practice has perhaps been most clearly developed by historians. Fuelled by their own theoretical concerns, particularly their desire to scrutinise and to challenge the ways in which 'memory' and 'history' have been conceptualised as different kinds of social practice, historians have offered accounts of memory which foreground its rootedness in certain historical and social contexts. With specific reference to American history for instance, Thelen (1989b) argues that greater reflexivity is required by historians and that histories of memory might provide valuable insights for historians of history itself. Against this backdrop, the conception of memory as a social practice proves to be one of the most important insights which might be transferred. According to Thelen (1989b), memory can be said to be a social practice in so far as it performs certain kinds of functions in relation to present conditions:

> In the study of memory, the important question is not how accurately a recollection fitted some piece of past reality but why historical actors constructed their memories in a particular way at a particular time ... the struggle for possession

and interpretation of memory is rooted among the conflict and interplay of social, political, and cultural interests and values in the present. (Thelen 1989b: 4)

Similarly, in a wide-ranging study which challenges the supremacy of knowledge produced by professional historians, Samuel (1994) argues that perhaps all forms of historical consciousness which exist today can be understood only when situated within their proper social context. For it is the social, cultural, political, and economic conditions which communities are caught up in which lead them to value certain kinds of memory (and history) above all others:

> It is also my argument that memory is historically conditioned, changing colour and shape according to the emergencies of the moment; that so far from being handed down in the timeless form of 'tradition', it is progressively altered from generation to generation. It bears the impress of experience, in however mediated a way. It is stamped with the ruling passions of its time. Like history, memory is inherently revisionist and never more chameleon than when it appears to stay the same. (Samuel 1994: x)

Likewise the theme of histories and geographies of memory proved central to the French project *Les Lieux de mémoire* directed by Pierre Nora (Nora 1999, 2006, 2009, 2010). According to Nora the acceleration of history wrought by a restless, frantic and frentic phase of financial capitalism has created profoundly new conditions in which memory is being practiced. The 'flaring up' of memory, reflects a cultural need to slow time down, to preserve what is left before it is washed away, and to find a repository for tradition and the familiar. 'We speak so much of memory,' Nora observes, 'because there is so little of it left. What is secreted is a series of *Lieux de mémoire*, 'realms of memory' or better still 'sites of memory'. These sites of memory include festivals, heritage industries, landscape conservation, genealogy, monuments, literature, song, dance, poetry, folklore, public marches and so on. Memory has gained new social, political, economic, and cultural capital because it is a practice which speaks in profound ways to the cultural needs of populations living through a turbulent present.

Questions about the status of knowledge produced through oral history interviews then must proceed by questioning what this particular act of memory gathering, negotiation, production, reproduction, and ordering accomplishes at different points in time and space. What work do oral histories do in different social, political, economic, and cultural contexts? Here, the social relationships which exist between interviewer and interviewee, mediated by social class, gender, age, ethnicity, disability, cultural capital, and so on need teasing out. The location of the interview and the agenda behind the interview would need reflecting upon. The embeddedness of the commemorative practice being adopted within the university setting and within the discipline of history, sociology or geography would emerge as important. And of course the prevailing political, economic, social, and cultural conditions in which the discussion is situated would need critical inspection.

Introducing the new oral history archive

Part II of this book now turns attention to a substantial new oral history archive which was collected by the author between 2000 and 2002. This archive consists of 67 interviews with 76 members of the Irish Catholic community in Scotland, incorporating first generation settlers to fourth generation descendants, which solicit family stories of migration from Ireland to Scotland and which document family experiences of settlement in Scotland. Before departure it is necessary to document how interviewees were recruited, how and where interviews were conducted, the interview schedule which was used, the socio-economic characteristics of the participants individually and in aggregate profile, relations between the interviewer and interviewee, and finally the strategy which will be used to identify and cross reference interviewees in the main narrative to follow.

The vast majority of the participants who took part in interviews were drawn from the west of Scotland, and in particular from the city of Glasgow. This reflects in part the concentration of Irish Catholic migrants who settled here. But Irish Catholic migrants also settled, albeit in fewer numbers, further afield, including in the cities of Edinburgh and Dundee and in the coal mining and farming villages of Fife. Consequently the study recruited a minority of participants from Scotland more broadly. It is likely that the Irish Catholic encounter with the west of Scotland was different from the Irish Catholic encounter with the east of Scotland; there is a belief in some quarters for instance that anti Irish Catholic sentiment was and is more pronounced in the west of Scotland. It is perhaps wrong then to gather all interviewees together under one roof. This study does speak more clearly to the story of west of Scotland and perhaps ought to be labelled more frankly to convey this fact. Where especially necessary the more specific designation of Irish Catholic in the west of Scotland is therefore invoked. But given that some of the cast were drawn from Scotland more generally it was felt more appropriate to deploy the wider title as the routine and underscore this qualification in this methodological prologue.

The first task was to recruit members of the Irish Catholic community in Scotland who were prepared to give up their time and recount their family stories. Two adverts were taken out: one in July 2000 in Scotland's leading Catholic newspaper the *Scottish Catholic Observer*, and the second in October 2000 in the *Celtic View*, the official magazine of Celtic Football Club (Figure P.1). These adverts enlisted fifty two responses and led to forty one actual interviews. A strategy of snowballing was then adopted; interviewees were asked if they knew of any friends or relatives who might participate in the project and a follow up letter was sent to potential leads. A total of sixty seven interviews were conducted between May 2000 and October 2002; sixty with individuals, seven with pairs, or triplets or quads, giving a total of seventy six interviewees. The seven interviews which incorporated more than one individual were not initially intended to be multi-contributory; in each case on turning up to a house the author was informed that for company, confidence, or self assurance the initial contact wondered if it would be possible for a partner, friend, or relative to sit in. This 'sitting in' ended up becoming a conversation and useful data was collected. In every case the additional participants had Irish Catholic lineage too and this was recorded.

TALKING ABOUT IRISH MIGRATION TO THE WEST OF SCOTLAND?

Volunteers are sought for a research project examining the memories of Irish migrants and Irish descendants currently being conducted by the Department of Geography at Strathclyde University. The purpose of this project is to collect a range of stories about when and why families migrated to the west of Scotland, and how Irish people now look back on their experiences of settling into life in Scotland. Volunteers will be expected to give up an hour of their time to talk over their recollections. As we are interested in seeing how memories are passed down, as well as first generation migrants, we would welcome interest from second, third and even fourth generation Irish descendants. Anyone interested in participating in the project should contact:

Mark Boyle, Department of Geography, University of Strathclyde, 50 Richmond Street, Glasgow G1 1XN, Tel. 0141 548 3762, e-mail: mark.boyle@strath.ac.uk

Figure P.1   Advert which appeared in the *Scottish Catholic Observer* and *Celtic View*

An overwhelming majority of interviews were conducted in participants' houses. During each of the interviews, respondents were asked to provide factual information about themselves and as much factual detail about their forebears as they knew. This latter knowledge was often sketchy and occasionally participants would be apologetic about imprecisions or gaps in knowledge. A decision was taken to record what was known rather than request participants to research their family histories further to get more comprehensive and detailed background. In fact the level of memory which interviewees were able to offer was taken to be an interesting finding in itself. All interviews were fully transcribed. At the end of the interviews participants were asked if they would be willing to have an anonymised transcript of their testimonies lodged in an oral history archive which would be open to the public. This archive currently runs to over a million words and it is intended to open it to a wider readership once prepared to professional standards. Finally, and especially in the light of this initiative, a copy of each transcript was returned to each participant for checking and some took the opportunity to amend, add to, or delete sections.

Although adopting an open format, most of the interviews enquired into the stories participants possessed about they or their forebears' migration to Scotland; recollections of their/their families' initial place of abode in Ireland; understandings of why migration occurred and the routes taken to get to Scotland; thinking behind the initial choice of location of and in Scotland and subsequent relocations; life in Scotland including the importance or otherwise of religion, experiences of employment, the importance of family networks and marriage, political views both in relation to Ireland and Scotland, feelings of attachment to Ireland and Scotland; continued links with Ireland: the family's aggregate experience of assimilating into Scottish society, including what forebears might be most proud of, most disappointed of, and most surprised about; whether their family's experience might have been any different from that of other families; and finally, whether future generations might be more or less interested in Irish heritage and culture than present or previous generations (Figure P.2).

Background Information

Personal Background: *age/sex/location/marital status/occupation/*
                           religion
Irish Connections;   *If first generation - County of origin/date of*
                           migration/age at migration
                           If not first generation – generational links by County of
                           origin/date of migration/age of migrant/on maternal and
                           paternal sides

Interview Prompts

Ask interviewees to provide a panoramic overview of their/their forbears historical links with Ireland. Establish what is known and what is not known about specific migrant moves.

Take each migrant in the family biography in turn and enquire into -
- Recollections of place of initial abode in Ireland
- Levels of knowledge as to why the person migrated and the route they took to get to Scotland.
- Where in Scotland the migrant moved to and any subsequent relocations.
- Levels of knowledge about migrants' lives in Scotland including; the role of religion, experiences of employment, importance of family networks and marriage, political views both in relation to Ireland and Scotland, feelings of attachment to Ireland and Scotland and links to Ireland maintained.

Irrespective of generation, ask each interviewee about how they/their family have personally found life in Scotland including: the role of religion, experiences of employment, importance of family networks and marriage, political views both in relation to Ireland and Scotland, feelings of attachment to Ireland and Scotland and links to Ireland maintained. Explicitly enquire into their sense of being Irish, Scottish, British, and so on.

Ask each interviewee to provide a summary overview of their family's aggregate experience of assimilating into Scottish society, what they think their forebears would be most proud of, most disappointed of and, most surprised about regarding how things have turned out for the Irish, and whether they think their family's experience has been any different from that of other families.

Ask each interviewee to look to the future and offer views on whether the next generation is liable to be more or less interested in their Irish heritage than the present or previous generation. Why?

Figure P.2   Schedule for the oral history interviews

Tables P.1 and P.2 provide detailed summaries of the cast who took part and should be consulted throughout the book. Of the 76 interviewees who participated, 51 per cent were female, 49 per cent male. The youngest participant was a male aged 19, the eldest, a female aged 86; meanwhile 30 per cent of participants were aged 30–49, 43 per cent were aged 50–69, whilst 24 per cent were aged 70 or over. The west of Scotland was home to 82 per cent of respondents (mainly Glasgow, Lanarkshire, Ayrshire, and Renfrewshire). Whilst 43 per cent of participants were employed in a range of occupations, 36 per cent were retired. Of the seventy six participants, fourteen were first generation and sixty two were 'descendants'. Of the sixty two descendants, fifty six had second generation ties to Ireland, forty had third generation ties, and seventeen had fourth generation ties. Whilst participants traced their origins back to a number of counties in the north and south of Ireland, County Donegal was the most common source region. First generation migrants traced their move back to as early as the 1930s, second generation traced forebears' migration to as early as the 1890s, third generation to as early as the 1870s and fourth generation to as early as the 1850s.

Table P.1   **A summary overview of the oral history archive**

Dimension	Summary overview
The cast	
Overview	Total of 67 interviews held: 60 with individuals, 7 with multiple interviewees. A total of 76 people took part. Of the seven interviews held with multiples, 2 were with couples, 3 with sisters/brothers, 1 with a mother and her children, and 1 with friends.
Gender	Of the 60 interviews held with individuals, 28 were with females and 32 were with males. Of the 7 interviews held with multiples, 11 females and 5 males participated.
Age	The youngest participant was a male aged 19, the eldest a female aged 86. Of the 76 people who took part, only 1 was less than 20 years of age (1%), 1 was between 20 and 29 (1%), 11 were between 30 and 39 (14%), 12 were between 40 and 49 (16%), 16 were between 50 and 59 (21%), 17 were between 60 and 60 (22%), 13 were between 70 and 79 (17%), and 5 were older than 80 (7%).
Location of residence	Of the 76 participants, 34 (45%) came from Glasgow, 16 (21%) from Lanarkshire, 7 (9%) from Ayrshire, 5 (7%) from Renfrewshire, 4 (5%) from Dunbartonshire, 3 (4%) from Inverclyde, 2 (3%) from Fife, 2 (3%) from Edinburgh, 1 (1%) from Stirlingshire, 1 (1%) from Perthshire, and 1 (1%) from Dumfries and Galloway.
Marital status	Of the 76 people who took part, 41 were married (54%), 4 were divorced (5%), 4 co-habited (5%), 8 were widowed (11%), 1 had separated (1%), and 18 were single (24%).

Dimension	Summary overview
Occupation	Of the 76 participants, 33 (43%) were employed in a range of occupations, 27 (36%) were retired, 5 (7%) were students, 5 (7%) were housewives, 4 (5%) were priests, and 2 (3%) were unemployed.
Generation	Of the 76 participants, 14 were first generation and 62 were 'descendants'. Of the 62 descendants, 56 had second generation ties, 40 had third generation ties, and 17 had fourth generation ties. Among the 62 participants who were descendants, 3 had links on the maternal side only, 8, on the paternal side only, and 51 on both sides.
First Generation	
County of origin	Of the 14 first generation participants, 7 were from Donegal, 2 from Cavan, 2 from Mayo, 1 from Tyrone, 1 from Tipperary, and 1 from Antrim.
Date of arrival in Scotland	Of the 14 first generation participants, 3 arrived in Scotland in the 1930s, 3 in the 1940s, 4 in the 1950s, 1 in the 1960s, 1 in the 1970s, and 2 in the 1980s.
Age at migration	Of the 14 first generation participants, 2 were under 10 years of age at the time of arrival in Scotland, 4 were aged between 10 and 19, 7 were aged between 20 and 29, and 1 was aged between 30 and 39.
Second Generation	
County of origin	57 counties were cited as source counties by second generation descendants. Of these Donegal was cited 29 times (51%), Tyrone 5, Antrim 5, Fermanagh 4, Down 3, Carlow 2, Tipperary 2, Sligo 2, Roscommon 1, Armagh 1, Mayo 1, Cork 1, and Kilkenny 1.
Date of arrival in Scotland	53 second generation descendants estimated the date their forebears left Ireland for Scotland. 5 cited the 1890s, 4 the 1900s, 7 the 1910s, 12 (23%) the 1920s, 12 the 1930s, 7 the 1940s, and 6 the 1950s.
Age of parent who migrated	Second generation descendants identified the ages of 56 parents at the time of migration. 8 were under 10, 22 (38%) were between 10 and 19, 21 were between 20 and 30, 2 were aged 30 to 40, and 3 were aged 50 to 60.
Third Generation	
County of origin	18 counties were cited as source counties by fourth generation descendants. Of these Donegal was cited 4 times (23%), Tyrone 3, Antrim 2, Armagh 2, Cork 2, Down 2, Tipperary 1, Meath 1, Fermanagh 1.
Date of arrival in Scotland	30 third generation descendants estimated the date their forebears left Ireland for Scotland. 1 cited the 1860s, 3 the 1870s, 5 the 1880s, 6 the 1890s, 8 (27%) the 1900s, 1 the 1910s, 5 the 1920s, and 1 the 1930s.

Dimension	Summary overview
Fourth Generation	
County of origin	40 counties were cited as source counties by third generation descendants. Of these Donegal was cited 13 times (33%), Antrim 7, Sligo 4, Armagh 3, Mayo 3, Monaghan 2, Dublin 2, Leitrim 2, Meath 1, Tyrone 1, Cavan 1, Clare 1.
Date of arrival	17 fourth generation descendants estimated the date their forebears left Ireland for Scotland. 1 cited the 1850s, 4 the 1860s, 5 (29%) the 1870s, 1 the 1880s, 2 the 1890s, 3 the 1900s, and 1 the 1910s.
Practicalities	
Location of interview	61 interviews were conducted in the interviewees' own home (91%), 3 were conducted at Strathclyde University (4%), and 3 were conducted at another location (the participants place of work and a holiday caravan) (4%)
Length of interview	Of the 67 interviews held, 1 interview lasted between 40 and 49 minutes (1%), 4 lasted between 50 and 59 minutes (6%), 14 lasted between 60 and 69 minutes (21%), 24 lasted between 70 and 79 minutes (36%), 10 lasted between 80 and 89 minutes (15%), 6 between 90 and 99 minutes (9%), 4 lasted between 110 and 1 20 minutes (6%), 2 lasted between 130 and 140 minutes (3%), and 2 were over 140 minutes (3%). The shortest was a single interview with a female and lasted 40 minutes, the longest was a single interview with a female lasting 180 minutes. The average time for all interviews was 79 minutes, for single interviews with females it was 76 minutes, for single interviews with males it was 82 minutes, and for multiple interviews 79 minutes.
Transcript vetted	The average time it took for the author to return draft transcripts to participants was 4.8 months. 40 interviewees (60%) returned transcripts, 27 interviewees (40%) failed to return corrected drafts. The average turnaround time among those who did return drafts was 5.2 months, and for those who did not was 4 months, suggesting length of time to return transcripts had little effect on likelihood of corrections being submitted.

It will now be clear that the purpose of the interviews was to make sense of the debate over Scotland's shame by foregrounding Britain's colonial history in Ireland and its displaced, derivative, and mutant offshoots, whilst at the same time allowing the multiple other tendencies which have shaped the Irish Catholic encounter room to breath. Although not worked out as clearly at that point, the broad thrust of adopting a topological/topographical/cartographical approach to render intelligible the Irish Catholic encounter with Scotland was *de facto* fundamentally the agenda of the author from the outset. But it was not only the author who of necessity brought an agenda to bear on the work.

The participants themselves came forward and volunteered their stories freely and with their own interests. It is impossible to say why participants contacted the author but it is clear that their involvement mattered to them at a number of levels. Among the more prominent reasons cited by participants for their involvement were: simply because of a passion to get involved in all things Irish; the need to 'offload' a harrowing family story which was more easily told to a stranger; to commit to posterity memories of deceased parents and relatives; for company and to overcome loneliness; to help 'one of their own' publish a research book; to ensure a point of view was put forward which might otherwise be overlooked; to check out the political credentials of the author; to display and validate personal knowledge about Irish history; to ensure their role as a public figure in the diaspora was recognised; and simply out of personal curiosity. Whatever the reason, it is obvious that participants actively sanctioned the sharing of only a subset of family stories and framed these stories according to the way they wanted them to come across and what they felt the author was looking for.

A comment is required on the labels afforded to each of the interviewees in the main body of text. Initially it was thought that it would be sterile, especially in a book of this sort, to refer to participants throughout the narrative as interviewee 1, interviewee 2, and so on. Nevertheless to refer to participants by their real names would be to breach confidentiality. Initially a whole collection of new names were invented to personalise the text without risking public disclosure of any individual's identity. It was realised however that the naming of people was in itself a cultural practice and that members of the Irish Catholic community had a relatively distinctive collection of names which the author's inventory did violence to. A compromise was found in that only first names were used and the list of first names was rotated. In other words, each interviewee was awarded a different first name, this first name being taken from the list of names pooled from the actual cast. But this in itself became tortuous and resulted in one aged female being given the name Kylie! Consequently it was decided to stick with the interviewee number given on Table P.2 below. This might seem overly technical and obstructive in a book of this sort but the practice of naming is fraught with personal and political challenges and these challenges proved in the end too prohibitive to overcome.

Table P.2   Biographical details of the oral history interviewees

Interviewee number	M/F	Age	Location of current residence	Marital Status	Occupation or status	1st Generation	Descendants Maternal side (most recent migration) Generation, County(ies) of origin, dates of migration, age at migration (second generation only)	Paternal side (most recent migration) Generation, County(ies) of origin, dates of migration, age (second generation only)	Length of the interview (Mins)	Place where interview was held (Home, University, Other)	Turnaround time for returning transcript (in months) and corrections made by interviewee (YES or NO)
						County of origin, date of migration and age at migration					
1.	F	30	Knightswood/ Glasgow	Cohabiting	Community Worker	Cavan 1987 17			75	H	3N
2.	F	46	Pollokshields/ Glasgow	Cohabiting	Law Student	Cavan/ Donegal 1976 22			70	U	4Y
3.	F	59	Clarkston/ Glasgow	Married	School Secretary	Donegal 1945 4			75	H	6N
4.	F	60	Clarkston/ Glasgow	Widowed	School Secretary	Donegal 1945 5			80	O	3Y
5.	F	68	Greenock/ Inverclyde	Widowed	Chapel Housekeeper	Donegal 1955 24			60	O	4N
6.	F	69	Bridgeton/ Glasgow	Married	Retired	Tyrone 1957 26			80	H	6Y
7.	F	84	Cupar/Fife	Widowed	Retired	Mayo 1936 20			50	H	5N

Interviewee number	M/F	Age	Location of current residence	Marital Status	Occupation or status	1st Generation	Descendants		Length of the interview (Mins)	Place where interview was held (Home, University, Other)	Turnaround time for returning transcript (in months) and corrections made by interviewee (YES or NO)
8.	F	86	Strathkinnis/Fife	Widowed	Retired	Mayo 1936 20			40	H	5N
9.	F	30	Kings Park/Glasgow	Married	Housewife		Second Donegal 1955 10	Fourth Donegal 1910s	50	H	3N
10.	F	38	Burnside/Glasgow	Divorced	Student		Third Antrim late 1920s	Second Antrim, 1950 17	70	H	9Y
11.	F	39	Paisley/Renfrewshire	Single	Custom's Office Official		Second Donegal 1950s 20s	Second Donegal 1940s 20	85	H	3N
12.	F	42	Dunlop/Ayrshire	Separated	Civil Servant			Second Donegal early 1930s 15	90	H	4Y
13.	F	42	Prestwick/Ayrshire	Cohabating	Secondary Teacher		Second Tyrone 1948 18	Third Sligo 1920s	75	H	6Y
14.	F	53	Cambuslang/Glasgow	Married	Housewife		Second Antrim 1911 4	Third Donegal/Tyrone 1890s	75	H	4Y
15.	F	56	Kilmacolm/Inverclyde	Married	School Meals Auxiliary		Second Donegal 1930s late teens	Second Donegal 1930s mid 20s	60	H	5Y
16.	F	58	Saltcoats/Ayrshire	Married	Retired		Second Tyrone 1917 1	Third Donegal 1880 and 1904	70	H	3Y
17.	F	62	Elderslie Village/Renfrewshire	Married	Retired		Third Antrim and Donegal 1870s	Second Donegal 1910s mid teens	65	H	3Y
18.	F	63	Croy/Lanarkshire	Married	Retired			Second Armagh U/A U/A	65	H	4N

Interviewee number	M/F	Age	Location of current residence	Marital Status	Occupation or status	1st Generation	Descendants		Length of the interview (Mins)	Place where interview was held (Home, University, Other)	Turnaround time for returning transcript (in months) and corrections made by interviewee (YES or NO)
19.	F	67	Giffnock/Glasgow	Single	Retired		Third Monaghan U/A	Second Mayo 1920s early 20s	70	H	5Y
20.	F	69	Knightswood/Glasgow	Single	Retired		Second Donegal 1929 late 30s	Second Donegal 1910/11 16	70	H	4Y
21.	F	70	Wishaw/Lanarkshire	Widowed	Housewife		Second Tipperary 1908	Second Tipperary 1908 21	90	H	9Y
22.	F	82	Clydebank/Dunbartonshire	Widowed	Retired		Second Donegal 1914/1915 mid 20s	Second Donegal 1914/1915 mid 20s	75	H	3Y
23.	F	83	Milton/Glasgow	Single	Retired		Second Down 1901 19	Second Antrim 1898 19	180	H	3Y
24.	F	43	Ayr/Ayrshire	Married	Solicitor		Fourth Armagh 1860s	Third Donegal 1901	80	H	3Y
25.	F	55	Troon/Ayrshire	Married	Housewife		Third U/A U/A	Third Dublin U/A	110	H	3N
26.	F	64	Uddingston/Lanarkshire	Single	Retired		Third Donegal 1890s	Third Donegal 1870s	75	H	3Y
27.	F	77	Paisley/Renfrewshire	Married	Retired		Third Mayo 1840s-1860s		75	H	4Y
28.	F	41	Govan/Glasgow	Married	Student		Fourth Armagh 1870s	Fourth Donegal 1870s	70	H	4Y
29.	M	39	Greenock/Inverclyde	Single	Priest	Tipperary 1986 25			75	H	4N

Interviewee number	M/F	Age	Location of current residence	Marital Status	Occupation or status	1st Generation	Descendants		Length of the interview (Mins)	Place where interview was held (Home, University, Other)	Turnaround time for returning transcript (in months) and corrections made by interviewee (YES or NO)
30.	M	62	Glasgow	Married	Caretaker	Donegal 1956 18			60	O	6N
31.	M	64	Calderbank/Lanarkshire	Single	Priest	Donegal 1961 25			65	H	10N
32.	M	72	Govanhill/Glasgow	Married	Retired	Donegal 1945 15			80	H	5Y
33.	M	19	Rutherglen/Glasgow	Single	Student		Third Antrim U/A	Second Donegal U/A U/A	70	U	4N
34.	M	36	Glasgow	Divorced	Manager		Second Donegal 1948 21	Second Fermanagh 1930 7	60	H	3Y
35.	M	50	Royston/Glasgow	Single	Priest		Second Donegal 1932 19	Second Donegal 1932 19	50	H	4Y
36.	M	50	Perth/Perthshire	Divorced	Engineer		Second Donegal 1932 14	Second Donegal 1936 20	65	H	6Y
37.	M	55	Bearsden/Glasgow	Married	Retired		Second Donegal 1920s early 20s	Second Donegal 1920s early 20s	75	H	5N
38.	M	56	Lochwinnoch/Renfrewshire	Married	Engineer		Third U/A U/A	Second Donegal 1930s 17	65	H	4N
39.	M	59	Baillieston/Glasgow	Married	Union Official		Second Donegal 1928/29 15	Third Cavan 1888/89	80	H	2N

Interviewee number	M/F	Age	Location of current residence	Marital Status	Occupation or status	1st Generation	Descendants		Length of the interview (Mins)	Place where interview was held (Home, University, Other)	Turnaround time for returning transcript (in months) and corrections made by interviewee (YES or NO)
40.	M	60	Coatbridge/ Lanarkshire	Single	Priest		Second Tyrone 1936 31	Second Tyrone 1941 28	110	H	3N
41.	M	62	Paisley/ Renfrewshire	Married	Joiner		Second Tyrone 1917 16	Second Donegal 1913/1915 20	115	H	5Y
42.	M	68	Bearsden/ Glasgow	Single	Freelance journalist		Second Roscommon 1932 25	Third Armagh and Mayo 1895/96	135	H	5N
43.	M	73	Shotts/ Lanarkshire	Married	Retired		Second Kilkenny 1890s 7	Third Dublin U/A	55	H	3Y
44.	M	76	Cathcart/ Glasgow	Married	Retired		Second Antrim 1897 7	Third Armagh U/A	70	H	5Y
45.	M	33	East-Kilbride/ Lanarkshire	Married	Council Worker			Third Antrim 1900s	70	H	9N
46.	M	34	Hamilton/ Lanarkshire	Married	School Teacher		Third Donegal 1920s	Fourth Meath and Antrim early 1900s	90	H	3Y
47.	M	41	Baillieston/ Glasgow	Married	School Teacher		Third Antrim 1930	Fourth Cork 1873	135	H	5Y
48.	M	43	Knightswood/ Glasgow	Single	Careers Advisor			Third Donegal 1910	75	H	6Y
49.	M	46	Baillieston/ Glasgow	Married	School Teacher		Third Donegal 1900s	Fourth Tyrone 1890s	80	H	5Y
50.	M	47	Drumchapel/ Glasgow	Cohabitation	Senior Social Worker			Third Monaghan early 1900s	80	H	3N
51.	M	53	South Side/ Glasgow	Married	Social work Co-ordinator		Third Belfast early 1900s	Third Armagh 1890s	90	H	9Y

Interviewee number	M/F	Age	Location of current residence	Marital Status	Occupation or status	1st Generation	Descendants		Length of the interview (Mins)	Place where interview was held (Home, University, Other)	Turnaround time for returning transcript (in months) and corrections made by interviewee (YES or NO)
52.	M	59	Clarkston/Glasgow	Married	Printing Trade Printer		Third Mayo and Sligo 1880s	Third Sligo U/A	115	H	3Y
53.	M	59	Troon/Ayrshire	Divorced	Customs Officer		Third Leitrim 1890	Third Donegal 1880	80	U	5Y
54.	M	63	Motherwell/Lanarkshire	Married	Commercial Artist		Third Antrim U/A	Third Meath 1907	170	H	6Y
55.	M	72	Motherwell/Lanarkshire	Married	Retired		Third Clare 1879	Third Donegal early 1880s	65	H	3N
56.	M	21	Troon/Ayrshire	Single	Student		Fourth Donegal 1900s	Fourth Antrim 1880	65	H	5Y
57.	M	45	Royton/Glasgow	Married	Taxi Driver			Fourth Fermanagh 1850s	75	H	3N
58.	M	65	Dumfries/Dumfries and Galloway	Single	Retired		Fourth Down 1860s	Fourth Tipperary 1860s	65	H	9Y
59.	M	71	Vale of Leven/Dunbartonshire	Married	Retired			Third Donegal 1890s	65	H	5Y
60.	M	73	East Kilbride/Lanarkshire	Married	Retired School Teacher			Fourth Down 1859	60	H	8N
61a.	M	78	Clydebank/Dunbartonshire	Married	Retired	Donegal mid 1950s 33			75	H	2N
61b.	F	61	Clydebank/Dunbartonshire	Married	Bereavement Counsellor		Second Donegal U/A	Third Donegal U/A	75	H	2N
62a.	F	82	Moodiesburn/Lanarkshire	Single	Retired	Antrim 1910 1			90	H	3N

Interviewee number	M/F	Age	Location of current residence	Marital Status	Occupation or status	1st Generation	Descendants		Length of the interview (Mins)	Place where interview was held (Home, University, Other)	Turnaround time for returning transcript (in months) and corrections made by interviewee (YES or NO)
62b.	F	76	Moodiesburn/Lanarkshire	Widowed	Retired		Second Carlow 1910 18	Second Carlow 1910 20s	90	H	3N
63a.	F	36	Kingspark/Glasgow	Married	Business Systems Administrator		Second Fermanagh 1954 23	Second Fermanagh 1954 23	85	H	9Y
63b. S	F	43	Glasgow	Married	Classroom Assistant		Second Fermanagh 1954 23	Second Donegal 1940 late teens	85	H	9Y
63c.	F	44	Glasgow	Single	Personal Assistant		Second Fermanagh 1954 23	Second Donegal 1940 late teens	85	H	9Y
64a.	F	58	Crookston/Glasgow	Married	Unemployed		Second Sligo 1930s late teens	Second Sligo 1920s late teens	70	H	9N
64b.	F	37	Crookston/Glasgow	Not know	Social Worker/Carer		Third Sligo 1920s		70	H	9N
64c.	M	30	Crookston/Glasgow	single	Unemployed		Third Sligo late 1920s		70	H	9N
65a.	M	58	Leith/Edinburgh	Married	Tax Inspector		Second Antrim 1928 20	Fourth Tyrone 1870	70	H	8Y
65b.	F	58	Leith/Edinburgh	Married	Housewife		Fourth Tyrone 1870	Third Leitrim 1890	70	H	8Y
66a.	F	72	Cumbernauld/Lanarkshire	Widowed	Retired		Second Donegal 1915 late teens	Second Down 1898 1	70	H	5Y
66b.	F	68	Falkirk/Stirlingshire	Married	Retired		Second Donegal 1915 late teens	Second Down 1898 1	70	H	5Y

Interviewee number	M/F	Age	Location of current residence	Marital Status	Occupation or status	1st Generation	Descendants		Length of the interview (Mins)	Place where interview was held (Home, University, Other)	Turnaround time for returning transcript (in months) and corrections made by interviewee (YES or NO)
67a.	M	72	Newarthill/ Lanarkshire	Married	Retired		Third Donegal 1900	Second Cork 1904	90	H	5Y
67b.	M	75	Carluke/ Lanarkshire	Married	Retired		Third Donegal 1900	Second Cork 1904	90	H	5Y

Note: U/A means data was not available from the participant

Chapter 4

National Identity, Estrangement and Belonging: Who are Irish Catholics in Scotland?

Introduction

The purpose of this chapter is to scrutinise the category Irish Catholic in Scotland and, through an examination of claims to national identity which members of the Irish Catholic community in Scotland make, to establish the ways in which this category has sponsored a number of derivative identities as it has taken root in Scotland. As such, it represents something of a preparation for the journey which will be taken in the next four chapters. It is at this point that we recognise that the category Irish Catholic in Scotland, whilst having a level of coherence in itself, is sufficiently primal so as to permit a wide range of claims to national identity. I first sketch out a number of key narratives of the Irish nation to set the context. I then gather together tales of alterity from the archive to establish the ways in which some members of the Irish Catholic community use these narratives to construct differences between this community and indigenous Scottish communities. But moments of alterity have not defined the primary loyalties of the Irish Catholic community. Besides tales of estrangement and discrimination reside stories of new roots and new senses of belonging. Next I examine the claims to national identity which participants make, particularly with respect to their Irishness and Scottishness. The aim is to show how the idea of Irish Catholic resonates with at least six different constituencies who mobilise it in different ways and for different purposes. The Irish Catholic community has moved beyond its roots and although these roots continue to inform who they are they do not determine in any simple way the national identities which people identify with.

Key narratives of the Irish nation

The Irish Catholic community in Scotland recognises itself to be an offshoot of the Irish Catholic community in Ireland. We must begin therefore with a reflection of the key narratives of the Irish nation. Boyce (1982) refers to Irish nationalism as constituting a 'crowded landscape' comprising a 'confusion of beliefs ranging from democratic theory to Jacobinism, from constitutionalism to revolution, from comprehensive nationality to sectarianism, from French republicanism and enlightenment to the 'seminarist gallantry of Trent', from Marxism to near Fascism (Boyce 1982: 380). According to Hutchinson (1987), the clearest expositions of Irish nationalist historiography can be found in Ireland's cultural nationalist movements. Hutchinson argues that there have existed three periods in which cultural nationalism has flourished. In each case, an initial preparation period, led by romantic intellectuals (poets and scholars), is followed by a period of crystallisation (in which scholarly and cultural institutions take up the cause), and finally a period of articulation when an effort is made to popularise the cause among the wider public (by say intellectuals, journalists, politicians and pamphleteers).

Ireland's first experience of cultural nationalism begins with the largely Protestant antiquarians of the mid-eighteenth century, progressing through the activities of the Royal Irish Academy and ends with the work of the Society of United Irishmen, the *Belfast Journal*, and the *Northern Star* in the late eighteenth and early nineteenth century. This was followed by a second campaign, which began with the activities of scholars and poets in the 1830s, was championed by the *Dublin Penny Journal* and the *Dublin University Magazine*, and which exploded onto the mass public with the work of the Young Ireland group of journalists and their publication *The Nation* in the 1840s. The final phase of cultural nationalism began with the activity of poets and folklorists in the 1880s, which was picked up by the Gaelic League and Irish Literary Theatre, and developed through Arthur Griffith's journal *United Irishmen*, and other journals like *The Leader* and the *United Irish Peasant*. This tradition rests upon five central historiographical narratives.

> *Narratives of origin* – Comprising myths of ethnogenesis, homeland and foundation myths, and myths of descent. These recall the arrival of the Goidelic Celts (the Gaels) between 500 and 300 BC, the legitimacy of the land claims made by the Gaels over their new homeland on arrival, the foundation of Gaelic society as a distinct polity, and the continuous and harmonious descent of the Gaels over the first millennium. They include the heroics of such legendary figures as Cú Chulainn, Fionn mac Cumhaill and the Fianna, and Cathleen Ní Houlihan. The Irish nation is founded properly in c. AD 500 when St Patrick converted the population to Christianity. The *Lebor Gabála Érenn* (Book of Invasions) is appealed to as the essential guide to the period.
>
> *Narratives of a golden age* – which seek to recall the greatest achievements of Gaelic society at its pinnacle before (subsequent) foreign intervention. Invariably, these tend to focus upon the period from the sixth to the eighth century when Ireland became the European centre of religious and secular learning, and the leading guardian of European Civilisation.
>
> *Narratives of British colonisation* – These myths track British involvement in Ireland, representing the British as driven by imperial greed, capable of acts of evil and at times cowardly aggression in pursuit of cultural and

economic supremacy, and immune from any appreciation of the rights of other peoples. British rule is invariably traced back to the landing of Strongbow in 1169 and thus occupation is represented as occurring over an 800 year period. Among the more popular tales are the Tudor conquest and the crushing of associated rebellions, the defeat of King James II by William of Orange III in 1690, Cromwell's brutal regime, the instigation of the Penal Laws in 1703, the oppression of the United Irishmen and the Act of Union 1801, the crushing of Irish rebellions throughout the nineteenth century, the Anglo-Irish War of 1918–21, partition and the systematic discrimination of Catholics in the North, the failure of power sharing and the Anglo-Unionist repression of the Irish Catholic and/or nationalist and/or republican movement in the North.

Narratives of the Irish diaspora – which record the ways in which the British repression of Ireland proved to be midwife to massive out-migration peaking in the period 1845 to around 1920, and to the formation of one of the world's largest diasporic communities (estimated today to be around 70 million in strength). These myths record the flight from religious and political persecution, and the poverty and general economic retardation of Ireland that resulted from British mis-rule. The Irish Famine of 1845 to 1852 is taken to be the chief exemplar.

Narratives of rebellion and uprising – which seek to portray the stoic suffering the Irish have endured under British colonisation and colonial rule, the heroic acts of resistance and rebellion they have put up to this rule, and the assertion that Ireland's Gaelic past will never be extinguished and that British rule will eventually be broken leading to a United Ireland. The role of the Irish diaspora in supporting nationalist movements is attested. Among the most celebrated events are, the great rebellion of 1641, the Jacobite war of 1689–91, the rise of the United Irishmen and the republicanism of Wolfe Tone in the 1790s, Robert Emmet's doomed rebellion of 1803, Daniel O'Connell and the Catholic emancipation movement, the literary genius and political agitation of Thomas Davis and the Young Ireland movement in the 1840s, the Fenian rising of 1867, the rise and fall of Charles Stewart Parnell and the Land League, the rise and fall of John Redmond and the Irish Parliamentary Party, the Easter rebellion in 1916, the War of Independence, the Truce, the Treaty and the establishment of the Free State in 1921, Éamon de Valera's new Republican constitution of 1937, the border campaign of the 1950s, the civil rights movement of the 1960s, and the Northern Ireland 'troubles' from the early 1970s.

An overview of claims to alterity

Irish migration to Scotland brought these key myths of the Irish nation into a direct confrontation with key narratives of the British nation, and relatedly key narratives of the Scottish nation. For some, the result was a sense of alterity, displacement, estrangement, and alienation from the indigenous host. A focus upon moments of alterity, and alerity's more extreme and particularly ugly manifestations in encounters with bigotry and sectarianism, is helpful in the attempt to establish the critical properties invested in the category Irish Catholic in Scotland. One could compile an endless list of stories of Irish Catholic estrangement from Scotland. The following testimonies represent only a small subset culled from the archive. Notice the criteria which is being used in specific accounts to judge why alterity is a sensible emotion to invest in in particular circumstances.

- Interviewee 48 recalls how his father changed his name on arrival in Glasgow (circa 1910) to try to get a job but continued to have difficulties because other aspects of his background would be brought up at interviews. By 1945 he had decided that this strategy was ineffective and changed his name back to its more recognisable Irish form.
- Interviewee 55 recalls his father working down a coal pit (circa 1940s) and having to walk nearly half a mile to the pit shaft where a hoist would lift them to the surface. A bogey fortunately was provided to ease the journey but if it was full, the foreman would say 'you Irishmen, get off the bogey and let me on'. The Irishmen had to walk to the shaft as the other workers passed on the bogey.
- Interviewee 43 recalled his time in Edinburgh University as a student of English in the 1940s. Coming from the mining town of Shotts, he admits to being acutely aware that he was one of only a few Irish Catholics on the course. He recalls the experience as lonely, isolating, and alienating and sought regular refuge in the local Catholic chaplaincy.
- Interviewee 9 records how her mother and aunt were bullied at school in the Gorbals in Glasgow (which was 'quite an Irish area' (circa late 1950s)) for speaking Irish Gaelic and how they were taunted mercilessly by school children. Sick with nerves every morning, her mother nevertheless persisted in misery, but her aunt 'faded away' so much that she had to be sent to relatives back in Ireland.
- Interviewee 15 related a childhood experience when she befriended a Protestant neighbour (circa late 1950s, early 1960s). She recollects her shock at being challenged by other children when she visited a Protestant Church with her friend to see a wedding. She also recalls the difficulties she had in making sense of childrens' comments, for instance she was asked if she was a Catholic when she attended a Sunday School party with the same friend. She recalls thinking 'What IS this all about?'
- Interviewee 65a recalls being caught on a boat from Northern Ireland to Scotland with a large number of Glasgow Rangers FC supporters in the late 1950s and being terrified and wondering if he would be confronted and challenged as to his allegiances. Whilst displaying no decorative features of note, he felt he 'looked' Irish.

- Interviewee 58 records how growing up in Dumfries and Galloway in the 1950s and 1960s, he was acutely aware that many professions would not employ a Catholic: newspapers and printers, banks, the county council, and the carnation milk factory. The only jobs available were in nursing and in the railways and even then managerial positions would be closed to Catholics. It was just accepted that that was the way it was.
- Interviewee 27 reflected on how in the 1960s she changed the name of her newly born son from Kevin (the pre birth preference) to Gregory because relatives told her he would never get a job with a name like Kevin.
- Interviewee 38 recounts how, whilst working in a shipbuilding firm (*circa* late 1960s), he was told only Protestants were allowed to use the washing facilities. In response, he was deliberately ambiguous about what school he went to and was allowed access to the washing area. When it was discovered that in fact he had attended a Catholic school he was thrown out and had to go home dirty.
- Interviewee 40 who is a Priest, grew up in Larkhall, an area known for its strong Loyalist tradition. He recalls a frightening incident in early 1970s when people who he did not recognise visited his family house and told his father he needed to leave. He had no idea why but thinks it was to do with gun running activities to loyalist groups in Northern Ireland from Larkhall which his dad had witnessed by accident and the protagonists feared their 'cover might be blown'.
- Interviewee 63b conveys how her mother, who was a nurse with a strong Northern Ireland accent, hated doing house visits in the 1970s and 1980s after an IRA atrocity for fear of being challenged and confronted as to whether she was a terrorist sympathiser, which patently she was not.
- Interviewee 13 recalls reading about the troubles in Northern Ireland and circling bits about the conflict in newspapers. She recalls her father being frightened that the bin men might see her doodles and her family might be targeted for abuse.
- Interviewee 26 conveyed how she had deliberately exploited the ambiguity inherent in the name of her school to secure a job in a city centre shop (*circa* late 1960s early 1970s). The interview panel however, probed further as to why they had never come across such a school before and she was forced to admit the truth. She never got the job.
- Interviewee 18 admitted to exploiting the ambiguity of the title of her school to get a job as a secretary in a Protestant school in the 1970s. Again repeated questioning about where her kids went to school resulted in the truth coming out.
- Interviewee 13 records how her mother has an almost paralysing fear of drawing attention to her roots. She notes that this was in spite of serving as a nurse for forty years, giving her a wide exposure to life. She recalls how she was terrified when she applied for an Irish passport and refused to allow her to send her application documents from her home address.

She remembers how panicky her mother became when she got the innocuous Irish publication the *People's Friend* magazine sent by post to her father as a Christmas present. Indeed, she muses how her mother told her 'no good could come' from giving the author an interview as part of this research.

- Interviewee 33 recollects a relative's fury when applying to join the local golf club. Having called the club secretary his relative was told the waiting list for prospective members was closed. And yet thirty minutes later when a friend called with a less Irish sounding surname he was informed that there might be a possible opening and to complete and submit an application form immediately.

- Interviewee 33 laments the way in which his father and mother switch off tapes of 'innocent Irish folk music' when visitors call for fear off offending. He says 'if it was Scottish or English folk music nobody would bother their shirt with it', so why should Irish traditional music take on meanings and be burdened with stigmas that other folk music does not.

- Interviewee 39 is a union activist and cites the difficulties he has in trying to raise issues about Ireland even among union officials. All too often, people misinterpret concerns about social justice issues in Ireland as being tantamount to tacit support for the IRA, even though this is clearly absurd.

- Interviewee 12 whose married name was 'bland' and whose work took her to Northern Ireland recalls the racial taunts that were banded about the office by male colleagues who did not appreciate her background. She describes how her stomach was in knots and how appalled she was and how it made her realise the ways in which Catholics in the North of Ireland were treated.

- Interviewee 14 expressed her concerns about allowing her children to wear Celtic FC strips in the light of the sectarian murder of Mark Scott (a young innocent Celtic FC fan), and to display their crucifixes and medals of St Jude and St Lucy. Interestingly she notes how she was happy enough when they wore crosses but crucifixes 'upped the anti' and gave her an elevated fear about their safety.

- Interviewee 28 remembered how she had been subjected to 'humour with a serious undertone' by an employer when she returned to work with ashes on her forehead on Ash Wednesday. Her employer jibed that he would not have given her the job if he realised that she was 'one of them'.

- Interviewee 45 recalls a frightening experience of being challenged and confronted by a group of men whilst walking through Bridgeton Cross, an area with a strong Loyalist tradition, with a Celtic FC scarf on.

- Interviewee 51 expresses the awkwardness he feels in looking at books in the Irish section in Borders Books store in Glasgow. If anyone is looking over his shoulder he wonders if they are waiting to see if he will pick up a book by Gerry Adams or whether he will play it safe and consult Conor Cruise O'Brien instead! He feels this small event reveals his more general concern about people finding him offensive or misinterpreting his motives.

- Interviewee 58 recalls feeling uncomfortable going through airports especially if he is going to Ireland. He admits to a heightened sense of being under surveillance when travelling to Donegal in particular. From his career in the British army, he acknowledges that such heightened surveillance is likely.
- Interviewee 46 recalls starting a new job and a Protestant colleague creating furore in the canteen at his expense by asking him if had been 'put through a sheep dip', before entering the building and enquiring when the company 'had changed their policy towards hiring "retards" and "tinkers"'.
- Interviewee 14 has a daughter who is engaged to be married to a British soldier from England. She has had to sanitise her house of tri-colours on the wall, Wolf Tone albums, religious pictures and memorabilia for fear it offends.

Claims to national identity

But to cast the Irish Catholic experience of Scotland in terms of a warring between two tribes, host and newcomer, is to fail to give due weight to the rich variety of embroilments which exist; stories of alterity and bitter estrangement cannot and must not be the point of conclusion to any study of the Irish Catholic entanglement with Scotland. In no sense is the story of the Irish nation wholly incommensurate with the story of the British nation, and certainly not with the invented traditions through which the Scottish nation imagines itself. Whilst recognising themselves to be 'other' in important ways from Scottish people, few members of the Irish Catholic community in Scotland deployed the category 'Irish Catholic in Scotland' in any simple way. In the archive, this was especially the case when participants were asked to put a label on their primary sense of nationality. The category Irish Catholic in Scotland provides a point of departure for a range of complex, contradictory, and often 'in-between' hybrid claims to national identity. It does not represent a stable or essentialised or definitive sense of belonging in and off itself. The purpose of this section is to examine the ways in which participants construct a sense of alterity from and belonging to both Irishness and Scottish, so as to arrive at their primary sense of loyalty. Because in many cases identities are hybrid and positioned somewhere in between these two poles, discussion will be structured in terms of the spectrum of identities claimed, from Irishness to Scottishness.

Before departure we should note that many of the participants felt particularly uncomfortable about aligning themselves exclusively with the concept of Britishness. The majority admitted that whilst that they were reasonably content to identify themselves as 'British' in official forms that was 'as far as it went'. Only when speaking about their family's involvement in the first and second world wars did Britishness emerge as a potent identity. For instance, recalling the Battle of Britain and the heroic efforts of Sir Douglas Bader, the exploits of his uncle whose valiant endeavours at Dunkirk earned him the rank of Major, and the terrifying broadcasts of Nazi propagandist Lord Haw Haw, one participant reflected that he was a 'signed up member of Brittania' during the Second World War. Another interviewee made the interesting observation that not only did the Second World War affect attitudes to Britishness but at that point the idea of Scottishness was simply not developed enough to offer a meaningful alternative marker of assimilation. Others nonetheless appeared to be more confused and defensive about the enlisting of grandfathers, fathers and brothers into such regiments of the British army as the Cameronians and the Connaught Rangers. Whilst proud of their efforts in 'defeating Fascism', there was a clear recognition that there was something 'surprising' and 'ironic' about fighting for King/Queen and country.

Some participants chose to call themselves principally Irish. Among those who did were a number of first generation immigrants, a war evacuee who had stayed in Ireland as a child, and a number of second generation descendants who had taken regular holidays in Ireland as a child, who had close family ties still in Ireland, and/or who grew up in such Irish neighbourhoods in Glasgow as the Gorbals and Govan Hill (affectionately known as Bengal-Donegal' by dint of its concentration of families from Donegal and from Asia). Interestingly, some of these participants even argued that the concept of Irishness itself needed to be refined; migrants belonged to particular sub communities dependant upon the county they came from (Donegal, Mayo, Tyrone, etc) and where they settled in Scotland (the industrial west, the tatty farms in Ayrshire, Fife and Tayside, the hydro-electric schemes in the North of Scotland and so on).

In its more regressive moments the Irish Catholic community has recognised its cultural distinctiveness on the bases of blood and genes. For some, the term Irish Catholic simply refers to one's biological inheritance. Being Irish and Catholic meant being born with a certain DNA and migration could not, at least in the short run, change one's pedigree and blood line. Several participants claimed that there were no 'crossbreeds' or 'racial mongrels' in their family and that they could trace their ancestry back to the Kings of Gaelic Ireland. Whilst they lived in Scotland they 'didn't have one drop of Scottish blood in them'. Even though their children were born in Scotland the fact that they were born of Irish parents meant they were genetically Irish; 'just because you are born in a stable does not mean you are a horse'. Intriguingly, Irish Catholic people were said to look different; with females being either Spanish/Gypsy in appearance with black hair and dark eyes or sporting long red hair with pale skin and lots of freckles, and males being plump with rosy cheeks, or tall and lanky with long arms and big ears!

For those born in Ireland, place of birth is often cited as critical. Interviewee 2, a first generation migrant, paints a moving story of how her sense of genetic distance from the Scots, has created for her a certain feeling of loss and a struggle to belong:

> Last night I was at the Eddi Reader concert and I thought that's good, she's one
> of us and I thought that's some sense of me feeling Glaswegian, but on the other

hand I would say what I do miss is that complete sense of belonging so that it was very acute when my first child was born and I remember walking along the streets at Battlefield and thinking he is related to so many people in this city and I'm not related to a soul here, nobody here belongs to me except him and he has this huge connection. My husband has 80 first cousins so this wee baby, who is my wee baby, belonged in this city and I didn't and I still feel that, and my sister is here now but that is still not the same kind, I still don't completely belong and I suppose in a sense I belong through my kids and I would never want to go back to Ireland, I would think that was penance, if somebody said, you have to go back and live in Ireland, I just wouldn't do it, although, perhaps now things have changed a lot and I could go and live in Dublin or Cork or somewhere like that and find likeminded people. I don't think I would go back anyway, my friends, everything is here now. But I miss that sense of belonging and I quite like to go to Wexford, where all those, not just your parents and brothers and sisters, it's about that whole wider family thing but way back generations there is a wee bit of you there and I feel quite emotional when I go there I feel that really strong sense of there being a wee bit of genetic material sort of there. I met somebody recently and they said I met somebody and she was exactly like you and they told me who this person was and we traced her and this person is a relation! You see the family similarities going over there and they say, my god, you are so like so and so and they get out photographs and I like that sense of belonging. (Interviewee 2)

For some who were born in Scotland genetic inheritance is more important than place of birth and location of childhood in defining national identity. The genetic transmission of Irishness through the parental line means that residing in Scotland should not be equated with being Scottish. Irishness is in the 'blood' line and even manifests itself in certain cultural traits that appear to have genetic roots:

I'm proud of being Irish. I wouldn't change it for the world. But as I said I do have cousins here that were born in Scotland. And some of my children say 'I'm Scottish' and I laugh and say 'oh no, you're Irish. Both your parents are Irish and you can be born in a stable and not be a horse, look at our Lord. (Interviewee 6)

My mum was very, very proud of her Irishness, and the fact that she actually was born there. People used to say to her, 'oh but you're Scots' cos she was obviously brought over when she was a tiny baby. 'If I was born in a stable would it make me a horse?' she used to say. No, she was very, very Irish. (Interviewee 16)

When people talk about me they say 'your mum was Irish'. I would say, 'but I'm Scottish born'. But they'd say, 'you're Irish. There's not an ounce of Scots blood in you'. There isn't. I've got no Scots ancestry at all. It's all Irish. I know that one of my cousins says to me, she's Irish and lives in Ireland, she says, 'you're very Irish'. When my husband and I met in Donegal he thought I was Irish. We were

both in Donegal on holiday. Like I say, I'm Scottish but I feel very, ultimately
I'm Irish. (Interviewee 15)

Interviewee 20, a second generation descendant distinguishes herself as racially
Celtic, something different from being Irish, and for her something which sets
her apart from British and curiously even Scottish people. Her account portrays a
significant commitment to biological essentialism that defies the importance of a
Scottish birth to claims to nationality. She speaks disparagingly of what she terms
'mongrel identities'. She also appears able to reconcile the essential traits of the
Celts as on the one hand socialist and on the other hand monarchical:

> I think the Irish have a certain sense of socialism. It's a Celtic thing. No matter
> who you are and where you are, you can't change that. Even if I'd been born
> and brought up in America, I would still be Celtic by race and you can't change
> that. As far as nationality is concerned I'm not Irish, but in race yeah, I'm Irish
> by race, Celtic by race and I can't change that and I know it's there. I know
> I'm different from the English and the Scots. But then again most of them
> are crossbred, I'm not. You can go back as far as you like in my lineage and
> you'll find I'm not cross bred anywhere. A lot of them are just mongrels, racial
> mongrels, I'm not, my family can be traced going back to the Kings of Ireland.
> You can look it up if you like. (Interviewee 20)

For other participants it was social attitudes and outlooks rather than biological
factors that were key. Caricatures of the authentic Irish and the authentic Scot were
often depicted. The genuine Irish national would; be blessed with the gift of the gab
or the craic; be literary inclined and a master of the craft of linguistic playfulness;
breeze through life with a humorous and light-hearted gaiety; participate in Irish
societies; follow Celtic Football Club; be a devoted and practising Catholic; be
part of a large and extended family network and have a large number of children;
name their children Pierce or Dillon or Sinead or Niamh; have a sympathy for
the underdog in political affairs, display an extra hunger for socio-economic
advancement; have an elevated respect for the sacrifices their forebears made
and the hardships they had to go through to allow their children to live as they
currently do; reveal a healthy degree of self criticism and realisation that one has
come from nothing; and have a belief that vanity comes before a fall.

The authentic Scot would by definition be straight laced and dour; be
economical with words and emotion; be interested in and have a bent for science
and engineering; be supportive of cultural organisations such as the Boys Brigade
and the Girl Guides, and even the Freemasons and the Orange Order; be followers
of Rangers Football Club; have responsible family sizes and relatively limited
interest in the extended family; name their children Hamish, Gordon, Hannah, Ian
and Wendy; have cold, clean and sterile houses; be politically conservative and
supportive of hard work and thrift; be supportive of the monarchy; have an interest

in defending positions of authority and protecting domestic interests first; and be keen to promote the virtues of citizenship more than the values of welfare.

Interviewee 22 observes that in spite of good friendships with neighbours in Scotland, there was a secure sense of Irishness in her family home, borne from an alienation from Protestant Scotland and the British Monarchy:

> My mother was always Irish. She got on well with her neighbours, her Protestant neighbours and Scottish neighbours, but we knew we were Irish. I was always quite happy to be Irish. My hackles would go up if anyone said anything about the Irish, and still would. But times have changed and you have to be ecumenical. There has been a change. We had good Protestant neighbours. My best friend, when I was wee was a protestant, Cissy Baxter, and she stayed in the same close as us. We got on well with the neighbours, but I knew I was Irish basically. Aye, I felt Irish. I felt Irish because we went there every year and stayed six or seven weeks, and we heard talk in the house. I enjoyed Ireland but I had friends here and I enjoyed it here. But I knew I was Irish. I felt like an alien sometimes in different company. I would go to different things and I felt like I didn't belong there at all. There was of course religion and different attitudes to things. Loyalties and things were different. They were very Royal, some people, that was an anathema to us. It was terrible. The old Queen and King, we couldn't be bothered. (Interviewee 22)

For Interviewee 9, culture and in particular religion, was pivotal to Irishness and the sense of being different from Scottish people.

> My mother was Irish through and through, she was always very proud of being Irish. She has made no excessive efforts to assimilate at all. She pretty much takes the view that her culture is important to her and her faith is extremely important to her and people should accept her for that, and if they don't then she's not particularly interested. She expected the same from us. She always gave us the feeling that we shouldn't, in any way, hide who we were or where we were from. (Interviewee 9)

Interviewee 3 meanwhile speaks of the strength of her Irishness, in spite of her Scottish accent and her residency as a child in Scotland. For Interviewee 3, being Irish meant doing Irish things:

> I never had a problem about feeling Irish. I always was Irish and I never felt that I had to identify myself as anything else. I was Irish and OK I've got a Glasgow accent because I happened to go to school here. Probably if there was anything I would have changed, it would have been I would have liked to have grown up in Ireland. But the fact that you're doing Irish things here means you're making a statement that you are Irish. (Interviewee 3)

For Interviewee 66a, religion and family and kin relations helped to define her mother's sense of Irishness. This maternal sense of Irishness was in turn inculcated into her own family life so that she too feels more Irish than Scottish:

> I would say she [Interviewee's mother] was still Irish. She was Irish in her faith and that shone through in so many ways. That came first and foremost in her life. She did all her work in one room and in another room there would be a time of the day and I would go through and she would be sitting saying her prayers and always quiet. That was always part of her life. So as regards that she was Irish to the core. She inherited that and passed it on. I would say in her family the bonds with the other people in Ireland were kept going. She kept in touch by writing and sometimes she would go and visit them. I would say I feel more Irish than Scottish in my make up too. I was born in Scotland but I think we've got so many roots from the Irish side of our family that I think that is really predominant in my own make up and my outlook. That has come from contact with my Irish grandparents and parents. I think our life was, to a certain extent, dominated in our childhood by Irish things and Irish ways of living and the Irish outlook on things. And laterly by keeping in touch with the Irish people, I think you feel your roots are there. (Interviewee 66a)

People who were born in Scotland but who felt predominantly Irish occasionally sensed a need to be apologetic about their conundrum. For interviewee 19, for whom the Irish flair for the dramatic, the literary, the arts, and music, was pivotal in her own alignment with Irishness, to be 'technically' a Scot but 'emotionally' Irish was something to be wrestled with:

> You see when somebody says to me something about, how do you feel?, I feel Irish. In spite of the fact that I have spent so many years of my life in Scotland, emotionally I'm Irish. And when anything happens on television and Ireland is maligned, I am upset. I don't feel a Scot. It's terrible because Scotland has done so much for me. I honestly don't feel a Scot. I don't feel a Scot. I love Scotland and I love Glasgow, and any time I go abroad I tell them, in fact I'm like the Scottish Tourist Board. They all laugh. I remember going to America and I was telling them all about Glasgow and about Scotland. And I remember at a party, them saying, 'gee Glasgow must be a fantastic place'. And it is, if you think about what we've got here. And Scotland is so beautiful. I think Scotland is, I love it. I love it to pieces but I don't feel a Scot. That's the truth. I feel I'm Irish. Now I don't know whether, is that normal or is that unusual? It's very much an emotional thing isn't it? I think on the whole, the Irish tend to be more dramatic. One of my friends said to me, 'you're awfully dramatic'. Now I don't think I'm dramatic but she says, 'when you're telling me a story you're very dramatic'. Now I think the Irish on the whole are very dramatic and they're also very imaginative. I think too, the Irish have got more appreciation of the arts. That's a ridiculous thing to say, but they seem to think very highly

of literature, poor Scots, and they're very interested in music and art. Yes that's right. I think too, maybe I'm wrong here, but the Irish that I know tend to be more optimistic. When you are in their company there's laughing going on and there are jokes. But I've also noticed that, and this is true of my dad, just like that it can turn from laughter to tears very quickly. But the Scots are more reticent. I think maybe that's the difference. (Interviewee 19)

Likewise, for interviewee 49, privileging Ireland over Scotland, for example in a competitive football match between the countries, is something which one might do but not 'feel proud of':

If I were asked, would I pass the Norman Tebbit test? If Scotland were to play the Republic of Ireland on whose side would I go? I'm not quite sure. I love it when I can sit here and enjoy Scotland gubbing England. That in a way is an inverted, it could be xenophobia, it could be racism, it could be a disturbed form of sectarianism. But when Scotland is playing the Republic of Ireland or when Scotland is playing Ireland in sporting events, I suspect I want Ireland to win, but I don't feel very proud of that and my kids don't feel like that and they're astounded by it. They're astonished by it. (Interviewee 49)

Whilst some participants could securely present themselves as Irish, others felt that they were ill served by the categories of both Irish and Scottish. Their identity was positioned somewhere in between both and they felt neither acceptable nor accepted among those who essentialised each. Interviewee 35 notes how he felt Scottish in terms of his place of birth, accent, and schooling, but was forced to confront the fact that he was not accepted as such as a consequence of anti-Irish Catholic practices in his place of work. He describes the experience as 'disillusioning':

I think we were disillusioned. We didn't know if we were Irish or we were Scottish. We didn't know where we were. As I said, we all felt as though we were second class citizens and certainly where I grew up there was no Catholic school, so we had to, it was a multi-religious school. I've got to say at school we never came up against any anti-Catholic feeling. When I started work I came up against it. I certainly came up against it. And yet the thing was, I was as Scottish as anybody else. I had a Scottish accent and was born and brought up in Scotland, but Scottish people didn't think of me as being Scottish. I was an intruder into their country and it was often said, there was an Irish joke about Wimpy and Wimpy actually meant 'we employ more Paddy's every year'. That was a joke that used to do the rounds quite often. Most of these jokes were derogatory jokes. The intention was to belittle the Irish person that was listening. (Interviewee 35)

Interviewee 54 provides a more meandering musing on the question of national identity. In part his testimony reveals the context specificity of enquiring into the question of belonging. But in using the words 'bastard' and 'illegitimate', Interviewee 54 is making a clear declaration that he feels he falls between a number of identity categories and occupies a nomadic position:

> Well I don't feel Scottish and I don't feel Irish. I think I'm a bastard, illegitimate is the word that comes to mind. When I'm in Ireland I do feel Irish and I don't associate with Britishness in any way. When I'm at Celtic Park I do feel Irish, an outsider from Scotland. Sometimes I think I'm a Scotsman. I'm living in Scotland, I'm staying here and all the rest of it and I'd have a slight affiliation with 'we're all Jock Tamson's bairns'. But as you get older you become intransigent and you move away from that. I can't find the words, I don't have the ability to actually feel Scottish. That's a sad thing. It's quite sad that, for me to be here for sixty-three years. But having said that if somebody said to me, are you an Irishman or a Scotsman?' I would say I'm a Scotsman. I'm Scottish. So I mean, I've got a foot in two camps. I am a Scotsman. I feel, I've been here all my days and my father was here. A lot of the things that people speak about what Scots people do I've taken that on board. I've been up early in the morning and I've been scrubbing and all that. So I've tried to assimilate into another sort of thing, so I'm not actually one thing or another. Can I honestly say I'm Scottish, no in truth I can't. I think I used the word illegitimate before. (Interviewee 54)

Although in no sense statistically representative, the greater majority of participants identified themselves as principally Scottish but in most cases this claim was tempered with the assertion that their Irish Catholic heritage played an important role in conditioning what kind of Scot they were. It was both impossible and undesirable to forget one's roots and begin afresh. Having an Irish background produced a specific kind of Scottishness, a Scottishness infused with Irish ways. This brand of Scottishness shared a number of characteristics with traditional Scottishness but it also differed from traditional Scottishness too. Being of Irish Catholic heritage meant that it was possible to feel a certain kind of Scot without feeling that one belonged entirely to the Scottish nation. Interviewees 1, 24 and 55 summarise this claim to identity well:

> I actually feel both! I certainly don't feel I'm not Scottish. I know more about Scotland than I do about Ireland because I left there when I was 16 and I'm 30 now. As a kid you don't think about your country in big terms. I think I'm both. I've lived in Scotland for more of my life than I lived in Ireland. I'm a Scottish-Irish person if you like. Nobody round here anymore would make any reference about me being Irish. (Interviewee 1)

> We know our roots but I think we're now Scottish really. But we've got a certain affection for Ireland and certainly we're very pleased to hear when Ireland is doing well, North and South. We'll always remember where we came from and it'll always be part of who we are. But we're now Scottish and that's where our concerns lie. (Interviewee 24)

> I would say I was an Irish-Scot. I would say I was Irish but I would also say that it is time that we got more integrated into the Scottish life, without giving up things that are precious to us. (Interviewee 55)

'In betweeness' of course means different things to different people. For Interviewee 48, having a family who were born in Scotland was an important component of his father's transition from an Irishman to an 'Irish-Scottish person' or more specifically a 'Glaswegian from an Irish background':

> My father had a lot of strong links with Ireland and was proud of his heritage, but he was a Glaswegian as well. He was an Irish-Scottish person if you like and he was quite happy to stay here. Maybe he would have gone back to Ireland had things been different before we were born, but I think when we were born he was more or less prepared to stay. I think he would say he was a Glaswegian from an Irish background. (Interviewee 48)

For interviewee 56, being born and reared in Scotland meant that he recognised himself to be principally Scottish. His affiliations are first and foremost with Scotland. Indeed as a consequence of living in England for some time he claims to enjoy a heightened sense of being Scottish. But in no way does this diminish the sense of importance of his heritage. The Irish inheritance has travelled far and remained influential world wide and down through the generations. It was no different in Scotland. Being Scottish but with an Irish background means being in tune with and empathetic with the lives, ways and attitudes of the Irish in Ireland:

> I class myself as Scottish with an Irish background, I wouldn't class myself as Irish purely because it would be frogjumping, I couldn't. My Father, he classes himself as Irish, at least has done in recent years. When there is an international match on he'll watch the Ireland game instead of the Scotland game and to me I find that strange as well, purely because, I mean it's like, you know you are of Irish descent but you are Scottish. Scotland has given you your home and your life and you are certainly from Irish descent but you are still Scottish. I've always seen myself as Scottish, certainly living in England and latterly living back up here I've always classed myself as Scottish. I have Scottish blood in me therefore, I'm Scottish. The Irish part comes into it going back, it's like, if you went to America and Australia and you talk to people there whose great grandfather jumped on the boat back in the 1840s or whatever and they will class themselves as Irish-Americans or class themselves as Irish-Australians. It's that

part of you, you are Scottish, you are settled here, born here and always lived here and down the line your family have lived somewhere else in a different country and that's where you are originally from. That's where the Irish blood comes from and in that respect you are, how can I put it, sympathetic to all the things that go with the Irish background. You feel as if you could feel the same about things as somebody who has lived in Donegal all their life. That's how I feel anyway. (Interviewee 56)

For Interviewee 9 again being born in Scotland means that one's primary identity is by definition Scottish. But there has lingered a sense of closer cultural proximity to Irish ways of life than to Scottish cultural traditions. Alterity persists and manifests itself in levels of comfort and ease in different kinds of company. Here the alleged 'coldness' 'logical' and 'emotionless' qualities of Scottish Presbyterianism seem to be being contrasted with the warmth and collegiality of Irish Catholicism:

Well I would, generally speaking, say I am Scottish. I was born here and brought up here and it would be silly to say otherwise really. But that belies what you really feel deep down inside, which is that you're not. Scottish, you equate it with Presbyterianism and lots of other things that you know you're just definitely not. There is a conflict that goes on in your mind cos you think to yourself, the vast majority of Scottish people, well the vast majority of people anywhere, are just dead nice, decent ordinary people, and working class people have a lot in common, obviously. But you just know that your culture is different, and this sounds terrible, but you can generally speaking, there's always a wee connection. I don't even know what it is; I can't even put it into words really. Between Irish people, there just seems to be, you know even Irish people with very different personalities, there just seems to be a common way of going: a way of communicating that involves being light hearted or whatever, that you sometimes don't get from Scottish people. (Interviewee 9)

Interviewee 47 meanwhile defines his primary identity as Scottish but is clear that he would not be the type of Scotsman he is if it was not for his Irish background. He displays a clear awareness that some might question his right to claim Scottishness in these terms and seeks to assert the 'healthiness' of recognising identities as hybrid. He claims that expressions of Irishness in Scotland are as legitimate as expressions of Scottishness in the United States. Those who do not see the parallel betray duplicity and contradictory judgement. Ultimately assimilation and integration has run its course and primary loyalty lies with Scotland.

I don't feel Scottish and I don't feel Irish, but I feel both. Sometimes I feel more Irish and sometimes I feel more Scottish, but I don't feel one or the other. I feel like a Celt as opposed to one or the other. But sometimes I don't feel Irish because I don't know enough about Ireland itself, if I went into Irish company they would have their own sense of humour and things that would be peculiar to their own situation. For example if Billy Connolly said something we would find it hilarious and other people wouldn't. So they would have their own comedians and singers and things which would be funny to them which I would maybe miss. So from that point of view I don't feel Irish, in the sense that I'm not there every day and I think you need to be there everyday to really appreciate it. But I feel very proud of my Irish roots and I'll never ever allow my own family to forget it. They must appreciate where they came from and never to forget it. But we've got to move on and be Scottish. My kids are certainly more Scottish than what I was at their age. I remember my dad refused point blank to support Scotland. I quite like to see the boys supporting Scotland. If Scotland played Ireland at football, I would want Scotland to win because we're here. The unfortunate thing is some Scottish people don't like Celtic players in the team and some Irish background people don't like Scotland anyway because they're seen as against us. But I think we've got to a stage now where we are integrated and there's no doubt about that. But I still think that we should keep that identity which says, 'I'm Scottish by and large, but I'm never ever going to forget about where I came from'. What does bug me about Scotland is that they keep going on about culture and flying the Irish flag at Parkhead and the whole Catholic thing and how can we not just forget about that? But the same thing happens with Scottish people when they go to Canada or America. They still have Rabbie Burns Clubs and quite rightly so. They'll still have the kilt and the haggis and the bagpipes and quite rightly so. So why should Irish people in Scotland forget about where they came from? I'm proud to be Scottish but I'm also very proud to have that Irish background and I don't think I would be the person I was if I didn't have the mix of the two of them. That's the thing I like about Celtic FC as a club, because you've got both there. They're not one and they're not the other, they're both and I think that's healthy. (Interviewee 47)

Interviewee 67a likewise recognises his final and ultimate loyalty is to Scotland and is pleasured by and proud of Scottish cultural traditions. But his Scottishness is a blend of Irishness and Scottishness, the combination of which makes him a 'better person'. His claims to Scottishness are always tempered by the fact that he has Irish parents:

I think they've blended both cultures because basically they're both Celtic races. Take for example the kilt, I've never worn a kilt in my life, but every wedding I go to I see kilts and it gives me a wee bit of a thrill, because we come from the same source, if you like. And we're embracing the culture of Scotland. I've got two relationships, Irish and Scottish. I'm aware of both and I try to blend them both to become a better person. I'll tell you one thing, we went to see Scotland playing Ireland at rugby one time and John Down, my nephew, asked the question of Bridget: 'Will Jimmy be shouting for Ireland or for Scotland?' I said, 'I'll be shouting for Scotland'. He was sitting beside me shouting for Ireland and I was sitting shouting for Scotland. But between the two I definitely felt an affinity for both, but when it came to the crunch, I'm a Scot with Irish parents. (Interviewee 67a)

Meanwhile, Interviewee 58 asserts that in spite of being a 'Scotsman' he is 'very much aware' of his Irish roots, and not least the poverty and oppression visited upon his forebears. Interestingly, he draws out a comparison between the optimism of the Irish and the tenacity of the Scots. These are cultural traits that have been creolised to produce people like himself:

> I think the one thing that they had was optimism. I think they had hope and I think they had optimism. I think that came from their Catholic background. If their Catholic background gave them anything, it was hope, maybe not much else but it certainly gave them hope and a sense of their worth. They had that kind of human quality. I think they rolled with the tide. Things weren't going to be easy and they didn't expect things to be easy. But when it was good it was good and they enjoyed it. But when things went against them they didn't lose hope. I think they had a certain optimism. And a certain sense of humour, a dry humour sometimes, but they certainly had that. I think Scotland gave them tenacity, which I think is a very strong Scottish characteristic and I think they absorbed that tenacity. I think the Scottish tenacity is the thing they have absorbed into their system. And they don't let go. They just don't let go. I'm a Scotsman, but I'm very much aware of my Irish roots. I'd be very much aware of that. Four generations later I'm aware that my forebears were poor downtrodden peasants who were looked on with contempt. Yes I'd be very much aware of that. (Interviewee 58)

It is simply untrue to assume that first generation migrants identify more with Ireland, that Irishness becomes diluted through time, and that later generation descendants feel more Scottish than their forebears. Nor is it true that first generation antipathy towards Ireland was replaced with an elevated patriotism among the second generation which is now dwindling. Nevertheless the assumption, that Irish influences are progressively losing their salience and that there is an intergenerational shift across the spectrum from Irishness to Scottishness did feature in some accounts. For Interviewee 26, as exemplified primarily by levels of contact with and travel to Ireland, there exists a degree of dilution in matters Irish:

> I think I would have to say I'm Scots with an Irish background. I would admit to being Irish to a degree but I was born here and brought up here, and now at my age I think I'm really an indoctrinated Scot, but I would always admit that I had Irish blood in me. It's about I think a difference in attitude. I find the really true Scots very dour and very, not straight laced, but very dour and very singular. They keep themselves to themselves. But anyone with Irish blood, the people coming up and down the road talking to me, you usually find that most

of them are of Irish descent. They'll tell you their family secrets whether you want to know them or not. So I think that way, I still see that divide and that line. The true Scots keep themselves very much to themselves. But I think it's getting better. I think everybody is integrating a bit more, here, not in Ireland, but here I think here they are. I don't think there's as much bigotry, or else it's because the bigotry has been turned around now off the Irish on to the coloureds or something. They talk about 'them' coming and 'taking our jobs'. That's what was said about the Irish. So it's maybe just that they've got another focus now.

I would say yes it has been watered down, in as much as I don't really think about it on a day to day basis, but when I go across to Ireland I suddenly become Irish. In fact when I was a child, they used to say I came back talking with an Irish accent. I acclimatised myself and I was just Irish to the core when I came back. Then it would go out of me again. There was a period there when I hadn't been in Ireland for a number of years, and I was the outcast of the family because I started going abroad. Oh, I remember the first holiday I took in Italy. Oh it was terrible, I hadn't gone to Ireland that year at all! So there was a few years there I hadn't gone over for a visit, but the year before last I went over to Dublin, and again, suddenly it all came back and I didn't want to leave it. It's funny, it's there inside you somewhere and it comes out, even if you don't want it to it does. But overall, I think some of my generation, and certainly most of the next one to me, their Irishness is watered down definitely. You never hear them talk much about Ireland unless it's about the troubles. You never hear them saying, 'oh I'd love to go and stay in Ireland'.

I'm comfortable here now, but I wouldn't like to think that I would never go back to Ireland for another holiday. I enjoy Ireland very much and I know so many people there. I'm comfortable there. But I don't think it's just as strong as it was in my mother and father's generation. To them, they just longed to be able to go to Ireland. They faced the fact that they couldn't and that Ireland couldn't give them a living, but they longed to be able to go there. If my father had won the lottery or had come into money, I'm quite sure he would have gone back. His father wouldn't, as I say, he was bitter. Ireland had let him down. But my father would have gone to live in Ireland. (Interviewee 26)

Interviewee 39 however detects a renewed interest in Irishness in Scotland. Children and grandchildren are displaying a passion and interest in Ireland which suggests a rekindling of patriotism and interest in heritage. Interestingly, he attributes this to the easier lifestyles of the present generation and the time people now have to even think about the roots and routes of their forebears:

Maybe in a couple of generations it might water down, but I still think, I feel that this generation in Scotland just now are even more interested in their Irishness, because our people in the past were so busy working to keep their head above water, never mind having time to read a book, they did not dwell on it as much! The younger ones now are asking about where their people came from and are very interested in it, as I say, all that definitely makes you what you are. It's like the black people in America want to know about their African roots, you've got to know your own identity and while I'm proud to be Scottish, I'll probably live here till the end of my days, I am also very proud of my Irishness and I don't feel any conflict between the two. (Interviewee 39)

Many participants then appeared to be comfortable with the concept of Scottishness. Nevertheless, in spite of its integrative potential, few chose to identify themselves as singularly and exclusively Scottish. Those that did were often people with bitter memories of poverty and religious and cultural conservatism in Ireland and who had benefited from Scotland's comparative modernity, not least in terms of standards of living and welfare services:

Oh no I wasn't born there. I was born here. This is my home. I would never think of Ireland as my home. I never have any special feeling towards it at all. In fact if anything I hate it more than anything. My parents did find a better way of life here than what was in Ireland, but then the one in Ireland was so awful that you could go anywhere and it would be better than that for most of them. Most of them had to leave because of the land, they wouldn't be getting any land so they would have to leave. But they all did very well in Scotland, that's what they would think to themselves. My father was ill and I said, 'if anything happens to you do you want to go back to Ireland?' I meant if he died, did he want to go back to be buried in Ireland. 'No' he said, 'I don't want to go back there. If anything happens to me I would want to be buried in the country that gave me a living.' He liked Scotland. He thought it was a great place. He thoroughly enjoyed it. He did enjoy it and my mother would have enjoyed it very much too, except she was ill for such a long time. But her great thing was about what great doctors they had here and great hospitals. She could never have survived in Ireland with the amount of operations she got and the very difficult operations she needed. Sometimes it was the first time they were ever done in the Western Infirmary. Away back during the war she had nine major operations in eleven weeks. Her whole stomach was all taken away and they had never done parts of those kinds of operations before, it was cutting edge. They got to the stage where they said 'Mrs. Swinney there's nothing more to take away'. They just had to leave it then and hope for the best. And she lived on until 1967. It's quite amazing. That's from 1944 to 1967, it's a long time. My parents would have liked it here and felt this was their home. I think that nearly everybody that came here would have said that they did the right thing. That it was the right thing to do and that it was a marvellous country. (Interviewee 20)

A lot of people assume that I'm Irish and I say I'm not I'm Scottish, I think it is just as nice here up in the highlands as they have over there. I can't understand why my brothers, my two younger brothers, would be quite happy to get over there and stay. Yet, if somebody asked me where do you come from, I would say I'm Scottish. If I'm filling out forms they ask you what's your nationality, well I'm British, so it's British because it's a form. But if anybody asks me, I'm Scottish, my parents are Irish, but I'm Scottish. I think my brothers would consider themselves more Irish than Scottish. But not me. This is my only home. I am Scottish, this is where all my family live. (Interviewee 11)

Some participants identified friends and relatives who had embarked upon a kind of self-imposed 'ethnic cleansing' in a bid to submerge their Irish heritage. For these 'lace curtain Irish', prim, clinical, clean, and Calvinist Scotland offered a superior ethic to repugnant, decadent and primitive Ireland and all traces of Irishness were to be erased from the family scrapbook. Given the nature of this research project and by implication the type of participants recruited, none of the interviewees placed themselves in this category:

> The lace curtain Irish, they were a certain type of Irish that didn't want to associate with their past. All their houses were nice and clean. They were always polishing up things. They were trying to improve themselves by education and learning. A slight ego was there as well, they thought they were good and all that kind of stuff. I've got to be correct here, PC is the word. I mean my grandfather's brother Johnny, I don't know the full story, but I always had this wee idea that the brother Johnny, old Johnny, who was his brother, would not be considered in the Irish lace curtain type. He always said things like, his brother who was my grandfather, was a Lloyd George man. Now the connotation I assume was that he was veering towards the establishment, SDLP sort of thing. My grandfather was a member of the lace curtain Irish. Whereas old Johnny was more of a Sinn Féin'er blowing up bridges and statues of King Billy in County Meath you know. So this appealed to earlier people, whereas my grandfather was more inclined to be more right wing and keep things quieter. (Interviewee 54)

> Here in Saltcoats they've a habit of saying to you, 'and tell me this hen, who was your granny?' And I'll go, 'well, you wouldn't have known my granny cos she was Irish, but I'll bet yours was as well'. And I think that's true, but I think a lot of them have conveniently forgotten their roots. My father used to say, 'they threw their rosary beads away on the Irish boat on the way over'. They don't want to remember that they came from Irish culture, but I think it shows in a lot of the things they do. (Interviewee 16)

Conclusion

It is clear then that the Irish Catholic community in Scotland displays an open variety of claims to nationality and that they variably align themselves with properties imagined to be distinctively Irish and Catholic does not mitigate against their preparedness to migrate towards a range of complex and creolised claims to identity. I take the idea of 'Irish Catholic' to resonate with six particular groups of people who now dwell in Scotland but who have an attachment to or awareness of their Irish Catholic heritage. These six groups of people in turn help to populate the category with content and invest it with meaning. They may be titled 'Irish', 'Irish Scot', 'Irish and Scottish', 'illegitimate' or 'neither Irish nor Scottish', 'Scottish with an Irish heritage', and 'Scottish with a repressed Irish Catholic past'. Based upon the above analysis the chief characteristics of each might be identified as follows:

- *Irish*: There exist a group of individuals, often first generation but not always, who define themselves as exclusively Irish Catholic. Their move to Scotland has in no way diminished or diluted their Irishness and if anything they exhibit a heightened patriotism and exaggerated Irishness. They offer essentialist, and often genetic and biologically rooted, accounts of their Irishness.
- *Irish Scot*: Another group define themselves as offshoots of the Irish nation, chiselled and moulded into a modified form by dint of their encounters with Scotland. These are people who see themselves as primarily Irish Catholic but who concede that their Irishness has become Scotified; improved, tarnished, mediated, and filtered through their encounters with Scotland. 'Irish Scots' remain recognisably Irish but bear a different stamp from Irish Catholic communities in Ireland and in other parts of the diaspora
- *Irish and Scottish*: a third group identify themselves as both Irish Catholic and Scottish and seem able and content to live with a dual allegiance. If one educates oneself beyond the caricatures, it is possible to see that the Irish and the Scots are not that dissimilar after all. Both exist on the margins of Great Britain, both have Celtic roots, both have suffered under British imperialism, and indeed socialism and class has figured more in Scotland's history than Ireland's.
- *Illegitimate*: others again felt unable to identify with either Ireland and Scotland and mourned the fact that they felt they were 'illegitimate'. Although Irish Catholic they were different from Irish Catholic people in Ireland. Albeit living in Scotland their Irishness mitigated against any secure sense of being Scottish. For these participants 'in betweeness' was confusing, disorientating, and at times paralysing. Being of 'no fixed abode', dwelling in displacement in an interstitial and in between space, was more of a burden than a liberating experience.
- *Scottish with an Irish heritage*: Another group, mainly although not exclusively, later day descendants, were Irish Catholics who saw themselves as primarily Scottish but who still held their Irish Catholic heritage to be important. Questions of national identity were reduced to the ways in which those with Irish roots were different kinds of Scot from those who do not. The Irish had leeched and bleached Scotland and Scottish national identity was in part a product of the Irish influence.

- *Scottish with a repressed Irish Catholic past*: A final group of lace curtain Irish Catholics displayed a certain embarrassment about their Irish Catholic roots and sought to repress and stifle their origins. These Scots refused to permit their Irishness to affect their sense of Scottishness and sought to embrace a purified Calvinist, clean, orderly, prim, and conservative lifestyle.

The remainder of this book seeks to better understand these complex and in between senses of belonging with respect to issues of the production of images of Ireland among diasporeans, Irish political influences both with respect to Ireland and Scotland, social, cultural, and religious attitudes and behaviours, and work, welfare, economic mobility and class.

Chapter 5

Imagining Home: Holidays, the Farm and the Craic

Introduction

How was Ireland, or for some 'home', imagined within the Irish Catholic community in Scotland? Albeit mediated in important ways by class, gender, and family composition, it is inter-generational variations in the depiction and imagining of Ireland which emerges as of particular importance. First generation migrants clearly had more realistic and more ambivalent attitudes to the country of their birth. Their memories are marked by bitterness and anger about the poverty and backwardness they experienced. The invention of Ireland as a paradise or repository of a precious way of life emerged only when collective memory of the hardships of life in Ireland were safely left behind and contact with the country became structured through more pleasant interludes. Of course not everyone held this view, those with prolonged experience of visiting Ireland, for example war evacuees, provide a more balanced and at times sobering depiction of traditional Ireland. But principally triggered by family holidays to farms and homesteads of origin, there has steadily emerged, especially within certain second, third, and fourth generation descendants, a vigorous romanticisation of Ireland, its landscapes, communities, and ways of life. With the demise of family holidays and rise of the Celtic Tiger since 1993 images of Ireland as a utopia have come under threat. The purpose of this chapter is to ruminate over these competing framings of Ireland, and in particular to scrutinise the ways in which family vacations contributed to the reinvention of Ireland as a paradise and wonderland.

The plight of the first generation: Ireland as a place of hardship, melancholy, sorrow and bitterness

First generation migrants who moved to Scotland did so for a wide variety of reasons. These included to flee from community hostility to mixed marriages; to avoid the shame and humility imposed on young women who fell pregnant out of wedlock; to pursue a romance with and often to marry a Scots man or woman; to serve as a priest following graduation from an Irish seminary; to avoid political and religious persecution and discrimination; to achieve freedom from what could be experienced as a stifling, conservative, and insular culture; and to avoid imprisonment for either political activities or more everyday acts of criminality.

Nevertheless one underlying explanation of migration emerges as by way and far the most significant; poverty. For many in the first generation, traditional Ireland was a place characterised by limited opportunity for advancement, long tortuous working conditions, no secondary schools, industrial schools, walking two to three miles in bare feet to school, frightening religious strictness, cramped living conditions, no electricity, cooking only on turf fires, fetching water from distant wells and springs, and restricted and rationed diets. Ireland had done nothing for them; home was little more than a life of grind and misery.

Interviewee 32 first moved from Donegal to Scotland for work in 1945 at 15 years of age. He recalls the central importance of poverty in his decision to migrate and its especial salience in peripheral parts of Ireland:

> It was hard to move to Scotland especially at the age of 15 when you're just a boy really but the only thing was you had money coming in. See in Donegal, nobody had any money, not in our place anyway. Even before I was fifteen, I used to be cutting a day's turf just the same as a man, but they had nothing to give you. They were very lucky to be able to get regularly fed. North West Donegal was the most neglected part. That and Connemara and Achill Island were the most neglected parts of Ireland in my time. (Interviewee 32)

Interviewee 17's father moved from Donegal to Glasgow in 1924. She recalls the vivid memories of biting poverty her father frequently recounted:

> He told me of dreadful, dreadful poverty. When he was serving his time as a Cooper he had to walk three miles to his work and he was there all day. One day he took the last slice of bread from the house and he got in to real bother when he got home that night for leaving the rest of the house with nothing to eat. He said but I had nothing to eat and I had to work all day. That's how tight it was. He had terrible memories. (Interviewee 17)

Interviewee 30 left Donegal for Glasgow in 1956 at the age of 18. He notes the ways in which migration to Scotland became a way of life for young men and women left with no other option. Scotland was preferred as the cheapest passage to something better and chain migration became important in the routing of people:

> Everybody was poor so we were all in the same boat. You were away from school as soon as you were a man, about sixteen or seventeen. You wanted to get over here and that was it. My father had worked awhile here in Scotland, whereabouts I couldn't tell you. Every one of us came to Scotland at some point, you know. I've still got two brothers here. They're older than me. Well as I say I never experienced any heartache. You had nothing but you didn't know any better. Scotland was the land of milk and honey I suppose. All you were used to was hand-me-downs. Then a boy maybe two or three years older than you would go away and the next time you seen him, oh a lovely suit on and the

works, you know. You'd say, oh flip I need to get over there. Why not America or somewhere like that? Why Scotland? Well, when would you have the fare for America? Nearly everybody had somebody ahead of them in Glasgow to take them in when they came here, a relation or a close friend. (Interviewee 30)

Interviewee 31, a priest, moved to Scotland in 1961 at the age of 25 following his ordination. He also recounts the habituated nature of migration to Scotland and the role of family members and other local worthies who went ahead and sent messages back about the opportunities which Scotland provided:

Coming from the west of Donegal, there was so much coming and going of people from Glasgow, that's all we talked about. And the men from around my locality were part of building the hydro electric schemes here – Pitlochry, Loch Sloy, Loch Awe. I knew all those names because my father had a pub, so I was in serving all these guys when they came home, so I knew all these names and I knew all about the work they did and where they lived. Then a lot came over here and worked on the farms in Perthshire and some of the families that I grew up with, they came altogether and settled down in Perth. My best friend growing up was a wee boy at home, his family left because there was no work for them. The father went first and got a place to stay and the wife and the kids followed. I remember the day they left. I wouldn't be more than seven or eight years of age. He lived up in Perth. That was the community I was born into, a community of coming and going to Scotland. Of course during the Glasgow Fair they all came home on holidays and you met them again. So I knew so much about Scotland. They were just over there because there was no work in that part of Donegal and as you know they were really good workers those guys, building the tunnels and the railways and the roads. A lot of them had very responsible jobs, they called them 'gangers' in those days, they were the bosses. Some were called them the 'tunnel tigers'. They were known as the tunnel tigers these guys. That was the nickname they had. I remember hearing that name so often, they're home on holiday, the tunnel tigers crowd, you know. So Scotland was very much in the news for me growing up as a lad. (Interviewee 31)

Interviewee 35's father and mother left Donegal for Scotland in 1932, both at the age of 19. He too portrays migration from Ireland as a necessary 'habit', a way of life which was a natural and routine response to the destitution and family poverty which existed in Ireland:

They never expressed any kind of reason for coming to Scotland but you could see it was obvious. My father's side, he was one of the oldest in the family, there was no money coming into the house, my granny would be selling pigs and eggs to get a few bob and once you reached a certain age it was just natural for you to move on. My father came over here and his brother came and another brother went to America and two sisters went to America but then, the other two sisters

stayed in Ireland. It was a natural progression for the men just to move away. My
mother as well, she was one of five sisters and one brother, he wasn't too well,
he was never fit, so she was the oldest so it was natural for her to move away and
get some kind of employment to send money to bring up the younger ones in
Ireland. It was just a natural progression, there was no kind of thought of 'why
are we doing this'. (Interviewee 35)

Interviewee 36 offered a particularly poignant story. His father had moved to
Scotland in 1946 at the age of 14 from Donegal. Against the backdrop of crippling
poverty on the farmstead, he had been forced to move to Scotland to work on farms
to generate remittance monies for the survival of his family. Forced migration
in turn was blamed bitterly on British rule in and mismanagement of Ireland.
Starting in June in Girvan and Ayr, he made his way up to the East coast for the
final harvests of the year in Fife and Tayside in November. In telling the story of
his father, Interviewee 36 broke down in tears and had to leave the room to re-
gather himself. He expressed bitterness that British failures in Ireland had 'robbed'
his father of a childhood. The wounds inflicted on a mere child had clearly left
emotional scars that ran deeply in the family too:

> My father told me on a number of occasions that generally speaking they were
> half starved. They had very little food in the house. There was no running water,
> no electricity. Moving to Scotland wasn't a choice. The family needed money
> and the idea of coming over to Scotland was to earn money and send it back. It
> wasn't to come over here and earn money and have a good time. It was to send
> money back to support the family in Ireland. The money had to be sent back and
> if it wasn't sent back, that person was in trouble. I think deep down, he was very
> bitter about the way in which he was denied a childhood. At the age of fourteen,
> he disembarked at the Broomielaw in Glasgow. At fourteen he was taken away.
> (Interviewee 36)

This story has parallels with the account offered by Interviewee 10. Aged 38,
Interviewee 10's father came from Rathlin Island, a small island off the north
Antrim coast in 1950, and settled in Glasgow. This participant conveys her father's
dislike of romantic views of Ireland in the following terms:

> There is one pub and one shop. No policemen, no doctors, no secondary school.
> My dad didn't have a secondary education there. There is just a primary school.
> So, he doesn't talk fondly of there. He talks about how he never got a chance
> to go to school. He's quite bitter he never got a secondary education. He hates
> animals and farming. There are only a hundred and fifty nine people live there
> now. So he's not really got fond memories of there. Since my granny and
> granddad died, about ten years ago now, he's only been back once. He hates the
> whole thing. He hates it all. He thinks there is no future there for young people.
> We all look at Rathlin romantically and say, 'oh we'd love to live there'. He says

'don't talk rubbish. There's nothing to do there and in the winter the boats don't even come'. He is very realistic about it. He gets quite annoyed about the way we go on about Rathlin. He says it was my home. It was never your home, yet you are all, 'oh Rathlin ....' He gets quite angry with us. (Interviewee 10)

Interview 26's grandfather was born in Donegal but moved to Scotland in the 1870s in search of a better life. She recalls her grandfather's bitterness about moving:

> My grandfather spoke bitterly about Ireland. All he could remember was not having enough food to eat and things like that. He was always bitter about Ireland. He never ever spoke about going back. To him it was bitter memories of not having enough food and travelling the countryside from morning to night looking for work. He was glad to get away to Scotland Then of course he had no family left there. One of his brothers, his oldest brother went off to America, and as he didn't read and write he never heard from him again. He never ever heard from him. Tragic, isn't it? My grandfather couldn't read and write. I can remember helping him to sign his pension book. We taught him to write his name but that was all he could read or write. Work was very important to him. He kicked the boys (his sons) out, 'get work'. Work was everything to him, to earn money and have enough to eat. In fact I don't remember my grandfather ever going for a holiday to Ireland, ever. I always thought it was that he blamed Ireland for not being able to give him what he wanted. He was bitter. That's what I remember, the bitterness in him, that Ireland had let him down, so therefore he didn't think any more of it and that was it. (Interviewee 26)

Although born in Donegal in 1941, Interviewee 3 was brought to Scotland in 1945, aged 4, by her parents, and settled in Glasgow. She offers the following account of her father's views towards Ireland:

> It was important for my father to have money. When he was in Ireland he didn't have any money and he was always of the opinion that there was nothing in Ireland. Whereas he came to Glasgow and he got married and he reared a family and he had a house and it was important to him that he had a couple of pound that he could leave to his family. That was very important and if you were to ask him he would say in Ireland there was nothing whereas in Glasgow there was. To him, Ireland had done nothing for him and probably his generation; maybe they would all have thought the same way. Whereas they came to Glasgow and they made their home here and they were never hungry and I would think that's probably what they would think of Glasgow. They made their living here and my father is buried here and probably my mother will be buried here too. Ireland didn't have anything for him but Glasgow had. I remember my mother's brother talking about having the toothache and running up the road crying with the pain and they didn't have any money to take him to a dentist. You can understand how

people have those kinds of feelings because there was no money for anything. When you think how many people must have died because they couldn't afford to get to the doctor. (Interviewee 3)

Interviewee 3 also recounted in a more humorous vein, what happened one year when her father quite unexpectedly took up her offer to come to Ireland with her family for a visit:

Every year we would go to Ireland and we would say, 'dad why don't you come?' He'd say, 'no'. This particular Sunday night we left and had kidded him on, 'why don't you come?' He of course was, what we thought, spinning, 'right I will'. So fine we came home and we were getting ready, and my mother by good luck phoned about nine o'clock and said, 'and what time are you picking your father up?' We went 'what?' If she hadn't have phoned we wouldn't have picked him up. We thought he was kidding us on. She said he's going to Ireland tomorrow with you. And I remember leaving him in his own home in Ireland in the street he grew up in. I looked out the back window of the car and I thought, oh my god he'll go crazy there for five days, cos there was no car there at that point. The brother had no car. I don't even know if there was a phone in the house. I remember saying to my husband, 'he'll go crazy'. And I know for a fact he stayed overnight and went down to Strabane and stayed there for the rest of the time. We arranged that we were going to pick him up and going to take him to visit my mother's sister and take him to visit people that he knew. But I remember seeing him standing in that street and I thought 'oh god'. (Interviewee 3)

Is there any significance in the fact that many accounts such as these recalled the attitudes of fathers and grandfathers in particular? Given that many young women also had to flee to Scotland to take up hard labour 'in service', it would seem disingenuous to claim that negative perceptions of traditional Ireland among first generation settlers were gendered. As alluded to in these accounts nevertheless, the consequence of imagining Ireland as a place of hardship, sorrow and bitterness was that many first generation, and first generation men in particular rarely visited for a holiday and could not share the fascination for the country held by their siblings. Whilst they might return for funerals, baptisms and marriages, Ireland did not hold any especially significant attraction for them (Figure 5.1). It is fair to say that women in contrast did tend to accompany their own children when sending them back to Ireland for holidays and consequently perhaps retained slightly stronger bonds. Moreover, in some instances, disputes with relatives over the dispensation of inherited land and property meant that even these kinds of visits were curtailed. Once again given that it was the eldest son who normally inherited the farm, it is possible that conflict over land rankled males to a greater extent, investing them with heightened levels of bitterness and estrangement.

Figure 5.1 **Broomielaw, River Clyde, 1899. A place where migrants arrived to set up a new life in Scotland and from where family holidays to Ireland began and ended (Courtesy of Glasgow City Archives and Special Collections)**

Mixed encounters with Ireland: the 'war evacuees'

Whilst a majority of second and third generation descendants based their perceptions of Ireland upon childhood recollections of summer holidays, some were able to articulate memories which drew upon more prolonged exposure to their forebears' counties of origin. In some instances, the closeness of extended family ties meant that children who were visiting on holiday actually selected to stay on in Ireland to live with aunts, uncles and cousins. What was intended to be a brief stay, only a few months or thereabouts, on occasions expanded to years. Included in this cohort would be those children who were evacuated to Ireland during both the first and second world wars. This was a particularly common practice among migrant families living in the more heavily industrialised parts of west central Scotland, particularly of course Clydebank, Glasgow and Lanarkshire. It was especially significant during the Second World War (1939–45) by which time Ireland was a neutral country and as such could offer a relatively safe refuge for children. The length of time spent in Ireland varied but in some cases stretched across the entire war period.

Given their extended engagement with the vagaries of Irish country life, the war evacuees offer a sober, complex and critical picture of what rural Ireland was like in the early 1940s. Their stories represent something of a fulcrum between outright bitterness towards the oppressiveness of traditional Ireland and a certain exoticisation of this very same traditional Ireland. The stories of two particular evacuees will be used here to reveal the varied ways in which relocation at once enriched and threatened childhood innocence. Interviewee 19 is now 67 and lives in Glasgow. She is second generation Irish on her paternal side, her father coming to Scotland in the early 1920s from Mayo. Aged 7, and along with her mother and two sisters and a brother, Interviewee 19 was relocated to a small village in Mayo to live with her paternal grandparents for the duration of the Second World War. Interviewee 20 is aged 69 and lives in Glasgow. She is second generation Irish on both sides of the family, her father coming from Donegal around 1910, her mother arriving later in 1929. Aged 9, and along with her younger sister, Interviewee 20 was evacuated to Donegal for virtually the entire war to stay with more distant relatives of her mother. During this time, her mother was ill and remained back in Glasgow.

Interviewee 19 clearly had a more pleasant experience of evacuation than Interviewee 20. Above Interviewee 19's mantle piece hangs a hand painted picture of the original family cottage. She describes the way in which just looking at the picture stirs deep felt emotions and fills her with 'pure joy'; 'because you feel when you go to our village that every stone and every bush is in your blood. You look at an old hedge and think that hedge is beautiful. It's really an old scraggy hedge but to me it's beautiful'. Visiting the village is like a 'drug'; she needs a 'fix' on a regular bases to feel at peace again. Interviewee 20 in contrast recounts a cold and hostile place that left a permanent scar on her. She can only conclude that; 'a lot of these people who are very nostalgic about Ireland maybe never spent a lot of time in it'. Clearly moving to another country under war conditions presented a daunting challenge to young children and had the potential to generate angst and insecurity. The difference in the experiences of both participants can be attributed to the varying levels of love, affection, and support they received from both immediate and extended family members. Whilst Interviewee 19 stayed with her mother and brothers and sisters in the home of her grandparents which she describes as being 'filled with human warmth and real feeling', Interviewee 20 resided with distant relatives and had the support of her younger sister only to rely on. Her home life was 'miserable' and she felt constantly stressed by the laborious chores set by her hosts. The differential support structures both evacuees had around them in turn fundamentally affected their different perceptions of the rigours of country life and in particular their varying experiences of the disciplinary regime at school.

In 1998, Interviewee 19 was asked to write down her memories as an evacuee for a booklet which was to be circulated as part of a centenary celebration at her old school in Mayo. During the interview, Interviewee 19 requested that she read aloud extracts from her essay as these conveyed best her most cherished memories of school life:

School was a whole new world. Hail, rain or shine we trekked two miles to and fro over bog, bovine and stream to arrive there. Unless someone mentioned it, we didn't think there was anything unusual in walking that distance daily. Everyone told us that we were great girls, so we just accepted that we must be. We hadn't spent long at school in Glasgow so as far as we were concerned our primary school experience was in County Mayo.

In today's educational world, we are constantly informed that the content of our school curriculum must cater for the child physically, intellectually, emotionally and socially. On reflection on my school days in Mayo, having been evacuated from Scotland, I can appreciate what a wide, interesting and rich education we had. Our programme all those years ago embraced almost all of the above aspects. Generally at that time, we followed many of the subjects studied in today's curriculum, English, Irish, History, Geography, Needlecraft, Singing and Arithmetic. I don't recall learning about the natural environment or studying Science, however living on a farm and having a grandfather who was a born teacher and who loved to explain to us the mysteries of plants and animals, we didn't really need to cover this again in school. I cannot remember physical education and games, but since we had walked several miles to school, we probably didn't need any more exercise. The map of Ireland hung on the classroom wall and is clearly imprinted on my memory. I knew its contents well and we, the pupils, seemed to repeat over and over again catchphrases like, 'the Shannon rises in the chalky mountain in County Cavan'. Much of our schoolwork we learned by heart.

Religion was part and parcel of everyday life. Most activities began with an invocation to god to bless us and we wouldn't dream of going to bed without the family rosary. Canon O'Malley with his black walking stick visited us annually to test our knowledge of the Catechism. We had spent months in preparation and we knew our stuff. The Canon was thorough in his questioning. If there was any dubiety in our minds as to whether the answer should be 'yes' or 'no', we were helped by the teacher's nod of the head in the appropriate direction. The teacher normally stood behind the Canon and our eyes darted from one to the other. Another highlight of the year was a visit from an Inspector to test our knowledge of spoken Irish. The whole family attending school was taken together and we had to carry on a conversation in Irish with the Inspector. My grandparents basked in reflected glory when my sisters Julia, Helen and I passed and were awarded the princely sum of two pounds, a lot in those days.

Some school memories are positive and some otherwise. It was exciting to learn to sew and knit to an advanced level. The singing in English and Irish was most enjoyable. I won't dwell on my memory of being whacked with a rod. Because of the latter experience, I made a resolution as a teacher never to punish children with the belt, which was in use when I started to teach. I can still recall the sense of humiliation of the rod. (Interviewee 19)

Interviewee 20 recalls her experience of school life as being tantamount to 'child abuse'. Her account pays testimony to the vulnerability of children to Institutions and to the ways in which the mistreatment of children through institutional bullying and belittlement can leave lifelong emotional scars. Interviewee 20 interestingly speaks about an event that also featured in the memory of Interviewee 19, the visit by an Inspector to check that all children in the school were fluent in Irish Gaelic. Whilst Interviewee 19 passed the test and can remember receiving the £2 prize awarded to all successful pupils, the whole drama of the test clearly shook her. Her inability to protect her younger sister who, not surprisingly given her recent arrival at the school failed the test, was evidently profoundly unsettling. One can only imagine how harrowing the experience must have been for a frightened young school child who was living in an alien household with no one to support her:

> An Inspector came round every year to check that the school was teaching Gaelic properly. Honestly, it was like pure child abuse. It was shortly after Martha, my younger sister, had arrived in Ireland to join me and Martha couldn't speak Gaelic at all and she couldn't make head nor tail of it. Martha was in another classroom. I got called up to see the Inspector. Your name gets shouted out and you come walking up past the whole class and this man was sitting there with a uniform, like a policeman he was. He started asking you questions.
>
> After he had finished and I had more or less passed the exam, I had no time to be relieved because he says, 'and who else lives in the house with you?' I told him 'Mr Friel and Mrs Friel'. 'And who else, anyone else?' Well the Master was standing behind and he's mouthing 'nobody else there'. And this man is saying, 'who? Who is there? Anybody else?' I goes, 'YES'. The whole place went 'NO', I heard the whole class going 'OH NO'. Because he had more or less said 'oh well you're really entitled to the two pound' you see. He more or less had said that. You've answered the questions and the Master put a good word in for you as well. We know you weren't born here but even so, you're quite good at this language and we'll let you pass. That's alright we'll put you on the list for the two pound.
>
> 'Who lives in the house with you?' Then I mentioned Martha. 'And does she speak Gaelic?' You weren't supposed to speak any English at all. You were supposed to speak Gaelic all the time. 'Is this your sister? And does she speak Gaelic?' I said, 'she only arrived here four months ago and she hasn't had time to learn Gaelic but she was studying very hard but it was hard to learn Gaelic right away like that'. She was 'a wee bit nervous about coming to a new country' and all the rest of it. This was all in Gaelic. And 'is she at school?' 'Yes.' 'Where is she?' She was down in the lower room. 'Get her up here'. They called Martha up and started to ask her questions. Martha got such a fright getting called up like that. She couldn't speak with fright and she was pure white and could hardly remember anything at all. So he said, 'I'm sorry, no two pounds for you'. I didn't get the two pounds and both of us were disgraced in front of the school. Oh cruel? It was absolute abuse, real child abuse, is what it was. (Interviewee 20)

Enchantment: Where the Atlantic Ocean washes the doorsteps of little white cottages

Twilight in old Donegal

Have you ever saw a million stars together
Winking at the Romans down below
And you've landed in a hill of purple heather
Then you're lucky that's where I long to roam
Where the angels have lighted their tiny lamps bright
And the evening's beginning to fall
And the heather is sparkling with heavenly light
Then it's starlight in old Donegal
Round the peat fire glow sits the wee ones
Listening to tales of the bold
And out under the stars lovers telling their stories
When it's starlight in old Donegal
Tis the laughter of fairies way down in the glen
And the glory of god over all
You'll be nearer to heaven than ever you've been
When it's starlight in old Donegal
Have you ever been a roaming in the gloaming
In the evening when the dawn deserts the day
And the birds unto their little nest returning
And granny takes her old brown beads to pray
Tis the laughter of fairies way down in the glen
And the glory of god over all
You'll be nearer to heaven than ever you've been
When it's starlight in old Donegal
(Sung by Interviewee 41)

The family holiday: ritual, pilgrimage and homily

Further removed from the hardships of traditional Ireland were the sons and daughters of first and second generation migrants. Growing up as children in urban and industrial Scotland in the period from say the 1930s to the late 1970s, these descendants were often taken to family farms in Ireland on holiday. These visits could last for up to six weeks and would mainly take place during the summer months. In some instances, children were sent to stay with relatives themselves. Tagged with labels, they would board a boat in Glasgow and be picked up by relatives 'at the other side'. More frequently, mothers would accompany children to stay with either maternal or paternal in laws, and fathers would come across for part of the duration, normally the 'Fair Fortnight' in July. These holidays figure vividly in the memories of this particular section of the Irish Catholic community, many of whom describe them as the best days of their lives. Romantic attachments matured as the children who holidayed in Ireland grew to adulthood. As children entered adulthood, an Ireland which appeared a place of great adventure, a little paradise and a wonderland for children, blossomed into an Ireland of romance, enchantment and belonging. Ireland was no longer a wretched land of misery, hardship, poverty and hunger. Instead it was now revered as an almost sacred centre of pilgrimage, with local villages and actual family homes being invested with intense personal significance. Consider the following accounts:

> Every summer we went to stay, my mother and us as children, at the end of June or maybe the week before the school finished, we always got to Ireland and then my father came when the Glasgow Fair was on. So we would have spent every summer in Ireland in Donegal. In the area we lived in we knew all the locals. We'd go and we'd stay for six weeks and I could have stayed forever. (Interviewee 3)

> I remember school holidays, the older we got it was only two weeks we would go, but all through primary school right up to I was 14 we would go over and spend our entire holidays there and we would all stay at my Uncle Paul's. My mum would leave one day and come back the next with my dad then he would go home himself and she would stay till the end of the holiday. I would get moved now and again to an aunt's house, my aunt lived about half a mile down the road. It was good because you were allowed freedom. When I grew up it was like one row of tenements where I stayed and I think there must have been about 13 kids in that stairwell. If somebody went missing, one of the mothers knew someone wasn't there, everybody was out hunting for you, you were never out the front you were always out the back, you were not allowed out the front playing football. In Ireland you were up trees, you were on top of the roof, you were allowed to get dirty. You worked, but you never thought of it as work but that's what you did worked in the fields. That was fun when you were young. My brothers when they were younger they would drive a tractor, it was something you could do over there. (Interviewee 11)

> We didn't see the rawness that my grandfather saw and the people who stayed behind saw. We went there on holiday and they made it a holiday for us and they went out of their way to be kind to us. So we look back on that as a kind of nice time and I think when you're young too, from June to August is an eternity, whereas at my age 72 now, it's gone before it's started, just in a flash you know. I think the concept of time accelerates the older you get. That's a trite thing to say but it's true. I think you look back to those days and they always seemed to be warm days. I'm sure they weren't. I used to go down with the men who worked in the fields, gathering hay. We'd go down with flasks of tea and bread and scones to them. They would stop their work and we'd lie on the grass that had just been cut, the hay, and you could feel the sticky bits on your legs. They

would take their tea and have their sandwiches and have a smoke and then go back to work again. It was always idyllic kind of times. I suppose it gave you that romantic notion of Ireland. (Interviewee 55)

As soon as the school closed we went across. My father would be working and then he would come across for a fortnight for the Fair. So as soon as we went over there the first thing we would do was throw off our shoes and socks and that would be us more or less for the holiday, apart from Sundays, running about in our bare feet. It was great, there would be a big crowd of us, the cousins and we had a marvellous time. The tide would come in and we would jump in the river and things like that. You never saw a car, if you saw a car you would hear a car first of all. That was the whole idea to get away from city life. I remember thinking some of the days we would be coming back and you would be saying to yourself just think tomorrow we'll be in Glasgow and it was really a sad occasion and when the mini bus came to pick us up, there would be a dozen of us going back and one person would start crying and that started us all, and my oldest brother would go around saying cheerio to the hens and the cows and it was terrible. It is still a wrench leaving the place and coming back but in those days you knew that was it for another year. Coming back to Glasgow meant coming back to a concrete jungle, so I think the fact it was a rural community mattered. The other element, the wider family, it wasn't just your own family, you were very conscious of your cousins being there, but when you were back in Glasgow it was just all your own family. The friendliness of the people as well, adults would speak to you over there, it amazed me coming back, adults would say 'hello are you well boy?' So there was that friendliness which made it difficult to leave. (Interviewee 35)

My father was killed when I was seven. My mother had eight of us and the youngest was only four months and all her family was in Ireland, except for one brother who stayed in Clydebank. Every year my mother used to take us over to Ireland herself on the boat that left from Princes Pier in Greenock. I remember in those days you didn't get taxis but there was a taxi that came up to the house to take us all down. My mother used to pack this huge big hamper about a week before we went and anybody that got school prizes, they got put in to show my granny. That was all taken over to Ireland and it would be there when we arrived. The six weeks we were there, looking back now there is a bit of nostalgia and things, but then it was just a change of sink for my mother. It must have been horrendous for her because my granny had no running water and no sink, no toilet, no electricity, and this was my mother over there every year with eight of us for six weeks. You used to have to go out and help with the cows and this sort of stuff, and you didn't touch this cow because it kicked, and my granny used to be out throwing holy water over it. I remember my granny just going out and lifting a hen and ringing its neck and hanging it on the wee wall outside the house, and that was our dinner for the next day. When you walked to the village the first thing you done was you smelled the turf. I just remember all the things about my granny and everything getting up every morning and the bread was made and the butter was churned. I remember her baking bread on the big black, it was a big black range with a lid and she used to sit turf on top of it. (Interviewee 15)

It is impossible to underestimate the importance of summer vacations in cementing lifelong attachments to regions and villages of origin. When asked what it was that so caught their imagination, participants spoke about the 'feeling' they got when they arrived at the local village, or visited friends and relatives, or trampled through the remains of now disbanded cottages. In using phrases such as 'deep sense of belonging', 'enough to make you weep', 'sobbing to the point of a complete emotionally overflow', 'peace like you've never felt before'; 'excited and euphoric' and 'very very nostalgic', it became clear that the experience was indeed deeply moving. In visiting Ireland, participants were seemingly reawakening their imaginations and thinking about where their parents and grandparents were born, the fields they ploughed, the rooms they slept in, the churches they were baptised and married in, the pubs in which they had wakes in memory of émigrés and dead relatives, the graveyards they were buried in, the places where they made the painful decision to migrate, and the feelings they must have had walking up the long road away from their farmhouses for the last time. Moreover, they were recalling their own holidays in Ireland when their parents were alive, when the summer days seemed longer, when they played innocently with brothers, sisters and cousins, when they enjoyed the tremendous sense of community and the support of the extended family, and when they had their whole lives ahead of them.

Participants kept these memories alive through a treasure trove of memorabilia. These included: rocks from the old farmhouse, on one occasion being used as a pen holder on an office desk; houses named after Irish farms and villages; pets assuming Irish place names; lucky charms positioned on the mantle piece; heather sprigs from the old farm replanted in the garden; pictures and paintings on the wall of the old farmhouse; and teaspoons, dishtowels, and whiskey glasses engraved with significant Irish symbols. In the case of one particular family who had settled in two separate areas, Clydebank and Glasgow, an annual card game *Chase the Lady* had become something of a celebrated tradition. Keenly contested, and cheered on with the best of craic, the winner was given a silver cup engraved with the name of the tiny village in Donegal from where the family had derived. The event was rotated between Motherwell and Clydebank, but had been held back in the local village hall in Donegal and even in Boston.

In searching for a deeper understanding of the kind of images of Ireland which second and third generation sons and daughters actively produce, reproduce, and circulate, the rest of this section will examine five themes of particular importance. The first I title the 'joy of melancholy' to capture the emotional and teary sense of tragedy and dislocation which the Irish Catholic community courts and embraces. The theme of 'exile' is indeed mobilised by the Irish Catholic community in

Scotland to express or more accurately to generate a sense of misery about being forced to leave beloved Ireland and a yearning to be reunited with their ultimate home. The remaining four themes emerge from oral accounts of childhood holidays in Ireland. They explore respectively, the journey to and from Ireland, life on the farm, the warmth of community and social gatherings, and the virtues of retaining a closeness with nature (Figures 5.2 and 5.3).

Figure 5.2   The family holiday, Connemara 1955 (Property of the author)

Figure 5.3   The family holiday, Donegal 1964 (Property of the author)

The joy of melancholy

It is a truism of a particular kind to say that the diasporic condition entails a longing for home. Estranged from one's beloved family and place of childhood by circumstances beyond one's control, homesickness and isolation emerge as perennial themes. Homesickness and melancholy can and do engulf some migrants' whole lives. And yet as observed many first generation migrants more often than not held bitter memories of life in Ireland and discounted attachments to the old homeland as romantic nonsense. For them the reality of hardship and poverty was simply too fresh to wallow in nostalgic self pity. It is within second and later generations that diasporic preoccupation with the pain of forced separation is most forcefully evidenced. It would be condescending to deny that second and later generation descendants might feel a genuine sense of angst about the way their forebears were forced to leave Ireland. Not wishing to actually return to Ireland themselves nevertheless this preoccupation clearly performs more complex cultural functions. There seems in particular to be a certain joy in melancholy and empathy with sadness that participants found to be stirring.

The plight of the lonely refugee arguably manifests itself most poignantly in song. During several of the interviews, participants either offered to sing, play, or to broadcast songs that they felt expressed the deep felt love the Irish have for their regions of origin. These songs brought to life in evocative and moving ways the landscapes and communities that characterise counties such as Donegal and Mayo and more broadly the rugged, remote, and mythic west coast in particular. They most often took the form of laments about the internal sorrow migrants had to wrestle with in reconciling their love of home with the necessity of emigrating and living in displacement. One song, titled *Moriarty*, aired during interview 38, serves to capture this genre well. Aged 56, Interviewee 38's mother migrated to Scotland from Donegal in the 1930s at the tender age of 17. So special does he hold the village from which she derived that he has named his house after it:

> Going over there, it was like a pilgrimage. The rest of Ireland didn't matter to me. I tell a lie, my wife and I were over for a weekend to Dublin. But that might as well have been in Glasgow. It didn't mean anything to me. But the village means it all to me. Oh it's still very, very precious. My grandfather took us all over to Ireland every year from when I was two years old right up till I was nineteen. I went every year, just like a pilgrimage. And I only went to my village. I went over there to work. My aunt was a spinster. She had a pub and a farm out in the country and the border ran through her field. I went over there and I worked all my school holidays. I loved the place. I just couldn't see past it.
>
> I seen it all through rose coloured glasses when I was in my teens. It wasn't a great big farm. It was big enough. But what did I know about farming? Nothing really. And they would say to you 'welcome home' and I was accepted. I was always the 'Scotsman' as well. But they always said, 'welcome home'. That was the first thing they said to you. In the morning I would go out and feed

the calves, milk the cows, that's when I was eleven, bring in the turf for the fire, go down to the well for the water and then go out and work along with the men from dinner time. And the reversal at night time. On a Sunday you walked two miles into mass. You had to tell my aunt who was all there and you had to come straight back again. Then after your lunch the pub was opened up but she kept all the shutters closed. So you came in through the house cos it was all part of the one building. I served the kitchen and she served the bar until it was six o'clock when I had to go and get the cows and get them milked and get them back out again. Then I'd go back in and get my dinner. That was your life. (Interviewee 38)

Interviewee 38 has amassed a significant collection of Irish artefacts, tapes and CDs, videos and DVDs. His enthusiasm for Irish music in particular is not altogether shared by the rest of his family and so he has a designated room in the house where he can retire at night to play Irish songs and reflect upon the lives of his forebears. In this sanctuary, Interviewee 38 feels emotionally in tune with his heritage and finds his mind alive to the trials and tribulations of those who fled Ireland out of necessity. Songs such as *Moriarity* provide fuel to these stirrings :

Moriarity: Sung by John Kerr

In a little pub in London Moriarty drank his beer
And recited wonderous stories of his exploits far and near
Sing an Irish song said Kelly best of order one and all
Then Moriarty sang for them The Hills of Donegal
There was cheering at her finish and the sound of a roar
Moriarty said, 'listen lads I can't sing any more'
So he stood there sad and silent and gazed into despair
Then his eyes they glistened at the starting of a tale
Are you going home for Christmas? the kindly barmaid said
Moriarty fixed his gaze on her and slowly shook his head
Sure I haven't been to Ireland now for twenty years or more
Me mother would hardly know me if I walked up to the door
I was born, said Moriarty, on an island off the west
The last place god created, the first place that he blessed
We were poor but we were happy in our simple little way
My god I wish I wish I was a boy again and to live my youthful days
My father god be good to him was drowned one woeful night
And my mother left all lonesome and myself to work and fight
It was with Donald McCarthy and young Michael O'Day
I came across to England to earn an honest pay
I told my dear old mother that I'd soon be home again
But the curse of drink came over me and enslaved me in its chains
So I haven't been to Ireland now for twenty years or more

But I know she's still there waiting for my footsteps at the door
Then someone started singing a song he used to know
Like an old bell ringing far away and long ago
Moriarty stood and listened then pushed his glass away
Then he made a solemn promise to go home for Christmas Day
So he scraped up every penny he could get into his hand
And coming up to Christmas he sailed for Ireland
His heart was filled with gladness and he felt content at last
It was a train rolled through the Midlands that brought him to the west
In the village of Kinsella on that night upon the shore
Across the deep blue waters he saw his island home once more
The stars were shining brightly sure they glistened like a dome
That little white washed cottage was Moriarty's home
Tis a grand night for the sailing said the boatman Thomas Bong
Moriarty didn't know him he had been away so long
So he climbed into boat and the boatman heard him say
Thank god thank god in heaven I'll be home for Christmas Day
In a little room in London, Moriarty's poor abode
On a table in the hallway a message lay unread
The message said Dear Danny your poor mother has passed away
She'll be buried in Kinsella after mass on Christmas Day

The Journey to and from Ireland

Whilst some migrants whose families derived from southern counties in Ireland travelled to Dublin, in most cases the 'Derry boat' was the preferred route. The Derry boat would leave from Ardrossan, Greenock Princes Pier, or further upstream from the Broomielaw. Journeys on both the *Royal Scotsman* and *Royal Ulster* passenger ships were recalled. Both had wooden trestles which creaked noisily in high seas. They were often full to top, with cattle as well as humans. Occasionally, when conditions were very stormy and bad weather had set in, water would come into the boat and participants recall the rosary being said for safe passage. The journey to Derry would last for around 13 hours whilst the sailing to Dublin could take up to 26 hours. Many participants remember their mothers bringing blankets for the overnight sail, and sandwiches to fortify spirits. Once disembarked, visitors would head to their favourite local café. Each family it seemed had cultivated a ritual of getting breakfast from a special venue, with the Lido Café in Derry a particularly favourite haunt. With taxis being a luxury, families would more often travel on by bus or train and invariably faced an exhausting long walk to the cottage as a finale to the journey.

Whilst the journey could be long and tortuous, it was an essential part of the holiday and was a source of fun for the children. To such children, the boats were 'huge and magnificent, and the journey was in itself a thrilling adventure'. Interviewee 43's mother came from Kilkenny to Scotland in the 1890s and took the family regularly back home to visit relatives in the 1940s and 1950s. Now aged 73, he recalls the visits he often made to Kilkenny which required a sail from Glasgow to Dublin and then a long bus ride onwards to his family home:

> We got the boat from Glasgow from the Broomielaw and it was usually Fair Friday because that's when the coal pits got a week's holiday at that time. So we left on the Friday evening about 5 o'clock and arrived in Dublin the next morning about 7 or 8 o'clock at night and it was rough! We sailed with the old *Burns and Laird Line*. They always put on a good boat for Fair Friday, they would bring up a bigger boat from the Liverpool run. But for the rest of the time and very often when we were coming back it was a cattle boat. We would be there as they were taking the cattle off and then they would go down with hoses and hose out the place where the cattle had been and we went straight in there. The smell, oh my god! It was rough and yet the entertainment was of the highest value. Everyone was on great form and there was usually a fair colony of church people going over there. We would usually have an accordian, I play that myself. I used to take that to Ireland. The craic was mighty! The bus run to Kilkenny took about 2 hours and that was great entertainment too. The same driver and conductor were on it for years, and they used to ask me, have you brought, they called it the 'yoke', that meant the accordian. We used to play on the bus and sing. The drivers seemed to know everyone down the road and stopped to do all sort of odd jobs and to hand off parcels and just to speak to people, it was great entertainment on the bus. We were in great form (Interviewee 43)

Interviewee 65a is second generation Irish (Antrim) on his mother's side, She moved to Scotland in 1928 following the death of her father. Her two brothers had already moved and she joined her sister in Edinburgh working 'in service'. Interviewee 65a was born in 1940 and lives in Edinburgh. He first visited Ireland in 1946 with his mother and her sister and visited thereafter every year where he stayed with his grandmother and his uncle. Interviewee 65a has compiled a rich account of his holidays, which he has committed to text. The story of the journey is only part of his account:

> Some of the other children at school went to Fife (30 miles away) on holiday and many did not go on holiday at all but we went all the way to Ireland! No one went abroad at that time. The journey itself was an adventure. The cases were packed and taken to the station a week or more before we left and sent as luggage in advance. They would be waiting for us in Ballymena Station when we arrived. The most important items of luggage were Wellie boots for the farm. The journey started by train from Edinburgh to Glasgow. We were occasionally on a train to visit an aunt in Kircaldy in Fife but not often so this was exciting. In Glasgow, we got a taxi to the Broomielaw Quay to board the boat. We were never in a taxi any other time.

The boat left at 9pm and sailed overnight to Belfast. We usually got a cabin with bunk beds and a small wash basin where we could be sea sick in private as mum and I were never good sailors. My brothers and sisters seemed to be better travellers. If we could not get a cabin we ended up in the dormitory which although very clean if some of the other passengers were sick the smell would guarantee mum and I would follow. After some years the boat from Belfast to Glasgow was cancelled and we then had to take a taxi transfer to a different station in Glasgow to get the train for Ardrossan where there was a daytime crossing to Belfast that only took 4 hours.

On leaving the boat in Belfast we took a taxi to the station for the train to Ballymena where our suitcases would be waiting for us. Without sending luggage on in advance it would have been a difficult if not impossible journey for my mother with four children. The final part of our journey was a taxi from Ballymena Station to the farm. The excitement of the journey was the anticipation of this arrival. Throughout the year as children, we played at going to Ireland, re-enacting the exciting journey by the different modes of transport, taxis trains and boats. (Interviewee 65a)

Life on the Farm

The hardships which so frustrated first generation migrants were by no means eclipsed when descendants returned for a holiday break. Participants recounted the simple, primitive, and self sufficient existences they encountered on arrival. Water had to be pumped from underground streams, some pumps offering only water sufficient for washing dishes and clothes and for personal hygiene. Drinking water often had to be secured from pumps further afield and buckets would be filled up and taken for storage in the pantry. There was no television, no doctors, no radio, and no phones. Living quarters were tiny and overcrowded. Stone floors and thatched roofs were common. The Byre was often used as a toilet. There were no living rooms, people conversed in kitchens and there was often only one or two small bedrooms. Lighting was restricted to the Tilley Lamps which hung from the roof, on hooks. Food was mainly sourced locally and cooked over a big hearth in the kitchen. The hearth was fuelled by turf which was freshly cut from nearby fields and stored at the back of the house. Boiling potatoes and making scone bread were daily jobs, as were churning butter, planting, harvesting, storing and cooking vegetables and tending to livestock. Most farms had a healthy flock of sheep but at most half a dozen cows and only a few horses. Milk was put through a Muslin Cloth to be cleansed of dirt and hairs that dwelled at the cow's udder. Disposal was regarded as wasteful and crochet and knitting were all party of a repairing and recycling culture. Shoes and socks were removed on arrival at the farm and returned six weeks later before departure for Glasgow.

Whilst these hardships were a source of resentment among first generation migrants, it is clear that they were perceived as part of the thrill for the migrants' children and grandchildren. It was part of the charm and the adventure to live a more simplistic and primitive lifestyle. Interviewee 54 captures this way in which grinding poverty and poor living and working conditions became exoticised and romanticised by visitors. Interviewee 54 is 63 and comes from Motherwell. He is third generation Irish on his father's side, his paternal grandfather coming from Meath in 1907. He recalls his first visit to the family home in Meath in 1948, aged 11:

> I went to my uncle's, I think it was 1948, and the place was like a midden. We arrived there as the immigrants that were going back, the new wave of immigrants and we were going to be extolling the sort of, we had left the shores and expanded ourselves and done well. So we were looked upon as being sort of toffs even, although we weren't anywhere near that. So we arrived up with cases and my uncle, who was quite old at the time and his wife, they had wellies on, big wellie boots. There were hens and chickens running about the place and his wife had a long black skirt, all old fashioned stuff. She'd got herself tidied up for us coming. You know the strangers were coming, the visitors were coming back. So we arrived and we had tea, and all the cups were cracked and a wee bit unwashed even. So we were to sleep in the best room, but it turned out it was the only room. All the walls were whitewashed and insects were crawling up. So we went into this big room and we lay down. They all went away and sort of peeked in and, 'have a nice night' and all the rest of it. And the hens outside were all squeaking. So I took the sheets off and the blankets. I felt they were a wee bit wet, sort of damp. So I'm lying in the dampness here. Anyway the next thing was, we woke up and we looked out and there was a cow looking in the window; this added to the charm of it all. So then we looked even beyond the cow and saw an old run down house. We were informed later that that was the old house before they had the new one. So we were lucky to be living in the lap of luxury in this place. If we'd have come three or four years earlier it would have been this other place we'd have stayed. So we were in the lap of luxury. But so what. We couldn't care. This was the first night, we'd arrived in the old country, and it was going to be great. This is where your grandfather was born and the stories and everything were being told. So the eyes were dewed. We'd heard all these stories about what happened. He was there before the first world war, the halcyon days. When he was a boy he done this, he played in the fields and he swam in the rivers. They were telling stories into the night about leprechauns and all that. So it was all coming true to me. This was where I hailed from. It was a dump to everyone else but I felt dreamy about it. (Interviewee 54)

Working on the family farm and learning farm work was evidently a major attraction. Never seen as hard work and always approached as an educational experience as well as a help to the family one was staying with, farm work often emerged as a central and core part of the visit. Interviewee 65a recounts in detail the nature of the farm work he undertook when visiting his relations in Ballymena in Antrim:

There were free range hens and one cockerel that we were afraid of. My memory is of only a small number of hens at the start, maybe 20, but later on my uncle got a couple of Arks (wooden hen houses) in the back field and I guess there must have been over 100 hens. We liked to collect the eggs so long as the hen was not sitting on the nest and there was 1 or 2 hens who liked to lay eggs among the bales of hay in the shed or in a self made nest at the end of the field and you always had to go looking for them or to follow the hen to find them. Eggs became uneconomic and their numbers reduced for home use only but one night a fox got them all and they were not replaced.

There were 3 cows and usually one or two calves and that is when I discovered that cow's milk dried up just before calving and they gave most milk immediately afterwards. A new Byre with a milking machine was built for 6 cows so there were then 9 cows, three of which were milked by hand. It was necessary to keep a constant supply of milk for the creamery lorry. After milking each morning my uncle took the 2 cans of milk down to the bottom of the lane by wheelbarrow, placed them on a platform, and left the barrow in a ditch. We had to bring the empty cans up later on in the day. I always liked to think I was helping around the farm and would clean out the shed after milking.

One day when I was eleven I would bring up the empty milk cans. The lane was about 250 yards long with a gate at the top and the bottom, a banking with bushes and barbed wire on one side and an open field on the other. This field belonged to an old man who was a bad tempered recluse but I convinced myself that I was not afraid and set off down the lane to place the milk cans on the barrel. It must have been a clever old cow because it waited till I was exactly half way up the lane when it came running at me. I knew I did not have time to get over the gate at the top or bottom and the barbed wire stopped me from escaping in that direction. I panicked and as the cow got nearer I could only run around the barrel. The cow followed and so the two of us ended up running round and round the barrel. It seemed like ages until my granny, thinking I was taking a long time, came out to the gate and saw us and she quickly called the dog and sent him down to chase the cow.

For a number of years there were pigs. There were two or three large sows and maybe 50–70 assorted sized young pigs. I remember my uncle nipping the teeth of the wee pigs to protect the sow when they were feeding. One sunny July day there was a sow about to give birth but my uncle asked me to look in on the sow and as the piglets were born to lift them over into the corner were there was a heat lamp and they were surrounded by bales of hay. I felt privileged and although I thought I knew where they would come from there was some doubt but I would not ask. I was right and it was a very memorable experience to be responsible for lifting 12 newly born piglets.

Before my time my uncle had a horse but it was many years after the horse before he got a tractor. My earliest memory of work in the fields is of a lot of women gathering the hay into sheafs which were then combined into stooks. This was for threshing to make grass seed for the next year. A neighbour would come with their tractor to cut and plough but after the hay was cut my uncle would turn it by hand with a pitchfork often several times if it rained to dry before it could be baled. I remember mum near to tears if the rain came and all the hay had to be turned again and again.

I often felt deprived that we were always there in July so I did not see what happened on the farm in other months. I remember when I was very young there was a couple of years when there was a field of lint or flax which had a blue flower in July. There was a lint pond where the harvest of lint was soaked but I missed that excitement and similarly I had never been there when the corn was harvested. Other members of the family in Scotland always went over in August but we did not go together mainly because there was not enough room but also it meant a longer spell of visitors for granny and uncle. With all our questions they were maybe glad to get peace when we all left. (Interviewee 65a)

Community and social gatherings

The joy of participating in community and social gatherings and being part of extended family support systems was another source of fond and happy memories for children. Of course the most popular events were community gatherings either in a house or in a local hall at which local dances would be held. Accordian players, fiddlers and dancers provided the soul of these events. Great fun was had in learning the routines that accompanied the 'Dashing White Sergeant' or a set of quadrilles. At some point in the night singers would be invited to take the floor to recite their favourite song and different locals became known as experts of different songs and stories. Of course gender roles would be strictly demarcated at these events and humour was often to be had as courting rituals unfolded awkwardly throughout the night. Beyond dances and sing songs participants also recalled the smacking of clay pipes in cramped kitchens as men played card games, the pride that accompanied being picked to host the stations of the cross in one's house and the great event that became, and of course families camped around the fire late at night listening to ghost stories. Ghost stories, supernatural tales of fairies and leprechauns, myths and legends, stories about weeping and moving statues, and folk cures and curses all fuelled children's imaginations wildly. In each village, there was often a good story teller who would gather everyone around and hush would descend throughout the house. Stories would be told with such conviction and artistry that everyone was convinced they must be true.

The *banshee* is probably the most widely feared figure of the story telling tradition. Most often appearing in ghostly form as an old, ugly, frightening hag, the banshee would visit people to inform them of impending doom. The visitation of a certain kind of bird (for instance the Corn Crake) or animal and strange changes in weather patterns were all signs that a terrible death was to occur in the community soon. Famine stories held that when stepping onto a piece of turf that was the precise spot where a victim of the Great Famine drew their final breath, walkers would instantly be overcome by hunger and would need to eat immediately to quell their famish. Among the more widely circulated folk medical cures were sticking ones feet in boiling water to remove warts, eating eel oil for sprains, and burying a person with German Measles alive for 10 minutes to cure them. 'Gartan clay' alongside religious medals was also advocated as a protector against travel accidents. Finally, the 'White Lady' was reputedly a young maid who was murdered by a local aristocrat who was never brought to justice because of his high social standing. She wanders the roads late at night as if seeking justice and revenge.

Interviewee 6 paints a vivid picture of the entertainment that characterised her family home in Tyrone:

> Well we had quite a small house with a great big kitchen. My mother played the accordion and my father was a good dancer. So all the girls and boys gathered at our house at night and my mother provided the music and through her being able to play the accordion my brother and my sister were good too at this. The rest that weren't in any way musical, they played cards. It was a game of twenty-five, maybe for ten pence. So we learned how to play Pontoon, counting up to twenty one and we were quite good at that. The entertainment was good because my mother provided it. The other advantage to that was, I've two sisters and a younger brother, and when my mother was invited to parties she brought her accordion along and of course we went too. So we were able to mix with the younger generation and some of the older ones and we learned all the Irish step dancing, which I was never any good at and I learned other kinds of country dancing, like The Dashing White Sergeant and the sets of quadrilles. We learned all that and it was cheap entertainment and as well as that it kept us together and it kept that neighbourhood together, so we were all like one big family. The neighbours were like an extended family. (Interviewee 6)

Interviewee 62a paints an intriguing picture of how the imagination often ran riot with disturbing consequences in the dark of night in the Irish countryside:

> We went back to Ireland to Carlow regularly and the superstitions we encountered were very real to us. I remember when a wee girl we used to go to the dancing with died. When we walked home from the dancing we used to come to the bit of the bend where we would meet her before she died and we would cross over the road to the other side before moving on. We had premonitions of death if we walked the same path we had always done. And we used to believe that if we lit a candle and put it up to the window and it blew in a certain way that was also a sure premonition of death. And if you had a number of candles doing the same thing it would mean death would come in two's and three's. We would also never go out in the 'night of the dead march.' This was the night of August 12th roughly the night when Cromwell had marched his troops through County Carlow. If you went out that night something bad was liable to happen to you. We knew someone who did and she was found dead the next day in a ditch. The 'hungry

grass' was another one. If you stood on a turf of grass where a person had fallen and died during the famine you would be overcome with intense hunger pangs. If other people died too you were to await them visiting you in dreams or coming back as robin redbreast birds on your window sill. It might seem silly to you know but in the deadly dark of the countryside at midnight in a cold winter's evening I can tell you the imagination can run wild. (Interviewee 62a)

Likewise Interviewee 30 portrays the social and community life of his home village in Donegal as follows:

Our greatest discussion at night was talking about bloody ghosts. That's right and you'd go to bed and you'd put the clothes over your head. See for all the old timers, have you ever heard of the word 'raking'? No, well up in our part of Donegal, if you went visiting at night they called it, 'Mark's away raking at Sean's house' or something. And that's what happened. Everybody went visiting everybody else. Everyone went 'raking'. In every Irish home there was a fiddle or a melodeon. If you got ten or fifteen people gathered in the one house for the craic, somebody would get the fiddle going and it would end up a dance. Or songs would be sung and probably that was where all the rebel stuff came out, but then it was a different kind of … it wasn't like the stuff you hear nowadays that you can't open your mouth and sing. It was all the old characters and good old people who had died for the country. 'Lonely Banna Strand' and 'Johnston's Motor Car' and all this kind of stuff. Well do you know I play the fiddle, and that was what I was mainly interested in all the time was traditional music, you know, and there was so many of us. One of the finest fiddle players and the most famous one, you've heard of John Docherty haven't you? Well I knew John extremely well, personally. He used to come round to our house, he was a tinsmith. John came round and I was very fortunate, I was just learning the fiddle, and John used to come and stay with folk and work his way by repairing stuff. And every flaming night I was over with that fiddle. And he never carried one of his own, never, and yet John could play the fiddle. That house would be full every night. (Interviewee 30)

Closeness to nature

Not surprisingly, given their urban and industrial habitat, exposure to the countryside brought to children a tremendous sense of being close to nature. Running across fresh grass in bare feet, partaking in an invigorating early morning swim in the Atlantic ocean, fishing in local streams, marvelling at the shape of the landscape and its quite literal forty shades of green, and working on the farm and learning the ways of sheep, cows, horses, hens, birds, and goats, as well as the lives of soils and crops proved to be a source of great fascination. Many participants noted that this closeness with nature brought with it greater physical exercise, a sense that one was breathing in fresh air, better appetites, and deeper and more refreshing sleeps. Country life may have been hard, but it was more integrated with nature and it was presumed surely must be healthier. For some participants, the childhood fascination with nature that trips to Ireland awakened proved to be midwife to lifelong interests in botany, agriculture, ornithology, and zoology.

Interviewee 12 provided perhaps the most significant example. Aged forty two, Interviewee 12 lives in a farmhouse in Ayrshire. She is second generation Irish on her father's side, her father leaving Donegal for Scotland in the 1930s. Interviewee 12 spoke at length about the vivid memories she had of visiting Ireland as a child in the late 1960s and early 1970s. It was during these visits that she first took an interest in horses. This interest has blossomed to become a core part of her life. It cannot be described as being a mere hobby; instead it has become a passion and central life interest. She describes the background to her interest in horses thus:

> One of my earliest memories concerns Sheila a very big heavy horse who lived on my uncle's farm. I was desperate to see her. We had heard all these stories about Sheila and we were promised we would get to see her. I was only three at the time but I remember nagging, when can we go and see the horse! My uncle took me to the top of the hill where she was grazing and next thing he put me up on her, no saddle! He put me on the front and my young sister on the back and she was holding onto me and I can still visualise it. I must have been tiny because I felt as if I was 30ft off the ground; it was huge and he walked us all round this rough ground, it was like a little mini paddock that they used for grazing and he walked us all round. Well, that was me, I was just hooked that day on horses and I have never forgotten it. I think I really did get the love of horses there and then.
>
> I was so small and Sheila was huge to me when I was that size. She was a Clydesdale and was bedecked with big white feathers. I was tiny and I couldn't have been more than up to the knee of this horse. And yet she was just a gentle big thing. I was aware of the strength of her one day when she was stepping in the yard; she was stepping forward and moving back I could sense the weight and size of her foot, it was like a soup plate. I remember standing watching my dad and my uncle Patrick shoeing Sheila. I was just fascinated and I just loved the smell of her and everything, she was jet black with a white face, she was absolutely gorgeous. At the end of one of our summer visits there was a race along the beach involving one or two big heavy horses. It was very important. The horses did not have saddles and only had a makeshift bridle or a halter, I remember watching the race in amazement. I just couldn't believe these huge horses could go so fast. We loved the thunderous noise their hooves were making and it was like, yahoo, and their ears and their tails were going like mad all along the beach and their feet were sort of bouncing along.
>
> From those days as a child. I just knew that that was what I wanted to do. I wanted to live in the country and I always had this dream that I would go back to Ireland. Obviously circumstances have meant that I've not done this but I have bought a house in the country and I also now own and run a racing horse.

It's quite expensive to keep it going but it's my passion. Ayr is his favourite course, that's the local course, but he has won at Ayr, Hexham and Wetherby. We call him Micky. That's him up there [points to the wall], look at the colours! See my colours! See the colours of my silks, that's my racing colours, green, white and gold! (Interviewee 12)

Keeping the glow: living the dream

As foreign holidays grew in popularity and as low cost airlines and fast and cheap ferry services became ubiquitous, the nature of holidaying in Ireland changed dramatically. Trips now tend to be taken more frequently but for shorter durations and for different purposes. Elderly participants continue to visit for short breaks, often timed to coincide with family events such as funerals, baptisms, and key anniversaries. These visits often take the form of organised bus tours or joint visits with children and grandchildren, brothers, sisters, and other relatives and invariably are focused around the village or town of family origin. But the days of extended family visits are over. It is therefore pertinent to enquire whether romantic and exotic notions of Ireland are losing their force.

Given the power of romantic images of Ireland produced by second and third generation descendants it is unsurprising that some families have made concerted efforts to transmit the 'magic' of traditional Ireland down to children and grandchildren. Whilst the need to consciously and actively encourage children and grandchildren to keep links with home was a theme which emerged in numerous interviews, the testimonies of two particular participants will be isolated for particular attention here. Interviewee 9 is second generation Irish on her mother's side, her mother arriving from Donegal in the 1950s, and fourth generation on her father's side, her great grandparents coming from Cavan and Donegal in the 1910s. She spent her school holidays up until she was a teenager in Ireland at her mother's family home in Donegal. Aged 30 and having just given birth to her first child, she too has become especially motivated to transmit the special qualities of Ireland to her offspring. Interviewee 14 is second generation Irish on her mother's side, her mother coming to Scotland from Antrim in 1911, and third generation Irish on her father's side, her grandparents coming from Tyrone and Donegal in the 1890s. Aged 53 she is married with seven children. Having spent her childhood holidays in Donegal she is highly enthusiastic about nurturing a love of Ireland within her children.

Interviewee 9 portrays beautifully the value attached within some families to preserving romantic images of traditional Ireland. The spiritual mysticism of Donegal she reflects 'is drummed into you from the moment of conception and it is impossible to rationalise it out!' When asked what kind of Donegal she has in mind when she pictures the county, Interviewee 9 replied:

When my grandmother talks about Donegal it sounds almost like a utopia. And when my mother speaks of her early childhood in Ireland, it all sounds pretty idyllic. The first time I went to Ireland was when I was seven or eight, and I clearly remember having this idea that it was some kind of paradise on earth, where you could run around in bare feet across fields picking flowers, because that's the kind of terms that she described it in. It sounded absolutely wonderful. You know, fishing in the stream outside the house and she had a horse called Fanny. It was a carthorse and she used to ride it bare back. I suppose there was an idea of loads of freedom, you know, when she was over there. And there was the idea that she was surrounded by a big loving family; aunts and uncles who adored them. And then of course there is the craic. (Interviewee 9)

Moved by the mystical qualities of Donegal Interviewee 9 recently purchased an old cottage close by the villages of origin of both her and her husband's families. The cottage was completely overgrown and having lain empty for forty years required modernisation and huge financial investment. Pregnant at the time and having just bought a house back in Scotland, the decision to buy was clearly a 'big decision' that was 'more driven by the heart than the head'. In accounting for why she bought the cottage, Interviewee 9 makes clear reference to the importance of protecting the intergenerational transmission of Ireland as a special place. It is clear that the cottage would be a home for the whole extended family, a way of reclaiming a bit of Donegal that they might call their own. The cottage would be the thread that would keep alive both her own and her parents' cherished memories of Donegal among those that would follow on behind them:

My husband and I thought we're probably never going to get an opportunity like this again. It's something that has always been a wee dream for our families. So we just decided to go ahead with it. It does give you a sense of having a wee bit of it back. In fact we bought a wee bit of the land at the back of the house as well. That was a bit of folly to be honest with you. That was my husband. A lot of that has to do with reclaiming something. And of course nurturing the importance of Donegal among the children of the family was a big part of it as well. The whole feeling of Ireland is important to my husband and I and we would like our children to have the same kind of feeling. It's difficult to recreate the kind of circumstances that help to create that feeling. John was brought up in the Gorbals and I was initially brought up in Govan Hill and it was the tenements. When you went to Ireland in the summer it was like, oh fields and cows and stuff, you know. We're actually saying things like, this will sound absolutely ridiculous, my husband said, 'I don't know if I want a big garden here cos I want to appreciate the grass there'. Ok we're taking this too far now. But hopefully it will be important to my daughter and nieces and nephews. I'd like that same kind of thing for my children. I'd really hate them to grow up saying, 'I hate it here (Ireland). I want to go to Florida' or something like that you know, and having no sense of how special it is to us. (Interviewee 9)

In 1997, Interviewee 14 began to realise that her family were growing up rapidly and that her eldest child could shortly 'fly from the family nest'. Whilst the children already had a strong interest in Ireland, through Irish dancing and Gaelic language classes, it had proven financially prohibitive to visit the old country. Concerned that they had not experienced Donegal in particular as a family unit she decided that the entire family should visit for a holiday. Borrowing a minibus from a relative and renting a cottage in Donegal for a week, the holiday was set up. Interviewee 14 describes the holiday as 'simply wonderful, one of the best the family has ever had'. The magic of Ireland that she herself had experienced as a child was being transmitted to her children who loved every minute of it. She was intrigued to see if 'they would get it, what it was all about' and was taken aback by just how sensitive her children's antennae was for Ireland and Irish ways.

What exactly were the children meant to 'get'? Whilst all of the romantic notions of Ireland outlined above were clearly important, it seems that the 'sense of community' and 'Irish ways of being with other people' were crucial. In developing her account, Interviewee 14 noted how one of her children was so smitten by Donegal that he decided to move there at the age of 16 for work. Accompanied by his sister, he secured work in a village hotel and began to settle into life in the countryside. She recalls a story told by his sister on her return which vividly captures the social mileu that was so precious:

> John went over to Ireland with his kilt on and carrying his bagpipes, at the age of sixteen he had some guts. Now one day there was a wedding on and an ordination on the same week so the village was packed out. One of his friends said, 'I'll give you a dare John, you do this'. So they all went over to the local hostelry and John followed them in with the bagpipes under his arm. He walks straight in and sits in the corner. This is part of the dare. And they were saying, 'who's that fella with the pipes?' There's not many strangers come through. So John stood up in this heaving pub and shouts, 'this one's for big Charlie Boyle', one of the well known locals. And he started to play one of his tunes. They went mental. They were roaring and screaming. So he sat down, and they said, 'give us another one' So he did another one, one of his wee fancy ones. They said, 'that's you, you've made your name in the Glenties'. 'Freedom of Glenties for the Scotsman.' That's John. He's a character. (Interviewee 14)

The Celtic Tiger and death of old Ireland

The Celtic Tiger economy which roared from 1993 to 2007 clearly transformed Ireland out of all recognition. The colonial calculus is steadily withering and ebbing and it is no longer possible to view Ireland as a periphery. The Irish Catholic community has being confronted by the rise of a new Celtic Tiger economy and its legacies. Some take pride in what Ireland has achieved and view the tiger economy as a direct challenge to colonial narratives that depict the country as an economic backwater, living on the brink of poverty and lost without the help of mainland Britain. For a time and before the current recession wrecked the story, the colonial pauper had seemingly outwitted the master and it was time for the Irish to lord it over its envious neighbour. Scotland's First Minister Alex Salmond had even come to Ireland and publicly admitted that he was looking for instruction and guidance. Some participants noted wryly that some Scots with a strong sense of Britishness go to extreme lengths to reject the claim that the Irish have been architects of their own success. They object that Ireland's achievements are little more than the product of European Union subsidies. Moreover, given the pivotal importance of US transnational firms in the Information and Communications Technology and Pharmaceutical sectors to Irish economic growth, Ireland is now little more than a neo-colony of the United States, the fifty-first state! And of course such critics lament the state that Ireland has now got itself into, the Irish cannot manage their own affairs and were always destined to ruin what success they had by pure fortune enjoyed. Undoubtedly the collapse of the Irish banking sector and the ignominy of the Irish state acceding to an EU/IMF bail out will further modify Scottish envisioning of Ireland. But it is clear that speaking of Scotland and Ireland in terms of cores and peripheries is now too anachronistic to be credible. Colonial depictions of Ireland as a social, political, economic, and cultural laggard, in need of a dose of metropolitan modernity, do not now serve as a potent source of alterity and seriality.

Whilst generally welcomed by participants who enjoyed 'Ireland's day in the sun' and the recognition Ireland was then getting, it is clear that for some, the new Ireland had downsides as well as upsides. In fact the image of the utopian paradise and the rural idyll is being erased and the country is now being framed as a cosmopolitan and thrusting nation, marching to the forefront of European economic development and restlessly and rapidly transforming its culture and landscapes. The following testimonies highlight the variety of complaints that lament what Ireland has lost as well as what it has gained by its success. Concern is with the loss of those virtues of the old Ireland which are celebrated: sense of community, ways of life, closeness with nature, hospitality, pace of life, traditional town landscapes, piety and religion, and anti-commercialism. Wealth has changed the Irish, sometimes for better and sometimes for the worse:

> I really wonder how anyone can afford to live in Ireland. There are beautiful homes, Spanish type villas, absolutely everywhere. Everyone has a couple of cars. The sons and daughters will now also have a car each. They have every shop under the sun and they are all super fashionable. All the latest wooden floors. But I don't think its been all good really. People have fallen away from the chapel. They are not going to chapel. People used to help each other out with the work and everything else but not now. You have to pay for everything. It's all contractors that do the handy work. (Interviewee 5)

On our last trip we started off at Derry and we went right down as far as Connemara, Galway and all of that. Aye, without a doubt its changed out of recognition. I've got relations in Galway now and it isn't real the way they're living. At one time they used to live in Donegal before they moved, and my mother used to send them shoes over every year, sandals for the summer, the Clarks sandals with the wee holes in them. My mother used to send over the first communion dresses for any nieces that were making their first communion. You wouldn't do that now. And they're living now in houses that are like something you'd see in Dallas. There's a big difference. (Interviewee 31)

Money is no problem. Around my rural Donegal where we had nothing, oh it's amazing the money they've got, the homes they have got, the cars they have got, the holidays they go for, the education that they've got, the jobs they have got. Of course affluence and money have affected them too you know. Marriage break down is terrible over there too. The faith isn't as strong any more. A lot of people don't go to mass either, which would be unheard of. Oh it has changed. You know the homes that they've built over there and the best of cars. It's not any rubbish car they're buying. The holidays, Spain, America and they have their houses in Tenerife and all this. It certainly is unbelievable. I think it has changed. They're not the same community caring over there, because its kind of we can look after ourselves now and we don't need our neighbours all that much. Ok when I go home a couple of the neighbours will pop in, but just a couple of the neighbours. I go round and visit the families round about just to say hello to them. A lot of that has gone Mark, you know. It's not the close knit community it was. (Interviewee 30).

Changes in Ireland? The Ireland of today is a brasher Ireland than it was in the old days. Its probably lost a bit of the neighbourliness, you know people rarely going in an out of houses and things like that. It's a more atomised society but I'm afraid that always comes with prosperity. I suppose its more international in its outlook. I don't go with the cliché about it being a European country. But it is certainly more outward looking. I hear a lot, and its done within Ireland itself, of slagging off Ireland in the 1950s and 1940s. It wasn't such a dismal place. There was happiness and spontaneous get togethers, dances in people's houses and so on. But you know the new Ireland is the new Ireland and the past is all sour and a time of soul despair for some of the more brasher youngsters of today. (Interviewee 42)

If my father went to Ireland now he probably wouldn't recognise it. My dad would have a vision of Ireland in the twenties and thirties when he was there in that very rural place and a very slow place. I think if he went to Dublin now, he would get the fright of his life, probably so would I. I think Ireland is changing quite dramatically now isn't it? I think the new breed of Irish person that is coming out is maybe a bit anti-clerical, anti-Catholic and much more liberal. I think he would have taken a dislike to them right away. He would have found it hard to live with probably. His image of Ireland would have been dented in a big way by seeing what is happening now in Ireland. (Interviewee 48)

When my wife and I went back a few years ago, we went to an Ireland that fleeced us. It was an expensive country to live in. When we went to a restaurant we felt we were being ripped off and I thought, there's people making a lot of money here. When I went a few years ago, we went to Mayo, which was particularly harshly hit by the famine. We were brought up for a meal by my wife's cousins one night and I was astonished by the wealth. This was not just comfortable. This was a house with about eight bedrooms and we were given a meal that was just sumptuous. It was like from the famine to the most fantastic salmon and this was just outrageous. They had satellite TV and they had a wealth beyond what my kids enjoy. The kids, they were on-line a few years ago. This was about five years ago when even the internet hadn't been appreciated here quite as much. (Interviewee 49)

With the boom Ireland is going to change and Ireland is going to become more like anywhere else. They call it progress, but I'm a traditionalist and I like it the way it was. Time wasn't too important. You didn't need a clock and yet everything seemed to go very nicely didn't it? (Interviewee 64c)

Ireland itself has changed. Since Ireland went into the European Community it has become very cosmopolitan. If you've been over to Dublin, I don't think it's the old Ireland there. If you've seen the palatial houses they've got and I don't think the faith is the same as it was. We used to go to Knock on pilgrimages, but I don't think that's as strong as it was. I think if you went to New York you'd get the St Patrick's day parade stronger than it is in Ireland But can you imagine the old folks who have passed over coming back to this world with all the terrible morals and all the things that are happening. That would be a different world for them to the world that they left. They wouldn't recognise Ireland. They would be shocked by it. (Interviewee 66a)

Pleased that Ireland is coming out of the doldrums and doing so tremendously well. Sadly though, Ireland is losing a lot at the present minute. My own family, my own friends listen to the young people in Ireland now evaluating their life in new ways, they are talking about their jobs, 25K, 30K and all that. Of course it is very important that you get some return in life but I think suddenly the Irish are about to lose what has made them special, they are possibly losing their identity, really that's what I feel most sad about. (Interviewee 40)

Conclusion

Images of Ireland and of 'home' produced and circulated by the Irish Catholic community in Scotland vary principally as a function of generation. First generation migrants left an Ireland that was harrowingly poor and which offered little opportunity save physical survival. They settled into a Scotland that was comparatively and noticeably more modern. Consequently they could only ever imagine Ireland as a peripheral backwater. It was always home and was meaningful in that sense but it was a poor country that generated bitter memories of harsh childhoods and fractured families. Some second and third generation children who were exposed to Ireland for a prolonged period, for example the war evacuees, also sensed and glimpsed this darker underbelly of Ireland. Shaped in fundamental ways by long summer family holidays in Ireland, other second and third generation descendants undoubtedly invented an Ireland that was scarcely recognisable to their forebears. Ireland was an enchanting wonderland, a place of family, farms, nature, landscape, and adventure. Ireland was more 'home' for these descendants than it was for first generation migrants. The emotive qualities evoked by Ireland now consisted of excitement, longing, desire, exoticisation, fulfilment, and freedom, rather than bitterness, sorrow, melancholy, fear, anxiety, and imprisonment. Finally, today and notwithstanding the economic difficulties which have beset Ireland since 2007, it is clear that the Irish Catholic in Scotland vista on Ireland is changing; Ireland is an exciting and cosmopolitan place where skilled Scots might want to work. It is a country to be envied and copied. But it is also a country in which the Ireland of old is rapidly disappearing. What is emerging may not be able to animate patriotic passions in quite the same way as the old Ireland did. We might conclude then that different generations have affirmed, propagated, reclaimed, recast, transcended and disposed off a range of competing images of Ireland. And of course it remains to be seen what the catastrophic collapse of the Irish economy from 2007 and the deep economic recession which has followed will do to emerging Irish-Scottish views of the emerald island.

Chapter 6

The Politics of Anti-imperialism: Activists, Agitators and Advocates

Introduction

It is clear that Irish politics continued and continues to interest and animate the Irish Catholic community in Scotland and that the politics of anti-imperialism and republicanism has also become refracted through Scotland so as to produce a range of different interventions in the politics of past and present Scotland. For some politics has been a marker of difference which has generated a profound sense of alterity from Scottish society. But it has also served as a beachhead through which the Irish Catholic community has connected and found communion with progressive social, economic, cultural, and political movements in Scotland. This chapter begins with an examination of one testimony which proves to be effective in opening up the complex issues which surround manifestations of Irish politics in Scottish life. The stories of two participants with personal experiences of subjugation and rebellion in Ireland will then be examined, one recalling events back in the period 1916 to 1921 in the run up to the establishment of the Irish Free State, and one offering more recent insights into the troubles which flared in Northern Ireland from the late 1960s. Attention is then devoted to the kinds of populist and schematic understandings of Irish history and politics which circulate in Scotland with specific reference to the development of what might be called a 'rebel music scene'. The bulk of the chapter explores the testimonies provided by a small number of more seriously engaged participants who have become involved in overt expressions of support for the Irish nationalist and republican cause. What proves fascinating about these activists is the many and complex ways in which their solidarity with the Irish cause has mutated into a diversity of competing and at times conflictual conceptions of what might constitute a progressive politics for contemporary Scotland.

Key themes in the political life of the Irish Catholic community in Scotland

Interviewee 49 is third generation Irish on his mother's side and fourth generation Irish on his father's side. Aged 46, he is married with children, lives in Glasgow, graduated with a degree from the University of Glasgow, and is currently employed as a teacher in a secondary school in the west of Scotland. Interviewee 49's story is intriguing in so far he compares his own politics with that of his grandfather and his

father. Important generational issues present themselves. I will use this testimony
to prise open some of the complexity which surrounds the political dispositions of
the Irish Catholic community in Scotland, with respect to Irish politics, Irish politics
from a Scottish perspective, and past and present Scottish politics.

Interviewee 49's maternal grandfather came from Donegal in the early 1900s
and settled in Lanarkshire. Given the hardships from which he fled, he had little
time for those who would pedal romantic images of Donegal. Known for reciting
the 'Star of Rabbie Burns' as much as for singing the 'Ballad of Robert Emmet' at
social gatherings, he demonstrated very little interest in Irish politics and 'did not
appear to be very republican'. Scotland in contrast offered him a chance to make a
living. Employed by a well known local entrepreneur, he rose to become a ganger
over a cadre of Irish labourers. Earning a reputation for his no nonsense approach
to hiring and firing he became respected and slightly feared. His role also brought
him into social circles which would otherwise have been alien to Irish settlers. His
politics in Scotland appeared to be more pragmatic than left of centre. As such,
interviewee 49 always thought of his grandfather as 'untypically Irish':

> He was a man, who moved comfortably in Scottish labouring circles if you like.
> He became quite well respected in his work. But he became well respected in
> an untypical way, because my notion of Irishness is of a downtrodden people.
> It was they who got the worst jobs and through talking to my mother about
> her father I discovered that he was not downtrodden. In fact he did a lot of the
> trodding! She also told me, whether it's true or not I've never established, but
> she told me he worked through the General Strike. And my notion of labour and
> justice made me think, 'that's a surprise'! That ran against a lot of the grain that
> had been expected in my family and a lot of the attitudes that I grew up with in
> my family. But the most striking thing about my grandfather was the extent that
> he could move comfortable in Scottish social circles. He drank in Orange pubs.
> Granddad could drink in the pub next to the Orange Hall. He was as comfortable
> drinking in places like that so he was a unique individual. He rose above a lot of
> things. (Interviewee 49)

When asked why he thought his grandfather moved so comfortably in Scottish
labouring circles, Interviewee 49 deliberated on the possibility that it was 'maybe
an Ulster thing'. In so doing he drew parallels between the cultural traits of the
Ulster man and the Scot:

> The Donegal man is obviously an Ulster man and I've always thought that
> the men from the North of Ireland are harder. I could be wrong there. That's a
> notional view. I've always felt that there's a harshness about the soul of, even
> Donegal Catholics, that might not be the case in parts of the South, but that's
> only a very unscientific explanation. It's just a notion and I could be wrong
> there but that might be what led him easily into the Rabbie Burns culture or the
> Scottish culture (Interviewee 49)

In spite of being third generation Irish, his grandparents moving from Tyrone to Scotland in the 1890s, Interviewee 49s father by contrast had greater difficulty in securing a sense of complete attachment to Scotland. Although interested in the politics of Ireland, like many who did not have the opportunity to study history in any detail his knowledge of Irish politics was schematic and rooted in a number of basic assumptions. Interviewee 49 recalls how he felt compelled personally to become better armed with the facts of Irish history and politics in the light of his father's experience:

> My father's views on history and politics are made up of a small number of selective facts and his attitudes are built around those and he would describe himself as socialist. He would drop into conversation things like the Red Clydesiders or James Connolly or MacLean or Collins and De Valera, but he never hung on to the bare bones of the flesh. My father presented me with the dots on the line but I had to fill in the blanks for myself. (Interviewee 49)

A devout Catholic, his father's experience of living and working in Scotland in the 1950s and 1960s had left an indelible mark on his attitudes to the country. To him Scotland was a place that had still to come to terms with the Irish Catholic community. He felt alienated from the Scottish National Party (SNP) and took little interest in Scottish independence. His politics always revolved around the Labour Party and organisations with an interest in defending the working classes. He was Labour 'through and through' and would never contemplate voting for any other party. The Labour Party understood and empathised with the Irish cause and stood up for the rights of the Irish Catholic community as they secured a foothold in Scotland. The Labour Party *were* the party of the Irish:

> My father has the view that the sons and daughters of the first generation Irish Catholics were downtrodden, because he experienced it. He would be appalled to be described as anything but a 'Labour man'. He hates the SNP. I have tried to convince him that this is the era of small nations. Scotland is a small nation. When I was growing up we had about thirty-two nations in Europe and we now have about fifty or sixty. So why can't Scotland be one of those nations, because it's got a lot to offer. We've got nations like Azerbaijan and Lithuania and the Republic of Ireland is set up as a model of success, but yet to people of my father's generation Scotland means, 'aye you'll not get your Catholic schools' and 'you'll not get a job'. (Interviewee 49)

It is against this backdrop that Interviewee 49 specifies his own politics. Trained as a teacher and intensely interested in Irish politics, Interviewee 49 clearly has a more sophisticated and informed grasp of the Irish question than his grandfather or father had. He clearly sees nobility in the Irish Republican cause and like many of his generation would see a united thirty-two county Ireland as the preferred and ideal end to Anglo-Irish political history. But his views show a command of the compromises which might need to be made for peace. Interestingly, he claims to identify the seeds of progress in the form of a (re)growing socialist consciousness within the Loyalist tradition. He sketched out his belief that perhaps a socialist controlled power-sharing executive for Northern Ireland might not be as remote as many believe and might indeed provide one road to redemption:

> As a teacher I couldn't afford just to have the bare bones. There has to be some factual evidence in there. I am obsessed with Irish politics. I have a hundred books up the stairs. I see a nobility to the Irish Republican history. Any reading of Irish history would surely lead to the conclusion that it is only right and just that that side should win. But I think we're getting away from the language of winning and losing. They may be your enemy but the Loyalists are just as much trapped in there and are as much victims of the whole history and geography as anybody else. I've become very conscious of the extent to which hard working-class Loyalism has become Republican. I hear Loyalist prisoners talking a language which is to me Republican. A lot of their experiences in the Maze prison has led them to believe that they too have been shafted by the 'squirearchy' for hundreds of years. They have been banged up by the very state they are fighting to preserve, a contradiction that must lead to some reflection. They are sitting with their arses out of their trousers in the Shankhill Road, just like the Catholics on the Falls. The working-class Irish Protestant has far more in common with the working-class Irish Catholic than James Molyneaux or Chichester-Clark, or Terence O'Neill. People like McMichael, Ervine and Hutchinson, it seem to me, need to have a bigger say. There was a strike in 1931, there was a march down the Shankhill road over welfare payments. Welfare payments were far less in Belfast because it was a regional parish. And a march came down the Shankhill Road from the Falls. That was breathtaking. The idea that these two people could walk hand in hand was inspirational. (Interviewee 49)

Interviewee 49 clearly feels strongly about the Irish Catholic cause and is proud of the ways in which Irish Catholics have always 'fought for the underdog'. He shares his father's class consciousness. He has a keen interest in republicanism, inclusivity, and social justice. He senses a direct alignment between Irish politics and progressive Left politics in Scotland. Nevertheless, his passage through university has led him to a greater appreciation of what the British/Scottish welfare state has done for the Irish than his father would have had. Setting out in life in the 1970s and 1980s, he personally cannot recount any experiences of anti-Irish or anti-Catholic hostility at job interviews or in the workplace. Moreover, his training as a teacher has led him to an appreciation of the complexities of Irish and Scottish history and he has real interest in Scottish nationalism. Whilst his father might have equated Scotland with Protestantism, Orangeism, and discrimination he sees much in Scotland's past that connects with Ireland's subjugation under British rule. Unlike his father then, he does not feel threatened by Scottish nationalism and feels able to align his socialist politics with nationalist politics in Scotland. As he has made socio-economic progress himself, interestingly though Interviewee 49 admits that he experiences some torment as to whether he is living as an authentic socialist in spite of occupying a higher class bracket. There is no direct inverse correlation between socio-economic and immigrant advancement and the politics of the left but it is clear that the former has the possibility of putting stresses and strains on the latter:

> I was always dead proud of working-class ideas and attitudes, because there was a sense of community and looking after each other and love, the whole basis of socialism, romantic socialism. What I sometimes think is the type of person that I've become is not what I am. The Thatcher years did make a lot of changes here and I suppose that I have not been untouched by them. When we got married just less than twenty years ago I had no notion to even buy a house. I had no notion to have a car and have foreign holidays, but I've fallen into those things. I suppose my parents were untypical in that respect as well. My parents did buy their own house. They actually bought their own house. It wasn't really a decision that that generation made. It was because we were living in this house that was pouring with damp and they were just so fed up that they wanted out and the only way to get out, there was an opportunity there and they could afford it. But I remember running around with these young lads and I was the only one to move into a semi, a privately owned semi, because we were the council house generation. I made that step. In that sense I'm not sure I could even describe myself as working class. I actually have this view of myself that I don't know if I deserve to be working class. My father never got his hands dirty. My father went to work with a collar and tie. I never felt that I deserved to be working class. I can remember people saying, 'we're working-class kids, we came from the flats'. I did come from the flats, which certainly made us working class. We never owned a car, we never went on foreign holidays, we never even went to England on holiday. But my father had got a tie on. He was always there for his kids. He never did shifts. The fact is that my father could put a jacket on and go to work and he was an office worker. (Interviewee 49)

In the testimony offered by Interviewee 49 dwell a number of themes that go to the heart of the politics of the Irish Catholic community in Scotland. They include: the complex pragmatic politics of the first generation; the circulation of schematic and populist narratives of Irish history and politics; the translation of Irish politics into support for the Labour Party and the antipathy some feel for Scottish nationalism; the role of third level education in both exciting but also tempering the politics of upwardly mobile descendants; the preparedness to contemplate seismic shifts in the Northern Irish political landscape; the ways in which a growing sense of belonging to Scotland has opened up the possibility of greater political support for the Scottish Nationalist Party; and finally the impacts of socio-economic progress on class consciousness. Each of these themes will now be considered in greater detail through reflection on the testimonies of a number of participants whose lives have been more directly embroiled in Irish history and politics (Figures 6.1 and 6.2).

Figure 6.1   Free Derry Corner 1972. Irish Catholic families often feared passing through Northern Ireland on their way to the Irish Republic but sometimes political curiosity took them off the beaten track and many a covert photograph was taken (Property of the author)

Figure 6.2   The Belfast Ferry 1972. Irish Catholics often found themselves on the boat to Ireland with Orange Flute Bands who were going across to Belfast to celebrate the 12th July parade and marching season. These encounters could be fun but they the could also be feared (Property of the author)

Biographical embroilments in conflict and struggle

> The Catholics never had much of a say. But the Civil Rights march opened up
> the eyes of the world and let them see what the Catholics had to put up with.
> I have a cousin called Father Sean and he is one of seven men and his mother
> died and on the mammy's anniversary he came home. So the seven brothers and
> the three sisters were all in the house with their dad. The helicopter arrived that
> night. The soldiers were dropped off. They came in and the first thing they did
> was they smashed the Sacred Heart picture and Sean said, 'what did you do that
> for?' and the soldier said, 'I thought there was a cupboard behind it'. The two
> girls were in their bed, they were young teenagers and Sean said to them, 'you
> can't go in there until they get up'. So the girls came out and they said something
> and they said, 'oh we know he's a fucking priest'. So Father Sean said to me,
> 'I don't think there can be any Catholics in that army at all because they couldn't
> have behaved in that manner'. They wrecked the house and they kept them there
> until eleven o'clock in the day because the mass was at ten o' clock. As well as
> that, Joseph's cousin, Father Joe, his cousin, was shot. He came over the border
> for a packet of cigarettes and it's one of these second class roads with no border
> thing on it. The police shot him with one single bullet through the head because
> he had lost his license for driving in the North. An old woman came out to give
> him Rosary Beads when he was dead and the police wouldn't let her near the
> car, but she stood there and she didn't go away until a priest arrived. Someone
> phoned for the priest. But if they wanted to stop the car they didn't need to shoot
> him. So that just makes things worse you see. Once you're hurt by that tragedy
> then you're no longer at peace. And there are still many unsolved mysteries in
> Ireland. (Interviewee 6)

Within the archive, two moments of violence and discrimination against Catholics
living in Ireland appeared to generate particular rancour within families. Amongst
older participants, especially those with forebears or friends who lived in the
north of Ireland during the period of 1916 to 1921, the terror wrought by the
Black and Tans is particularly foregrounded. The stories recounted were so
ruthless, bloody and terrifying that it is unsurprising that they remain vivid for
descendants. The Black and Tans were understood to be 'raving lunatics who
were let out of the asylums in England', 'bad animals', and 'mentals from the
mental house, headcases'. They had been sent across to Ireland by Winston
Churchill at the time of insurrection after the 1916 rising to intimidate rebels and
their supporters into silence. According to participants, they were responsible
for rape, pillage, indiscriminate murder, torture and brutality, and brought shame
to the British army. Secondly, some of the younger participants and those with
live relationships with relatives in the 'six northern counties' shared stories
of civil rights abuses and discrimination in Northern Ireland. In Stormont, the
Protestant majority had erected an institution that systematically discriminated
against Catholics, Nationalists and Republicans. The civil rights movement had

been brutally repressed. Fearing that 'the game was up' Loyalists and 'Unionists had sought to crack down on legitimate protest in order to secure what they had appropriated from the Irish'. If the history of British occupation of Ireland was littered with inglorious periods then the troubles which bubbled up from the late 1960s and which are only now coming to a conclusion were emblematic of some of its most ugly moments.

Of dark deeds and long memories: The barbarism of the Black and Tans

When interviewing an 83-year-old second generation woman from Glasgow, the author was asked whether he would like to hear the woman's mother's views on Ireland's history. Perplexed at the possibility of interviewing someone this age, he replied politely, 'yes, is your mother in the house today.' 'No', responded the women, 'she died in the 1979'. 'How is it possible then to conduct an interview?' The woman pointed out that just before she had died and unbeknown to her mother, she had tape recorded hours of private conversation with her mother. Whilst precious to her and never publicly aired before, she agreed to share these conversations with the author in what turned out to be a fascinating if surreal afternoon. Whilst the tapes covered substantial territory, it was the story of the family's encounters with the British state and more specifically the Black and Tans that stood out most significantly. An edited section of this story is repeated here. It is preceded by an introduction narrated by the woman and contains a poem at the end, both specifically requested by the participant as a condition of the public dissemination of her story.

Interviewee 23

I was born in Glasgow of Irish parents. My father was born in 1884 in County Antrim. He died in October 1950, aged sixty-five. My mother was born in 1882 in County Down. She died in December 1979, aged ninety-seven. My mother and father were both very interested in Irish history and told us many things about Ireland many years ago. She was able in her nineties to tell me bit by bit the history of the Ireland she knew. She came to Scotland when she was about twenty years of age. Since her brothers and sisters were still in Ireland, also her parents, she was in constant contact with them, particularly during the troubled times of 1916–1921. She is now going to tell us about the bigotry and hatred which went on through the troubled times and which appears to have escalated in the last few years. My mother is not relating these incidents with any hatred or bigotry, and they are not meant to hurt anyone who hears this tape who perhaps has a different attitude to the Irish question. But she just would like to let us know from personal experience how the Catholics fared during the troubled times.

Interviewee 23's mother

As the fight for Irish freedom still continued, the terrible years of the Black and Tans began. The Black and Tans were sent to Ireland to rid the country of those who wished to fight for Irish freedom. It's often asked, 'what kind of men were the Black and Tans?' It has been recorded that an advertisement appeared in the Sunday papers asking for recruits to fight in Ireland. This attracted a peculiar kind of man. There is reason to believe that some of them were released from penal servitude and there is no doubt at all had been in jail. Several of them had been convicted for robbery and some for murder. Lloyd George admitted that a great number of undesirables had got into the Black and Tans and two hundred and sixty-seven of the police had to be dismissed. The Black and Tans had done enough long before they left Ireland to dishonour the British Government, to defile the name of the British Services and to make Englishmen hang their heads in shame. I'm not saying that the Irish Republicans were all Saints, but after all, they were fighting for the freedom of their country and for independence, and as everyone knows they were outnumbered by the might of Britain. The Black and Tans on the other hand were an organized body of British agents who were sent to massacre and murder.

The police journal at the time stated that the purpose of the Black and Tans was to make Ireland a hell for the rebels, in other words to terrorise the civil population and to wipe out any support for Sinn Féin. A British Commission issued a statement that there was 'no justification under the law of war or even under martial law for assassination or terrorism as a means of suppressing insurrection', and yet said the commission, 'this is what the British Forces are doing in Ireland'. In a single week they shot up and burned Balbriggan and Milltown, Trim and Larne, murdering as often as not. In a single month they gave twenty-four towns a dose of the same medicine. They burned property in Cork to the value of three million pounds, including the Carnegie Library and the City Halls. They even shoved back the Fire Brigade and cut their hoses. They robbed shops, post offices and banks. They flogged, beat up and murdered.

They tried to murder Bishop Fogarty by throwing him into the river in a sack. They murdered Father Griffin. They also murdered the Lord Mayor of Cork and also the Lord Mayor of Limerick. They were both murdered in front of their wives. A young girl of eight was shot and a young woman with a child in her arms was shot too. They were described as scoundrels in uniform. When they were robbing banks and post offices they didn't wear their uniforms. They blamed Sinn Féin. A young woman was sitting on a wall outside the Catholic Church, she was pregnant. A lorry load of Tans passed and one of them fired. The woman was shot in the abdomen. Someone ran into the Chapel House for the priest. He came out and anointed the woman then he took off his jacket and put it over her.

In rural Ulster, lorry loads of Black and Tans descended on our village. My brother Hugh was a Sinn Féin councillor for Banbridge and he was highly respected by Protestants and Catholics alike. He tried to get better wages and better conditions for the mill workers. Because Hugh was a councillor our home was often searched. The house would be ransacked and the haystacks searched. The Tans eventually got Hugh while out working on his farm. He was taken to prison in Banbridge and then he was interned on The Argenta, which was a prison ship in Larne Harbour. Here the men were crowded in filthy conditions with poor food and no comfort. Since they were on a ship there was no communication with home. Religion was forbidden.

After two years Hugh was released, but internment had changed him. He was a fine healthy man when he was interned. On release his health had broken. He was only thirty seven years of age and he spent the last of his years quietly working on his farm. He died before he reached his fiftieth birthday. He could tell tales of dreadful brutality which no civilised government should have allowed. But Britain closed her eyes to the atrocities committed.

Even when Hugh was interned, raids still took place on our home. Late at night on the seventh of November 1921, the Tans arrived again. They put my mother and father out of the house, also my brothers and sisters who were at home. They searched the house but found nothing. It was a cold wet November night, and my mother was only clad in a nightdress. When they had finished their search, they hit my mother on the back with the butt of their rifles and then drove off. Three days later my mother was dead. Hugh, who was still on the prison ship was not allowed home for his mother's funeral. It's very hard to forget when your own mother is a victim. But she was Irish to the last and died without a word of bitterness.

Interviewee 23

I have no mother for she died when I was very young,
But still her memory in my heart like morning mist has clung,
They tell me of an angel that watched me while I was asleep,
An awful soft and gentle hand that wiped the tear I wept,
And that same hand that held my own when I began to walk,
The joy that sparkled in her eye when I first tried to walk,
They say a mother's heart is pleased when infants think about them,
I wonder if she thinks of me in that bright happy land,
I know she is in heaven now for she was always good to me.

Truth and reconciliation: Civil rights and Northern Ireland in the late 1960s/ early 1970s

Interviewee 2 is aged 46 and left Donegal in 1976 to come to Scotland aged 22. Whilst in Donegal she stayed in the border town of Lifford, a sister town to Strabane. Her story begins with the extent to which sectarianism had become so naturalised in the north that it was taken to be banal. As early as the age of twelve she became aware of the discrimination which Northern Irish Catholics encountered. She recalls visiting Strabane on a regular basis in 1966 and being shocked at adverts for shop assistants specifying *NCNA,* 'No Catholics Need Apply'. Even at that young age she recalls being conscious of the injustices of the voting system which was still based on ownership of property rather than universal suffrage. She remembers graffiti on a wall in Strabane that read. 'Catholics in Ulster are the Niggers of the North.'

Alongside these experiences was a growing awareness also of the civil rights movement. She recalls being taken up to barricades at the Bogside in Derry, at the time when 'Free Derry' was being declared. This was a 'really big thing' and she recalls the sense of electricity that accompanied an impromptu performance by the famous band the *Dubliners* at the barricades. She also remembers the events of Bloody Sunday vividly. She had in fact been in the hospital having her Appendix removed when Bloody Sunday happened and recalls being relocated to provide space for casualties. She has vivid memories of the sense of anger, bitterness, and resentment that was felt by Northern Catholics around this time and the great awareness that the civil rights movement had to prevail lest the North descend into a South African system of Apartheid.

In spite of her growing political awareness, Interviewee 2 laments how she still 'missed' a lot of discrimination that was visited upon her personally. In 1973, when her Protestant friends were given places at Trinity College Dublin, she presumed that she had got inferior grades and simply accepted a place on a social work course at the University of Ulster in Coleraine. The following year she discovered that in fact she had obtained better exam marks but had simply been overlooked. Even whilst in Coleraine, she described her political consciousness as a 'republican thing' rather than just 'an anti-British thing'. It was only gradually that she began to become aware that Coleraine had been built as a 'nice safe Protestant university' to counter the expansion of the more Catholic-oriented Magee College in Derry itself. On graduating in 1976, Interviewee 2 recalls how difficult it was for Catholics to secure employment as social workers in comparison to Protestant class mates, irrespective of what degree results they secured.

In spite of these experiences, Interviewee 2's resentment continued to bubble beneath the surface. Nevertheless, it was to burst asunder in the final year of her course at Coleraine when she was violently attacked by a Sergeant in the Police. One night, 'out of the blue' the Sergeant turned up at the door of her student flat and violently raped her at gunpoint. She recalls him saying, 'fuck off ya wee fenian bastard'. Not surprisingly this experience was seminal in her life and generated a furious reaction. Whilst she could never fully support or perpetrate political violence, she admits that she came close to considering it at this point. Her response was to leave the oppression of Northern Ireland behind her and to move to Scotland:

> In spite of what had happened, I wasn't into doing anything bad so I thought, 'fuck it' if I don't get out of here I'm going to be planting bombs. I was really angry and I didn't want to go but I would have been shooting people. I was really, I thought, if I don't leave this country then you know, I'll be up there and

be in jail and I was inflamed and I thought then, I will run away. On reflection I am so happy I said no, this isn't right or whatever. I was never keen on the violence and I just don't have the stomach for it or the bottle for it. If you are going to get into the IRA then you have to be prepared to do the bad bits you know, that's the deal and if you go along with something it's not just one person that kills everybody has to do their bit so there is no squealing. In any event I think there were too many idiots getting involved anyway. I suppose it's like any times of troubles you will always get the chancers and the bad boys that will join in and it does kind of scunner you, because you see these people in times of peace and you wouldn't have trusted them with a fiver of your money, never mind trust them with your whole kind of way forward and with your political aspirations. You know, they are just thugs and hooligans. (Interviewee 2)

Based on her own experience, she perceives a real need for a South African style 'truth and reconciliation process' if Northern Catholics are ever to come to terms with the subordination and humiliation they were forced to suffer. She concludes:

I don't think you ever fully exorcise the hurt, but you just try to remember it and you don't fester on it. You just say some things are wrong and they will always be wrong you know, and sure you would like to see peace, but I think the kind of stuff they are doing in South Africa, this truth and reconciliation process, I think there is a real need for that. Because I think without that there is a denial of people's experiences, even at the level of opportunities denied, you know which is not direct injury: that being second class, that just not being of any value, and I think how do you move on if people still store such resentments? I think most people who lived as Catholics in Northern Ireland will have those resentments and sure it is like everything, it doesn't have to sour you for ever but it does have to be acknowledged you know, in terms of moving forward. (Interviewee 2)

Propagating Irish nationalist history in Scotland: Rebel music and the rebel music scene

There exists a complex history of cultural exchange between Ireland and Scotland. The circulation of songs of rebellion and insurrection form part of this history. Rebel songs were the provenance of the nineteenth-century street singers and those singers who performed at small indoor reunions. Rebel music then became propagated through the growing popularity of Irish Céilídhs in the 1930s and 1940s and the parades of the Ancient Order of Hibernians in the 1950s and 1960s. More recently, there has emerged a politicisation of folk music and musical sessions culminating in the growth of a new *folk-cabaret scene*, where rebel musical bands play in working mens' clubs or other social club environments. In the 1980s and 1990s such a rebel music folk cabaret scene developed in Glasgow. This scene consisted of a range of 'domestic' bands (for instance *Athenry, Blarney Pilgrims, Charlie and the Bhoys, Saoirsie, Timbuk five*) and 'visiting' Irish bands (including the *Wolfe-Tones, Irish Brigade, Erin Og, Tuam, and Summerfly*) playing Irish rebel songs in clubs, pubs and concert venues, to audiences numbering anything from 30 people to 3,000, normally on a weekend afternoon or evening. Bands normally consist of four or five members and an entrance fee of between £3–£20 is charged.

Whilst acknowledging the power of rebel music to excite political interest in key events in Irish history some participants expressed concern about the kinds of people these events were attracting. Drunken youths sporting Celtic football attire and sporting ostentatious crucifixes around their neck often flocked to concerts clearly knowing nothing about Irish politics. One female participant whose partner was a performer on the scene noted that he did not really enjoy playing rebel songs to such an audience but that the scene afforded a source of finance that could not otherwise be garnered. She noted how 'rebel nights' held all over Ireland were 'proper respectable sit down dinner dance jobs' in contrast to those held in Glasgow which she called 'mental'. Her partner extended this viewpoint with a telling anecdote:

> Recently for example, I was doing a gig and I played this song called 'Back home in Derry'. It's a good song, Bobby Sands wrote the words for it and it's a good tune. Anyway, the next thing I knew this guy jumped up and shouted, 'never mind that shite, get the Brits out'. They've no real knowledge of music or of history. They have a superficial bevvied up view of things. (Partner of Interviewee 13).

The following notes derive from attendance at a 'rebel night' in the late 1990s in Glasgow Plaza a somewhat down on its luck concert hall in one of the most deprived areas in Glasgow city centre. The evening entertainment was headlined by a visiting Irish band:

Field Notes

> The audience consisted of 2000 younger males, most drunk by the end of the night if not the start. Many sported IRA memorabilia and some had paramilitary headgear and wore dark sun glasses. The hall was covered in Irish tri-colours. Around me, a number of people spoke in Irish Gaelic, greeting each other with the popular catch phrase Tiocfaidh ár lá (our day will come) but progressing then to more complex conversations. The night began with a large banging of a drum and almost hysterical screaming to 'Get the Brits out now'. Then the bands came on and played the usual range of rebel songs, some fast and stirring, others slow and remorseful. It amazed me how the mood of the audience could change, with anarchy, affray and fighting inside the venue giving way to tranquillity and lament. One song, mourning the death of Pearse Jordan, an IRA volunteer shot dead by the British army on the Falls Road in Belfast in 1992, resulted in

a spontaneous kneeling of 2000 people, in complete silence, hands clasped as if deep in prayer. At one stage, a Glaswegian member of the republican movement who had recently been released under the Good Friday Agreement was brought on to the stage to thunderous applause and shouts of 'No decommissioning' and 'Fuck the peace processes'. This was followed by a raffle, the first prize of which was a framed drawing of Bobby Sands, the first IRA H Block hunger striker to die in 1981. The night ended once more in anarchy where intoxicated with drink and propaganda, the audience exploded to the two favourites 'Go on home British soldiers go on home', and the 'SAM song', gleefully celebrating the IRAs acquisition of Surface to Air Missiles in the mid 1980s. Again in a bizarre mood swing, the crowd descended into almost total silence, everyone standing with their hands behind their backs and heads to the floor. The last song of the night was the Irish national anthem, the Soldiers Song, sung in Irish Gaelic. Super-pumped up, the audience flocked back on to the streets of Glasgow with the Strathclyde Police Force stewarding the event outside the subject of verbal abuse and threatening behaviour.

An effort has been made in Figure 6.3 to identify the most commonly played and popular rebel songs in the west of Scotland folk cabaret scene between 1994 and 1999. Although not claiming to be exhaustive, a total of 62 songs are listed as being sufficiently in circulation to merit inclusion. Two points are note-worthy, both of which point to the importance of the rebel music scene in the affirmation of particular models of masculinity; models which have come under threat in post industrial Glasgow. Firstly, the vast majority of the rebel songs focus upon some of the most traumatic, bloody, and violent events to have occurred in Irish history. Primary attention is given to the grotesque, the extreme, and the most violent episodes in Ireland's past. The privileged status ascribed to memories which recall tales of blood and gore, violence and death, is indicative of an appetite for models of masculinity which only the physical force tradition offers. Secondly, it is clear from Figure 6.3 that there is a general appetite for one particular type of rebel song in the west of Scotland, the hero-martyr genre. By recounting the heroic life of a variety of Irish martyrs in the physical force tradition, this genre is explicit in its endorsement of particular models of masculinity. The edification of the 'rebellious Gael' enshrines certain qualities as defining what it truly means to be a man of outstanding character; brave, bold, daring, fearless, robust, trustworthy, reliable, dependable, and noble: at least for this particular sub-culture.

1798
General Munroe Henry Joy The West's awake (*)   *United Irishmen's rebellion 1798*
Irish Soldier Laddie (*) The rising of the moon
The boys of Wexford Wearing of the green

1803
Bold Robert Emmet Anne Devlin   *Robert Emmet's insurrection in 1803*
Back home in Derry (*)

1848
A nation once again (*)   *Cultural nationalism of the Young Irelander's and*
        rising in 1848

1867
God Save Ireland (*) Bold Fenian men   *Fenian rising of 1967*

1916
Grace(**) James Connolly(**) Padraig Pearse   *Easter 1916 rebellion*
Banna Strand The foggy dew (**) The boys of
the old brigade (**) Soldiers song (**) Merry
ploughboy(*) Ireland un-free should never be at peace

1919-23
Kevin Barry (*) Michael Collins Beal na Blath   *War of Independence 1919-1923*
The broad black brimmer (**) Black and Tans (**)   *Civil war 1921-1923*
The rifles of the IRA On the one road (**)
Wrap the green flag round me boys

1942, 1957-62
Brave Tom Williams (*) Ireland's Fight for Freedom   *Northern Campaign 1942*
Sean South of Garryowen (**) Patriot game (*)   *Border campaign 1957-62*
1969 - present
Ballad of Billy Reid (*)   *IRA volunteer shot dead by the army in 1971*
Men behind the wire (*)   *Internment of suspected republicans 1971-1975*
The helicopter song   *Helicopter escape from Mountjoy Jail Dublin, 1973*
Bring them home (*)   *Transfer of Pearse sisters from Brixton Jail 1974*
Ballad of Michael Gaughan (*)   *IRA volunteer shot dead by the army 1974*
Joe McDonnell (**) Roll of honour (**)   *Death of 10 hunger strikers in 1981*
Bobby Sands MP (*) The people's own MP,
The H Block song Farewell to Bellaghy
Only our rivers run Free The time has come
Rock on Rockall (*)   *Conflict over ownership of Rockall crag 1981*
Little armalite (**) SAM song (**)   *Glorification of IRAs acquisition of the armalite and*
        subsequently Surface to Air Missiles in the 1980s
Nineteen men a missing   *Break out from Portlaoise Jail 1974*
Loughall Martyrs (**)   *SAS shooting dead of eight IRA volunteers*
Aiden McAnespie(**)   *Shooting dead of Sinn Fein election worker 1988*
Fighting men of Crossmaglen (**) Auf wiedershehn   *Exaltation of republican Crossmaglen, S. Armagh*
Crossmaglen (*)
Pearse Jordan (*)   *Shooting dead of IRA volunteer in 1992*
The Black Watch (*)   *Denigrating the Black Watch regiment of the army*
Provo Lullaby, My old man's a provo (**)   *General songs promoting the Provisional IRA*

General, non time-specific songs
This land is our land Four green fields,   *Crude panoramic historical vista on Anglo-Irish history*
Go on home British soldiers go on home (**)
Let the people sing   (*)   *Celebration of the place of rebel music itself*
Fields of Athenry (**)   *Cruelty of British landlord in the west of Ireland*

Notes
1. *Songs in bold form part of the hero martyr genre.*
2. *Songs followed by (*) are among the more popular.*
3. *Songs followed by (**) are the most popular of all.*

Figure 6.3   Most popular rebel songs in the rebel music scene

Activists, agitators, and advocates: Irish politics in Scottish Life

Within the oral history archive five individuals stood out as demonstrating an elevated solidarity with the Irish Nationalist and Republican cause. These five activists, agitators, and advocates cannot be said to be typical or representative of all activists in Glasgow or Scotland, and they are certainly not representative of the Irish Catholic community more generally. Each has come to political consciousness at different stages in the Northern Ireland conflict, each comes at the Irish question from a different vantage point within the Irish political tradition, each has displayed different levels and forms of activism, each has ancestry from the six counties of Northern Ireland and none were first generation Irish. It is interesting to note that that the five were men. In some of the accounts it is clear that the role of mothers and grandmothers in sowing the seeds of political interest and engagement have been pivotal. That only males came forward from this constituency though does reveal something about the links which exist between masculinity and the preparedness to be interviewed on matters to do with Irish politics. Let us consider the politics of each both with respect to Irish political activism and the ways in which Irish political leanings mutate and help to inform Scottish political activism.

The Irish question and trade union activity

Interviewee 39 is third generation Irish on his mother's side (his grandfather having come from Cavan to Glasgow in the late 1880s) and second generation Irish on his father's side (his father coming from Donegal in the late 1920s). His childhood and formative years were spent in the Garngad neighbourhood in central Glasgow which, alongside Townhead and Springburn and other areas in the west of Scotland and Lanarkshire had strong involvement in the Irish political movement. He has little difficulty in tracing his strong political interests to his upbringing in the Garngad and to his wider genealogy as a descendant of Irish stock. The political culture that Interviewee 39 was reared in was cemented in the period from the turn of the century to the late 1940s and early 1950s. Of central importance were the radical influences of Irish migrants from the northern counties of Donegal, Fermanagh, Tyrone, and Cavan, who brought with them a remarkable interest in Ireland's political past and present. Of course the rise of Sinn Féin from the start of the previous century, the Easter rising in 1916, the civil war, and the establishment of the Irish Free State, played a role in further igniting the Garngad Irish. The combustible atmosphere was fuelled not only by the Irish however, but also by dispossessed Highlanders, and Lithuanian, Jewish and to a lesser extent Polish migrants all hailing from Eastern Europe and all fleeing persecution. It would find its fullest expression in the events of the Red Clydeside and the heroics of Marxist activists such as John MacLean in the period of 1914 to 1919.

Growing up in the Garngad Interviewee 39 learned not only about the sympathy the Irish Catholic community had for the Irish nationalist cause but also the ways in which this community was prepared to play an active role in the struggle for Irish self determination. Interviewee 39 recalls how his mother was very political, more so than his father. Influenced by her own father, her politics were 'socialist republican'. He recalls how his mother knew the Irish question inside out. She would be an avid reader of local newspapers which would be posted over from Ireland like the *Cavan Celt, The Monaghan Argos* and the *Derry Journal*. He remembers stories about Michael Davitt, a leader of the Irish National Land League, and his visit to Celtic FC Park to open the new football stadium in 1888. He was immersed in a culture in which Irish Labour and Socialist leaders such as Larkin and Connolly were venerated. He remembers how Irish Republican leader Éamon De Valera's comment that, 'head for head the Irish in Scotland contributed more to Ireland's struggles for independence than the Irish in America' resonated with him. At one level this support was simply financial and moral and was channelled through Sinn Féin clubs that were active in the Glasgow area. Laterally in the late 1930s and early 1940s, Fianna Fáil clubs following De Valera's establishment of Fianna Fáil in 1932 became the political movement of choice. At another level however, support was more direct. He remembers vividly stories about the 'smashing of the van', when an attempt was made in 1921 to free IRA volunteers on way to a trial in a Glasgow courtroom. He recalls tales of how safe houses were provided for prisoners on the run, including Roddy Connolly, the Irish Socialist son of James Connolly. He remembers the support given to Countess Markievicz on her various political visits to Glasgow. He recalls how stories abounded that a local family had been caught sending arms to Ireland and that one of them had been injected and infected by the British state with tuberculosis (TB) as a punishment:

> There are some families in Glasgow now that are not too keen to be reminded of their role and it was not just fundraising. There was a hall in Castle Street down in Townhead where I remember my mum talking about where they had a Sinn Féin women's section and they would organise Celidhs and fund raising events but they were also actively involved in sending armaments to Ireland. I remember one women called Mary who was arrested for smuggling guns on to the Irish boat and it was said that Mary was injected with TB by the British while she was in prison. If you look up the archives in Dublin you'll see how Sinn Féin had many sections and battalions throughout Scotland, mainly in the west of Scotland but also as far up as fife and Dundee. De Valera said in a famous speech that per head there was more help from Scotland than any other place including America. (Interviewee 39)

Of course, reflecting schisms in the broader nationalist tradition, the Irish Catholic community in the Garngad was fractious at times too. There were lots of shades of green opinion and these were sometimes expressed in heated discussions when 'Irish men would gather socially'. Two schisms proved to be particularly bitter. First friends and family fell out over the decision by the local Ancient Order of

Hibernians' banch to support British efforts during First World War. The thinking was that if Ireland helped Britain then maybe Britain might grant independence at the end of the war. For many, this position was an anathema and the natural course of action for the Irish to follow was to join forces with Glasgow socialist and republican John MacLean and his anti-war movement. Secondly, the civil war in Ireland in the early 1920s proved to generate conflict within the Irish community in the Garngad. Whilst some saw Irish Republican leader Michael Collins' decision to sign a treaty with the British that was committed to partition and which offered only Dominion Status within the British Empire as disloyal and tantamount to a 'sell out', others saw the wisdom of Collins' position of using the treaty as a stepping stone for now and condemned the folly of those who wanted to fight on.

Following the signing of the treaty in 1921, political interest in the Irish question began to wane and whilst it never fully petered out, the Irish in Garngad slowly became engrossed in domestic political issues. According to Interviewee 39, the Irish played a significant role in the early growth of the Independent Labour Party (ILP) in the west of Scotland. He identifies John Wheatley in particular as playing a significant role in bringing the Irish vote to the ILP. The Irish began to translate their fight against oppression, imperialism and exploitation to the social injustices that they and other working people were subjected to in the west of Scotland. The two world wars further bridged the gap between the Irish and indigenous Scots, and integrated the Irish further into domestic politics.

Interviewee 39 is aged 59 and now lives in a suburb on the outskirts of Glasgow. Married with a family, he works in the graphic design industry. Possessing a strong commitment to socialism in general, and deep interest in equality of opportunity and fairness in the workplace in particular, he has been active in labour politics for the greater part of his adult life. A member of the Labour Party in the past he has now joined the Scottish Socialist Party. His socialist beliefs have, however, arguably found greatest expression in his involvement in the trade union movement. Today he serves on the National Executive of one of the leading trade unions in Scotland. He views his politics as directly derivative of his Irish upbringing:

> People ask me, how did you become a socialist, what did you read?! I feel I was born the way I am just now, I wouldn't dramatise it, but I was born with a feeling for the underdog! I feel that I would like to contribute. I believe that my Irishness has been very important to me because I have read so much about the works of Connolly and Larkin and I really believe in what they say. My Irishness is an important part of my heritage and who I am. (Interviewee 39)

Interviewee 39's interest in Irish politics led him to support the Glasgow Committee of the 'Free the Birmingham Six' campaign which sought to overturn the conviction of six Irishmen in 1975 imprisoned for republican bombing of pubs in Birmingham. All six convictions were eventually declared unsafe in 1991 and overturned by the *Court of Appeal*. He expresses his disappointment that some within the Irish Catholic community who have 'made it' in Scottish and British politics have kept their 'head down' politically. Upward social, economic, and political mobility has come at a cost of concealing one's roots, biting one's tongue, or selectively manipulating one's heritage depending upon the audience. Referring firstly to a decision taken to postpone a visit by the then Irish Taoiseach Bertie Ahern to Carfin Grotto, a Catholic place of pilgrimage in Lanarkshire dedicated to the blessed virgin Mary, on the basis of fears of sectarian trouble expressed by local Catholic MP Frank Roy, Interviewee 39 provides one reading of how Irish Catholic politicians manage their roots and attitudes to Irish political questions carefully:

> I think the Carfin thing showed a kind of quite frankly Tammany Hall type politics. People would sing about Ireland into the early hours of the morning but didn't particularly want to be seen with Bertie Ahern. What an insult! Bertie Ahern is the Taoiseach of Ireland. One of them is [famous national politician] who was brought up in a mining village just a mile up the road from here. He used to travel in the bus to Celtic Park and sing 'Off to Dublin in the green' and all the rest of it, the same as everybody else. When he became a senior politician, I know he said to one of his cronies he went to Parkhead with 'Do you think it would be appropriate for me to be seen here'. My god almighty. I think it's pathetic. I don't think he'll do any favours for the republican side at all, I think he'll bend over backwards to procrastinate to the Orange men, he'll speak with a forked tongue. He is a very clever guy but he can be too clever by half. I was involved in the Birmingham Six Campaign Committee in Glasgow. It was very difficult to get members of parliament in the west of Scotland to stand up and support the Birmingham six. Maria Fyfe occasionally, George Galloway, although sometimes you don't want to have George on your side (ha ha); these were the people that we could look to. Dennis Canavan, people like that who would bring up the Irish situation. John Reid, Helen Liddell, Frank Roy? Will they ever bring up the Irish situation in Parliament? No, they don't want to know. And they are the kind of people that should be. Why not? Tony Benn, god bless him, no Irish connections whatsoever, brilliant, first class. Give them a showing up! If these people could do it, why the hell do they have to be so silent? (Interviewee 39)

The Irish question and anti-fascism and anti-racism activism

Intervieweee 33, aged 19, is a student, and lives in an affluent suburb at the edge of city of Glasgow. Although he could not specify dates, Interviewee 33 referred to himself as second generation Irish on his mother's side (Donegal), and third generation on his father's side (Antrim). Reflecting upon his childhood, he concedes that his interest in Irish politics cannot be attributed to his parents or an especially politicised upbringing. Indeed, if anything his parents exercised a very cautious approach to displaying their Irishness. His journey to activism then is best characterised as a personal awakening of political consciousness through self education. Visits to Celtic Football Club led him to question why some supporters were singing songs like the 'Boys of the Old Brigade'. His questioning led him to take an interest in Irish Republicanism and he began buying the newspaper *Republican News*, which was on sale outside of Celtic FC Park after home matches. This in turn led him to join the Edinburgh-based James Connolly Society, a Society dedicated to the promotion of the Republican and Socialist ideals of James Connolly, a Scots-born leader of the Easter 1916 rebellion in Dublin. He now attends meetings of the Society once a month, visits the James Connolly book shop in Edinburgh regularly, and helps steward the annual James Connolly March which takes to the streets of Edinburgh every Spring. Moreover, he also writes for a number of Celtic Fanzines and helps sell republican publications.

Interviewee 33 describes his interests as republican and socialist and professes a hatred for racism and fascism and a deep opposition to the British National Party (BNP). As a socialist republican he is active in confronting and contesting bigotry, fascism and racism within contemporary Scotland. Against those who allege that anti-Irish and anti-Catholic sentiment peaked in the 1930s and is in the wane in Scotland, Interviewee 33 observes an upsurge in bigotry in recent years:

> It's getting worse here I think, definitely. To my memory, I can't remember Celtic fans having their throats slashed fifteen years ago. There's a church in Bridgeton where the priest has been threatened. He's had excrement put through his door; UDA sprayed over the walls. Churches in Rutherglen and Cambuslang have had 'UVF' and 'Fuck the Pope' sprayed on them, the plants and that ripped up. People feel threatened going into church. There's gangs of people hanging outside the churches sometimes. So in my view it's getting worse. Saying that I've heard that in the seventies, the Ancient Order of Hibernians (AOH) had to go out and protect people going in to church in Dennistoun, because people were threatened. I don't think that's still happening in this day but it could happen because people still hold these views. I consider myself an Irish Republican but I would never go to the Church of Scotland and threaten people going in to it. A few years ago when Rangers lost the cup final to Hearts, we were going to church on a Saturday night and a car went past and a boy hung out and shouted 'Fenian scum'. What can you do about that? He was driving past in a car. He's just a thug. I don't know anybody who would do that, pass a church and shout 'Orange scum' or something or spray paint 'IRA' on a church wall. In the media it's portrayed as 'Celtic fans are as bad as Rangers fans' but I think the facts prove otherwise. Celtic fans come out the games getting stabbed and murdered. Thirty eight reported assaults in Bridgeton in 1997. Celtic fans don't do that. The police don't do anything about it. (Interviewee 33)

Alongside bigotry resides the equal cancer of fascism and racism. Recognising that Far Right groups are actively repositioning themselves and securing greater credibility and electoral success, Interviewee 33 argues that anti-fascist and anti-racist groups like the James Connolly Society need to be alive to the needs of working-class communities in Glasgow. It is for this reason that he sees a natural progression from republicanism, to anti-fascism, anti-racism, and finally to grass roots neighbourhood politics:

> The James Connolly Society had a stall at the Festival for the Edinburgh Asian Community promoting anti racism and Republicanism. The Connolly Society are saying, we are totally against racism and the Asian community are saying well these people can help us in some way. In Glasgow, Anti Fascist Action drove the BNP off the streets. The BNP or the National Front, if they tried to hold a newspaper sale they would basically attack them and they would never sell a paper there again. But the BNP have just gone now to safer streets and are establishing new non violent community politics now. They're getting some electoral success. There needs to be an alternative to them, a left- wing alternative. That's why Republicans are trying to get involved in community politics. The Socialist Workers Party, I believe it's caught up in an outdated Marxism. It's not doing anything in the community. It's not going out there and appealing to working-class people. The National Front have opened up a branch in Paisley on the back of leafleting doors and asking people what is affecting them. It's holding newspaper sales and it's working for them. You cannae just let it go, you need to do something about it. So yesterday for example, we went to the 'Gorbal's Against the Gorbals Housing Sell Off' protest. We helped them leaflet at that. The Council were sending a bus around to sell the idea of council house stock transfer and we boarded it and occupied it for two hours. A couple of papers turned up. So we try to get involved in politics at a local scale. (Interviewee 33)

Interviewee 33 feels his politics is not reflected in any of the mainstream political parties in contemporary Scotland. He finds it difficult to see in Scottish nationalism and the Scottish Left a political position which is faithful to Connolly's socialism and his own anti-fascist and anti-racist commitments:

> I don't see any party that really supports me. Even Tommy Sheridan's party. They are the only left-wing party that don't support a United Ireland. I support an Independent Scotland but I don't really support the SNP. Their policies just don't do anything for me. I remember reading somewhere that in the 1970s, two SNP politicians went round the doors saying don't vote for Labour, he's a fenian bastard. The other went to a different place and said don't vote for Labour, he's an Orange bastard. (Interviewee 33)

Whilst republican beliefs can often be inculcated in the home, it is equally true that family networks also operate to stifle, tame, and control siblings' political interests. Interviewee 33 notes his own parents concern about his involvement in the James Connolly Society:

My mum knows I'm involved in it and she worries about me. She doesn't really want me to get involved in it, she would prefer it if I stayed clear. She says, they're all murderers. She knows I go to marches and I steward marches and she just says, take care of yourself and play your cards close to your chest. When you are ever in company never let anybody know who you are and what you do. (Interviewee 33)

Being young and relatively unknown to loyalist and far right groups, Interviewee 33 does not feel under any particular personal threat at present. But he does not underestimate the opposition which his political views might attract. He acknowledges that the British state films James Connolly marches and probably has agents among the crowd taking notes, photographs and names. One member was alleged to have been followed home from the James Connolly book store in Edinburgh to his house in Livingston:

His door was 'kicked down', and he was confronted with the people who told him they were from the Drug Squad. He said 'I'm not a drug dealer' at which point the agents said we know, just tell us all you know about the leadership of the James Connolly movement and about the people who come over from Ireland for the Celtic games. They offered him £15,000 to help him buy a taxi in return for information and when he refused they threatened him by saying that he lived in a known loyalist area and they might let it be known that a republican sympathiser was in their midst. (Interviewee 33)

The Irish question, Friendly Societies, and the defence of the right to march

Interviewee 57, aged 45, is a taxi driver and lives in one of Glasgow's inner city neighbourhoods. He identifies himself as fourth generation Irish on his paternal side with his great grandfather hailing from Fermanagh. Interviewee 57 finds it difficult to trace his interest in Irish politics to his upbringing. Indeed, having fought in the Second World War he reflects that his father would have had no problem identifying himself as British. He instead recalls how he became smitten with flute bands following Celtic's 1967 European Cup final win over Inter Milan when is father took him to Celtic Park to see the Coatbridge Shamrock Accordian band who were playing at the celebrations. His interest was further ignited when at the age of 15 he began buying the *Irish Weekly* newspaper which was on sale at the back of his local chapel. As his interest germinated he joined the Ancient Order of Hibernians, where he has been a member for the past 32 years.

Although its origins can be traced to the *Ribbonmen* of the eighteenth and nineteenth centuries, who sought to resist Britain's colonial subjugation of Ireland, the Ancient Order of Hibernians (AOB) is normally thought to have been formed in 1838. The aim of the organisation is to protect the interests of Roman Catholics and to defend and foster the Catholic faith. The AOB in Scotland has an established tradition of marching and these marches have become known for their bands, banners, and the colourful green sashes. In Scotland, around four marches are held each year, the principal ones being held on St Patrick's day (17 March) and around St John's day (the last Saturday in June). The heyday of the AOB came at the start of the twentieth century when it took on the role of Friendly Society as well as providing political support for nationalist movements back in Ireland. With the establishment of the Irish Free State in 1922 and the introduction of the National Insurance Act in 1947, the rationale for the organisation has been eroded and its membership base now comprises only several hundred.

Interviewee 57 recalls the early 1980s when the Hunger Strikes in the H Block Maze prison generated a renewed interest in Irish politics amongst the Irish Catholic community in Scotland. He describes himself as very bitter about the deaths of the ten republican hunger strikers who lost their lives protesting about their treatment as criminals and not political prisoners. At the time, fearing public disturbance, the Glasgow City Council and Strathclyde Police decided to ban all marches in the city, including several which sought to pay tribute to the humanity of the Hunger Strikers. He describes how he and several others made representations on more than one occasion to the Chief Constable and the Chief Constable's secretary to allow the marches to take place. He remembers the period as being particularly 'wild', with reports of the establishment of Glasgow loyalist organisations who, at the time of the papal visit in 1981, threatened to 'kick Catholics and Irish Republicans off the streets of Glasgow'. It wasn't until late 1982/83 that the first remembrance marches were eventually allowed:

> I'll tell you this the now. There was a number of 'H Block' marches, hunger strike marches, when Bobby Sands and the others died. At the actual time of the hunger strike regarding protest marches, the city fathers in their wisdom here put a blanket ban regarding protest marches. They done it for six months and then kept renewing it. So the actual first protest marches, really if you look at the aftermath of it, was actually about a year later, 1982/83, when they actually organised a remembrance, because folk were dead by that time. I was one of the people who went to the Chief Constable, or the Chief Constable's secretary, me along with other people went to visit. We went on a couple of occasions over the next couple of years because I felt strongly. I felt quite bitter. I even feel bitter today about that whole thing. I felt like the republican movement should have, when Bobby Sands won Fermanagh South Tyrone as an MP, they should have called it off. I don't think they should have carried it on and I am bitter regarding the British Government who should really have said, 'hold on a minute we realise you aren't criminals. We want to do a deal here'. I think that was done in the background. It was never made public.
>
> They didn't ban Orange Walks. The position regarding Orange Walks was that Orange Walks were traditional and they weren't political, which to be fair, there was actually a bit of truth in that. The slight problem there was they also banned, when they banned the H Block marches, they banned everybody else. They didn't unwind it if by chance you were hospital workers. It was a

complete blanket ban. It was a wee bit annoying when you realised that a lot of these folk, Labour councillors, were of Irish background. But I think along with them and the police that they panicked. My memory of the time or when I read about the Renfrew Fair it was pretty wild. We also knew the Loyalists and people fighting against us. There was a group set up called the Glasgow Loyalists and their idea was, roughly at the same time was the papal visit to Scotland, they said they were 'gonna kick Catholics and Irish Republicans off the streets of Glasgow'. I can assure you there were plenty of us who thought well if we ever get the chance we're gonna have a good go at you. We aren't Jews here in the 1930s going to bow our heads. We're gonna target youse and we did and we got to know a lot of them and they backed off when they faced opposition. You organise your troops together and they'll run just as bloody quick. And what was quite interesting at the time, the Orange Order, the official Orange Order leadership didn't want anything to do with the Scottish Loyalists and they backed right off them. (Interviewee 57)

Irish politics and liberal reform of the welfare state

Interviewee 50 is aged 47 and lives in a new private housing estate at the edge of one of Glasgow's peripheral council housing estates. He works as a social worker and identifies himself as third generation Irish on his paternal side, his grandfather coming to Scotland in the early 1900s from Monaghan. He recalls how his interest in Irish politics was first ignited by his grandmother and his father. Whilst both felt inhibited to talk about Irish issues when sober, alcohol lifted the lid on their true feelings. Etched into Interviewee 50's memory are the purple faces of both as they sat round a large brass fire hearth singing songs of rebellion which revealed a profound and deep seated bitterness:

> There were two stools around the fireside hearth and a big brass fireguard. My granny used to sit me on one of the stools and when she had a couple of whiskeys she would sing Irish ballads to me. I don't recall what the songs were but I remember her getting very purple and realising that there was something more there. My father was always very diplomatic until the whiskey kicked in and then it would come out. It would come out with such a venom force that I used to start finding it hard to comprehend and I always linked it back to my granny. I could see the same purple face. My father used to say it's natural for you to be like that. It's in your blood. But can it be natural if it's against the law? He said, 'fuck them'. But on the other hand, when the drink wears off he's going, 'you can'nae behave like that'. I said 'but you told me. You told me not to let they bastards …' (Interviewee 50).

Interviewee 50 also was heavily influenced by his aunt. At a young age she had gone on quite an adventure to Bulgaria to teach English to Russian students stationed there, but had returned to Glasgow at the time of the Red Clydeside movement in the period 1914–19. She spoke proudly of the work of the Glasgow socialist leader John MacLean and had strong Marxist tendencies. She was a member of the Communist Party. Fuelled by these influences he recognised himself to have an especially critical and enquiring mind:

> When I was in my teens, I started to develop a very questioning mind. I would question everything, on our side as well as theirs. I couldn't understand the blessed trinity for example, and I would challenge that. I would be saying, but how can there be three? It was a mystery. It wasn't meant to be understood. It was meant to be believed or not believed. So, I was a very confused youngster going into adolescence. I was developing trains of thought that no one was able to provide good answers to. (Interviewee 50)

By the early 1970s, he found himself pulled strongly to the Irish cause and was greatly influenced by a biography of James Connolly written by his daughter Nora. In 1981 he became very politicised by the hunger strikes. He recalls the 'powerful feeling of human and social injustice' that overwhelmed him at the time, and the sense that Margaret Thatcher should be tried for war crimes. It is clear by his own admission that he was not a serious 'player' and was more of a rebellious young man. But in the climate of the 1970s this was sufficient to warrant excessive attention by the state, which included being arrested and jailed on 'spurious' breach of the peace charges, having his house searched, and being 'quietly' advised that he should not travel to Ireland:

> In the late sixties and early seventies I found that I was becoming very, very pulled to the cause or the fight. I found myself selling Irish newspapers in a Celtic bar and I found Special Branch had put a tail on me. Obviously I was still a small minnow but I could still be potentially dangerous if I'm disseminating information. And there was a kind of shot over the bow, when I was arrested a couple of times at football games for Breach of the Peace, which was a total and utter nonsense. I never done a single thing that day but I got arrested out of seventy five thousand people and they just walked up and jailed me. I was sent to prison on a number of occasions after that. Obviously for very short sentences, but I was classified as a hooligan by the court system. There was one occasion when I refused to recognise the authority of the court. I got an extra thirty days on top for that. I was desperate to be political but I didn't know how to do it. So on one hand my behaviour was perceived as deviant to the Crown and on the other had there was certainly victimisation against myself from a police force that, at that time, I would have described as predominantly Protestant. (Interviewee 50)

On the brink of being persuaded to become more active in the Irish Republican movement, Interviewee 50 made a decision to channel his energies more peaceably and to venture down the path of education and politics instead. He successfully secured a qualification, became a trained social worker and, began to read seriously about both sides of the Irish conflict. He also embarked on a social policy course run by the Open University. He has taken part in activism which has changed the parole system in Scotland, and has appeared in public debates and in films and documentaries about reforms in the criminal justice system in Scotland and mental health problems in Scottish prisons. Whilst he continues to feel some anger and resentment over contemporary politics in Northern Ireland, he now recognises that education and learning techniques to control and better express oneself is 'the way to go'. It will only be through education that young Scots with republican sympathies coming through the ranks today will get the leadership and direction they need. They might productively harness this energy in concrete ways, not least by speaking up for voices normally lost in the welfare state and criminal justice system:

> What partly helped me to put things into a different context was education. I did take time out to read about Irish history from both perspectives. I also went on to do social work which forced me, well I chose to, adopt a position of objectivity. You are sworn into a code of ethics which I have honoured. I would never discriminate against anyone. I gave a commitment to serve everyone equally no matter what their colour, creed, religion, or political background. That kind of eased me a bit. Instead of going out and saying give me a sub machine gun and we'll fucking go out and I'll Kamakaze myself up, and right into parliament, I started to say if we are going to change the system maybe we can do it from within. The need to scream and shout and bawl was not to the same degree. (Interviewee 50)

Interviewee 50 has little appetite for Scottish National Politics and continues to see a huge gap between Irish nationalism and its Scottish variant: 'people who fail to see this difference worry me'. There is a superficial affinity with Scottish nationalism and an instinctive and patriotic level, 'the logic is that we will vote for the SNP because we want to fuck England at Wembley'. But probe deeper and the concept is too fractious to be taken seriously:

> The more I read and the more I see, it's just not there. Scotland is sitting in an entirely different situation from Ireland. Half of Scotland want to live in a free Irish Republic, and the other half want to swear allegiance to the crown and fly the Union Jack forever. Especially if the vote went on the basis of proportional representation you would not get a clear agreement on what Scottish people really want because there is no clear majority. In Ireland it was clear that the majority wanted independence. (Interviewee 50)

The Irish question, Scottish Nationalism and pan Celticism

Aged 36, a graduate, and a manager in a Glasgow business centre, Interviewee 34 lives in one of Glasgow's more affluent suburbs. With his mother migrating to Scotland from Fermanagh in the early 1930s, and his father arriving from Donegal in the late 1940s, he is second generation Irish on both his maternal and paternal sides. Interviewee 34 began by reflecting upon the extent to which his level of politicisation could in part be attributed to the influence of his mother, who had 'very strong views on Britain's involvement in Ireland'. As he entered his teenage years, he recalls being acutely aware of his mother's feelings about the challenges Irish Catholics faced in the North of Ireland after sixty years of home or Stormont rule. He remembers her particularly hostility to the B-Specials, an armed part-time group within the Royal Ulster Constabulary, which she characterised an 'armed militia who lorded it over the nationalists'. He remembers his mother buying the *Irish Weekly* and *Ulster Examiner* from the back desk of his local chapel, and has vivid memories of the quiet that descended over the house when RTE radio news bulletins were broadcast.

Whilst these maternal influences were fortified when a cousin in Northern Ireland was interned for participating in civil rights marches in the early 1970s, it was the anger that surrounded the IRA Hunger Strike in the early 1980s that propelled him to action. He recalls how the death of ten of the hunger strikers served as a seminal moment for many Irish Catholics in Scotland and ignited and reinvigorated interest in the republican movement and the plight of Catholics in the North. It was around this time that he got involved in what he referred to as Irish solidarity work. This work saw him join a range of Glasgow-based Irish republican organisations including Sinn Féin. From the outset, Interviewee 34 made a conscious decision that he was not going to get involved in anything illegal. Describing himself as a political activist, his work was confined to promoting flute bands and marches, selling papers, and getting involved in demonstrations. But he recognises his actions were not typical:

> Many folk come from a Glasgow Irish tradition but they don't articulate it. There was very few who would opt to be involved in a political organisation, very few. Most of them were Celtic supporters who supported the Wolf Tones. Even if you spent time with them and tried to educate them or politicise them, it didn't work. To me republicanism had nothing to do with any of that. Most of them were very young and it was just a kind of sub-culture for them in a way because there was no strong interest in the history. But I started reading early on, and then when I started reading I wanted to be involved politically and that's why I done it. But I'd say that there's very few who actually did it that way. There's very few that were active in the period when I was involved, the early eighties, that would still be that interested now. I meet people that are embarrassed to admit that they were politically conscious then, they just moved on to other things. It was just a passing thing, as I say it wasn't a conscious thing. (Interviewee 34)

Whilst largely unaware of it at the beginning, Interviewee 34 has now come to view his politics as part of the historical ebb and flow of Irish nationalism in the Irish diaspora. He notes that John Denver wrote a book in the 1890s about the Irish in Britain which described the Irish in Scotland as being the most loyal and committed of all the Irish. He further pointed out that records show that at this time, some 50 young Scotsmen fought alongside Pearse and Connolly in the GPO in 1916, that Sinn Féin boasted over 95 branches in Glasgow and that there existed a Scottish Brigade of the IRA which had 2,500 volunteers. Moreover, he roots his biography back to the radical, socialist, and anti-imperialist politics of the Red Clydeside period. He describes his political commitments as socialist, republican and anti imperialist and very much in tune with the Red Clydesiders:

> the essence of republicanism is that it has to be revolutionary. It's about social as well as political change. It's not about courting the establishment or getting into bed with corporate America or becoming part of the corporate state and aligning oneself with multinationals and the property classes. For me republicanism is about ordinary people. And even if you get a United Ireland tomorrow it certainly wouldn't be socialist. For me the struggle continues until you get a Socialist Republic. (Interviewee 34)

Whilst Interviewee 34's mother was very politicised and offered encouragement and support, his father was less enthused. Coming from Donegal, he had had less exposure to British rule in the North of Ireland and had come from a Fine Gael family (the main moderate pro-treaty political party in the Irish Republic). He also had little sentimentality towards Ireland, believing it to be a harsh country that offered little potential for advancement. Interviewee 34 recalls how his father opposed his involvement in politics and how his involvement caused conflict within the house as he grew up. This hostility reached a number of flashpoints, for example when his father brought the police to his house saying that he was an IRA supporter or when he got into trouble at school for selling republican newspapers:

> My father was quite down on the Republican movement. It caused conflict with me when I was growing up. My father thinks that you should keep your head down. Don't rock the boat, don't show your views because all it can do is bring trouble to you and hardship. Just get on with it. That was his outlook. My parents had arguments about me being involved. My father was very hostile to me being active. He brought the police to the house one time. He said I was an IRA supporter. The police were very hostile to me as you can imagine. Now I was only fifteen. My mother stood up for me. I got into trouble at school as well because I was selling republican newspapers at the school, and my mum was called up to the school to discuss it and my mother defended me. Basically they couldn't really say anything. But my father was totally hostile to that. (Interviewee 34)

Interviewee 34's conflict with his father however was not the end of his troubles:

> The Irish community was always a suspect community as far as the British state was concerned and Irish people were monitored, especially if they had any known political views or opinions. Certainly I've got experience of that, and there was always the fear that if you were outspoken that could get you into trouble. I had experience of both the Special Branch and MI5. I'm sure the telephone is tapped, but that is par for the course, you would expect that unfortunately. I found that every single time I went to Ireland, whether it was for political purposes or not, I was constantly questioned on the way back. There was never a time when I came back and it didn't happen. I felt it was extremely intrusive because I'm quite sure that they knew that I was never involved in anything illegal, but what they were doing was just a trawling exercise to find out who was involved and to assess the political opinions of those who were involved. I would describe that as harassment or intimidation, because they never ever asked any questions about illegal activity anyway. And of course that would have an impact because there would be people who would be too frightened or reluctant to get involved, in what should be legitimate political activity by a community, simply because they feared for their family or their employment. However, my fear would be from the loyalists more than the state, because the loyalists have shown in the past when they blew up various Irish pubs in Glasgow, that they've got a quite a strong network of support, especially in the west of Scotland. They have threatened and intimidated people who couldn't simply be described as IRA supporters, but just people who are Catholics or Celtic supporters. I'd say that they would be more of a physical threat than the state would be. (Interviewee 34)

These difficulties have generated an intense and painful emotional reaction and managing his anger has become an important part of Interviewee 34's life. Whilst many might have succumbed to the pressure to conform, he attributes his ability to cope with opposition to his confidence in the rightness of his position and the sense of deep community his involvement has brought:

> I go on because I have a conviction and a confidence in my belief that the republican argument is right. It's just and it's inclusive. It's just a deep held belief of the rightness of my argument. And I feel confident about it in a way that I don't feel confident about other areas of my life. I've always had that strong passionate belief in it, and that's impelled me to act. Looking back I've no regrets because it was an ideal I felt passionate about and I felt I was doing something worthwhile. You couldn't have met finer people, and the comradeship that you get from working with others who carry the same convictions is something that, to me, is priceless. I know of other people in the city who are veteran republicans. Some joined the movement in the 1930s and they still have the exact same convictions they had then. They don't have wealth in any material

sense but they have that satisfaction. You couldn't have met finer people and the comradeship is something which to me is priceless. (Interviewee 34)

Today, Interviewee 34 is a supporter of the ongoing peace process. He describes the armed struggle as a 'tactic that's been tried and failed' and that people are 'war weary and tired'. Republicanism is undergoing a change he stresses. Indeed, with the advent of the peace process he has observed a general dwindling of Irish political activity and considers flute bands to be among the last main remnants. There is not the same pressing need for activism today therefore. He remains passionate about Irish issues and continues to be committed to the republican cause in Northern Ireland. Moreover he continues to organise Irish marches and commemorations in the west of Scotland. But he has also turned his attention to domestic Scottish politics and is an exponent of what he refers to as pan-Celticism, more specifically the Celtic League, an ant-imperialist organisation. From this vantage point, and seeking to transcend the complicated relationship Irish Catholics have with Scottish independence, he has become an active supporter of the Scottish National Party:

I live in Scotland and I passionately support Scottish independence. I see the Irish struggle and the struggle of all the Celtic peoples as being one and the same. So one of the frustrations for me is that the Irish in Scotland have that kind of lukewarm attitude to Scottish nationalism. I think that the Irish in Scotland should be at the forefront in supporting Scottish nationalism. Not simply because it would advance a United Ireland by helping to bring about the break up of the United Kingdom. But it should be a natural empathy with what are essentially one people who have been falsely divided by an artificial history that has been created for them by an imperialist policy.

Why are the Irish so ambivalent? I think it's quite complicated. Compton McKenzie said, 'why should the Irish feel passionate about Scottish nationalism when very few Scots feel that strongly about it'. That certainly was the case in the past. The SNP was only founded in 1934 and didn't get its first seat till 1945. And it's also the case that in the 1920s and 1930s Scottish nationalism was perceived as being anti Irish or at least there was an anti-Irish strain to it. There were people like Dr Andrew Gibb who felt that the Irish coming to Scotland was a menace which undermined Presbyterian moral standards and threatened Scottish workers' employment. But having said that there was always Scottish nationalists who were pro Irish even at that time.

In the present situation it suits the Labour Party to present the concept of an Independent Scotland as a new Stormont or an old Stormont rather, whilst on the other hand there telling Unionists Home rule would be Rome rule. That's disgraceful. Catholics and people with an Irish background have nothing to fear from the concept of an independent Scotland and I'm glad to see more Irish Catholics are joining the SNP.

So, I'm a member of the Celtic League. It was founded in the 1960s and it promotes friendship, and it encourages an alliance between the six Celtic nations through an exchange of information about the various struggles that are taking place be they political, economic, or cultural. And as a body they support the struggles in any given country. It is a non violent organisation and although quite small has quite a bit of respect. I would also add that the Irish Republican movement has always supported the concept of Celtic unity which is quite a progressive position to hold. (Interviewee 34)

Conclusion

It is clear that Irish political history continues to interest the Irish catholic community in Scotland and is 'present' in and through this community in conscious and unconscious, explicit and implicit, and direct and indirect ways. The civil rights movement in the north and the politics of the troubles has evidently reignited a certain interest in Irish patriotism, and the death of ten republican hungers strikers in the early 1980s was evidently a seminal moment which prompted some to become activists, agitators and advocates for the cause of Irish unification. But in no sense are the constituencies under observation here representative of attitudes within the Irish Catholic community more generally. In fact, in spite of the widespread empathy with nationalist and republican historical understandings, other participants displayed an equally widespread diversity of views as to how the current troubles in Northern Ireland ought to, and will, work themselves through. There remained a strong constituency who believed that the only 'logical' outcome of the troubles was the establishment of a united Ireland. But others suggested that they no longer had any interest in the Northern Ireland situation and had become wearied with the conflict to the point of no longer caring about its outcome. Interestingly a group of participants noted that growth of the European Union had substantially reshaped the terms of reference of the conflict and maybe inadvertently had displaced its relevance. Many participants suggested that the only practical way to secure peace in Ireland was through the principle of power sharing irrespective of electoral strength.

It is also clear that Irish nationalism's republican, anti-imperialist and socialist heritage has also colorated and conditioned the contributions which the Irish Catholic community has made to Scottish political life. The Irish Catholic community has fortified left-leaning political, economic, social, and cultural organisations, institutions and parties and consolidated indigenous movements which have supported a range of progressive policies and agitated for social justice for the poor, marginalised, and dispossessed. Repeated references to Connolly, Larkin, MacLean and Wheatley press home the importance of the early twentieth-century Irish and Scottish Left politics in the long term formation of the political consciousness of the Irish Catholic community in Scotland. But Irish nationalism has sponsored a range of mutant Scottish movements and interventions and has journeyed in many different directions. Perhaps the biggest cleavage to have emerged is around the question of Scottish independence from the British Union. It is clear that whilst the Irish Catholic community has historically feared Scottish independence, especially in so far as an independent parliament might promote hostile attitudes to Catholic Schools and their funding, many are now prepared to countenance voting for the Scottish Nationalist Party. We now exist in a moment when those whose politics were formed around Ireland's long and turbulent struggle with Britain on the one hand, and the working class struggles which defined the history of the Clydeside on the other, are coming to regard the Scottish Nationalist Party as a natural heir for their aspirations. But the Irish connection with the Labour Party is long and deep and any transition to Scottish Nationalist Politics will likely remain a fraught one.

Chapter 7
Ways of Life and the Life of Ways: Culture, Faith and Family

Introduction

Whether it be through music, football, flute bands, dance, poetry, folklore, language, St Patrick's day celebrations, cooking, place and people naming, religion, family life or kin networks, the Irish Catholic community in Scotland has often rendered itself visible and distinctive as a consequence of its cultural practices. Although sometimes welcomed, courted and celebrated by Scottish society, some of these cultural practices have attracted an unwarranted amount of critical scrutiny. It is perhaps with respect to religion that cultural alterity has been at its greatest. Irish migration brought to Scotland in particular a fresh injection of Roman Catholicism and it is arguably the case that some Scottish constituencies who revere Protestantism as central to Scottish and British national identity have never been able to accommodate this cultural intrusion. Much of the debate over sectarianism and bigotry in Scottish society pivots around the question of indigenous hostility and intolerance towards Roman Catholicism. And it is arguably with regard to the question of denominational schooling, and in particular the virtues and vices of Catholic Schools and their educational and hiring practices, that the debate over Scotland's shame has drawn its energy.

The purpose of this chapter is to examine the Irish Catholic ways of life in Scotland. I intend to show that whilst markers of difference rooted in cultural practices have been of critical importance, the transplantation of Irish ways of life into Scotland has never been a straightforward process and has always been mediated by Scottish social and cultural life. I begin with an outline of the ways in which faith and family, music, language and football, continue to be seen as important badges of Irish Catholic identity. With a view to examining how cultural alterity is experienced, confronted, and at times transcended, attention is then given to the biographical accounts offered by six particular interviewees, organised in a continuum to reflect their degree of estrangement from and belonging to Scottish culture. The remainder of the chapter then focuses upon two central themes which mark the cultural life of the Irish Catholic community; secularism and the demise of Catholic piety and the changing status and structures of the Catholic family. My intention is to explore intergenerational transformations in investment in Irish Catholic cultural practices within the Irish Catholic community in Scotland.

Cultural markers of difference

Within the interviews a number of cultural markers of difference associated with the Irish Catholic community in Scotland were identified. For the greater majority of interviewees, the Roman Catholicism of their forebears, and the attitudes to family and kin which emanate in part from a Catholic outlook, were of critical importance for first generation settlers. Piety and reverence to the faith and for the priest were for the most part absolute. The nightly family rosary recited under either a picture of the blessed mother or of the sacred heart was a routine part of life. The regular visit from the priest to the family home was a significant moment demanding preparation, cleanliness, the best attire, the finest cooking, and impeccable behaviour and manners. Attendance at mass, stations of the cross, and confessions were a routine part of life. The rearing of good, and sometimes large families, was a pre-eminent value cherished by the Catholic Church. Families were best incubated within stable marriages and sex before marriage, cohabitation, and divorce were frowned upon. Loving and supporting brothers and sisters, mothers and fathers, grandmas and granddads, as well as cousins and extended families, was a celebrated virtue. The behaviour of children was taken to reflect upon their family and their faith and moral fortitude and righteous behaviour brought communal pride and validation. Irish family life was an important barometer of the standing of the Irish Catholic community.

For Interviewees 63a–c Irish traditional dance and Irish traditional music were also important cultural practices. In sending their own children and nieces and nephews to music and dance lessons these interviewees were in an important way affirming their love for their father, 'a Donegal man'. Likewise for Interviewee 41, the sublime joy of music, and in particular fiddle playing and singing, brought to his family home by his father, stimulated a desire to hand down Irish music to his own family. He regularly attends informal 'sessions' in the Victoria Bar in Glasgow and more formally participates in Comhaltas Ceoltóirí Éireann. For Interviewee 52, the Celidh bands and traditional church hall dances, held in places like the Claddah Club and the Donegal Club figured prominently in his 'courting years'. He recalls standing for the Irish National Anthem at the end of each evening. Meanwhile for Interviewee 57 the street marching music of the Ancient Order of Hibernians' flute bands was pivotal and captivating.

Membership of and participation in Comhaltas Ceoltóirí Éireann was a feature of many of the interviews. Established in Mullingar in 1951 to defend and promote Irish traditional music from secular trends, Comhaltas Ceoltóirí Éireann now boasts over 400 branches worldwide. The Scottish branch of Comhaltas Ceoltóirí Éireann, the *Irish Minstrels*, the first overseas branch to be created, was given life in Glasgow in 1957 by local legends Jimmy McHugh, Pat McNulty and Owen Kelly. Three other branches of Comhaltas currently operate in Scotland, namely the St. James the Great Branch in Pollok, the Johnny Doherty in Holytown and St Patrick's in Coatbridge. Likewise, the involvement of siblings in Irish traditional dance schools was mentioned in many interviews. Among Glasgow's most popular dance schools were the McLaughlin School of Irish Dancing, the John McKenna School of Irish Dancing, the O'Connor School of Irish Dancing, the Maguire School of Irish Dancing, and the Erin Go Bragh Irish Dancing School.

Described by Interviewee 33 as 'probably the world's greatest Irish sporting institution', a greater defender of the Irish cause than the Boston Celtics', and 'probably *the* monument to Irish Migrants in Scotland', Celtic Football Club has come to serve as a metaphor for the growing confidence of the Irish, their concern with charity and the plight of the poor, the socio-economic advancement which they have achieved, and their anti sectarian and inclusive beliefs. Celtic FC were officially instituted in November 1887 by a Marist Priest, Brother Walfrid, in St Mary's Church Hall in Calton in the East End of Glasgow. Himself a migrant from Sligo, Brother Walfrid's ambition was to use the football club to generate income to alleviate the poverty which pervaded parishes in the East End. Amidst its glittering history, the Club's fairy tale victory over the mighty Inter-Milan in the European Cup final on 25 May 1967 remains its most pivotal moment. Managed by the revered Jock Stein, a Protestant from an Orange background in Lanarkshire, Celtic FC became the first British Club to win the European Cup. If any one event was to confirm that the Irish 'had arrived' and were 'now a force to be reckoned with', this was to be it. Team selection at Celtic was based upon meritocracy and Celtic was a brand that attracted, welcomed, and nurtured people of all creeds and colour.

The use of the Irish Gaelic language among settlers and their families has been limited. Nevertheless speaking and writing in Irish remains a cherished skill set for some; a means of establishing and underscoring the importance of having an Irish Catholic heritage. Interviewee 17 grew up in a Glasgow household where, in spite of displaying a strong interest in their Irish Catholic roots, adults in the house never spoke a word of Irish. She married a man from north-west Donegal whose first language was Irish Gaelic and fell in love with the language. During visits to his family home in Donegal she became aware of her lack of linguistic competence. There have existed classes teaching Irish Gaelic in Glasgow for over a century and interviewee 17 and her daughter decided to join one class in Charing Cross in Glasgow. She became competent and then somewhat expert and was able to understand the nuances of the language, including provincial variations in its annunciation. Although there are thousands of native speakers in Glasgow very few of them offer to become teachers and at a time of shortages Interviewee 17 was asked to lead a class. She has taught Irish classes to adult learners ever since. She notes the continuing and indeed revived interest in the language shown by some, and identifies cultural and political motives among learners.

Encounters with cultural estrangement

Markers of identity such as these emerged as a source of alterity for many interviewees. This section will examine the ways in which such alterity has been rationalised and managed. The testimonies provided by six individuals will be drawn upon to reveal the continuum of responses which exist, from outright cultural estrangement to the negotiation of difference and the search for a new sense of belonging. I begin with an examination of two individuals who have internalised a sense of profound cultural alterity with devastating consequences. I then examine the moving story of a woman who never felt quite at peace with Scottish culture and who embarked on a quest to find her roots and 'find out who she was deep down', a journey that led her to rediscover and reconcile her sense of being other. Next I consider the case of two interviewees who in their own ways have managed to put cultural differences into perspective; in the first instance through genealogy and the muddying of assumed pristine biographical and racialised biographies and secondly, through recognising everyday shared experiences as productive of a common sense humanity. Finally, the testimony of an informed participant employed by the Catholic Church to co-ordinate social supports for disadvantaged groups in the west of Scotland is examined. Here can be seen an interesting account of the historical emergence of the Catholic Church in Scotland and its steady engagement in Christian ecumenical reflection and practice.

Experiencing cultural alterity with devastating consequences

Health inequalities between Irish migrants and host communities have been recorded in many cities and regions of destination. The aetiology of these inequalities is surely complex and is related to poverty itself, differential access to and use of health care infrastructures, diet and lifestyle, and the psycho-social impacts of migration and resettlement. For some Irish Catholics in Scotland cultural alterity has indeed been internalised with devastating health consequences and on occasions life-threatening health consequences. The importance of cultural alterity as a psycho social mediator of health emerged as central in the stories of two men. Each has faced a lifelong battle with alcoholism, a battle which they happily appear to be winning. Whilst both recognised the complex roots of alcoholism, each argued that profound feelings of being marginalised as a result of having an Irish inheritance lay at the core of their difficulties. Indeed, each felt compelled to participate in the research because they sensed that this was an important story that needed to be aired.

Now retired, Interviewee 37 is aged 55 and lives in an affluent suburb on the periphery of Glasgow. He is second generation Irish with both parents coming to Glasgow from Donegal in the 1920s. He started the interview with a striking admission, 'I'll talk as honestly and openly as I can Mark. I would say that a good part of my own journey through life was, to put it bluntly, fucked up by the whole Irish question'. He acknowledged that whilst he might be accused of being 'more sensitive than others', throughout his childhood and early adult life he could not help feeling that there was a 'marked difference between the O'Brien's and the folk round about'. Whilst he did not detect in his family any particular pride or heightened awareness of being Irish or Irish Catholic, he recalls the wearing of shamrocks on St Patrick's day, the music of Bridie Gallagher occupying the background to everyday life in his family home, an awareness of how Irish his surname was, annual holidays in Donegal, and the special craic that filled smoky rooms when other Irish families came to visit. Against this backdrop he developed an acute sensitivity to being different from Scottish people, a consciousness that led him to think of himself as Irish. This sense of difference was accentuated by experiences at his local school:

> I find it peculiar that I should still think of this so far back but in Kilduggans Primary School, I remember, it must have been in primary six or seven, there was a concert and I was to play a few tunes at the concert. So what did I play? A couple of Irish tunes. What would you expect? But what I can remember, and there's a resentment that still lingers here too, I remember me sitting down to play the Irish tunes and the headmaster sporting either a big smile or a laugh. It was more than a smile. Now I can see why he was smiling, but at the time I thought, 'that bastard's laughing at me'. You know what I mean? (Interviewee 37)

These feelings were reinforced on his holidays to Ireland where, in spite of being referred to as the 'Scottish boy', Interviewee 37 felt more comfortable and certainly more 'at home'. At the age of eighteen he left Glasgow to join the civil service in London. He acknowledges that he was already in a 'state of confusion about his identity' at this point in time and was 'quite far gone'. In London matters were to deteriorate further when for the first time, he came into contact with 'real' Irish migrants. Confronted with the 'true' Irish, Interviewee 37 was to find himself plunged into a deeper identity crises; 'they [the London Irish] put a mirror up to me and I thought, "I'm not Irish". But when I came back up to Scotland I knew that I wasn't Scottish either'. It was at this point in his life that Interviewee 37 developed a serious drinking problem that developed into full blown alcoholism. For the period of two years he was to develop an 'acquaintance with the gutter way of life'. This period was fraught with traumatic memories and to this day it remains something of an emotional open wound (Figure 7.1).

Whilst Interviewee 37 readily recognises that his alcoholism might have more complex roots, he himself cannot make sense of his descent into a life of tramping in London without referring to the overwhelming significance of his search for a secure and convincing sense of belonging. In 1973 he joined Alcoholics Anonymous and since this point has successfully rebuilt an alcohol free marriage and family life. Based upon his involvement with Alcoholics Anonymous (AA), Interviewee 37 feels that his story is noticeable similar to a number of other people of Irish Catholic descent:

> The interesting thing Mark about the AA, I would say that the Irish Catholics are well represented in AA. I've been in the AA for thirty years. I've been sober since seventy-three, but I've been around the AA for thirty-two years in fact, and particularly in Scotland, the Irish Catholics are well represented. It's to do with

identity and identity problems, but it's a lot to do with the fact that we've all, I can only talk for myself, for myself, I certainly never really felt that I belonged here and I didn't belong over there, so I didn't know who the hell I was. It's a funny thing to be talking about sometimes. You wonder why it should cause you problems, but it caused me problems. When we talk about identity there was an identity problem, but there was a big problem with inferiority, being an inferior person because I was Irish and because I was Catholic, because I was different. So there was probably low self-esteem. (Interviewee 37)

Figure 7.1   Pub front, Garngad, 1936. The working man's pub became a central hub for the social life of Irish men and a ubiquitous feature of the Glasgow landscape (Courtesy of Glasgow City Archives and Special Collections)

Interviewee 37 now feels that he has reached a position of compromise over his sense of national identity and feels comfortable referring to himself as an Irish Scot. Nonetheless he acknowledges that circumstances can often conspire to render this compromise fragile. Today he can perhaps best be described as self consciously managing his profound feelings of difference rather than resolving his sense of alterity fully:

Within me there are certain buttons that if they're touched, I'm not saying that I respond always to how I feel, but I certainly quite instinctively feel that I'm not

Scottish and instinctively feel that I really don't belong here. When I see things that are stereotypically Scottish, I can in an instant turn on resentment and anger and a degree of bitterness. (Interviewee 57)

Interviewee 59 is aged 71 and retired. He has stayed in the Vale of Leven (the 'Vale') for most of his adult life. He is third generation Irish on his paternal side, his grandfather coming to Scotland from Donegal in the 1890s. Interviewee 59 speaks of his life as being 'screwed up' by profound feelings of being an outsider in a hostile environment. He recognises that whilst his reaction to being perceived as different and other has been 'extreme' in comparison to friends and other members of his family, his feelings of exclusion have run so deep that they have cast a shadow over his entire life. Indeed, the central theme of his life has been the struggle to come to terms with 'being a Catholic in protestant Scotland, being Irish in a protestant country':

It seemed to me that everything was put together to make me different. It's awful to feel that you've been born in this country and everything about it is against you. I've known, ever since I was young, that in Scotland there has been a hatred for everything that is Irish and Catholic. Put the two of them together, that was me. A guy I grew up with used to say 'be bitter, you're living in a protestant country'. That kind of suited me. Everything is against me. I in turn go against it, rebelling against the Scottish protestant culture that was different and seemed to be out to suppress me. I felt if you were to try and fit in, the odds were against you, you know. As a matter of fact they didn't want you. There's no point in beating about the bush, they didn't want you. It didn't matter how much you tried to fit in. There were other fellas the same as me but it didn't affect them the same. They didn't feel it the same way as me. Maybe I was oversensitive and I believe I was in certain ways. But, my whole life has been a series of rejections because of the area I stayed in, because of my surname and because of my religion. And to this day, I've got no love of anything Scottish, bagpipes, highland games, Rangers FC, the Scotland football team, the Scottish rugby team, Scottish dance music, anything at all that's significantly Scottish I don't get interested in it. (Interviewee 59)

Interviewee 59 traces his feelings to his very earliest memories as a child. He recalls how locals used to refer to his grandfather as 'a gentleman in spite of being Irish: it was remarked once in the Vale how well my grandfather dressed and his shoes were polished and somebody says, "and he's Irish". They thought the Irish should have muck on their boots.' He remembers questioning why his protestant friends went to different churches and schools and different social clubs like the Boys Brigade. He recalls being referred to as the catholic boy when visiting protestant in-laws. Interestingly, he acknowledges that the Catholic Church and his school education played a role in consolidating the sense of difference being imposed upon him by the wider society. He laments the way in which preachers and teachers for instance, misinformed him about the works of Scotland's most famous poet Rabbie Burns:

> When I was young Rabbie Burns was a bad man. I've read Rabbie Burns' life story now and I find the man more Christian than some of the people who preached to me on a Sunday. Scottish, Presbyterian, Ayrshire. Bad combination. Bad combination for people like myself, you know. Misinformed information but he was a celebrity. He was in the same category as King Billy. They hated Rabbie Burns and his Freemason aprons and all that went with him, do you know what I mean? But you weren't encouraged to read Burns or participate. There were no Burn Suppers and if a Catholic went the rest of them wouldn't speak to them, you know. (Interviewee 59)

In spite of these powerful currents, Interviewee 59 sparkled at school winning the Dux or 'head boy' prize and going on to represent the school football team in the Scottish Cup final at the national stadium, Hampden Park. At the age of eighteen he joined the British Army and was posted to the Black Watch regiment. Feelings of being an outsider resurfaced. He was acutely conscious that only a few Catholics were in the regiment and that the culture of most of the Scottish regiments was a predominantly protestant one. He recalls being the object of humour because of his decision not to participate in a church parade. By the age of eighteen Interviewee 59 described himself as 'really screwed up and against everything'. He reflects upon the way in which he had become slightly anti-social, rebellious, and prickly to be with.

On leaving the army Interviewee 59 settled back into the Vale of Leven where he met and married his wife. It was at this point that he started to drink heavily. He acknowledges the extent to which his drinking affected his marriage. He found his personality changed and he became more aggressive. Eventually, in his own words, he became 'a total disgrace to everyone connected with me'. Whilst he believes that the roots of his alcoholism are to some extent hereditary, he argues that it is impossible to understand his particular problem without referring to the state of his mind at that point in time:

> The booze has played a big part in my life. We were over in America for a holiday and in America, alcoholism is described as the Irish disease. When I go to meetings for Alcoholics Anonymous in the Vale here, me being me I look around the room and if there are forty people there, then over thirty of them have been at St Patrick's High School in Dumbarton, or at Notre Dame High School. So I think there is some truth in the Yankee description of alcoholism being the Irish disease. I believe it's hereditary but I believe also that the feeling that a lot of these people have got about not fitting in, the booze lets you fit in. You know yourself when you've had a bucket you can fit in, that's it. (Interviewee 59)

At the age of forty interviewee 59 turned to Alcoholics Anonymous for support and has happily managed to avoid drinking for over thirty years. Whilst in the intervening period, he has observed a steady decline in overt bigotry and discrimination in the labour market, he still concedes he has a heightened sensitivity to anything which he perceives to be anti Irish and anti Catholic including the liberal use of freemason handshakes at the local bowling club, the jokes told in the old boys networks at the local golf club, anti-Celtic FC sensationalist tabloid journalism, and the way in which new acquaintances feel it their right to point out that his surname is Irish and to enquire into his roots. In spite of continuing to struggle to create a life in an environment which he perceives is largely against everything he stands for, he has now read the works of Rabbie Burns and professes great enthusiasm for them. He concluded his story with a humorous reflection on where his journey for self enlightenment has reached:

> I'm not a bigot. I'm definitely not. I know I'm not a bigot. But I don't like the Rangers. I've cleared everything else out of my mind about protestants, ministers, freemasons, I've read about freemasonary and I've found nothing wrong with it. All these things I'm clear of but I cannae clear the Rangers. If Rangers had eleven Catholics playing for them I still could'nae go for them. I just don't like the Rangers. (Interviewee 59)

Naming and claiming submerged senses of difference: Rediscovering one's Irish Catholic heritage

Aged 55, Interviewee 25 is a married housewife and lives in Troon in Ayrshire. She is third generation Irish on her mother's side (origin and date unknown), and third generation on her father's side (Dublin, date unknown). Her genealogical research was prompted by a desire to find answers to a powerful sense she had of being different from Scottish people. The sense that she was 'lacking something' and that something in her past was 'calling her back' nagged away at her for a long time and eventually grew to become an emotional burden. She was aware from an early age that there was an Irish connection on both sides of her family but her mother and sisters disclaimed any Irish background and indeed went to great lengths to proclaim their Scottishness. She recalls hearing stories of a great, great grandfather who was 'an outspoken and harsh anti-Catholic person' and who lined up children in the neighbourhood and gave a penny to the Scottish children and nothing to the 'ones that looked like papes'. And so her roots were buried from her. But still there was a certain 'calling there'. Her search for her Irish and her Catholic roots has been immensely therapeutic and has resulted in a profound feeling that she has at last found her true self.

Interviewee 25's emotional account of her search for her past begins with the 'cold' and 'painful' relationship she had with her father. Her father had always been a 'man's man', he was always 'very very distant' and 'found it hard to express his love'. Her estrangement from her father was compounded when her parents got divorced when she was fourteen-years-old. Perhaps driven by a desire to prove that she was not to blame for the poor relationship she had with her father and for the break up of the family, she had always felt a need to understand her father better. This in turn resulted in 'a subconscious yearning in me to learn more about his family'. But when she interrogated her father he was rarely able or willing to discuss his forebears' lives and how they came to settle in Scotland. Towards the end of his life and when bonds were growing stronger he would speak more openly but the knowledge he communicated was very limited.

As a child, Interviewee 25 also recognised a 'yearning' in herself to be a Catholic. Although brought up a Catholic, her mother had had very strong opinions on the wrongs of the Catholic Church and had long since left the faith. She had become aggressive in her decision to rear her own children as Protestants. But in spite of her mother's disapproval, Interviewee 25 always found herself drawn to the chapel gates to listen to the services and the music. She remembers feeling envious of those children who were making their first communion and marvelling at their first communion dresses. Interviewee 25 interprets her pull towards the Catholic Church as deriving from a past that was concealed from her but which lay dormant in her as a kind of innate desire to unearth who she really was. She felt different from other Scottish people but lacked the vocabulary to express why. Her need to become a Catholic was symbolic of the wider feelings she harboured that she could not be at peace until she found out who she really was, where her real home was, where her father came from, and who her people were. In her teens in 1967 she took instruction to become a Catholic, albeit keeping it a secret from her mother. When she eventually 'came out', her mother was really disappointed and only reluctantly accepted her decision to convert and subsequently to marry a Catholic partner. But tellingly no one else seemed surprised. They appeared to recognise that she was merely 'coming home' and 'finding herself ' rather than embarking on a new journey.

But doubts about her father's origins gnawed away at her. Her busy life as a mother meant that she did not pursue matters but simply learned to live with a certain sense of unease and insecurity. Then one night in 1976 she received a visit from a relative, an eighty-year-old nun who was based in Sri Lanka. Her (paternal) grandfather's cousin, this nun was originally from Ireland and had lost none of her Irish accent. She came at just the right moment for Interviewee 25 was feeling 'very low' having had just lost a baby boy. Her visitor began to educate her about her (paternal) grandparents' roots in Ireland. She was transfixed. From that day onwards she became especially 'hooked' and 'obsessed'. She began to construct a family tree. This research continued through correspondence with her relative on her return to Sri Lanka. The conversation continued until 1984 when her confidant and mentor died. At this point her research stalled much to her frustration.

She had become particularly intrigued with 'Brigit' her great grandmother. Brigit had left Dublin to go to Australia via Chicago, when her grandfather was a child. Brigit 'came to haunt her'. Some of Brigit's children suffered greatly from TB and other diseases and she too had lost children. Her adventure to the other side of the world, infact to Brisbane in Queensland, was both confident and bold. She died at a young age in Australia. Her great grandfather could not bring the children up alone so he returned to Ireland. Her grandfather who was a sailor then came to Scotland. He bequeathed a son who was to become Interviewee 25s father. For sure she was interested in the lives and times of her grandfather and his travails in Scotland. But Brigit became the person she fixated on: 'It was unbelievable, Brigit just possessed me! Every so often I would say, what difference is it going to make to my life if I learn more about her story and trace her down, absolutely none, but later we talked about it, my husband and I, he said you are obviously desperate to know what happened to Brigit'. (Interviewee 25)

In spite of rigorous research from Scotland, which also conscripted distant family relatives in Australia, Interviewee 25 found herself no closer to understanding what Brigit's life was like. When her relative, the nun, died, a fellow Sister in the Order she was part of got in touch. Amongst the nun's belongings was an address book with contact details of distant relatives who lived in Dublin. On receipt of the address book she wrote to these relatives explaining the background to her story. They were 'naturally suspicious' that she might be looking for land or money but quickly realised that she was on a personal crusade. And so a ten-year correspondence followed in which a bit more background to Brigit's life was gleaned. But Brigit remained an enigma and the search was not yet complete. So strong did her feelings become that one summer she decided to sacrifice a family holiday and made a trip to Dublin herself. Here she searched for clues as to why Brigit left for Australia in the first instance and what became of her family when they returned to Ireland after her death.

She describes her search for Brigit and Brigit's family in Dublin in the following ways:

> I started to feel quite vulnerable, this is crazy, this was lunch time and I thought I'm going home, this is just ridiculous, a 45-year-old woman, I've left my children and I'm wandering about Dublin. I don't know, I wasn't a well travelled woman, put it like that right, so I started to feel very vulnerable, and I thought, I'm going home. But I went into a coffee shop and had a cup of tea and went back on the trail because I couldn't let it go. But nothing was turning up. Then on my final day, I was actually going for my flight that night, I was getting frantic, and I went back to the Registry Office and found Brigit's marriage certificate, found the extract in the big ledger, got the certificate, I couldn't believe myself, I was hyper! That then led me to Glasnevin Cemetery where all the great Irish heroes O'Connell and Collins were buried. And there I found the grave of Brigit's husband, my great grandfather, and some of his children, my grandfather's brothers and sisters. I went straight up to the office. No bother at that moment. Straight in I went. And a wee man looked it all up and led me to it. It was an unmarked grave and I found it quite sad that seven people were buried in the plot. I came out, found my way to O'Connell Street and went in and had a drink, and it was the first time ever in my life that I have done that

on my own! I thought I have to celebrate this, I was ecstatic, I actually, can't explain what I was like, I was walking on air! I was walking down O'Connell Street thinking she did this, she lived here as a girl, she got married here. I could relate to everything about what her life must have been like and that was all I needed to know, well, for that day, that was all I needed to know about her and then, it was really quite funny, I went into Pierre Victoire's and sat and had a meal and a couple of glasses of wine on my own and I'm sitting saying this is really heaven! I've done what I came to do and if I don't find out anything else that's it. I've now been there, I've visited their grave, I've prayed for them. I feel as if I have an affinity with them. I now think that I was driven to do this, to find this out. I don't know why or what purpose it will ever serve but for me it was a self fulfilment thing. It was a mark of respect to look back at people who came through times like that. That day in Dublin I was ecstatic. I felt when I was young that I should have been something that I wasn't or I should have been a Catholic. I knew I should have been a Catholic. There was always something in me. I can't explain to you now what it was but there was always something. That day in Dublin when I found the marriage certificate I was very proud because I think it was something I was meant to find out. (Interviewee 25)

Genealogy as a pathway to ecumenical empathy

Interviewee 24 is aged 43, married, and lives in Ayr. A solicitor by occupation she is fourth generation Irish on her mother's side (Armagh 1860s) and third generation (Donegal 1901) on her father's side. In spite of being third generation Irish on her father's side, Interviewee 24 did not appear at first glance to be someone who had moved far beyond her Irish Catholic roots. She grew up in Coatbridge in Lanarkshire, an industrial town which was popular among Irish settlers. She admits that it was not until she got to university that she encountered and struck up real relationships with Protestants. It was important to both her and her parents that she married a Catholic and she remains a practising Catholic today. On graduating with a Law degree she started applying for traineeships and experienced discrimination first hand. Whilst acknowledging that institutionalised bigotry has now waned, she suspects that sectarian-related discrimination still exists in pockets of the west of Scotland. There is more to Interviewee 24s story nevertheless than that of an infant taking its first tentative steps into the world beyond the Irish Catholic ghetto.

Interviewee 24 was stimulated to undertake genealogical research as a consequence of teasing from her eldest aunt on her mother's side. She recalls how her aunt, who tended to 'live in the past', always used to be 'sniffy' about her father's possible Protestant background. Playfully they would trade insults such as 'you are from planter stock', and, 'ah but yours is a tinker's name'. Eventually she decided to research her family tree. Her research got obsessive. She joined the local family history club and has travelled as far as Adelaide in Australia in search of answers. Having compiled a dossier on her father's side of the family, Interviewee

24 has concluded that perhaps she has indeed come from 'planter stock'. Using the Donegal Ordinance Survey, she established that her forebears came from England (she suspects from Halifax) as one of fifty seven planters to settle in the area of Ramelton in Donegal. She found a tombstone erected in an ancient abbey in Donegal to commemorate the life of one of her relatives. She suspects that there was a lot of inter-marriage down the generations which tended to follow the rule of a Protestant man meeting a Catholic woman and marrying that woman and becoming a Catholic. By the time her grandparents decided to move to Scotland in 1901 they were both Catholic. This heritage has proven to be an eye opener for Interviewee 24. It has helped her to feel less alienated from Scottish society and more aware of the dangers of simplistic and essentialist identities. Instead of awakening and deepening her sense of difference and otherness, genealogy has served to complicate and diminish Interviewee 24's feelings towards Scotland:

> Yeah, we know our roots but I think we're now Scottish really, well from my point of view, I don't know what other members of my family think, when you do your research and you find that you're not just Irish Catholic, you're actually Church of Ireland and Presbyterian and English, you think oh well, we are all Jock Tamson's bairns to a degree. (Interviewee 24)

Moreover, her complex past has led her to place greater emphasis upon two hitherto under acknowledged facts in her family conversations: first, that poverty and hardship were not the exclusive provenance of Irish Catholic migrants but were central to the lives of Ulster Protestant migrants too; and secondly that Irish migrants have both learned from and contributed to Scottish culture. Interviewee 24 recognised the importance of socially progressive politics in the lives of her forebears. She herself admits that in spite of her own socio-economic advancement, she has always voted for the Labour Party, 'the Party of the ordinary person', and could never bring herself to vote Conservative, 'the Party of the self seeking'. From personal experience, she understood well the bitter struggles that working-class people had to endure simply to feed their families and to provide them with opportunities others took for granted. The 'great trade union interest' that ran through her family led her to accept the role of Shop Steward in her current workplace. Whilst the underdog label was most frequently appropriated by Irish Catholics destitution also blighted the lives of Protestant migrants. They too have had to sacrifice much to pave the way for the socio-economic advancement of their siblings. This point was often neglected by Irish Catholics who confused Protestantism with privilege and the establishment and Conservative political leanings. What working-class Scottish and Irish Protestant and Catholic people had in common often overwhelmed even their sharpest points of difference. Class unites even when religion strives to divide:

> My auntie told us a story about the mutual inter-dependence. In her father and mother's days the Protestants and Catholics lived in the same building in

Whifflet, and the good suit was sometimes pawned to help a man go out to the Orange Walk, you know, the neighbour. Or if there was a bit of food left over and someone was in trouble they would give them it. Poor people could sometimes see beyond the religious thing and say, 'well they're people in need'. I think one phrase one old neighbour had said to my grandmother was, 'it's your day today Mrs O'Malley, it's our day tomorrow'. You know if it was a St Patrick's day they'd see the processions and things that they had in those days, and if it was the Orange Walk then that was their day. (Interviewee 24)

In addition, Irish migration has brought Irish and Scottish culture together and in the ensuing romance each has changed the other for the better. Claims of ethnic purity are nonsensical: the cocktail which is still fermenting has of necessity created complex and hybrid cultural forms. Interviewee 24 points to two examples to make her point; the Calvinisation of Irish Catholicism and the injection of flair and artistry into Scotland's dour and scientific culture:

Well I think there's a difference between the Irish Scot's Catholicism and Irish Catholicism. In my view, I feel that part of the Church of Scotland and Presbyterian tradition has kind of knocked some of the edges, some of the silliness sometimes, off Irish Catholicism. It's maybe a wee bit less flowery and things you know. A good number of years ago I was going over to Ireland for a wedding and I was quite taken aback at how over the top some of the practices were. Over here that really wouldn't be done, and I think that maybe it's the influence of, we've had to keep Catholicism or certain practices a wee bit lower key so as not to attract attention, whereas if you're in the majority you can have your festivals. We have to be a wee bit more circumspect here. (Interviewee 24)

The Irish have given the Scots story telling and gaiety and Irish dance. I think the Irish sometimes, they are very cruelly portrayed. You hear these stereotypes on the TV that the Irish are meant to be thick. But they've won Nobel Prizes for literature so they can't be that thick, you know. They're flamboyant, that's also come down from the Celts who were the cultured ones of Ireland. That was their tradition, the written word. Their work came from the Gospels and they just carried this on into writing and thought, rather than building up the scientific mind. They've brought that to the Scots and helped the straight laced Scot become a bit more rounded. (Interviewee 24)

Transcending difference through sharing everyday practices

Interviewee 30 moved to Scotland from Donegal in 1956 at the age of 18. Now aged 62 and married with a family, he serves as a caretaker at a university in Glasgow. He describes his decision to move to Scotland as a direct response to the abject poverty and lack of opportunities which existed in Donegal. Rising to the status of scaffolder, a much vaunted position, he worked all over Scotland on projects of national significance; on North Sea oil platforms and at Sellafield nuclear power plant and Torness nuclear power station. Interviewee 30 opened with the claim that whilst he was 'so proud' of his Irish roots and whilst he would support the Republic of Ireland over Scotland in sporting contests, he felt otherwise 'as Scottish as any Scot'. This he attributed to the 'everyday' way in which he related to Scottish people as people rather than as objects. In spite of being first generation Irish, he had grown to love Scotland and felt absolutely at home in Glasgow. Describing Scotland as a 'tremendous place' in which to dwell, and the Scots as having 'given him everything', he harboured no ambition to ever return to Ireland or to be buried there:

> I've only ever met wonderful people here. I've been so lucky. I have so many friends I wouldn't know what to do with them, and they're all kinds. They're all sides of the fence. They're in here in the university and they'll go out and watch the 'Walk' and everything, and they'd give me the shirt off their backs if I wanted. So I've no complaints. It's a tremendous place. I think from a young age, I can say truthfully that I have had no animosity towards any religion at all or any politics. I could even see the Drumcree Orange Parade debacle and say, why the hell don't they let them march there? Why don't they compromise and come and go? At the end of the day we all end up in the bog six feet under. We've to meet God and what will he think? That's what it boils down to. The scripture tells us we should be loving one another instead of killing one another. It's as simple as that. (Interviewee 24)

Intriguingly Interviewee 30 noted that his capacity to strike up genuine friendships with Scottish people was helped by his total naivety and his rapidly acquired sense of humour. He had no interest in politics or religion. Debates on Irish history largely passed him by. He lived in a world that was so unconscious of the importance of difference that difference never became an issue for him. And this absence of a mentality to identify difference everywhere and in everyone would often lead to interesting and humorous encounters. He makes his point about the importance of everyday life in diminishing sectarian division in a clever and amusing anecdote:

> Remember I'd never in my life heard of Rangers and Celtic. Where I came from the Protestants and the Catholics, the only difference you knew was that you went to different churches. Apart from that we could all have been blood brothers. There was no such thing as bloody animosity in a wee local place. Then I came over and one day there was this John Drummond, John was a devil. He was a Celtic man. He said, 'Charlie, what team do you support?' I says, 'I don't support any team'. He says, 'Celtic or Rangers?' Now I used to read a lot of cowboy books and they were all about the Texas Rangers and I says, 'I suppose it'll be Rangers'. 'I thought you were a bloody Catholic?' I says, 'I am uh uh'. 'Well you don't bloody well support Rangers.' That's how green I was.

Then he did a trick, you'll laugh at this one. Think back to 1956, right. So one Sunday I was asked to come out and there was only two of us out. I was labouring to this John Drummond, he was a red hot Celtic man. Now there was a foreman there called John Dills and I didn't know it then, but he was a bitter, bitter Orange man. So we had our tea about half nine or something and went back up to the factory. John mixed a bit of stuff and we were working away and John says, 'Charlie, we'll need to get to mass'. I says, 'well we'll get it tonight'. He says, 'no, no we'll get it the flipping day, we're not waiting till night. We'll get it up in East Kilbride'. I says, 'oh that'll be good'. He says, 'I'll tell you what, you go down and tell John Dills that we're going up to mass in East Kilbride at twelve o'clock'. I said 'ok', so I went down, shy as anything and knocked the door. John shouted, 'come in'. I went in. 'Right young fella, what can I do for you?' I said, 'well me and John Drummond are going to twelve o'clock mass, we're just going down'. 'Oh for fuck.' He hit the roof. 'What? You're going up there to worship a bloody foreign God?' And all of a sudden he stopped. He said, 'who sent you down, young fella?' I said, 'John Drummond'. 'He did did he?' I says, 'aye'. 'Right you back up and tell John Drummond that John Dills said it was fine. The two of youse can go'. He said, 'remember that now, tell him it's ok, by all means go to mass'. So I went up. The penny still didn't drop with me you know. 'What did he say Charlie? What did he say?' I said, 'aye he said it's alright to go to mass'. He said, 'what else did he say?' I said, 'nothing, well he asked me who sent me down'. 'You didn't tell him I sent you down?' I said, 'aye I had to, there's nobody else here'. 'And what did he say? Tell me the truth.' 'He said we could go.' I was too thick to notice. I was too green. Drummond was outflanked too. (Interviewee 30)

Beyond sectarianism: Ecumenical work in Scotland.

Interviewee 51, aged 53, is third generation Irish on both his maternal and paternal sides; his grandparents moving to Scotland in the late 1890s and 1900s from Ulster. Currently he is employed by the Catholic Church and works to promote Catholic social support for disadvantaged and vulnerable groups in Scotland. Clearly well read in Scottish Catholic history, Interviewee 51 offers a fascinating account of the historical emergence of Catholicism in Scotland, noting its origins as an 'immigrant' and 'embattled' Church struggling for its existence against on the one hand a hostile Protestant milieu and on the other an atheistic Socialist and Communist constituency. This context inevitably resulted in a defensive Church and one that perhaps was not ready for debate over Christian unification nor for shared ecumenical worship and practice. Through time nevertheless, promoted by the reforms ushered into Scottish Catholicism following the Second Vatican Council (1962–65) and embodied in the ecumenical work of *Action of Churches Together in Scotland* (Acts), the Catholic Church in Scotland has matured and acquired the confidence to move beyond its walls:

I see it over a couple of hundred years, in Scotland, there was an enclave of Catholics from pre-Reformation times which continued. They tended to be North Banff and that sort of thing and some of the Western Isles. Massive emigration from Ireland obviously, but also Italy, Lithuania, and Poland, the massive emigration of the nineteenth century, brings in the whole Irish thing in. There is a tension then between the Irish and the Scottish Catholic Church. This is historical stuff. This was written and this can be archived. What you've got is a church that was looking for its identity. I don't think the Catholic Church in Scotland really found its identity much till late on, it was right into the mid twentieth century before it really began to relax with itself. It was just an immigrant church. It went through ministering to its own people and building hundreds of churches and church halls and societies and the rest. It was about 'look after your own'. It was about 'we're attacked on all sides and anybody who is not with us is against us' type stuff. So there was an embattled mentality. I think the whole rise of Communism made that even worse as far as the Catholic Church was concerned, because here was another enemy, you know. I think in the fifties there was a sense, and into the sixties more of a sense, that the Church had arrived, the Church was seen to be part of life. It wasn't always popular but even people in public life would now say it's almost in the establishment. Scottish public life will now say, we'll invite a Bishop to do this or an Archbishop and we'll call him Mr. and we'll do all the wrong things, but at least there were beginnings of that. I think in the sixties going into the seventies, I think the Catholic Church in Scotland found itself, cos the Vatican Council then said we'll open it all up.

We're about working with people and we're about working for social action and I think I could go into volumes at some time Mark if you want, about the Spanish Civil War and what it did to my dad's generation politically and culturally and the rest. But I think there was a sense of here is a Church that is actually seeing itself as relevant to what working people are all about, justice issues and the rest. So I think there was a sense of something and I think a lot of things came together in the sixties and I think the Catholic Church got a sense of it being independent of its Irish roots and certainly independent of England and Wales, cos we see ourselves as a quite distinct tradition. So I think here was a growth of what the Catholic Church was all about. So I think there was a growth of self-confidence at that point. Slightly later than that but not that much later, they went into the ecumenical dialogue, which tended to be closed-door stuff. A couple of people maybe in the Baptist Church would say to one of the Bishops, we would like to talk about a bit of theology or something. So there was a bit of that going on and relationships were building. The big breakthrough would have come less than twenty years ago when they started to talk about what they called the ecumenical instruments, the ecumenical instruments in Scotland, which was launched finally about twelve years ago. This brought the Catholics into the mainstream. Because previously Catholics didn't join councils of churches, cos they were seen to be on the Protestant side and the Catholics kept their own thing.

The one in Scotland is called ACTS, which is the *Action of Churches Together in Scotland*. There is another one, which covers the four nations as we refer to them, the Catholic Church in England and Wales, ourselves and there are observers from the Catholic Church in Ireland, which isn't obviously divided between North and South, it's one hierarchy for the whole of the island. All of the Protestant churches except for the Baptist Union in Scotland and a number of the Free Churches and the Free Presbyterians obviously are not in it, and some of the Evangelical Alliance. Most of them are not joining it because we're round the table and some have got problems with Reform Theology in the other Protestant Churches. They are purer than pure and don't want to get into the Church of Scotland backsliding and there's three hundred years of history and stuff. So there's a lot internal stuff there. But in the main denominational groups and that's everything from the orthodox to the minority churches, meet fairly regularly, every couple of years, in a major assembly and then we meet between times.

The social issue stuff, you can hardly put anything between us. You know the moral issues, things like the beginning and end of life, abortion and euthanasia, you will find a whole wide range from the orthodox Catholics who hold a certain line right through every gradation down to groups who see themselves in modern terms as liberal. I don't like the term but they would see themselves as liberal on some of these issues. But on things like poverty issues, on things like ethnic justice, you name it, on nuclear war, we're identical. In fact as often as not we're re-churning out one another's stuff and saying, we come up with the same conclusions. More and more what we're doing is we're grouping together and putting the joint conclusions to government or whatever and purely to add to the volume, we're adding our own bits to it. (Interviewee 51)

Secularism and the demise of the Catholic Church in Scotland

Whilst Catholicism persisted in pockets throughout Scotland before the arrival of the Irish, undoubtedly the Irish fuelled the resurgence of Catholicism throughout the country and in particular in the city of Glasgow. Irish priests, ordained in seminaries in Wexford, Carlow, Thurles, and Maynooth, were despatched to Scotland to minister to their fellow countrymen and women. Moreover, in some instances the children of first generation migrants, inculcated into the faith in strong Catholic households, went on to become priests and to serve in Scottish Dioceses. Trained in Scottish seminaries such as Blairs College, Drygrange College, St Peters College, Chesters College, and the Pontifical Scots College in Rome, these men asserted their Catholicism but in Scottish ways. Whilst the Irish were centrally involved in propagating the Catholic faith in Scotland they have nevertheless become absorbed into the general drift towards secularism within Scottish society and have presided over the demise in the status and importance of Catholicism (Figure 7.2).

Figure 7.2   The sacred in the secular, Dalmarnock 2007. The Church brought faith and purpose to lives that were otherwise lived in dire poverty and overcrowded housing (Property of the author)

It is clear that the Catholic faith and the Catholic Church were much revered within the first generation. Nevertheless there were more than a few cases in which first generation migrants discarded their faith for personal (occasionally a nihilistic family trauma of some proportion), professional (to secure employment and socio-economic mobility) and/or political (as part of a turn to Marxism and Socialism) reasons. There is certainly a need to temper assumptions about the virulence of Catholicism in the past and among the first settlers. In many instances Catholicism was rejected in favour of agnosticism or atheism rather than for another branch of Christianity or another religion. Interviewee 45 for instance noted his father turn away from the Catholic Church following harrowing war time experiences. The brutal loss of friends and the first hand experience of mass and violent death had shaken his belief in divine providence. His father married a Protestant but religion played no role in their household. By choice, his father was buried by a Humanist. His father had sent him to a non denominational school simply because it was closer. He concludes that perhaps his father's approach might have contained the seeds of more wisdom than some would credit:

> After the war my dad became an atheist. He saw too many horrific things. He said how could God do something like this? It made him think twice about God. A lot of people might have been drawn to God in those times but he went the opposite way. He respected people's religion. But he just didn't believe in it

anymore. My dad never rammed any religion down my throat. He just said. 'when you are old enough you can decide what you want'. I do believe in God but I don't believe in the religious aspect of it, if you can understand. I have actually got a deep, not religious belief, but a deep belief in God. But the other stuff, no. I believe I have good morals without needing any church to tell me. If my daughter married a Catholic or a Protestant it would mean nothing either way to me, as long as she was happy. My dad in the end refused to call himself either a Protestant or a Catholic. He wanted a Humanist to do his funeral and that's exactly what I got for him. He hated bigotry. He was hopeful that there would be a better environment and less bigotry in the west of Scotland. He hoped that the west of Scotland would be pacified once Northern Ireland was pacified. Religion meant nothing to him and he hated what it could often do to set people apart. (Interviewee 45)

The complexities of the piety of the first generation notwithstanding, the story of the importance of Catholicism to first generation migrants and the steady decline of both the Catholic faith and faith *per se* through second and third generation descendants was pivotal in many accounts. Second generation offspring, often now parents themselves, acknowledged the 'shock' their parents might feel if they could see the disrespect for and ebbing of Catholicism among the younger generation. Indeed the notion of 'shock' pervaded many testimonies, suggestive of the fact that recent developments were seismic in proportion. Some conceded that they felt guilty that they had 'failed' in some way to inculcate the faith in their children. Some felt disappointed when siblings and relations stopped attending mass or going to confession. Some lamented the shallowness of some who marry in the chapel and baptise their children in the chapel but fail to practice the faith. They scorned the trend towards cohabitation before marriage. Some mourned the drift towards interfaith marriage and the bringing up of grandchildren Protestant and observed that they had had to keep their views to themselves lest a serious family upset develop. Others framed the rejection of the Church by siblings and kin as unfortunate but hopefully not permanent. In any case, all was not lost, people who had left the Church were often good people and that is what mattered. Likewise non Catholics who had married into the family were invariably 'fine and upstanding people' and one had to be thankful for that. There was little point in trying to hold back a tide.

Interviewee 6 speaks of her parents' strong commitment to Catholicism. She discusses her family's (both brothers' and sisters' and children's) drift from the Catholic Church and how disappointed and shocked her parents were and would still be with this development. But she secures consolation in the fact that those who have left the flock have, to a person, turned out to be good people with strong family virtues which would have pleased her parents:

I think everybody needs to go somewhere to learn the right from the wrong. It's a breather away from this mad world. I'm not too happy if my kids don't go and

I tell them so in no uncertain terms. The best present they can give me is to get themselves up and get to mass, because there's no excuse now. In the days of my childhood you had to fast from midnight to go to Holy Communion which meant nine o'clock the previous night for us. We had to walk miles to mass and we couldn't even have a drink of water. We'd go to early mass and then walk home again. I think my mamma and daddy would be very disappointed that some of my children only go to mass on special occasions. I think that would be the sorest point in their lives. I think they would be disappointed in my husband and me because in our house in Ireland, at home, the family rosary was said every night. We do say our prayers but not the family rosary. That was a great tradition in Ireland. You would never miss out because if there was a party or a dance the rosary was brought forward and recited earlier. (Interviewee 6)

For Interviewee 16 growing up as a Catholic meant being part of a family whose itinerary was constructed around Catholic prayers, practices, and rituals. Not surprisingly then, had her parents still been alive the drift from the Catholic Church would have been among those developments of the Irish Catholic community they would have been most disappointed in and least proud of:

It's unheard of now but when I was young we used to kneel and say the family rosary in our house. That's unheard of now. And if there was a thunder storm or anything like that, my mother went about with holy water, sprinkling it all over. And when we were in bed at night my mother would come in and say goodnight and she would put the holy water in the room as well. That's practically unheard of now isn't it? I can remember the priest used to come into the house all the time, which doesn't happen very often now, does it? We went to October devotions, we went to May devotions. My mother used to go on a Sunday morning to half six mass. That was in the days when there were five masses in the morning. She'd go to half six mass and she'd come home and we were all ready. We all went to ten o'clock children's mass. My brother, on a Saturday night, had to polish every shoe in the house, my oldest brother, for mass on the Sunday. Like I said, we used to say the family rosary. We went to confession every Saturday. Then you didn't go to communion unless you went to confession.

I would say that the decline in the faith or of the faithful would be the big thing for my mum and dad, because there's so many people now just don't bother. That's how now you've only got two masses on a Sunday. St John's is the big parish in Port Glasgow. There used to be five masses in the morning and now you've got two. I would say that would disappoint them. And I would also say the way families are now, I would say my mother would be quite shocked, because folk don't even bother getting married, and they're all parading about with these weans. My mother would have been shocked. But that's just the way it is now. She would be shocked that way. And I would say religion would be disappointing to them, because they were from the old school, and a priest doesn't do wrong and what a priest says should go. (Interviewee 16)

The reasons second and third generation Irish Catholics offer as to why they consider the Catholic Church of less relevance and interest today are substantially complex. For some, the credibility of the Christian story fails to persuade, indeed for a few, the central narratives of Christianity are literally incredulous if subjected to serious scrutiny. For others, the patronising attitude of the Church towards its flock and the failings of priests themselves emerge as a key repellent. Excessive expenditure on housing, an obsession with raising church funds, drunkenness within the clergy, and recent allegations of the physical and sexual abuse of children, had resulted in a loss of faith in the institution. Others again have withdrawn from the Church because it fails to fit with their views on matters such as homosexuality, the role of women in society, the use of contraception and, the status of other faiths. Moreover, some interviewees found it difficult to reconcile their left-leaning politics with a Church which they felt was more attuned with Conservative viewpoints. And then of course there were some who found mass and the liturgy 'boring' and disengaged not out of principal but because the aesthetic experience was a 'turn off'. Sunday was spent amidst the spectacles of the new cathedrals of consumption, the shopping malls.

Aged 60, Interviewee 40 was born and raised in Scotland from parents who moved from Tyrone to Scotland in the 1930s and 1940s. He was raised in a staunch Catholic household and was strongly pulled to the religious life throughout his teens. He was ordained a priest and has served throughout a number of parishes in Glasgow and Lanarkshire. He charts the decline of the Catholic Church to the 1960s and notes that in his view it might have been the 'watering down' of the Church which followed the Second Vatican Council which was most responsible. Perhaps the solution to the decline in the commitment to Catholicism shown by the Irish Catholic community in Scotland might be the reassertion of solid fundamentals and doctrinal rules; after all fundamentalism would appear to be resonating with many as an antidote to the uncertainties which pervade the changing and restless world of today. The Church might survive by becoming more Conservative rather than less:

> I think the Vatican Council had something to do with the current difficulties. The Vatican Council moved from the Latin Mass to the vernacular; you were putting the liturgy and the scriptures, the prayers, you were putting it all into the language of the people. In the old days the ordinary person might not understand that much about theology, scriptures, and so on but they said their rosary, their prayers, they prayed for their family, their intentions of a new house, a job, to win the pools, whatever it was but they prayed their own prayer during that time. Suddenly now they were told to discard all that and to a certain extent we lost a bit.
>
> There is another side to this and that is my own hobbyhorse, it's that we went for far too intellectual a line. I remember in my early days in the Cathedral Parish in Motherwell when the reform of liturgy had just taken place and they were working on the translations and the Monsignor in Motherwell and

the Scottish Bishops had to draw together a new book. Who did we consult; a parishioner or someone who might actually use the language? No! We got in a big guy from England who was a Professor of English at Oxford University, a Catholic. We were just trying to find a translation of the Mass and what really inspired them was the King James version of the reformation translation. We ended up treating the work as an act of literature making rather than what it was to be used for in practice. Never mind what it is actually saying, does it read professional enough! Does it meet the technical criteria?

It is not timeless anymore, the whole idea of the vernacular is that it should be set in the present day, incorporating all its chatter, gossip. Its not timeless and as trustworthy. I mean suddenly in the 20th century you started to make revised versions, you know revised versions of the King James translation, now the Good News version and all that. In a couple of hundred years it will have drifted like Chinese whispers. And then they wonder why the people kind of shut off a wee bit!

It's always been one of my exercises to ask people what the priest means at times, you stand up on Sunday or even during the week and you introduce the mass, we have the Confession, and then the open prayer, and the open prayer sets the theme really for the day's liturgy, then you sit down. Now you ask somebody what was said and they couldn't tell you. You could be lucky if you could remember what you actually said. It might as well be in Latin even for the priest reading it, it is written in a language which we don't use, but we have been doing that now since 1967 or 1968 since I have been ordained. Since I have been ordained 33 years ago, a generation of people have grown used to the language of the mass in the vernacular but it is a language that people are not hearing as it is not the language of the *Daily Mirror* or the *Sun* that people read. (Interviewee 40)

Interviewee 33 is one such person who has stopped attending mass. A former Altar Boy, he notes that his mother had a weaker faith than her own parents and this afforded him a certain permission to withdraw from the Church. He concedes that he may return to the Church as he gets older and has not severed his links permanently on the basis of any immovable conviction. Interestingly, he also notes that in spite of reservations he himself harbours he gets defensive when the non catholic media attacks the church or its leaders. It is perhaps a reasonable conclusion to draw that the notion of being a Catholic has greater symbolic than theological importance for some:

I stopped going to mass a month or two ago. I just got fed up with it when I saw all the child abuse scandals, I said I'd just give it a break for a while. My mother still goes to mass every Saturday night. She used to help out in the hall in the Church every Friday morning in the tea room. Her friends are really involved in the Church. But my mum, I think she's waned a bit from the church. She often says to me that she'll still go to the Church, but she'll never hold the same respect and fear of the priest that there was when she was younger. She said when she was younger, what the priest said was law. It was laid down, but she says now the sermon doesn't mean as much now and she won't listen. She says that a lot of what they say is irrelevant. She will still go to Church and pay her respects and that, but she doesn't hold the same beliefs that she once did.

I was an Altar Boy for seven years, when I was seven to fourteen. I just got too big and I thought, I'm daft, I'm as big as the priest on this altar. I was actually bigger than one of them. Who was the other guy? Bishop Devine, he's the sort of, it's the Diocese of Motherwell my parish in Rutherglen comes under, so he makes an appearance quite a bit. I don't really agree with most of the teachings of the Church. It just seems awfully irrelevant to me and often, as I believe in Irish Republicanism, it comes into conflict quite a lot with the Church. Saying that, there have been priests who have been involved in Republicanism but the two always seems to be in conflict. And over in Ireland there is sometimes open conflict. Sinn Féin will come out and say, we agree with abortion. It should be done. And most of their constituents are probably Catholics. I agree with abortion. They used to show us videos in school of abortions taking place and I used to think that was a bit propaganda led that. Make your own mind up. Give us the facts! Once I came out of school I realised that they are playing too much of a role in our education. It was the only subject you had to go to and it still is by law. Most people never turned up for it. I had to go because I was getting a bursary, so I had to have good attendance. But I just used to sit in silence, not wanting to open my mouth and say too much because I knew I didn't agree with anything this guy is saying or this woman is saying. I just think they have too much of a role in the schools and personally I don't really have any great longing for the Church or any great belief in it. I probably will still get married in a chapel and my children will still get christened in it but personally I don't really have much to do with it.

Sometimes Cardinal Winning, he just appeals to a right-wing clique of people. Most of his views are right wing. But saying that sometimes when I read criticisms in the paper about Cardinal Winning, I think what are they saying? They've no right to say that. I don't know why I'm thinking that but I do think it. I don't know, he seems to open his mouth for attention I think. He's trying to improve his status with Rome. Most of what he's saying is not relevant to 21st century politics. It's in the past. Most of the Catholic people in Scotland don't follow what he's saying on issues of contraception and that. Most families only have two kids. Very few people have big flocks like they used to do. Even my mum, she's against abortion but she said before that you would never know if your daughter of fifteen got pregnant, you wouldn't know what to do. I think he is wrong on a lot of things, but sometimes I don't like him being criticised. I don't know why that is. (Interviewee 33)

Interviewee 47 presents an equally complex story. He reflects upon his naive and shallow rejection of the Church in his early years at university. He recognises that his views at this time were more part of his search for a new and cosmopolitan outlook and that he unfairly paraded his new attitude whilst still living with his parents. But he also concedes that his return to the Church was not motivated by a deepening in his faith but out of obligation to fulfil a promise he made when his wife was seriously ill. It is clear that the rules through which people chose to attend or to reject the faith are often more happenstance, practical, and circumstantial than theological or philosophical. There remain many people who have disengaged or partly disengaged from the Church intellectually whilst still going through the rituals of membership, whether out of habit or for personal reasons:

> I made the decision where I decided I wasn't lying. It was an interesting touch point in my life. When I got to university I decided that going to church just didn't fit with this Bohemian uniform I was wearing. I was now some smart arsed undergraduate. I was probably a pain in the arse with it. It upset my mother and father alright as I was living under their roof and it maybe was unfair on them. But I had decided it was a lot of bloody nonsense and I wasn't interested. I see my parent's religion as a habit. I've been on holiday with my dad in Crete and he was always 'I must check out the church times. I must get to that church even if it is at the top of a mountain and I need a taxi'. And that was evidence to me that he just had to get there. It didn't matter what was being said, he obviously couldn't speak Greek. He just had to be there. But then again I won't deny a lot of it. A lot of good things my parents handed down probably came from there. The Church shaped them we've never been deviants or criminals. We're generally decent people. And I go now myself. But my reasons aren't really that genuine. A few years ago my wife took ill. I viewed God in the face and I prayed for a result. And I got a result. I went to the wee chapel in the Royal Infirmary and I prayed for a result. 'If you get me out of this one I promise you I'll do you a turn.' That was six years ago and I've never missed mass once. I'm not a spiritual person but I don't renege on my promises. I won't forget if I commit to something. And I'm going up the mountains as well now. I'm not a convinced catholic but I'm going up the mountains as well too. (Interviewee 47)

Now aged 30 Interviewee 1 moved from Cavan to Scotland at the age of 17. Her story reflects the difficulties a patriarchal church faces in convincing and persuading a growing community of educated and independent thinking woman. When speaking of the Catholic Church Interviewee 1 admits to being quick to anger and her rejection of the Church runs deep. Some wounds, it seems, might never be healed. Educated to degree level at Glasgow University, she wrestles with being pigeon holed as a submissive Irish Catholic girl, burdened by a suppressed sexuality and cherishing little more in life than to be a wife and mother. She rejects the Catholic Church as an institution which supports only a passive role for woman in society and laments the attitudes of priests in particular to independently minded and free thinking women. Her feminism has brought her into direct conflict with Church figures. She recalls:

I don't usually tell this story but there was this Irish priest, he was horrible actually. I was working in the Glasgow University Union and I was doing bar work. You know what the GU, that Union is like, the Scottish upper class, old boys networks, they really still don't like the Irish people. I used to work in there, and there is a place in the back called 'The Bridle' and it usually sits about 50 people and it's always guys, mostly 'all men dinners' and they call themselves the 'winers', and all that kind of stuff. They exist to do each other favours and I was working up there and it's only very recently they started to allow women to work up there. They didn't like that at all, but anyway, at one of these dinners there was this priest at it, and these three guys came to the bar and I thought this guy was dressed up as a priest! I really did! I thought, is it a priest, what's he doing here, and he had an Irish accent and I thought this was a young Irish guy being really funny dressing up as a priest. The guys he was with said he really is a priest and they told me the parish he was in in Glasgow and all that. So anyway. I'm looking at this priest, drinking with a load of 'winers', and we all know who the 'winers' are, with a big lovely really expensive black coat on, and he was dead loud and his face is all gushed with the drink. I went out and I thought I'm going to noise him up about religion you know, I didn't really want to do it, but I felt it would be challenging, and anyway, I can't remember how I approached it, I can't remember what I first said, but I said to him 'what do you think about women priests?' He went into all this kind of stuff, God intended women to bring up children, God intended women to be mothers, and then all of a sudden I heard nothing, just words coming out of him like you know, hell, which was funny. I didn't expect words like women, babies, mothers, God and all this came out, because he had a big red face, all I could see was this big priest's face! I just stepped back and I thought, oh! It wasn't like I was scared, it was because it was so ingrained when I was younger, you don't ask priests questions especially about their jobs. When he finished all this stuff I just wasn't listening to him, so I said, does that make nuns some sort of freaks!! He was completely and utterly disgusted with me. He just left his glass down and walked away from the bar. I left him gobsmacked, I just loved throwing every preconceived idea he had right out of the window, about being a working class Irish girl.

But secularism always has its limits and the Catholic Church, it seems, continues to reverberate even in the most unlikely places. Interviewee 29 is first generation Irish having moved from Tipperary to Paisley in 1986 at the age of 25 following his Ordination to the priesthood. Currently he ministers in Inverclyde. He acknowledges that some of his most taxing and rewarding pastoral work centres on his visits to the local prison. There he meets people who find comfort in the Gospels in a particularly profound way and who depend upon and support the Catholic Church as part of often life-changing experiences. The Catholic Church continues to do good in places where good is most needed and it is on such occasions that its future might be rendered most secure:

I remember the first time I went into the prison. My heart was pounding. I had all those assumptions about prisoners too that I now know to be part of the problem. I get 15 people regularly attending my Sunday mass in prison. That might not seem a lot to you but it is important to me. And I would say of a Catholic population of 250, I would see about 200 prisoners during the course of their sentence. They are like everyone else. They desire a reassurance from somebody else that their lives are not worthless and that they are loved. I know in doing the prison work that this is what the faith is all about. That's why I was called to serve. It matters and I know I am making a difference. (Interviewee 29)

The Catholic family and the fractured family

For Irish Catholics, there can be no doubt that the family, both immediate and extended, has performed a central and cherished role. Parents and grandparents inculcated the idea that loving each other and caring for each other, practically, financially, and emotionally, was of pivotal importance. It is not surprising then that childhood memories are filled with positive stories of visits from uncles and aunts, brothers and sisters, and sons and daughters. Family gatherings, around for instance birthdays, Christmas, First Holy Communions and Confirmations, are recalled with much affection. Nevertheless it is important to appreciate that within the Irish Catholic community family life was substantially complicated and often far from idyllic. In many cases, the nuclear family broke down and family life became fractured, twisted, and novel. At an early age children were forced to leave home and to move to Scotland in search of work. Many shouldered the burden of earning remittances. Moreover, children were often sent to Ireland or received from Ireland and spent their childhood and teenage years in relative's homes as part of relative's families. In addition, mortality was higher than it would be today and life expectancy was lower, and in some cases a parent would die before children reached adulthood. Further, the curse of alcohol blighted family life and created misery in many homes. And above all else, the stress and anxiety created by poverty exacted a high toll on many marriages and mitigated against a happy and carefree households. The image of the happy and loving Irish Catholic family then needs to be tempered by a sober analyses of the complex family formations which existed.

Interviewee 21 recalls the particularly brutal childhood her mother had to endure. Sadly, her maternal grandmother died shortly after giving birth and with a large family to raise her father quickly remarried. But the woman he married had little time for children and certainly not for children who were not biologically her own. She presented a cold and cruel figure and haunted the children's lives. Working on the farm in Ireland ought to have been fun but childhood memories were only infected by painful images of being beaten, punished, and emotionally abused. Clearly her father understood what was happening and intervened when relationships soured particularly badly but much of what occurred took place out of his eyesight whilst he was working. Fortunately the children bonded together and remained to their death close and supportive. And the experience was to result in her mother being the 'perfect mother', someone who knew what children needed keenly as she was denied these very supports:

> Everybody used to say to us, your mother's just a lady. She didn't go anywhere unless we were with her, because she didn't have a good mother herself. I'll tell you a story about my uncle Jack, my mother's brother. My mother's stepmother used to go into the market every day and she sold the eggs and the butter in the market. And yet they were allowed only one egg on Easter Sunday and one egg on Christmas day. The rest of the year, eggs were banned. This day the stepmother had gone to the market and my uncle Jack had said to my mother, come on we'll go in to the hen house and we'll get some eggs. They didn't have any electricity and it was a turf fire. So the two of them went into the hen house and they got two eggs each and they put them on the fire to boil and my uncle Jack happened to go to the window and said, 'oh no here she's coming'. She was coming up the road on her bike. So my uncle Jack took the eggs off and poured the water out and he put his two eggs in his trouser pockets. My mother hadn't any pockets so she put them down her jumper and she nearly roasted the chest off herself.
>
> The stepmother seen this and she gave my mother such a beating and then she flung her into a bedroom and locked the door. My grandfather, he was out in the field and he came in and my uncle Jack and my uncle Michael were there. My mother was maybe about fourteen or fifteen and I think she must have left school. Anyhow, when my grandfather came in he said to the mother, 'where's Katie?' She said, 'she's in the room'. He went to the door and he said, 'what is the door locked for?' He opened the door and he could hardly get my mother out. He said, 'what are you trying to do to the child? Are you trying to kill her?' And that is when my grandfather, his nephew had asked him if he would let my mother look after his children and to be a sort of nanny. She had to leave home then and she went away to be a nanny. That's when she came to Scotland. That particular day as well she battered my mother so much, my uncle Jack ran out into the barn and you know how they've got the thing that they lift the hay up with and he pinned her up against the wall. He was going to kill her that day because she did that to my mother. He was seventeen I think at that time. My grandfather had to take her away.
>
> But it affected my mum hugely. And she was a brilliant mum to us because of it. She used to take the two of us, me and my sister, on her knee and she put her arms round us and she'd say, 'I love you' and we'd say, 'I love you too' and we'd kiss her. She never got that herself and she would lavish it on us. I think it was a type of compensation or whatever. But it made us feel very loved and secure. (Interviewee 21)

For Interviewee 4 family life was marked by the absence of a strong father figure. The forced transnational existence of her mother meant that she spent the early part of her life in Ireland with her own mother. From this experience she learned the central importance of a strong maternal figure in the life of a child. Her mother had an impressive and strong personality and her rules were strict but fair. She was resourceful, thrifty when necessary but always prepared to work hard to provide for the family on matters of importance. When Interviewee 4's own husband died in 1974, leaving her to raise four children by herself, these were qualities which she herself inherited and put into practice. She makes little apology for being a 'domineering mother' and feels that strict boundaries are important. But the love for family is crucial too and it is clear that bringing up children as a lone parent, to be moral and successful citizens, is her greatest achievement in life:

> My mother was in Ireland waiting for my father to set up home. My father was here, then he was re-housed. He got a new house. He had an old house down in the Gorbals and he was then re-housed and then my mother did come across, but again she wasn't all that long here until her granny became very ill, so my father said, 'you're needed there. Go there'. So she went away back across to Ireland and she nursed my granny, who incidentally didn't die until 1949. So after that commotion was over she came back over, but I don't know how many times she was over and back, just for short periods. Then in 1939 the granny took ill again and then she was back over to Ireland. I know my father was over in the summer time and now my mother was expecting me and war was looming. He said, 'stay here until we see what's happening' cos war was looming. Of course war broke out. My mother was in Ireland and my father was here. My mother couldn't get out of Ireland; he couldn't get into Ireland. Letters went back and forward but that was it.
>
> I was born January 1940. I had never met my daddy and my daddy had never met me. My mother was trying to get out of the country. War was now over and she tried to get out of the country. When did war stop? Was it about May? May forty-five. My mother went over with a passport to get it stamped to try to get out of the country. Now she tried to do it legally through the right channels but she wasn't allowed. The next time she tried was from Dublin and at that point she managed to get out of the country on the tenth of December 1945.
>
> When you think these days, my mother went out and worked and she had no qualifications or anything. She had to go and housekeep for people. In those days they called it a 'charwoman' and my mother was a big outgoing person. The happiest person that ever walked on two feet. You'd never think that she came through what she did come through. Even in her young life losing her parents so young. She had such a happy go lucky nature. She worked very, very hard. My brother went to university and in those days there were no big grants or anything. He's just three years older than me. The grant that he got, that would have been a full grant, was twelve pounds a year. Even in those days that wasn't a lot of money. But he was very good and he would work in a holiday camp

in the summer and at Christmas time he would work at the Post Office, so any money he got, that also went into his schooling. It was Maths and Physics that he took and the books were very, very expensive and my mother worked all the harder.

I had a very, very stable upbringing with my mother. She was a very strong Irish domineering mother. At the age of twenty I was told to be in at half past nine, and by jings I was in at half past nine. I left the dancing and came home at half past nine. My mother's cousins were in that Sunday night and they went, 'oh my, you're in early.' And my mother said, 'what are you doing in so early tonight?' I didn't like to say, 'you told me to.' But I would not dare cross my mother. So in turn, I suppose, I'm an Irish domineering mother as well. I have four of a family. Three girls and a boy, in that order. My husband died in 1974. I was only thirty-four years old and I was left with these four children. The oldest was ten and the youngest was two, but I had to be tough, and I was a tough mother. And I say to them now, sometimes I would say, 'no you're not doing it or you're not getting it', but I'd be crying inside when other kids were going places or getting things. I had to make rules and I had to abide by those rules. I think the Irish mothers, they have that toughness that Scottish mothers don't have, but they also have that caring.

I worked for lawyers for seventeen years. There were girls in the typing room who would say, if their daughter was leaving home or going into a flat, 'that's one away' and that kind of talk. And I thought I would die if my family would leave the house before they got married. I remember saying to one girl, 'I think that is the biggest insult. Your daughter is leaving home to go to a flat. That's the biggest insult that I have ever heard of.' The other one would say, 'oh don't be daft. It's great. We can't wait till they're away'. I thought, No! My family came on holiday with me. They were in their twenties. We all went abroad together. We all went as a family. I never ever allowed them to go away with boyfriends. I never allowed my son to go away with girlfriends. I used to say, 'if the boyfriends want to go on holiday with you, they can come with us.' But you know they abided by those rules.

One of my daughters, who is a lawyer, she was twenty-eight years old when she got married. She's now thirty-four. And I remember sitting in here one night. Ian her husband to be was wanting to go somewhere for the weekend, hill-walking and things like that. She said to me, 'mum next weekend do you mind if I go to Arran?' or wherever it was. I was sitting reading. 'Ian and I are wanting to go hill-walking'. So I just lifted my head and I said, 'no you're not going'. And I put my head back down again. Now that wasn't mentioned again. She was twenty-eight years old. At the same time I'm thinking, I'm reading this and I'm thinking, what is Ian thinking? But I thought, I don't care. She's my daughter. If anything ever happens to any of my daughters I know that I've done my best. My friend who was there too said to me, 'I cannot believe that I heard what I heard in this room tonight'. I went, 'what do you mean?' My daughter didn't even question that. She wouldn't dare question it. Even now, if you were talking to them, they would say, 'we wouldn't dare cross Mum'.

Because of my upbringing, I could make a pound stretch to ten pounds and I still can to this day. My friend says, 'aye, by not taking your purse out with you when you go out'. But I was always very careful with money. The widow's pension, I even ran my car off the widow's pension. The week I couldn't afford to put petrol in it, I didn't. The week I could, I put it in. I taught my children the same. They can all make a pound stretch to a tenner to this day. I always think the main thing in the house is the mother, isn't it? If the mother is a squanderer god help the poor man. (Interviewee 4)

Conclusion

It is clear that the cultural identifiers which mark out the Irish Catholic community in Scotland as distinctive vary in their salience through time. The resurgence in Irish traditional music and dance which has reverberated in the years following the phenomenal global success of Riverdance has been somewhat surprising. The Irish Gaelic language meanwhile has continued to attract a small but enthusiastic constituency of speakers and learners. Levels of support for Celtic Football Club in some respects vary according to the vicissitudes of sporting success and failure but it remains a pivotal part of the social and cultural life of the community. Curiously, arguably the most virulent marker of difference of them all, Irish Roman Catholicism, has experienced a steady decline in respect, membership, and practice. The Irish Catholic community has not been unaffected by the secular trends which have weakened Christianity in many advanced capitalist societies. These trends have also reworked attitudes to sexuality, contraception, marriage, divorce, cohabitation and, family formation within the Irish Catholic community and this community has steadily drifted away, substantially so, from the ideal of the large, married, nuclear family. In fact this type of family formation has never been completely hegemonic and the Irish Catholic community has always displayed complex and at times fractured family structures. But for all its decline in virulence within the Irish Catholic community itself Roman Catholicism remains a central badge of difference; perhaps a cultural practice to be invested in for symbolic rather than theological reasons.

If the cultural distinctiveness of the Irish Catholic community has become diluted to a degree through time, it still remains the case that negotiating cultural difference remains of critical importance if the blight of sectarianism and bigotry is to be contained and combatted. It is clear that to date some members of the Irish Catholic community have been consumed by cultural difference and have interiorised a profound sense of alterity and estrangement, often with harmful and life threatening consequences. It is perhaps too much to hope that such people might ever secure a strong sense of attachment and belonging to Scotland. For others, a growing interest in heritage and genealogy has served to heighten a sense of difference which was otherwise subsiding and becoming lost in time. But whilst the growing industry of genealogy can sharpen differences which might otherwise have lain dormant it can also function to muddy assumed pristine biographies. The complexity of intermarriage in many families' pasts is for some a surprising, and perhaps a surprisingly positive and welcome outcome of the search for one's roots. Interestingly, ecumenical bridge building has also been a feature. At one level, the sharing of everyday life has meant that differences have occasionally been resolved through bracketing. Everyday life produces new sets of meanings that relegate and replace cultural differences. At a more conscious level, it is also evident that formal ecumenical strategies are being prepared and enacted by office bearers from different faith communities in Scotland. Even if theological differences might never be reconciled a new spirit of mutual respect and interfaith dialogue at the level of church leaders is emerging. And among its most fruitful consequences is the galvanising and fortification of progressive Christian social policy and advocacy in defence of the marginal, vulnerable and most disadvantaged.

Chapter 8

Immigrant Advancement:
Poverty, Education and Equality

Introduction

At the heart of debates about discrimination and bigotry in contemporary Scotland is the question of the extent of upward socio-economic mobility of the Irish Catholic community. There exists much debate within the social scientific community in Scotland over the extent to which Irish Catholics have caught up with their Scottish counterparts, in terms of earnings, occupational status, education, housing, health, and consumption patterns. This debate centres upon claims and counter claims as to the veracity and scale of different statistical data sets and the quality and objectivity of analysis of these data sets. Nevertheless a balanced and measured conclusion would seem to be that whilst more and better data and clearer and more rigorous analysis is required, there is a significant body of evidence to suggest that the Irish Catholic community has enjoyed an intergenerational rise to prominence, wealth, and economic parity. In many respects, many migrants and descendants have risen to form part of a confident and assertive Irish Catholic middle-class community in Scotland.

This chapter concerns itself with the stories the Irish Catholic community tell themselves about the strides they have made in Scotland, from humble roots to equals. It explores the challenges, hurdles, unexpected routes and detours the Irish have followed as they have searched for upward social mobility. Discussion is structured around four key themes: migrant encounters with Scottish modernity; stories of socio-economic assimilation (including the toil and hardships faced by the navvies, the immigrant appetite for socio-economic progress, and the importance of memories of forebears struggles); intersections between class and nationality in the tempering of immigrant advancement; and finally the defensive practices Irish Catholics themselves instituted and the duplicitous mind sets which underpinned some of these practices. My intention is to examine the ways in which socio-economic integration has diluted Irish Catholic alterity from modern Scotland whilst remaining cognisant of the ways in which being Irish and Catholic has on occasions retarded the speed of socio-economic assimilation. I conclude that the Irish Catholic community itself harbours a sense of having arrived and that this new-found security is pivotal to any understanding of why this community has displayed a certain boldness and confidence in the Scotland's secret shame debate, and in challenging the remaining vestiges of discrimination.

The sights, smells, and sounds of Scotland's comparative modernity

> I'd never had such a culture shock in my life. It was terrible. Picture it, there were very few motor cars, you cycled everywhere in Donegal in 1956. Maybe one or two cars were about the place and maybe one of them would be the local taxi and things like that. And I came over here and stayed in Hayfield Street. The Co-operative had their garage there and all their lorries, and their workers, I think they started at bloody one o'clock in the morning. At the time I was going to sleep they started up and you were shooting up in bed, Christ! From the tranquillity of the countryside where you only hear cows lowing or something like that or people shouting, to suddenly hearing all these engines firing up in the wee small hours. And then it was all the tram cars. I could hear them clattering down early in the morning. Oh aye I was scared. (Interviewee 30)

In contrast to 'traditional Ireland', 'modern Scotland' offered economic opportunity and security, modern, world leading and technologically advanced industries, laterally spacious houses in vast planned estates with modern amenities and utilities, a growing and exciting metropolis with a strong civic culture and modern transport infrastructure, and an expanding welfare state that provided tertiary as well as secondary education, free health care, pensions and unemployment insurance and recreational and library facilities. What were migrant encounters with Scotland's comparative modernity like? Interviewee 23's mother died in 1979 at the age of 97. Aged 19, she had moved to Glasgow in 1901 from County Down. Prior to her death, Interviewee 23 secretly recorded her mother as she told stories about her early years in Glasgow. Amalgamating hours of tape, she produced an edited summary. Although deeply personal, Interviewee 23 generously agreed to share these recordings with the author. In the words of her mother, it is possible to see a vivid account of what early twentieth Glasgow must have seemed like to a young Irish woman:

> When I was about nineteen years of age, my mother and father decided to close up the house and come to Glasgow for a better chance for the family to get on. My father came to Glasgow a few weeks ahead of us and had a nice house for us all to live in. I remember when I arrived in Glasgow Central Station I was astonished at all the din and noise. We got out on to Union Street and went down and crossed Jamaica Bridge. That was a wonderful bridge. It was very nice indeed to go down Nelson Street and come to Dale Street where my father had a house for us. The house was up a close and was very nice indeed; two stairs up above people. I never saw anything like it before. Neighbours would run up and down and pass you on the stairs just like they would in the street. The sitting room looked out on to Nelson Street and it was really very nice, with all the horse drawn cars.
>
> When I was in Glasgow I got a job in a week or two in a hosiery place as a knitting machinist, and I liked it very well and the girls were very nice, and to this day I can do a knitting machine good. I remember when the first electric

trams went. It was funny to watch them going along the way with no horses on them. I was taken to Crown Street and to see them going back and forward, it was astonishing. There was an exhibition in 1911 in Kelvingrove Park and I was sent to Kelvingrove Park as a knitting machinist, to demonstrate at the exhibition. I remember the Art Galleries was open at this time and I went through it at the time and really thought it was a lovely building. During my working days in Glasgow, I had a sail on the canal. The boat was called *The Gypsy Queen*, and it went from Port Dundas to Kirkintilloch. We had a picnic there and then it was back to Port Dundas. At this time the water works in Milngavie were open. We got the day off work to celebrate but that was a day without pay.

We were not long in Glasgow when there was a plague. Several people died as a result of it. At first no one knew what it was and what caused it, but a doctor discovered it was a Bubonic Plague. Once it was known what it was, the Glasgow Health Department acted quickly. I was working in Glasgow when the first old age pension was introduced. It was paid to men over seventy years of age. This was a wonderful thing, as it helped to pay the rent for the old people.

When I look back on my early days in Glasgow, I think there was more to amuse people than there is today, or else we were more easily pleased. We enjoyed places of interest and having a sail on the river. We also enjoyed reading a good book and taking an interest in the city. We had a sail on the Clyde on a kind of boat or water bus. It sailed on the Clyde between Victoria Bridge and Whiteinch. When we reached Whiteinch we got off and spent the evening at Whiteinch Park. We'd take the tram back to the city. The youngsters all cheered when we were going under a bridge, and it was great fun. The ferries crossing the Clyde were very well used. Sometimes they were that well packed you were feart they were going to sink. The Clyde looked very black and dirty when you were in the ferry boat. Now the ferries are gone and they've built more bridges. (Interviewee 23)

Interviewee 4 arrived in Glasgow from Donegal nearly half a century later, in 1945 at the age of 5. She offers a similarly colourful and insightful account of how Glasgow looked and felt to a child coming from the countryside:

My mother gave us a quick tour of the house. It was only a small two bed-roomed house. You have got to remember that we had never seen electricity, we had never seen water coming from a tap, we had never seen a radio. I had never seen a bathroom and I was saying to my brother, 'how did Mammy say we got all that water?' Charlie said, 'I don't know, I can't remember.' It was just too much for us to take in. I put the penny and the halfpenny in the overflow slot in the basin thinking that will get water out. Of course it didn't get water out, but my mother came in to see what we were doing and showed us the water. This was a miracle. In Ireland, we had a well that would always dry up and you had to walk a mile to the tar road as we used to call it. There was a pump there and we used to pump for water if there was no water in the well. So that was the first thing. I couldn't believe that you just done this and on this water came.

Glasgow at the time couldn't burn coal so people were burning anthracite or coke in the fireplace. I remember boking, physically boking at the smell of this. I'd never before encountered this kind of smell, and I remember being physically sick and saying to my Mum, 'I'm six and I'm sick.' I had to put my face right up next to the fire, cos that was the place where, the smell was weakest. But it was an absolutely horrible, horrible smell.

And then you simply switched a switch on the wall and these lights came on. We were amazed because we never had any electricity. We had just the wee lamps or the Tilley lamps. The Tilley lamp gave a fabulous light but you had to keep pumping it all the time. Then of course the radio. This radio would come on and we thought we wouldn't hear it unless you stood right up against it. My mother would say, 'no you can walk about the house and still hear it' and all this was just so new to us. We'd never seen oranges, we'd never seen bananas, we had never seen any fruit. So obviously Ireland wasn't getting these things. On the farms you're self-sufficient, growing your own vegetables.

The only thing was, I had never gone to school in Ireland cos my mother kept thinking we were going to Scotland and we'd be going to school there. Anyway because we came from the country we didn't have the immunity that city folk had, it was months before we got into the school because we took everything that was going. We took Chickenpox, we took Measles, we took Scabies. That was the most horrific thing. The wee boy next door took Scabies so we took them. We only had them on our knees but we had to go to a clinic once or twice a week. They stripped you off and put you in this bath and actually scrubbed you with a scrubbing brush and then they painted you with a big whitewash brush. This is what they done. That was horrific. (Interviewee 4)

In so far as different Irish migrants relocated to Scotland at different stages in its encounter with modernity it is clearly unwise to attempt to draw out universal conclusions. Nevertheless, from the stories told by these two participants alone, seven themes would appear to arise which might provide clues as to the complex ways in which Scotland's comparative modernity rubbed off on the Irish and contributed to their early years of settlement. Firstly, Glasgow did not only look different from Ireland but it sounded and smelled different. Intriguingly, it is only when migrants talk about the 'din' and 'clanging' of the busy and industrious city, and the 'stench' and 'choking smells' of the coal-fired industrial economy, that one fully appreciates that modernity was experienced in a corporeal way. Second, encounters with Glasgow's modernity were thoroughly ambivalent. It is obvious that migrants were excited by the adventure of living in a futuristic environment but their accounts are also underlain by a sense of anxiety and apprehension. Glasgow was magnificent, confusing and even a little dangerous in equal measure. Thirdly, tenement living is often assumed to have inculcated a strong ethos of community. But neighbours also passed one another in the tenement stairway as one would pass someone on the street. Estrangement from each other coexisted with communal living and one often had to learn to live in 'proximity without intimacy'. Fourthly, the standards of living in the city were clearly superior to that available in Ireland. This was not only true as a consequence of the social welfare provisions on offer and the quality of the houses migrants now lived but, also was made visible by the availability of everyday items such as fruit. Fifthly, technology and its ubiquitous manifestations made a huge impression on new arrivals. Communication technologies, (whether it be in the form of horse drawn cars, or electric trams, river and canal boots, bridges, or radios), industrial machines, electricity, and water and sewerage facilities, appear to have been particularly novel. Sixthly, health was a significant preoccupation among migrants by dint of their exposure to cramped and overcrowded living conditions. Coming from the countryside their bodies had not been hardened to particular kinds of infectious disease. Finally, civic life was clearly a feature of Glasgow's modernity that proved attractive to new arrivals. Along with its new found wealth of course, public officials in the city strove to spread modernity to 'the people' in the form of libraries, museums, parks, and public spaces, and art galleries. Whether it be in terms of the use of canals or river boats on the River Clyde, visits to national exhibitions in Kelvingrove Park or Bellahouston Park, or an appreciation of the magnificence of Kelvingrove Art Gallery, celebrations of progress and improvement evidently touched the lives of Irish migrants settling into the city (Figures 8.1 and 8.2).

Figure 8.1   Fountain, Phoenix Park, Cowcaddens, 1911. Glasgow's late nineteenth century liberal and civic ethos permeated its public spaces and announced for later generations the city's comparative modernity (Courtesy of Glasgow City Archives and Special Collections)

Figure 8.2   Hope St, Central Glasgow 1950. Glasgow city centre danced to the noise and the din of a thriving modern metropolis (Courtesy of Glasgow City Archives and Special Collections)

Stories of the socio-economic assimilation of the Irish Catholic community in Scotland

Toil and trouble: the perils of performing dirty, menial, and dangerous jobs

First generation migrants had to take on the dirty, menial and sometimes dangerous jobs. Children, teenagers and young adults were charged with the responsibility of finding work in Scotland and sending remittance monies back to the farmstead to support the rest of the family. It is difficult to overestimate the challenges which these young migrants faced and overcame. Initially many would go 'tramping' in Glasgow, living on streets and begging for food for survival. Interviewees reflected upon how their families came to Scotland to work as navvies and unskilled labourers on Scottish farms from Ayrshire to Fife and Tayside, on hydro-electric construction projects in Pitlochry, Loch Sloy and Loch Awe, in the coal pits of Ayrshire, Lanarkshire and Fife, as navvies in road and rail construction throughout the country, as labourers in the shipyards and heavy engineering and metal manufacturing firms on Clydeside, in nuclear power stations such as that in Torness, and as nannies, cleaners, and in general service for the city's well heeled.

These were jobs that placed the Irish Catholic community at the bottom of the social strata but they did have a platform from which to build.

Whilst reflecting upon the toil which first generation migrants must have had to endure to avoid starvation, intriguingly many participants demonstrated an awareness of the literary works of Patrick MacGill. Patrick MacGill was born in Glenties in Donegal in 1889 (–1963). At the age of 12 he was presented to land owners in Strabane (County Tyrone) for hire as an agricultural worker and entered the brutal and exploitative world of child labour. At the age of 14, he migrated to Scotland to work as an itinerant labourer, firstly as a 'tattie hawker', then as a railway worker, and finally as a navvy. It was during this time that he developed a strong sense of class consciousness and social justice. He detested the exhausting, harrowing and often hazardous work which the unskilled labouring class had to perform to avoid starvation. At the age of 21 MacGill self-published a volume of poetry titled *Gleanings from a Navvy's Scrapbook* which sold over 7,000 copies. Shortly after he moved to London to pursue a career as a writer but his experiences in Scotland had left an indelible mark. In 1914 McGill chronicled the perilous life of the Irish navvy in Scotland in his best selling book *Children of the Dead End* and his sequel *The Rat Pit.*

The story of Interviewee 30 is intriguing in that it has some parallels with Patrick's MacGill's biography, a fact Interviewee 30 himself pointedly alluded to. He was born in Donegal in 1930. Currently aged 72, he lives in Govan Hill in Glasgow, an area renowned for housing first generation Irish immigrants. Like MacGill, he recalls being 'sold' to wealthy farmers at a hiring fair near Strabane as a teenager. After only six weeks on the job, he was asked by the Police to return to the 'Free State' on account of the fact that too many 'Free Staters' were taking jobs from locals and driving wages down. Suffering from biting poverty in Donegal, like MacGill he migrated to Scotland as an itinerant worker in 1945 at the age 15. Like MacGill he secured work as a 'tattie hawker', in his case in Kilmarnock in Ayrshire. He recalls the filthy and dehumanising conditions he was forced to live in; at the end of a fourteen hour working day cows were driven from the byre and the labourers would move in to sleep for the night.

Concentrated into the more riskier occupations, the threat of injury or even death at work was a constant source of worry within many first generation families. With little or no employment rights and/or insurance protection, being unable to work or being killed at work carried enormous financial implications for families. Not surprisingly then, stories of death or injury at work, and their life long direct and indirect implications, figured prominently in some of the oral history testimonies. Migrants had been injured or killed as a consequence of working down the mines, being swallowed into vats of molten steel, being trapped under water in the North Sea whilst exploring for oil, falling from poorly erected scaffolding, being under falling rocks, being jammed between two railway engines, working with dangerous substances including asbestos, being poisoned with lead, and being crushed by animals (Figure 8.3).

Figure 8.3   **Twomax factory and William Wiseman & Sons, Cleaning Waste Manufacturers Hutchesontown, 1956. Working men and women often toiled in gritty industrial environments, some of which could be comparatively dangerous and hazardous (Courtesy of Glasgow City Archives and Special Collections)**

A similar fate was to blight the life of Interviewee 32. At the age of 20, he began to work as a labourer on construction projects across the country. During this period he earned 'good money' but admits to spending the bulk of his wage packets on excessive drinking. Then in 1965, at the age of 35, an event was to occur which would change the rest of his life. Whilst working on the building of Loch Awe power station in Scotland, he fell from a roof 110 feet high. Narrowly escaping death, he shattered his legs:

> You could put two cathedral size buildings inside the power station at the time I was working in it. You couldn't even see the roof. This day I was doing very little because we were waiting on work being completed before we could do our bit. We were all waiting at the top of the scaffold and so I said to the rest of the lads 'away down for a walk. Away you go cos you've nothing to do anyway'. So I was just doing things myself as normal and the next thing, see the joints, I seen the blue sparks coming out of the joints. The lift hoist that was taking men up and down started to shake and fell down and I knew the scaffold was next and that I was going to fall. Next thing I was falling and I was falling towards a sharp edge on the lift hoist that was now on the ground. I knew that if I kept my

legs together I had some chance but if I kept them open I would have been sliced up the centre. And I tell you, I felt lonely till I hit the bottom. I hit the bottom and I remember it well, I heard one of the men saying, 'pull the lift hoist up, his legs are through the bottom'. It wasn't a prayer I said anyway I can tell you. As soon as they lifted me, I flaked out. I broke the two femurs, you know, lateral fractures of the femurs. I lost the kneecap on this one. But I survived. I was very, very lucky. I was in the hospital for twenty-six weeks. I was twenty four of them in bed. I was only two weeks up before they let me home. I tell you I was in a bad state. See lying in bed, I thought there was nothing wrong with me until the nurse or the physiotherapist said, 'right put your legs over the end of the bed'. So I had to sit over the end of the bed. He said, 'as soon as your feet go black give us a shout'. When your feet go black? But it wasn't long, he was right, and they turned jet black. (Interviewee 32)

Following his accident, Interviewee 32 was unable to go back to work as a construction worker. He recovered the ability to walk but could not cope with heavy manual labour and lost the large pay packets he once earned. He secured work as a cobbler however and combined with state assistance has been able to have a reasonably good quality of life. Throughout his 'forties' he recognised that he was 'becoming steadily lonelier', a fact that was not helped by the onset of arthritis. At the age of 50 he met a recently bereaved local woman and got married. His wife now furnishes him not only with love and companionship but also the practical assistance he needs if he is to remain mobile in his remaining years.

Interviewee 20 also recounts the story of her father who came as a labourer to Glasgow in 1910/11 at the age of 16. The danger of the work he and others did was something she recalls with surprise and curiosity:

What he came out in the end to be was great at digging. He was famous for how he could dig holes. A place he was famous for digging out was Bishopton. It was a munitions factory. It's now the Royal Ordnance Factory. But before that was ever built it was just a big horrible place that no one had ever dug up. When they did dig it up the biggest problem was rats and they had to get rid of mountains of rats. Finally they dug it all out and my father got a job there, moving bombs, carrying bombs. Nobody else probably could do it. They made the bombs down there and they loaded them onto the trucks and took them down to England. He also worked under water. Even before Rosyth Dockyard was built they had to get people to go there, to get down under the water to lay the foundations under the water. But at that time they didn't have things like they have now to go under water. To go under water in the North Sea just now, they go under in these wee submarine type things, tiny submarines with two or three people and they fill them with different gases so as you can breathe. In my dad's day they didn't have that. They put them down in tin boxes and filled it up with stuff and put them down. People could only go down twice a day for six weeks and if you survived the six weeks you would live and if you didn't you would die in the box down below, under the water. My father lasted nine weeks but he came up and he suffered from the 'bends'. They say he suffered form the bends so he always had a bit of problem walking and then it started a deafness in his ears as well. (Interviewee 20)

The appetite for immigrant advancement

The archive is replete with references to personal upward social mobility and to the ascendancy of parents, children, and/or relatives in the Scottish housing and labour markets. Whilst 'normal' upward socio-economic drift alone might account for some of the success which the Irish Catholic community enjoyed many appeared to believe that the motivation to succeed was especially high among Irish Catholic families. The Irish Catholic household had a burning hunger for socio-economic advancement and progress meant more to them than even to ambitious indigenous Scots. Of all the values transmitted down the generations, the importance of getting an education and getting on to well paid and prestigious career paths, were amongst the more popular. Referring to what forebears might have been most proud of were they still alive, sentiments such as these then, were repeated in virtually every interview:

> I think they would be pleased to see that areas that were denied to them have been reached by their descendants and now you find that the Irish in Scotland are in every area of the profession, law, medicine, anything and it all. They are competing at least on equal terms with the others. There is still a thing against us but it's held by the denizen element of the Protestant world that aren't Christian at all and who don't go near church. And for some reason or other in built to the psyche was that we were inferior people. They believed that and I don't know why it is so. That would be the thing they would be most proud of, that we've come a long way since they came over as the hewers of wood and drawers of water. (Interviewee 55)

> I think the thing they would be most proud of would be the way our kids have all got on. My mother thought the sun shone out of them all. I suppose they just wanted to see us get on and achieve things. I remember my father being so proud when we got our first car and when my brother in law got his. Getting a new car was a big big thing. (Interviewee 21)

> I think they would have been most proud of the fact that so many Irish names appear in the forefront of newspapers and on television. They've actually moved up from the status of underdog and have become prominent members of society. My dad I know would have been proud to think that from arriving as scrubbers, it's hard for me to imagine, but to arrive on a boat homeless and penniless, foreigners in a strange land, his descendants had turned it around. They are now the ones who in a sense hold the reigns of power. (Interviewee 48)

Given that we came from nothing, the family did well. And I think that's true of a lot of Irish families. They came over here and they took the most menial jobs because it was all they could get and they crowded into houses. When you look around and see what the Irish have achieved it's total amazing. (Interviewee 16)

The importance of us getting on in life was extremely important to my mum. When the Pope came to Glasgow in 1982, he said 'don't just be content with what your forefathers achieved for you, you must achieve yourself'. The pope said 'achieve, achieve, achieve' and I always remember my mum being delighted at that. (Interviewee 9)

I think people of my father's age had certain difficulties but we were beneficiaries of his efforts and we will never forget that. The Irish had to take the menial jobs, but he would have taken great delight in their children rising above this and beating the system. They felt they had done the right thing because 'my son is now a teacher' or 'my son is now a joiner'. They took great delight in that. They left because there was no work in Ireland and they wanted to make a better life for their offspring. And when their offspring achieved anything it kind of justified their decision. We knew that and realised what was required of us. (Interviewee 64a)

I think what would make them most proud is the fact that they have become more educated. They might have been backward but they were only backward because they hadn't been enlightened enough and they couldn't get into the education system. The fact that they have become more educated and have become more professional and have bettered themselves in general, I think that is what would make them most happy. My granddad would be glad and would say 'I made the right decision. Look at my offspring'. He would be happy. He would be doing cartwheels, he would. He would say this is like a holiday every day of your life and we were breaking our back for this. I've still got to go to work, I don't think it's any holiday, but to them it would be like that. And I think it would make them feel as if they weren't leeches. They weren't leeching off society because they would be able to see that we have contributed something and we've taken something from it and we've not taken it for nothing. I think the Irish people who came here, they would be glad we are contributing so much and getting so much back for it. (Interviewee 52)

I think they would be pleased at the way that Irish Catholics have thrived in Scotland. I would say that a lot of them are in the top sections of a lot of the professional jobs, especially in Glasgow. I think even to look at a list of top jobs that, if they're not filled by the Irish now, they've been filled by Irish people at some point and they've all done exceptionally well, which means they've obviously taken the chances they've been offered and made something of it. (Interviewee 66a)

I think he would have been pleased with the material success of his descendants measured against his circumstances, their survival. I think that would be the biggest thing that his family survived materially and were now an awful lot better off than he ever was. And a lot better educated than he ever was. And there are more opportunities opened up for them now. So the survival of his family, their material advantages, I'm using him as a yardstick, the educational advantages, again comparing him as a yardstick, though he obviously was an intelligent man, and the opportunities that have opened up for them, he would be very happy with all that. (Interviewee 58)

There can be no doubt that education amounted to the holy grail for many first generation settlers. Education provided an escape route from a life of hard manual labour and relative deprivation. Consequently, children were strongly encouraged to take education seriously. Some families even lived on the brink of financial ruination so that they could send the brightest members to leading local Catholic private schools such as St Aloysius in Glasgow. To be able to read, to add and subtract, and to write letters to relatives, employers and, public officials, was a critical aspiration; to be able to converse knowledgeably about current affairs among friends and family was a marker of esteem; to pass the 'eleven plus' exam and enter into secondary schooling was an achievement; to proceed to a college or even a university was to earn even more prestige; and to graduate as a doctor, teacher, lawyer or accountant was more than could be hoped for. Educated people had the privilege of working in an office, using their brains rather than their brawn. Sitting comfortably behind a desk in a warm and modern office, owning a brief case, going to work wearing a suit, shirt and tie, these were all markers of real achievement and were highly prized. In such esteem were the professions in particular held that a visit to or from any doctor, teacher, lawyer, or accountant amounted to a big occasion for the family; one that was filled with fear and dread as well as excitement and honour. If a sibling or grandchild scaled such lofty heights him or herself, great credit, pride and glory would reverberate across the whole family and among the wider community:

I was awfully proud a couple of years ago. My cousin's girl, she is now a doctor in the Royal Infirmary and she was married in the Glasgow University Chapel. Now you have got to have gone to the University to get married in there. It was a big happy occasion but as the service was going on, I thought of her grandmother from Redhills in Cavan. She came here in the middle of the last century and worked as a skivvy at 15 years of age in a big house half a mile from the University. The man she worked for was a Victorian dictator and when he found out she was slipping out to go to mass he tried to sack her; 'we don't employ Catholics in here'. The wife argued on her behalf and they kept her on; big deal she was probably working like a slave in the house. I just thought, two generations on and here is her granddaughter getting married as a doctor having graduated out of this very university. We've come a long way. (Interviewee 39)

Education was very important to my mother and father. You want to hear this word 'Catholic emancipation' that was spoken about. I used to think, what's this fancy word 'Catholic emancipation?' They were really desperate about that. They used to go absolutely crazy if some lad made it up to the higher echelons. He's passed his exams, he's going to university, no matter whose laddie it was as long as he was from your stock. They used to put great stock in that and they rubbed their hands with glee knowing they had produced something that was of that status. The status thing was incredible, doctors in particular were revered so much that even I used to think it was absolutely ridiculous. (Interviewee 67a)

Of course success came at a price. Those Irish Catholics who were among the first to attend university may have been pioneers but they were often lonely pioneers. Journeying into unknown terrain was undoubtedly exciting but it was also frightening and intimidating. Often, Scottish universities were experienced as cold and alienating; they offered few cultural landmarks which were familiar and comforting. Interviewee 43 captures well the complex emotions, ambitions, fears, and coping strategies which surrounded his attendance at Edinburgh University where he was admitted to read for a degree in English in the late 1940s. He was the first in his family to go to university, one of the first in his local town, and certainly one of the few to attend Edinburgh University rather than Glasgow University. He describes how living at home and commuting to Edinburgh and, taking refuge in the local Catholic Chaplaincy in the university, became part of his coping strategies:

I felt out of it in Edinburgh. I would rather have gone to Glasgow, what happened was Glasgow was full up at the time, it was difficult to get into university and I had actually gone back to Our Lady's High School in Motherwell to do a sixth year which wasn't common then, that's kind of the norm now but in those days most people left in fifth year, but when I couldn't get into Glasgow I went back to Our Lady's and started sixth year. Then somebody, a friend of ours, said that we should try Edinburgh and so I went to Edinburgh. I knew absolutely nobody, if I had gone to Glasgow there were quite a number of people that I might know, but up there in Edinburgh, I didn't know anybody. I travelled every day on the train, it was a good train service. I got a train at 9.20 in the morning and was in the lecture room for 10.05, but I felt pretty much out of it. Eventually I got to know a fella called John O'Donnell and he was pretty much of our stock and we used to sit in the big Refectory and we would whistle an Irish tune (ha ha) to see if anybody would recognise it. If you whistled the same tune here up in Dykehead you would have got a reaction all right! But we used to do this. The east of Scotland as you know is not quite the same as the west of Scotland but we used to try this to see if there was any reaction but there never was. I couldn't say I enjoyed my university life, and of course travelling every day to some extent was probably a bad thing because I then didn't enter into the life of the university very much. I used to go the Catholic chaplaincy because you knew where you were there and I enjoyed the people there. They were quite friendly, although I met people there that were different! Catholic upper class, I had never encountered them before. It was always a wee bit of a chip on the shoulder I think but however we are survivors you know. Now, the following year my friend then came to Edinburgh and I think it was maybe partly because I was there and we knew each other quite well. It kind of built up a bit then. (Interviewee 43)

On humility: the importance of acknowledging and valorising forebears

The precious wisdom that the first generation had accumulated through harsh experience risked being casually ignored and was susceptible to erasure unless revalorised and handled with care. Whilst the Irish Catholic community has risen from the bottom of the status hierarchy and now boasts a respectable educational and occupational profile, it harbours, dwells on, valorises, and cherishes memories of forebears' struggles which in fact provided the essential platform from which such a steep climb has been possible. These memories help to keep the Irish Catholic community grounded, sober about its achievements, and able to demonstrate an empathy with the weak, vulnerable, dispossessed, and marginalised which often runs against its current class status. The value attached to material advancement has persistently returned to questions of social justice, equality of opportunity, and concern for the underdog. At the core of the Irish Catholic story in Scotland then, is a struggle for socio-economic assimilation which is inflected simultaneously by an elevated respect for the sweat and labour of forebears, most of who were simply uneducated and unskilled 'common men and women'.

Whilst first generation migrants devalued their own efforts by placing a premium on formal education, intriguingly later generation descendants betrayed a sense of humility and deference to the work of their forebears. This most often began with a recognition of the ways in which the formal education system has devalued practical knowledge and eroded the importance of the organic intellectual. 'Education' ought to be defined as the wisdom, knowledge, and common sense required to perform the practical work required in everyday life. To be educated is to be well versed in 'useful knowledge'. In fact, as brutal and dangerous as many of the jobs were it is clear that there did exist a professional pride of sorts within the labouring classes. No matter how demeaning a task might appear to be, if approached in the correct manner it could be turned into something very fulfilling. Navvying itself could be thought of as an art form; a trade with its own craft, specialist knowledge, and benchmarks of achievement. Only a very skilled person had the capacity to dig holes of considerably size to millimetre precision in rocky ground and ground prone to flooding; to build a straight and flat road using only the eye as a leveller; to be able to identify crops and co-exist in harmony with nature; to erect scaffolding quickly and safely; to lay bricks regularly; and to master a sewing machine so as to be able to produce beautiful garments.

Again referring to Patrick MacGill's novel *Children of the Dead End*, Interviewee 38 painted an evocative and emotive picture of the importance of remembering the hardships faced by the navvies who grafted in Scotland. MacGill's characterisation of Glasgow paints a world which Interviewee 38 felt he knew well from the stories his grandfather told him. And yet many of these navvies have ended up homeless on the streets of Glasgow living rough and in poverty. These are the 'forgotten Irish'. Interviewee 38 felt compelled to do volunteer work to support these people. He talks of the importance of respecting their dignity and wisdom and of how much they have to offer if anyone bothered to listen. He speaks of the anger which envelopes him when the forgotten Irish are disrespected or put down in public. He has also taken up the cases of many vulnerable Irish migrants, acting as their advocate and helping them to fight their corner in legal and other battles. Interviewee 38 has built a successful career and has raised a high achieving family but he has retained a fundamental commitment to commemorate and support those members of the Irish Catholic community who came to Scotland before him and who have made his life possible:

> That book, Patrick MacGill's book, *Children of the Dead End*, that ties it all in. MacGill wrote short stories for newspapers, and he kept doing it and kept doing it and he ended up being a journalist in London. That man, Mark, was twenty-one before he had a knife and fork in his hand. It's scary isn't it? Look at the education that man must have, he navvied up in the North of Scotland on the hydro electric schemes up in the middle of nowhere where they just lived for gambling. The book tells you all this. I know it's authentic because my grandfather confirmed that.
>
> My grandfather used to go up to the Barras Market in Glasgow, he got up there and started men. I remember going up there. I don't know what for. I just remember crowds of people in the Barras. But I remember the Irish part of the Barras if you know what I mean. That lay dormant in mind for all them years, thirty-five years, forty maybe. And I was walking through it one day and I seen the old guys standing there, with the black suits and the brown shoes and the bunnets, only an Irishman can wear a bunnet a certain way. And I thought, God almighty. And it just brought it all back to me.
>
> That pub, I think it's the Tudor they call it, they all stood there. And I went over and I stood about four or five feet away from them just listening to them, and it was just what I'd heard before. Then the next day I went up I went a bit closer. And then eventually, I can't remember what happened, but one of them looked at me and said 'hello' and I just kinda said hello to them, but I kept the mouth shut and the ears open. I just let them cos if you tried to go in too quick they would just throw you out. So I stood there and stood there and they used to say, 'here's the oil man coming' cause I worked on the Rigs. And I always shook their hands when I meet them. And they go 'hello' and they put their hand out, and going away I shake their hands again. That's an Irish thing as well isn't it? That goes back to the days of bidding. Now I'm accepted. It's great.
>
> I used to go to the pubs in the Gallowgate as well. You'd go in to a pub and the guys looked as if they'd had a hell of a life. It was written all over their

faces. You start talking to them and the background to these people, even if it's not been a dramatic story, even if it's just that they've survived down the Barras with a stall for forty years, to survive down there for forty years is something.

There's always somebody behind a face and I want to know what's behind a face. One time I got speaking to this old guy who was sitting on the wall. He obviously had had a few drinks in him. He offered me his bottle of wine. I said 'look I'm driving but thanks all the same'. I wouldn't insult him you know. He was talking away and he said 'I used to be on the Donaldson boats going to Canada'. I said, 'did you ever take any of the prisoners of war across'. Aye he said, we took across Otto Kretschmer; casual as anything. He then talked about the journey with Kretschmer. He blooming knew Otto Kretschmer.

Have you ever seen a lathe or a machine working and you see a white water, it's like a cooler they call it. It was in Rolls Royce. And this guy, the chuck was spinning this water out on to the floor and he could quite easily have stopped it. He could have stopped it and put it back in what they call the pan. I says, 'watch what your doing'. 'Ach the labourer can get that', he says. Now the labourer was a big quiet fella and I never knew anything about the guy, but I talked to him. That guy was a teacher at one time and he took a bit of a breakdown. That guy couldn't have laced his boots! The labourer can get it you know. That really bugged me. I don't like people that say 'oh so and so, he's only a labourer'. I say 'don't ever say, that you don't know who you're talking to'.

I'm always on the underdog's side of it, always. I've got a filing cabinet there with replies that I've written away on behalf of folk. My mother said, 'you're just like your grandfather'. Cos he was always fighting and writing and I can't, I don't feel any great, it's just the thing to do. I just can't bear to see anyone getting a raw deal. (Interviewee 38)

As he matured into adulthood, Interviewee 47 became aware that he knew little about his own family origins in Ireland and became motivated to construct a family tree. As early as 1978 his uncle had advised him that his great grandfather had come to Scotland from a small village in County Cork. He went to the Irish Tourist Office in Glasgow who located the place exactly. Work and family commitments meant he did not pursue the matter further at that point but his enthusiasm was rekindled in 1986, just a few months before his first son was born. Initially, he was only interested in tracing factual information, births, deaths and marriages. As he obtained this information he realised that he really wanted to know more about the kind of life his great grandfather would have had. He wrote to Cork City Library and secured information about the geography of his ancestral village. He also retrieved letters, photos, bills and certificates that were held by different members of the family. Slowly, he began to learn of the real hardships which his great grandfather had had to face. Taking a particular interest in the impact of the Great Famine 1845–52, he reflects on several cuttings from local newspapers published at the time:

This came from a book and it's about the Famine and this is County Cork in 1847. This one tells you how bad it was and gives you some examples. I've put it in because my own great grandfather would only have been eight when this took place. It talks here about this man, a countryman, almost deranged, obviously he is losing it because of what's happening. He's actually asked [the government] for help and when they couldn't give him help, he took out his own dead son or daughter and left them on the counter in desperation and just left. He didn't have the money to get the baby buried. So it seemed the Famine did hit the South hard. The graveyard is in the centre, on the main street, and there's several entrances. The gates were closed as people just could not afford to bury the remains of their family or friends and there were too many deaths. The coffins were placed on a wall and abandoned. I think it just got to the stage where people couldn't take it anymore. (Interviewee 47)

Interviewee 47's now extensive genealogical research has been 'written up' into a formal family history album which traces the family's history and crucially tries to place this history into the context of the geography of the village (prominent mountains which were signal landmarks) and the social and economic conditions of the period. His insistence on commemorating his Irish Catholic heritage ultimately stems from his deeper desire to transmit a social conscience and historical awareness to his children and grandchildren. He hopes this album will help keep his sons' feet on the ground:

I want these boys to hold on to their roots as well as to realise where they started from. I've done this so that my own family will appreciate the comfort they have grown up in and that they mustn't take this for granted. They must realise that this is what happened to their relations away back and is also still happening in the world today. Hopefully in their easy lifestyle they will appreciate where they've come from and the difficulties that members of their family have had to go through. It would be totally shattering. I want my own boys to appreciate that computers and TVs just didn't happen. Somewhere along the line somebody has had to work hard to get out of the mire and their life has been horrendous. It's a sort of social struggle, and hopefully at each stage, each branch of the family will get just a wee bit better, not just better off but better people. (Interviewee 47)

Intersections between nationality and class: Encounters with bigotry and discrimination

Arriving in Glasgow as a cripplingly poor migrant community, the Irish Catholic community faced an uphill struggle to secure socio-economic progress simply on the basis of their class, skill levels, educational status, and position at the foot of the occupational hierarchy. But being Irish Catholic, they also faced the added

challenge of securing equality of opportunity and due reward for merit and effort.
Upward socio-economic mobility has been achieved in spite of the existence of
a residual and hostile indigenous mentality which at times has sought to restrain
immigrant advancement. This rocky road to parity within the indigenous labour
market and prevailing class structure has left an indelible mark on the memories
which exist within the Irish Catholic community. Within every family there exists
a rich lexicon of stories about the elevated difficulties Irish Catholics faced in
securing equality of opportunity and advancement through merit. There can be
no doubt that bullying, harassment, and discrimination were endemic in many
Scottish workplaces. Of all the tales of prejudice that circulate within the Irish
Catholic community, by way and far the most prominent are those that take to
do with lost career opportunities or abuse whilst in work as a result of one's
background. Whilst some participants recalled job adverts titled 'No Irish Need
Apply' from the 1920s and 1930s, the majority of experiences reflected more
subtle discrimination with people recognising that some firms in some industries
were not worth applying to, being denied jobs after being asked which school they
went to, being denied promotion in jobs in spite of superior performances, and
being harassed out of workplaces by bullying and intimidation that often paraded
itself as banter and humour.

The sensation of being seen: harsh lessons from the factory floor

Industrial labour markets such as those which persisted in the shipbuilding, heavy
engineering and construction sectors through to as late as the 1960s, were sites
where workplace bullying and intimidation was particularly acute. Interviewee 54
was born in 1937 and is third generation Irish Catholic (Antrim) on his mother's side
and third generation (Meath) on his father's side. Leaving school at the age of 15,
he secured employment as a trainee signwriter in a signwriting firm in Lanarkshire
and from a position of innocence, 'cocooned in a nice decent respectable Catholic
family', he found himself plunged into another world, the harsh world of male
working-class labour. He was to last a year in this establishment before moving
on to better things. Interviewee 54 provided an amazing stream of consciousness
description of the year which stands as a unique and memorable testimony of what
the period was like. So brilliant and vivid is his story that it will be recounted in
full here:

> At that particular time [early 1950s] you either went into higher education or
> you got a job in a shop or better still you got a trade. Now if you got a trade, it
> was looked upon as quite good, because it was half way between the top jobs and
> the labourers. A lot of people told me labourers done what people told them to do
> and all they needed was a big pair of hands, strength. But a tradesman had to use
> his brains. His hands had to be used for dexterity. So I thought, I'd like a trade,
> because by definition, I was quite thin and frail and I couldn't be a labourer. I'm

not saying that in a bad way, but I just couldn't be a labourer because I didn't physically have the acumen to do it, so I had to get a trade.

I did not have a great education whatever that means. But I was able to paint. I was quite good at art. There was a trade called signwriting. Now the irony is, of all the trades, signwriting is looked upon as being one of the top trades. It's looked upon as being a higher class of trade. It was very hard to get into. Other trades, like platers and joiners and electricians, you could get into that. But even within the trades, a signwriter was looked up to; it was art and there was always a wee bit of mystique about art. Art was ephemeral. So it took it away from the other trades. But how the hell was I going to get into it? This is where my family came into it.

Now my mother was brilliant but she didn't help my chances. At the age of fourteen, I used to turn up to interviews with her and she would always pipe in with comments like, 'he's good at drawing the Sacred Heart by the way' and would poke me in the side to encourage me to show the guy a picture of the Sacred Heart I had drawn! You can imagine I didn't get too far with that! But one of my uncles had come back from the army a war hero, discharged as a Major. He spoke very well and built up a variety of businesses with his brothers. He came back from the army in 1946. I'm talking about 1952, so in that period of time he built up a haulage contractors, and had greyhound tracks, ran coaches to Lourdes, owned fruit shops and even post offices. They done everything.

So he had said, I'll see what I can do for you. So there was a signwriting company in Wishaw that he gave his lorries to for years but which was rife with anti Catholicism. He blackmailed them. He told them, 'I've got ten lorries, if you don't let this guy into this trade, the ten lorries that I send to you every year to get painted and re-sprayed, I'll take them elsewhere'. So from being in the position where, 'I'm sorry there's no jobs', there is a job there. Aye, oh yeah. In my opinion it was hard to get into any trade at that time, but to attempt to get into the best type of trade, that was impossible, no way.

So at the age of 15 and wet behind the ears, I arrived in this place and what a shock it was. Immediately it was looked upon as if I was tainting the situation. I was an alien. We [Irish Catholics] were revolutionary type of people. We actually went to the trade unions right away and we were left wing. You're out to cause aggro. Anything that's going to upset the establishment is bad news. Even if you're not that way inclined at all, if you're in the Irish camp and your name is Sean or Seamus, you will act in this way and we don't want to know you. I'm sure they thought, you're far better not to have anything to do with these people cos they're going to cause you aggro anyway. Whenever they do get in they'll bring in their friends, so keep them in a lower position where we can handle them and they're not going to be going anywhere. And for me to get into a top position was ridiculous.

So I appeared up at the place. I quickly found out that there were about three people who were Catholic and they were quiet, cos they had to be quiet. If they said anything they would be laughed out of court. From time to time you'd hear stories about the Pope's red socks and all this. Everybody laughs, you get a good laugh. Ha Ha. We're all laughing. So you just go about your work quietly with the head down, just going through it, cos I mean there's about eighty people there and they are big strong guys, f***ing and c***ing at you and all the rest of it, you can't fight it. The only way you can fight it is if you leave, and that's what they want you to do.

So the first thing they said to me was, 'the only brush you'll see in here is a f***ing sweeping brush, so you'd better get used to sweeping the place and I mean sweep the place. I mean clean it. One guy said, 'now probably the house that you come from will be unclean and clatty'. He said, 'so just remember you're in a different place here now and we want this place clean'. The inference was that I had come from a hole in the wall. So the next thing was I then had to go every day as I say this was 1952/53, I was sent down to Wishaw High Street to get rolls and ham and Penguin biscuits. I was told explicitly not to bring a Penguin that had a green cover. Now this was the level of intelligence of these people, and remember they were questioning my intelligence! So when I came back you want to see the smile on the guy's face as I proffered into his hand a blue coloured Penguin. What was inside was totally irrelevant. It was the colour of blue and the daft Fenian had got it for him. He went heady. It was better than a bloody half of whiskey to the guy.

So this was the standard of intelligence that I was in, and me coming from a position of low self esteem, I began to question then whether I was as thick as I had imagined. Because I warmed to it because the more I saw this kind of behaviour I said, this is going to be so f***ing easy it's not true. So anyway they thought they would test my educational credentials, this would be a good laugh for them. They began to give me more complex orders. I want a roll and egg with HP sauce on that one, a roll and egg with no HP sauce. I want a hard roll and a soft roll. I want a roll from this shop here and I want another roll from down in the Main Street. And they gave me ten minutes to get it. So there I am running around like mad sweating in case I'm late.

Now, they then began to tease me about whether I could count and whether I was capable of giving them all the correct change. They would say, 'I gave you a pound, this is the wrong change. But anyway, there's no point in arguing with you cos you're that bloody thick you can't add up anyway'. So I got fly. I used to take a float of my own. So I had in one pocket a float of my own so that if I was over or under, I always had the right amount of cash. So this was my first attempt to fight back. I had arrived in this world of aggro totally ill equipped for it and was being confronted by an element of people I'd never come across before. So in an effort to fight back, I've brought in my own float to save face.

Now this one fella was a particularly horrible character. He used to go out of his way to demean me. I used to say, 'what is it you want back in change?' And he'd come away with something outlandish that bore no resemblance to the truth and he always got it cos I was adding to the money or taking it away to fit whatever. So he always got what he asked for from the float. In his mind he was saying, 'the boy's is that bloody stupid he doesn't know what he had and he's spraying money about stupidly. He hasn't a clue about adding up. He shouldn't be giving us this money back, he's bloody daft.' But infact I was being fly. I had a vested interest to settle myself in, in the first two or three weeks to be able to see the tilt of the land. So everybody had a smile on their face. Now I didn't care whether they thought I was daft, but I had to use a float to a certain extent to make it work. But I was moving in and all of a sudden, from being in a position of real aggro, I was settling in quietly and getting my head down quietly and moving quietly.

Now, there was another guy called Billy. He was eighty-one but was still working. He was a brilliant artist. This wee guy was in the Freemasons, so he really should have nothing to do with me. I and my type were a threat to him. But fortunately there are good people all over the place. And he used to say to me, look, don't bother about these guys. They're just all second class, just don't bother with them. I've been lucky. There have always been people who along the way that I have met who have been good at their job and I have liked them and I've got on with them and they've told me things that have helped me. Wee sparks, wee things. These are people who are coming from positions who shouldn't have had anything to do with me. There are good people going about.

So this other crowd used to be upset by the fact that the guy who was the best artist and the best signwriter, spoke to me and he was telling me things and I would ask him things. So there was a two way thing. I was getting things from this guy by being ok, playing it low profile. I was keeping the head down, everybody was getting the right change, I was running about daft. They had told me, 'you won't last the pace' so I had to last the pace. But it was hard cos I was about fifteen years of age and going into a situation that was totally alien to anything I'd been in before, totally, completely. From being totally innocent I was thrust into a situation of absolute aggro and it was the first test.

Now, in those days if you were in a trade, it was the thing for a new person coming in to be initiated. The initiation was that they took down your trousers and they painted you whatever colour was the most obnoxious. So they kept on saying things like, 'it'll not be long now son till you get initiated'. So over a period it built up this big fear. So anyway this day, it was a Friday afternoon and about twenty guys grabbed me, pulled down my trousers and got red, white and blue oil paint and painted me all over the place. And of course for me it had to be red white and blue. Now it wasn't done in a way that, you know, 'you horrible character blah blah blah'. It was all done in a joke. And they probably were upset that I didn't join in the laugh. I was not enjoying it. So they were having a good laugh. It took me about two hours to clean myself. That was me initiated.

So at the age of 15 from coming from a sheltered background I was quickly introduced into working life in the west of Scotland. Welcome to the soap opera. I was being told I was that thick I couldn't count, that had I had to run around after them, that the house I came from was filthy and I was painted red white and blue. But I had survived it and if anything was growing in confidence because I was thinking, 'I am going to make something of my life not only to spite you b******s but because you are so thick you will be easy to take'. I don't mean I felt superior, I don't mean that at all, but I don't think I felt inferior. I used to think, 'they are saying that they are the people but we are the bloody people'.

We are the oldest church. There are more Catholics in the world than any other Christian religion. The Pope can speak twenty-five languages or whatever. To me, every Pope I've ever heard about can speak about ten languages. Celtic FC were absolutely fantastic. We take anybody in regardless of colour or creed. We are fantastic. Johnny Thompson was killed by a guy called English. He was a Protestant but we don't care. We take in anybody. We started off to help the poor people. They stole our land in Ireland. Our people were burnt out by the Black and Tans. Michael Collins was fantastic, we had all the heroes. They caused the famine and they put us in old rickety boats. Cromwell was a mass murderer. We were always in the camp of the people who were keeping back the forces of the Protestant Church. Who are they? The King? The King wanted to get f***ing married again and the Pope says 'no'. So he said, 'that's ok, it's a lot of crap. I'll start my own church'. So the King starts his own. He's got eight wives. What kind of guy is this? This is the guy who is in charge of the Protestant Church. This is a lot of nonsense. They change their tune whilst we have stuck to our values for over 2000 years. We are the people. The guy [points to a crucifix] there doesn't change and he's got the keys to the Kingdom. We are the people. If you go to the High Street in Glasgow, that church there was a Catholic Church. They took everything off us. They plundered the loot. So this was the kind of thinking that led to me to feel not superior but not cowed by my experiences neither. We always had the good people, the poets who were bulging with brains. In the thinking of that time and even to a certain extent now, there was always great things that could be brought out to prove our brilliance. (Interview 54)

The above account clearly makes for a memorable and illuminating read. To be sure, a degree of the experiences recounted here might be said to be typical of any apprentice who started in such a workplace in the 1950s, whether Catholic or Protestant. But there is surely more going on here that demands greater attention be given to the complex intersections which occur between age, gender, class, nationality and religion. In this light, the following points of conclusion to the above account might be offered: the ways in which trades were regarded as superior employment that were difficult for Irish Catholics to get into; the way in which the socio-economic advancement of one Irish Catholic brought with it new openings for family members who would benefit from the newly found leverage held by the family to secure jobs for relatives and friends that would otherwise be closed; the ways in which racialisation of the Irish as 'dirty, stupid, and subservient' permeated workplaces and created a climate where bullying and harassment based on nationality and religion were endemic; the levels of endurance, tolerance and patience under-prepared young men had to display to survive and the ways in which they put their heads down and developed strategies to keep a low profile; the ways in which class and sectarianism intersect so that more enlightened Protestants, even if they belonged to organisations that were reputedly less tolerant like the Orange Order and the Freemasons, were sometimes more paternal and supportive than workers on the factory floor (sectarianism breeds on ignorance not difference as such) and; the kinds of stream of consciousness arguments that tumble over in discriminated minds that protect them from internalising the hostility and aggression directed at them and which buffer them from self esteem and confidence problems.

Anti-Catholic practices in the professions

Whilst employment in the industrial and factory workplaces of the west of Scotland proved to be particularly demanding, often overlooked was the discrimination Irish Catholics faced in the white collared service professions too. These stories are rarely as prominent. Discrimination was perhaps less overt and more subtle. Moreover fewer Irish Catholics moved into these professions in the first instance. Interviewee 44 provides a fascinating insight into the politics of hiring at the University of Strathclyde in Glasgow as it developed following a merger between two city colleges. He recounts the experience of a colleague who was asked a question about his religion as part of an interview for promotion and reveals the profound ignorance of the panel member. Interviewee 44 asserts that in the 1940s and 1950s only a handful of Catholics had made it to Professorial level in either of the city's main universities. He was one of them and as such occupies a position of holding rare knowledge and insight. Interestingly, he speaks of engineering subjects as proving less attractive than 'ghetto' subjects, which he defines as subjects deemed useful by the Catholic population and subjects which Catholics had a greater degree of success in. Interestingly though, this testimony also reveals the steady secular turn within the University of Strathclyde and its desire eventually to dissociate itself from religious affiliation ('applied superstition') and in particular from Protestantism. The interviewee shows disdain for this himself, ridiculing it as 'political correctness gone mad', and eventual supports the appointment of a Protestant Chaplain. But a weaker Protestant hegemony continued to prevail. Interviewee 44 notes the steady withering of this hegemony, firstly with respect to the declining importance of engineering subjects and secondly with respect to the hiring of Principals from outside the Scottish educational system. He concurs that discrimination today is not as bad as it once was but refuses to discount its significance fully. It continues to operate albeit at a less visible, less overt, and less effectual level:

> Let me tell you a story told in Strathclyde University circles, which I think highlights the situation as it was. As you know, Strathclyde University was the result of a shotgun marriage between two colleges. Now on the staff of the

Scottish College was a guy called Tom Rogerson who was a Reader. Tom was a delightful man and he was a Major Acting Lieutenant Colonel during the war. I don't think his duties could have been all that arduous because he took his Masters during the period. He wrote a thesis on the Orinoco. What else is one going to do during the World War? When you think about it Randolph Churchill said how he drafted his novel parachuting into Yugoslavia, but anyway. Tom Rogerson once applied for a job as Senior Lecturer at the then Glasgow and West of Scotland College. So he turns up for the interview and he sits there and he's already taught degree level at a very prestigious Grammar School. He's done his Masters and he's done his PhD. At the end of the interview, the Chair of the panel says to other panel members, 'have you got any more questions for Mr Rogerson?' The guy who was the Secretary of the College said, 'yes, yes I've got a question. What denomination are you?' Tom Rogerson was very taken back and said, 'I'm a Methodist'. This was not clear as far as the questioner was concerned but he rallied and he said, 'don't equivocate, are you a Protestant?' Here's a man whose knowledge of Protestantism was so pathetic that he doesn't recognise that Methodism was an integral part thereof, but knows what is of interest to him and doesn't want a lot of bloody papists about him. So there was that kind of prejudice around in the forties and the fifties.

Now to its credit, the Scottish College had a fair amount of Catholics on the staff, but the Royal College didn't have all that many. But you're not comparing like with like, because the predominant disciplines of the Royal College were Engineering and Chemistry and Science and the Catholic community didn't go in for those sorts of things. The Catholic community like the Jewish Community, tended to go for ghetto employment. They did Law, they did Dentistry, they did Medicine, they did Accountancy. They did things where, if nobody else employed you, your own lot did. But they didn't leak to Civil Engineering because if you went to a big civil engineering company, the mark of Zorro was on you, you're a Catholic, goodbye.

So when the merger took place it was noticeable, but nobody commented then on it. However early in the Senate there were discussions as to whether or not we would have a Chaplain. So they set up a committee of eight and there were six who were nominally Church of Scotland, because Presbyterian agnosticism is the established religion in Scotland, and Tom Rogerson and myself. And the only two who did any work in that committee were me and Tom Rogerson and eventually we came up with the recommendation that there should be a Chaplain and the person should be an ordained minister of the Church of Scotland. The University Chaplain should be an ordained minister of the Church of Scotland. Some of the Church of Scotland people on the committee were not at all happy about this and said at one point, 'well it'll be alright as long as he doesn't wear a dog-collar. It'll be alright as long as he doesn't go about with a Bible'. And I said, 'what the hell do you want him to do, distribute Coca-Cola to Muslim students and ask them how their third wife is getting on?' And they said, 'exactly'. And I said, 'well engage a Social Worker. There's no point in taking an ordained minister from 121 George Street in Edinburgh to employ him that way. He'd be better preaching up in the Shetlands than footering about here with a lot of bloody Muslims and Confucian students'. But there was this sort of ambivalence and that. They were, 'ah but you would say that'.

But so far as actual advancement was concerned, I couldn't honestly say that there was much opposition on the grounds of religion. Mind you I had the advantage that I had managed to pick up a Senior Lectureship while I'd been at Scottish College and part of the merger agreement was that all Senior Lecturers kept their Senior Lectureships. So that got me half way up the tree. Nonetheless when I took over a small department, I wasn't given Professorial status although the person before me was given Professorial status. However I didn't mind, the salary was good. That was in 1975. In 1979 they told me that I was a Professor and I thought it was a personal Professorship. It was only when I got the documentation that I'd discovered that I had a full Professorship without a further interview. But what was interesting was that we did a quick check at the time, and as far as we could see, in 1979, there were only four or five members of the Professoriate in both the University of Glasgow and Strathclyde, who could be described as practising Catholics. Alf Brown at Glasgow, who eventually became Vice Principal, Pat Walsh at Glasgow, who became Vice Principal, Tom Marcus at Strathclyde and myself, and I forget who the fifth one was. Quite a number of them were lapsed Catholics.

But since then the situation has changed dramatically. You might say, 'why?' Well I think as far as Strathclyde is concerned, it is the death of the 'ancien régime', the domination of the old Scots Presbyterian clique. All the Mechanical and Dynamic Engineering departments, all that has gone or substantially gone. And there's a lot more people with a British background rather than a Scottish background around the place. I think it's significant that you've had two non Scottish Principals, Graham Hills was from Australia and John Arbuthnott, although Scottish had been both in England and in Trinity Dublin, and he had a much more open attitude to the whole thing. But the opposition now is nothing like as open and blatant as it was. They would never get away now with saying, 'what denomination are you? Don't equivocate man. Are you a Protestant?' That degree and intensity of religious discrimination could never come through now. But it's the odd wee nudge and the odd wee remark and so on. (Interviewee 44)

The shame of defensive practices?

In spite of often harbouring and professing politically progressive ambitions, in encountering discrimination in housing and labour markets immigrant groups sometimes react by developing a number of defensive practices. These practices accomplish a number of social goals; they protect new arrivals and offer them a bridging point into their new environments, they provide added social security in times of family bereavement and illness, they provide comradeship and help to combat alienation, and they can facilitate upward social mobility. Whilst starting out as benign in intention, defensive practices can themselves become discriminating; powerless groups can consciously or unwittingly drift into the category of oppressor as opposed to liberator. Walking this tightrope is something which the Irish Catholic community in Scotland is very wary about:

> The hierarchies of many Labour run councils were Connollys, Donnellys, and Murphys and they were looking after their own. I hate that. I think Malcolm X said to Martin Luther King, 'Man, you're a racist. We have blacks doing this and we have blacks doing that'. Malcolm X said, 'you're a f***ing racist'. I've got a friend across the road. He works for Chivas Regal. Chivas Regal, for years, it could be myth again, was notorious for its anti-Catholic practices. But my friend got into a managerial role. And he'll not employ a Protestant. He's quite proud of that. They did it to us and this is our chance. When Honeywell's came over from America in the 1970s their practices were different from the Wee Free engineering shops like Anderson Strathclyde who had the 'Dalziel High' syndrome. These American companies didn't operate like that. Educated Catholics could now get in there. But what did they do? They done the same thing, which I hate. You're only perpetuating the same sectarian cycle if you end up doing that. And I think that's happened too in the west of Scotland political scene. You look after your own. Like Airdrie is the Orange and Coatbridge is the Green. A lot of Catholics in many towns have grabbed the Labour Party by the throat and have engaged in a kind of Tammany Hall corruption, in Motherwell and Coatbridge. They have adopted attitudes that they themselves were victims off in the thirties, so it's all right to look after your own. (Interviewee 49)

In the oral history testimonies, participants themselves constructed a debate over the merits of four particular kinds of defensive attitudes and practices; the control of labour markets to hire and promote only Irish Catholic men; the use of the Labour Party to gain access to items of collective consumption; the function of Irish/Catholic social and cultural support groups, and the attitudes of descendants to contemporary refugees and asylum seekers. In each case, a historical association with and commitment to emancipation and liberation, and opposition to discrimination and bigotry, ensured that advocates of defensive practices felt doubly exposed and defensive. Whilst some groups and individuals on some occasions have undoubtedly 'crossed the line', insistence by the wider community on meritocracy clearly plays an important role in restraining some practices from becoming damagingly and virulently xenophobic.

Interviewee 2 is aged 46 and left Donegal in 1976 to come to Scotland aged 22. Having met a Scotsman and had children, and having pursued a successful career in social work in Scotland, Interviewee 2 has now firmly settled into life in Scotland. She has enrolled for a law degree at a local university. As a young left leaning (more 'in tune with Tony Benn than Tony Blair'), republican minded, independent and ambitious woman, she observes how she left Ireland with a lot of anger and resentment. Her troubled relationship with Ireland was not confined to her aversion to the British presence in the North. Describing herself as a 'recovering Catholic', she acknowledges that she resents Irish Catholic attitudes to family and the place of woman in society in particular. She describes how moral codes permeated everyday life even in her own family in ways which tried to stifle and suffocate her own ambitions. Any women who even spoke 'out of turn' about patriarchal dominance or had a view on current events was belittled and sneered at:

> Irish Society is very male orientated and particularly if you think back to those times 25 years ago, for women to be listened to just, you would be required to be a saint or a nun or something. But as an ordinary women, you were just some kind of f***ing mad featherless bird. I remember one of my brothers saying to me what man will ever want to marry you? We argued, we had friends in and I would argue with them about things, you know, don't behave like that that's not how nice girls behave you were supposed to be good or obedient or not step out of line and not to have any opinions contrary to the male view or whatever. I wouldn't want a girl like that to marry me they said! Everybody goes ha ha. (Interviewee 2)

Interviewee 2 is critical of discriminatory employment practices and was keen to state that male managers within the Irish Catholic community could be as oppressive in this regard as indigenous Protestant managers. That she identifies discrimination within the Irish Catholic male community is interesting. Whilst she understands that 'people need to get organised if they are to fight back', she is acutely aware of the possibility of the poacher turning gamekeeper. Her sentiments derive in part from her belief that the Irish have now colonised some sectors of the economy and sections of the state to the extent that they run the risk of controlling too much power. In some instances, meritocracy and ability have been overlooked and discrimination in favour of Irish Catholics might be being practised. But not only do such practices discriminate against non Catholics, they also on occasions act to exclude Catholic women:

> I'm always suspicious of the oppressed becoming the oppressor. It's about the bullied becoming the bully. It just seems to be that you then learn nothing and nobody moves on or whatever. Oppression is bad whoever is doing it and if you are being oppressed I think that you are under a particular duty to try and ensure that you don't oppress other people, but it doesn't always work like unfortunately. Often people who have been oppressed become more bloody oppressive themselves you know. I think this is dead important to get over to my kids about not being an oppressor and not being a bully and no matter what not taking part in that because even at a small level let alone at a political level you know it's just the kind of worse thing to be you know. I think the danger is you get this backlash so that Catholic people only employ Catholic people. We'll never achieve this but I'd like to see the goal being that people get employment

not on the basis of who they are but on merit. When I worked in social work
in Scotland I have to say you could see a big rise in particular areas of male
Catholic managers and they were all supporting each other and bringing each
other in and I think this is bad and aggravating the problem and it angered me. I
lose out again because I'm a woman as well. (Interviewee 4)

According to Interviewee 44 the Irish in the west of Scotland have historically
used the Labour Party in the same way that the New York Irish would have used
the Democratic Party in Tammany Hall. He asserts that in securing access to items
of collective consumption, and in particular to housing, who one knew was often
more important than what one knew: 'do you know somebody? I'll have a word
with Mr. so and so. A lot of that social contact stuff went on, and in effect it was
the lubricant of political action'. Votes for favours were equally important as votes
for ideological endorsement. Intriguingly, he then goes on to offer an explanation
for why the Irish are so attracted to patronage politics and clientalism:

I think it's one of the side manifestations of the differences between Catholicism
and Calvinism or Presbyterianism and Protestantism generally. Catholics pray to
saints and they say that he or she is letting me down very badly at the moment.
Even a saint of lost causes St Jude. St Martin for a sore throat, or somebody
else for a sore throat. So there's always somebody who's got a special interest
in your special need, and what you've got to do is find the appropriate saint
and ask for the right intercessions or say the right novena and you're in with a
shout. Now that is totally alien to a Protestant, it's God you pray to. Why bother
with intermediates? But you find this again and again. Protestant families will
go immediately to the head of the organisation. The Catholic family will say
'do you know anybody that works for so and so that could have a word with?'
They do things in a circumlocutory sort of way. They are nothing like as direct,
nothing like as direct. (Interviewee 44)

Perhaps the most visible controversy which this kind of politics has given birth to
is that which took place in the 1984 Monkland's by-election called when former
Labour Party leader John Smith died. In this instance, the hegemony which Catholic
Councillors enjoyed on the now abolished Monkland's District Council (situated
on the eastern fringe of Glasgow) had allegedly resulted in a disproportionate
amount of new public facilities being located in the town of Coatbridge reputedly
more Irish and Catholic, at the expense of the town of Airdrie, reputedly more
Protestant. In addition, claims of nepotism in council employment practices were
raised. This debacle was referred to by a number of participants and whilst an
independent enquiry failed to produce definitive evidence, the jury remains out
over whether any wrongdoing did occur. For Interviewee 39, a former member of
the Labour Party, rumours like this bring discredit to the Labour movement and
'discrimination in reverse' needs to be abolished. This said, it is disingenuous for
critics to call for an inquiry into this council only:

I remember a few years ago when the stramash went on about the Monklands, now I was in the Labour Party for 24 years and nobody needs to tell me about all the in fighting that goes on in politics, not just in the Labour Party. There was a lad working beside me at the time and I was getting a lot of complaints about what the Monklands' Catholics were doing. I said, 'if we're having an inquiry into the Monklands, lets have an inquiry into the whole country'. Here you had a small molehill where discrimination had been practised, I know loads of people in Coatbridge, their attitude is, they done it to us, why shouldn't we do what we're doing, they didn't see anything wrong with it. I don't think two wrongs make a right, I don't think that's right, I want to see people employed because they are best at the job or good enough to do the job, a level playing field, not looking for favours. But you can't look only at the Monklands. (Interviewee 39)

In investing pride in Irish Catholic cultural organisations and Friendly Societies some participants were especially keen to defend such organisations against the charge of inverted sectarianism. On balance, the Irish National Foresters were alleged to be the least sectarian, with the Ancient Order of Hibernians next, and the Knights of St Columba suffering the greatest criticism. The Knights of St Columba (KSC) was instituted in Glasgow in October 1919 by an Irish Catholic immigrant from Cork. The organisation was to be modelled on the Knights of Columbus order which had been established in the United States in 1881. Defining itself to be an 'Order of Catholic laymen' or 'lay apostolats', the primary purpose of the KSC is to assist the Catholic Church in enhancing the social and moral welfare of the local community and in supporting and nurturing the family unit. Members are expected to display the virtues of charity, unity, and fraternity in their everyday lives. The organisation expanded greatly between 1925 and 1950 but experienced a decline in membership from the 1960s. At present, it has over 8,000 members and 340 Charter Councils spread across the UK. Prior to 1966, initiation ceremonies were ritualistic and secretive, however a new generation of members have eliminated all traces of secrecy from the organisation.

In some families, forebears who held official memberships or who served as office bearers in the KSC were held in high esteem. For such individuals, the demands of membership occupied much time and effort. Members could build their entire social life, and for some their central life identity, around the organisation and its demands. Family albums contain cherished photographs of fathers and grandfathers marching in full uniform or performing a central role at a local meeting or conference. Nevertheless in other families reservations and concerns were registered about the motives and ambitions of the KSC. The Knights of St Columba were most often compared to the Freemasons and this comparison was enough to dissuade some Irish Catholics from joining. No Society should be a secret Society and any Society that felt the need to be secret was to be viewed with suspicion:

My father didn't like the Knights, it wasn't for the benefit of anybody but themselves that joined them. It was too similar to the Masons. If you were a Catholic and a Christian, you shouldn't need to be getting a help up from some secret society. He didn't approve of secret societies put it that way. He didn't like anything that was going on and nobody knew about it, you know. That wasn't right. He didn't believe they were doing the right thing. (Interviewee 22)

My father thought they were as bad as the Freemasons. He thought that the Knights of St Columba was like the Freemasons in reverse. He didn't approve of secret societies or anything like that. (Interviewee 28)

I was invited to joint the Knights of St Columba and my wife said, 'you're not doing that. They're like the Masons'. So I never took it any further. (Interviewee 30).

For advocates of the KSC this criticism is wide of the mark and displays a staggering ignorance of what the organisation is and does. A clear difference existed between the KSC and the Freemasons. The KSC only existed to serve the collective good, not to advance individual agendas and aspirations. It was something to be proud of and not ashamed of. As a consequence, some participants were keen to defend the KSC's true mission against 'false and ignorant assumptions':

My dad was in the Knights from whenever I can remember. He held every position in Council 22 and became the Grand Knight. I remember thinking 'oh my dad's a Grand Knight.' I was about fifteen at the time. It was very, very important to us. When I got engaged it was at a Knights of St Columba's dance. It was the only way he could show allegiance, if you like, to the church, to his Irishness, although it wasn't so much an Irish organisation. But most of the people that were in it were west of Scotland second generation Irish, and I think to him, it was the brotherhood. It was the solidarity of it more than anything else. I don't think he'd have looked at it as a way to get on. I think if he'd wanted to get on he'd have gone into the Masons. You should have heard him about them. My dad had absolutely no time for them. He'd say, 'there's all the difference in the world between the Masons and the Knights of St Columba. We're just there to help people and to do lots of charitable stuff'. He'd say, 'the Masons are all just there to get on and all the rest of it, with their funny handshakes'. I used to wind him up quite a lot. He used to take it off me. 'It's a secret society, just the same.' But I was very proud of the fact that he was in the Knights. I think that showed when I put it in his memorial. He worked all his life on the railway. He was good at what he did. He was a good tradesman. But I think the Knights was his achievement if you like. I think it was his way of giving something back to society. (Interviewee 16)

When reflecting upon the defensive practices which the Irish evolved to counter the difficulties they experienced in settling into Scotland, some migrants and descendants lamented the ways in which a minority of their peers were acting in racist ways towards other immigrant groups. It was profoundly ironic and contradictory that a group who themselves were on the receiving end of centuries of discrimination could find amongst their members people who thought nothing of using racist language casually and being complicit in acts of discrimination. Some participants spoke with regret about the racist views they were introduced to at home in regard to the migration to Scotland of Asians (principally from Pakistan, China, Bangladesh and India) in the 1950s and 1960s. Many more described their disgust at the ways in which some of their relatives, friends, and colleagues were talking about refugees and asylum seekers at present. Only in one instance however, did the author come face to face with a participant who seemed comfortable talking about the problems she personally had with new arrivals.

Interviewee 28 is aged 41 and lives in Glasgow where she is a student at a local university. She is married and is mother to nine children. She identifies herself as fourth generation Irish on both her maternal and paternal sides; her great grandparents coming from Crossmaglen in Armagh (1870s) and Donegal (1870s) respectively. In the testimony she offers, it is clear that Interviewee 28's views are complicated by class and gender as well as nationality. But her account could be repeated in many households. It is worth repeating in full here since it serves to foreground the paradox that confronts those from an Irish Catholic background who find it difficult to accept the level of state assistance afforded later waves of migrants.

Interviewee 28:

I think there's going to be real problem in Glasgow with the racial tensions. I think what the Muslim community is doing is going to turn around and bite them right on the bum.

Where we stay, ok it's a big flat and all that, but I have absolutely no chance of being re-housed in the city of Glasgow unless my name is Mrs Mohammed Kahn. There is such positive discrimination towards Muslims and against people in my situation. Everybody knows what I am. They look at my application for a house, nine children, of course they're going to go like that, 'Catholic'. It just jumps out of the page. Before I got the house I'm in, I had applied to fifty Housing Associations throughout the west of Scotland looking for, I had seven children at the time and I was expecting the eighth, looking for a larger flat than I was in. Govan Hill Housing Association were just completing a new project and the largest house they had available was four double bedrooms, living room, dining room, kitchen and two bathrooms. There were seventeen families in for it and I had the most children, so by all rights I should have got this house and I didn't. I got a phone call and was told to come down and to bring down the Family Allowance Book so they could prove that all the children were living with me. I was told to get down at two o'clock on the Tuesday afternoon. I went at two o'clock on the Tuesday afternoon and the house had been let to an Asian family on the Tuesday morning with less kids than me. But nobody would do anything about it.

Author:

Do you see any parallels though, between Muslims coming to Glasgow and the Irish coming over years ago.

Interviewee 28:

The Muslims make no attempt to integrate, none whatsoever. They insist on speaking their own language. Fair enough, I've no problem with that. But it shouldn't mean that their children get nursery places. When the families are second and third generation and their parents speak English, fine, it shouldn't mean that their children go first in the queue just because they're speaking Urdu or something else at home and deliberately doing it till the child reaches five. I think that's wrong. The places should be allocated on need or to whoever's first in the queue or whatever but not just because they are Muslim.
Irish Catholics, they were amongst the first coming over here. You had to integrate. You had to keep your head down. You had to take the shitty jobs in order to feed your family. Muslims coming over now, they're coming over to established communities where they've got their own welfare systems. There's a welfare system here now set up by the Government that they can tie into. That was never there for the Irish. I do believe that people here are getting really resentful at folk coming in.
        Mind the big stushie about the Kosovans coming over to Glasgow and they put them into Sighthill. I thought that was the wrong place to put them anyway because Sighthill is one of the poorest areas in Glasgow. Folk there haven't been able to get repairs done for about two or three years. I'd say about fifty per cent of folk living there are on long term benefit of some description. There's a big drug problem. The area is really run down. And all folk could see for weeks was painters, decorators, furniture, carpets, all these flats getting done up. They couldn't afford new furniture, they couldn't afford to get their places done up, they couldn't get repairs done. And then it's in the newspapers that these folk are coming in and what they're getting and folk are going, 'I've lived here all my life and I've never got that'. And all they could see was folk standing around the bookies with mobile phones and dripping in gold. And they're going like that, 'who's poor here?' And of course it's caused resentments and it's going to cause even more resentment unless it's handled very, very, very sensitively. There's going to be a real problem in this city. I hate to sound like the prophet of doom, but I really see it coming. Because you can't legislate for how people feel,

and if they perceive folk coming in getting more than they've got when they've got very little anyway, they're going to fight and kick out against that.

Author:

What is the solution do you think? A more fair system with no positive discrimination?

Interviewee 28:

No positive discrimination. I think people seeking political asylum, there should be a better way of doing this. I don't remember who told me, but someone told me that they don't even have a proper computer down south where this is all getting done. There is no way of cross-referring and tracing folk and things like that. I think there should be a distinction made between genuine political, folk seeking political asylum, and economic refugees. It's the economic refugees that are going to cause problems. You couldn't fail to be moved, there was a documentary on a few weeks back, and you couldn't fail to be moved by the girl from Rwanda who had lost nearly every member of her family and had escaped with her child. There is no way you would send somebody back to that kind of thing. Absolutely genuine and deserves a rest after what she's been through, deserves to stay. And then you get the other ones. My brother in law is a solicitor down in the Borders, and he was to defend, they were Romanian Gypsies, they've been breaking into houses. There's real money round about the Borders. One of the women was eight months pregnant, and they couldn't find the jewellery. It's because she'd stuffed it up her vagina. Eight months pregnant! And screaming blue murder, because they'd got a doctor, about her rights being violated. (Interviewee 28)

Conclusion

It is sometimes commented that the sensitivity the Irish Catholic community betrays towards equality of opportunity and fairness in the workplace borders on that kind of political correctness which is excessive. The Irish Catholic community is simply too prone to lamenting past deeds and misdeeds and approaches the present with a predisposal towards injustice, looking for wrongs everywhere and in everybody. Whatever may or may not have not occurred in Scotland's past, the Irish Catholic community have successfully navigated its way through the Scottish labour market and exhibits an educational and occupational profile which is on a par with the domestic population. Complaints about the difficulty of the ascent to the summit should now be tucked away into the past. To continually commemorate incidences of hardship and discrimination is to reveal a lack of confidence and a basic status anxiety; it is to demonstrate a chip on one's shoulder.

Establishment Scotland should not be walking on eggshells to avoid attracting the wrath of a community consumed with rights which are almost universally met but which generate disproportionate fury and noise in the rare instances when they are not. The right of the Irish to cherish and recall memories of past misdeeds is to be questioned, and even for some denigrated and scandalised

This chapter argues that indeed memories of the journey from poverty to parity constitutes a central thread of the narrative of the Irish Catholic encounter with Scotland, and crucially one narrated by the Irish Catholic community itself. The trials and tribulations of the journey taken by forebears, wrought by both class and ethnic discrimination and struggle, remain etched in the memories of descendants. Two conclusions present themselves thus. Firstly, it is impossible to stress enough how young, vulnerable and poor migrants were on arrival. The thousands of stories of belittlement which have undermined self esteem so as to corrode lives and restrain achievement matter to people. To die having secured a modicum of advancement and a better base from which families might set off into the world is not something which sons and daughters easily forget. The pervasive interest in commemorating success from an unpromising point of departure and on occasions in an inhospitable environment has undoubtedly produced a class consciousness which is uniquely unrelated to the actual class status which the community now enjoys. This can be referred to as political drag. Secondly, it is precisely because of their success in securing upward socio-economic mobility that the Irish Catholic community now has the confidence to speak out about lingering vestiges of anti-Irish and anti-Catholic prejudices. It was clearly more difficult in the past to contest discrimination from a position of vulnerability and weakness. A more confident and middle class Irish Catholic community now finds itself better able to defend its interests and to challenge any residual bigotry and discrimination which remains. In important ways the Scotland's secret shame debate reflects the outworking of a century of acquiring sufficient capital to secure a confidence to speak; I refer to this as capital's tongue.

PART III
Cartographical Reflection:
Method and Dialogue
Under Scrutiny

Chapter 9

Masses, Spontaneity and Tribe: In Search of the Intelligibility of the Irish Catholic Adventure in Scotland

For my generation, he has always been one of the great intellectual heroes of the 20th century, a man whose insight and intellectual gifts were at the service of nearly every progressive cause of our time. Yet he seemed neither infallible nor prophetic. On the contrary, one admired Sartre for the efforts he made to understand situations and, when necessary, to offer solidarity for political causes. He was never condescending or evasive, even if he was given to error and overstatement. Nearly everything he wrote is interesting for its sheer audacity, its freedom (even its freedom to be verbose) and its generosity of spirit. (Said 2000: 1)

Introduction

This book has sought to frame the Irish Catholic encounter with Scotland against the backdrop of Britain's long colonial and imperial adventure in Ireland and the legacies, reverberations, mutations and reincarnations of this adventure in Scottish social, political, cultural and economic life. I take the Irish Catholic community in Scotland to occupy a very specific geographical and cultural location; it exists as a community of former colons, and their descendants, who now reside in diaspora in a metropolitan heartland of the former colonial power who once ruled over them, and their forebears. Based upon this point of departure, I have approached public disputation, controversy and recrimination over past and present attitudes in Scotland towards the Irish Catholic community – what has been labeled 'Scotland's secret shame' – through the lens of critiques of metrocentric both populist and social scientific over determinations and over readings of concrete colonialisms. There is an undoubted frustration within both the Irish Catholic community in Scotland and some constituencies within Scottish society that the 'other side' simply cannot hear their story; their listening position puts it beyond their comprehension. What one side regards as obvious the other side simply cannot see. What sense might be made of this incommensurability? Can one camp be proven right and the other proven wrong? In debate, both constituencies make strong assertions of the truth of their stories but tellingly both are pervaded by a degree of concealed insecurity, uncertainty, and fear. I have argued that recent debates and disagreements over the extent of sectarianism and bigotry in Scotland are infact best apprehended as manifestations of classic metropolitan anxieties over the intelligibility of histories of colonised populations. Accordingly, this book has set out to take seriously the charge of metrocentricism as it bears on the search for the meaning of the Irish Catholic community in Scotland and has refused to permit any simplistic interpretation of the intelligibility of this community and the logic of its historical emergence. Nevertheless in this closing chapter, I will attempt to bring Jean Paul Sartre's theory of colonialism into a provisional and partial dialogue with the Irish Catholic story of settlement in Scotland. In so doing will court, indulge, ruminate on and expose my own specific metrocentricism and metropolitan anxieties.

Within Postcolonial Studies there is now a well established wariness of the metrocentric tendencies of postcolonial theory itself. For some the charge that postcolonial theory continues to interpret the history and culture of colonised societies through metropolitan frames of reference can be traced to the seminal theory of colonisation developed by French philosopher, novelist, and political activist Jean-Paul Sartre. Chapter 2 of this book subjected Sartre's theory of colonialism to critical scrutiny and qualified this claim. It located Sartre's philosophical works and political activism against the backdrop of a twentieth-century Parisian intellectual life marked by fierce struggles over the future of Marxism. It showed that Sartre's metrocentricism was tempered by his tortuous efforts to write existentialism into the Marxist canon, a theoretical endeavour which led him to replace Marxism's eschatology and linear teleology with a series of circular histories based upon the complex ways in which separate anti-colonial movements spiral off following their own contingent, creolised and anarchic trajectories. I argued that Sartre's desire to contest and rethink rather than submit to and seal metrocentric framings of colonialism and anti-colonialism derived from his weddedness to a historicised phenomenology of existence as spatial. I share in what might be called a new metropolitan anxiety over the capacity of modernist and social scientific enquiry to capture the telos of colonised populations. My objective was not to make the case for a revalorising of Sartre's theory of colonialism which, after all was also ultimately constructed based upon a metropolitan mentality. Instead my goal was to scrutinise, qualify, specify, and ruminate on the circumstances, conditions, terms, and bases under which Sartre might still be considered to offer insights which are meaningful, useful, and progressive.

Critiques of the colonising tendencies of metrocentric theory reflect a certain Indian hegemony within Postcolonial Studies. Here the question of the intelligibility of subaltern groupings presents an altogether different set of intellectual problems and challenges. This case study is clearly different. The British colonial adventure in general, and in Ireland specifically, stands as a unique and specific instance in the wider history of colonialism and empire. Moreover, this confrontation between coloniser and colonised is located not in a past or present colonised country but instead in a former metropole itself, between diasporean and host. This study has parallels with but differs in important ways from studies say of the Algerian community in France, the Indian community in London, or the Argentinian community in Madrid. Whilst racism on the basis of skin colour is central to these cases this study foregrounds racism within the category of whiteness. Finally, whilst the ongoing troubles in Northern Ireland have excited a new wave of interest in the island of Ireland's political status, the Irish Catholic encounter with Scotland continues to be mediated by a cultural politics which is historical, derivative and mutant, and not live, immediate, and of the moment. This study concerns manifestations and legacies of an increasingly distant colonial past in the postcolonial present.

To address the virtues and vices of metrocentric framings and over determinations in this specific context I have specified five sets of demands on any attempt to theorise the Irish Catholic adventure in Scotland. Any framework worthy of consideration must be able to incorporate:

- The pivotal importance of the long history of British colonial aggrandisement in Ireland as a backdrop for emerging relations between Irish Catholic settlers and their offspring, and the Scottish host.
- The multi-faceted and varied ways in which different Irish Catholic families experience, interiorise, and act on alterity from and belonging to Scottish society.
- The pro-active ways in which families – and *inter alia* the Irish Catholic community – have emerged from this historical experience as a distinctive social and cultural formation, in some ways incomparable with Irish Catholic communities in Ireland and indeed Irish Catholic communities throughout the Irish diaspora.
- The central importance of the gelling of Irish Catholics and progressive social, economic, cultural, and political constituencies in Scotland and the co-authoring of humane practices in everyday life as well as larger progressive social and cultural movements.
- The risk that some families might be touched by anti-racist racism and the importance of capturing ongoing struggles between Irish nationalist and anti-colonial sentinments.

To these ends I have outlined a framework which has drawn upon the geographical metaphors of topology, topography, and cartography. In its topological moment this book has made a case for recovering and considering anew the seminal theory of colonialism offered by Jean-Paul Sartre. The core of the book then pivoted around a topographical mapping of the complex trajectories of the Irish Catholic community, in the process mining a substantial new oral history archive collected by the author himself between 2000 and 2002. In this conclusion the fruits of bringing topological and topographical framings into dialogue will now be considered. I refer to this as a cartographic moment; a moment when I place under critical scrutiny the cartographic tools I have used; what I have identified as the progressive-regressive method and the oral history method; to begin the task of a) mapping the Sartrean lexicon onto the complex topographies of the Irish Catholic story and, b) mapping the topographic cacophony onto Sartre's more polished symphony. To be clear, it is not my intention to apply Sartre's thesis in any simple way to explain the oral history testimonies or to use the oral history archive to test the truth or falsity of Sartre's thesis. I resist the temptation to ruminate over the extent to which Sartre has got it right or wrong, is capable or incapable of explaining the social, economic, political, and cultural history of the particular community under scrutiny here. Instead my goal is to inspire the reader to search for the traces and spectres of Sartre's topology that reside within the topographic mapping and to consider the contributions which the topographic mapping might make to the mediation and calibration of Sartre's topological vista.

Sartre's theory of colonialism might be mobilised to ask a number of probing questions about the Irish Catholic encounter with Scotland. Which constituencies in Scotland mobilise anti-Irish and anti-Catholic discourses, when where, and how? Can sectarianism in Scotland be conceived without a consideration of the *scarcity* of resources, whether they be jobs or services or houses? Under what circumstances do Irish Catholics succumb to seriality, which groups suffer most, and how is this seriality experienced? Which kinds of groups in fusion are then secreted, where and why? Have all anti-sectarian groups been spawned from the interiorisation of alterity? Who are the third parties that are currently totalising these groups in fusion, what techniques are they using, and what kinds of contingent totalisations are emerging? In what ways does objectification and vilification of the Irish and the Catholic alienate bigots themselves from their own humanity? How is the loss of humanity experienced, why is it tolerated by the perpetrator, and why does it persist in spite of its existential burdens and costs? What kinds of alliances exist between Irish Catholic and non-Irish Catholic groups seeking to contest sectarian and bigoted practices and to rescue the humanity of both the colonising and the colonial subject? How are groups in fusion ossifying and to what extent have Irish Catholic organisations themselves lapsed into a new form of seriality and evolved into encrustations and 'crippling monstrosities'? Is emancipation possible through movements structured around religious, national, or racial identities? Does anarchism of Sartrean vintage really offer a way forward?

If imposed more strongly, a Sartrean topology would mobilise Sartre's theory of practical ensembles and characterise the history of the Irish Catholic community in Scotland in terms of the circular development of groups in series, groups in fusion, and groups in metastases – or as represented here cultural formations which are best characterised in terms of the concepts of 'masses', 'spontaneity', and 'tribe'. The Group in Series would characterise moments when a particularly oppressive indigenous gaze has cowed the Irish Catholic community, resulting in interiorisations of alterity and the withdrawal of overt displays of Irish Catholicism in the public realm – the Irish Catholic community exists as a serialised mass. Groups in fusion born from such othering and intimidation might then be viewed as totalising through different third parties, with various degrees of success and to varying degrees of universality. These groups would be anarchic and emerge through unpredictable and happenstance juxtapositions. The sheer throwntogetherness of different stories would produce novel cultural forms. The category Irish Catholic in Scotland would be a fluid category, ceaselessly emerging and bringing newness into the world. Where fused groups have solidified and gelled into encrustations themselves, the Irish Catholic community might be characterised in terms of the Group in Metastases. Groups in metastases announce a moment where the search for redemption, which started out with hope and optimism, degenerates itself into a machine for oppression, bigotry, and sectarianism. The Irish Catholic community crystallises into an inert tribe, a new but equally alientated mass.

Of course before departure I observe that Sartre's theory of practical ensembles needs to be tempered if it is to enter meaningful dialogue with this substantive case study. Whilst Scotland is indeed a place in which the vestiges of a colonial look lives on in spite of any empirical reality to support its existence it is clearly different from the kinds of visceral colonial projects Sartre was interested in. The extent and depth of seriality in Scotland has rarely been total or engulfing. Because anti-Irish Catholic sentiment in Scotland was rarely violent, was always experienced differently by different migrant groups and descendants, and has probably waned through time, any application of the theory of practical ensembles needs to exercise a lightness of touch. Anti-Irish sentiment has rarely been wholly interiorised or contested outright and the Irish community has bubbled and frothed with varying degrees of anger but rarely with a violent loss of temper. In addition whilst the Irish Catholic community displays moments of defensiveness and inverted racism, it would be misleading to claim the existence of a metastases of liberating anarchy into an ossified collective. It is perhaps too strong then to talk about the existence of well-developed Sartrean practical ensembles in Scotland. Instead, it is more accurate to speak of the existence of an embryonic circular dialectic. Masses, spontaneity, and tribe are recognisable cultural formations in the history of the Irish Catholic community in Scotland but are less pronounced, less visible, and often obscured by a century of additional cultural debris, jewels and detritus.

Let us bring Sartrean thought into conversation with the five stories introduced in the second part of the book dealing respectively with questions of national identity and belonging, images of Ireland and the Irish, anti-imperialism and political attitudes and activism, social and cultural practices, and socio-economic advancement and class consciousness. Here I will show the ways in which the multiple and complex threads of biography captured above complicate, calibrate, negate, and retranslate, Sartre's theoretical manoeuvrings. In excavating Sartre's thesis from the historical contexts in which it was produced and reconsidering its utility as a framework for rendering intelligible the Irish Catholic encounter with Scotland, I reflect on two key topics; the place in which the colonial gaze is encountered and the merits and limits of approaching the Irish Catholic community in Scotland as a Sartrean Group in Fusion. In so doing I supplement the Sartrean lexicon with a raft of new concepts and therein seek to contribute to the dusting down, resuscitation and wider development of the Sartrean theoretical project.

Placing the encounter with the colonial gaze

A universal feature of all colonial projects is the promotion by colonising powers of representations of those who are colonised as lagging socially, politically, economically, and culturally behind the core metropole. Central to these geographical imaginaries are binaries such as civilisation and barbarism, development and backwardness, enlightenment and parochialism, technological and primitive, cultured and philistine, rational and superstitious, morally disciplined and morally degenerate, clean and dirty, and disciplined and lazy. These binaries are mobilised so as to legitimate colonialism as a civilising mission, a moral imperative bestowed upon the coloniser, perhaps even by divine mandate. By othering the colonised as somehow culturally inferior, at a primitive stage of development, and in the most extreme cases as actually subhuman, the colonial look serves as a powerful generator of alienation. Whilst the extent to which metropolitan projections of Ireland and the Irish ever approached these depths is open to question it is clear that in its worst moments and among its worst citizens Scottish representations of Irish Catholics have been at the least unflattering and demeaning. A deployment of Sartre is in order to the extent that such a colonial gaze has existed and has proven to be historical formative. But crucially, in this case the colonial gaze has been fixed on Irish Catholic diasporeans who now dwell in Scotland. I use the ideas of 'colonialism's double look', 'the diasporic vaccine', 'mandatory Manicheanism', and 'integration as a progenitor of alterity', to point to four crucial ways in which this specific meeting place has mediated histories and geographies of Sartrean practical ensembles.

Colonialism's double look

I submit that there is a history to be written of the role of Britain's colonisation of Ireland in the determination of the experiences of the Irish Catholic community in Scotland. But for Irish Catholics in Scotland, struggles over alterity articulate both processes of othering which occurred as part of British colonial rule in Ireland and processes of othering which occurred as both communities, indelibly marked by this first encounter, were then forced to confront each other all over again only this time in the metropolitan core. Of course both moments of encounter cannot be reduced to a common denominator; local conflicts do not represent a displaced politics of colonialism and struggles over Anglo-Irish relations cannot be read as a displaced politics of Irish settlement in Scotland. But nor can they be separated. It is critical to appreciate the amplifying effects of the double intermeshing: local difficulties in Scotland would not excite the same controversy without the backdrop of historical relations between Britain and Ireland, and historical battles would not be commemorated so virulently if local disputes did not exist to stoke the patriotic flame.

Again, in its worst moments and among its worst citizens Scotland might be understood to have played a key role in the wider production, reproduction, circulation, and policing of racialised caricatures of the Irish. As late as the 1930s, some factions within Scottish society were still warning of the economic, cultural, political, and social, menace the 'Irish virus' presented to Scottish society and the need to repatriate Irish Catholics back home. For these constituencies binaries such as civilisation and barbarity were routinely deployed and promoted. These Scots depicted Irish Catholics as illiterate paupers and strike breakers, political radicals and insurgents, and staunch Roman Catholics. Irish Catholics were it seemed going to have difficulty in settling into the competitive labour markets which prevailed in urban/industrial Scotland, in finding communion with constituencies marked by their conservativism, imperial triumphalism, Loyalism, and Unionism, and in securing hospitality among those whose confessional preferences were for Calvinism, Protestantism, anti Popery and Orangeism.

The residues of empire have been kept alive in Scotland by a whole series of localised socio-political processes which have relentlessly bullied, buttressed, prodded, poked, and jockeyed this underlying structural asymmetry so that it has endured well beyond the conditions which gave it life in the first instance. The simple existence of Celtic FC and Rangers FC have played a key role which is too often underestimated. There is surely no such a thing as a ninety minute bigot. Other key local processes include the rise of the new Scottish parliament, the coming to political power of the Scottish Nationalist Party, fiscal pressures and deficits, the expansion in access to higher education, deindustrialisation, changing labour markets, a resurgence in interest in heritage and genealogy, altered gender relations, secularism, new migrations to Scotland, privatisations of public spaces, equal rights legislation, and transnational investment and changes in the structures of ownership of Scottish businesses. In a whole series of complex ways these local developments have reworked the ways in which Scotland 'looks' at its Irish community, and the ways in which this community experiences Scotland, sometimes elevating differences unwittingly.

The diasporic vaccine

It is classically true that diasporic groupings imagine 'home' as a kind of romanticised and idyllic utopia, a special and magical place capable of stirring otherwise dormant emotions and passions. Dwelling in displacement fosters a heightened sense of nostalgia and encourages an elevated valorisation of the sights, sounds, and smells of the country of origin. These imaginations are often more pronounced among second and third generation descendants than first generation migrants. For the Irish Catholic community in Scotland, Ireland is indeed ubiquitously imagined as a wonderland, a repository of precious ways of life, virtue, tradition, family networks, and communal life. Often to the incredulity of parents and grandparents who left Ireland at a time of crippling poverty, sons and daughters and grandsons and granddaughters venerate visits to Ireland much as they would a pilgrimage to a special and blessed holy place. These visits are framed by and in turn constitute a love of qualities often depicted as counter to Scotland's modernity: tradition, community, nature, and the oral tradition.

The Irish Catholic community in Scotland has developed practices of imagining Ireland which have to a large degree vaccinated them against negative and wounding images of Ireland as backward and peripheral. The periphery has become centred. In particular being in diaspora and intoxicated by a diasporic longing for home, a fictitious and irrational longing lacking in any real interest in actualising a return to that home, the Irish Catholic community has reclaimed the periphery as a mystical and romantic place of emotion, spirituality, and belonging. Images of Ireland have served as a most powerful antidote against interiorisation of negative stereotyping and stigmatisation. Of course it might be argued that inventions of Ireland which valorise its peripherality are simply reproducing colonial and hierarchical imaginaries, changing how poverty and backwardness is viewed does not change the fact that it is poverty and backwardness which is at the end of the viewing tower. Such a reading however would not do justice to the rich affective qualities of senses of belonging which diasporic peoples feel and their profound attachment to an Ireland where the wonders of childhood and the love of parents and extended family are felt with tangible consequences. The diasporic location of the Irish Catholic community in Scotland then, has led to a particular way of imagining and inventing Ireland, and to some extent has cut across and blocked out interiorisations of inferiority and processes of seriality.

Mandatory Manicheanism

Because the Irish Catholic community has formed its groups in fusion within the metropolitan heartland, arguably it has had to seek Manichean solutions to Manichean problems more aggressively. This of course has positive and negative features. I might speculate that since the turn of the last century, there have existed at least three species of groups in fusion which have been triggered by the Irish presence in Scottish history and which have had a major influence on the course of history; based respectively upon Christian Liberalism and Calvinist Humanism, anti-imperialism and anti-Fascism, and socialist politics and class struggle. Whilst each betrayed a different vision for Scotland and assumed different kinds of politics, all three can be said to be decisively progressive. Moreover each involved to varying degrees a destruction of the Manichean stranglehold characterising the Anglo-Irish estrangement and a co-authoring of social movements motivated by liberation, emancipation, and the restoration of the dignity of the wounded, exploited, and powerless.

- *Christian Liberalism/Calvinist Humanism* – The first moment came with the rise of certain species of Liberalism in Glasgow in the second half of the nineteenth century and start of the twentieth century, and the concomitant rise of Christian Humanism and a new era of bourgeois philanthropy. The political culture of Glasgow was permeated with a new civic ethos which whilst paternal and at times patronising was empathetic to the plight of poor Irish migrants suffering from poverty and living in squalor. Public education, parks, recreation, wash houses, and libraries were to be developed as lasting and precious resources. Whilst many might reject the analytic purchase of the idea of the Group in Fusion in this instance, lamenting the motives of Protestant reformers, there nevertheless exists a case that in its finest clothes the civic ethos of the Liberal period embodied a transcendence of indigenous alienation from the humanity of impoverished migrants. Moreover, the role of the Catholic Church in charitable work, albeit subsidiary to Protestant bourgeois philanthropy, is an important additional adjunct.

- *Anti-imperialism and anti-fascism* – The second moment stems from the rise of Irish nationalism in the west of Scotland, from the Fenian period and latterly and especially in the late nineteenth and early twentieth centuries. The Irish Catholic community in Scotland played a significant role in a range of both pacifist and violent Irish independence movements, providing moral, political, financial, practical, and soldiering support. From the Irish National Land League to the Home Rule Movement to violent revolutionary insurrection, the Irish Catholic community in Scotland participated in Ireland's search for independence and in Ireland's civil war. The rise of the troubles from the 1970s stimulated a new generation of support, on this occasion for nationalist communities in Ulster. But anti-fascism has also created some unusual bedfellows evidenced by Irish Catholic participation in the First World War (1914 to 1919) and in particular the Second World War (1939–45). Many Irish migrants of course stood against Fascism in the Spanish Civil War (1936 to 1939) and whilst both world wars were considered by some to be bourgeois wars, it was natural and rational for the Irish Catholic community to unite with the indigenous Scot to resist the march of Fascism, National Socialism, and Nazism in Europe. Irish Catholics fought and died alongside Ulster Protestants and Scottish Presbyterians as part of the stand against German imperialism and military conquest.

- *Class Politics* – The third moment can be traced to the period 1914 to 1919 and to the rise of the Red Clydeside movement. Substantially co-authored with Irish Catholic migrants, the Red Clydeside movement sought to contest skill dilution and inhospitable working practices in heavy engineering and shipbuilding firms, and domestic rent rises and the shameless rent hikes imposed by property owners. But it had much wider connections to emerging socialist, anti-capitalist and anti-imperial movements internationally. Its leaders tellingly included John Wheatley (Waterford born, leader of the Independent Labour Party (ILP), and a Catholic), Willie Gallagher (a Communist leader whose father was Irish and whose mother was from the Scottish Highlands) and John MacLean (a leading Marxist of Calvinist and Highland origin). Irish Catholics in

Glasgow played a significant role in the development of the British ILP. In the inter war period and in particular the period from 1945 to the oil crises in 1973, socialism and class politics in the west of Scotland was at the heart of the expansion of the British Fordist Keynesian welfare state and in particular the provision of mass social housing. In conjunction with the indigenous Labour movement, Irish Catholic politicians played a central role in planning slum clearance, providing new social housing estates in Glasgow, and building new towns to house overspill populations.

Integration as a progenitor of alterity

In Sartrean terms, it is possible to view the debate initiated by James MacMillan in 1999 and occupying Scottish public life for a decade, as the latest in a series of more established and mature groups in fusion. A number of activists and advocates from the Irish and Catholic community have been forced to confront the seriality imposed by the wider community and through personal struggles with alienation have engaged in processes of fusion. In no way is the Scotland's secret shame debate characterised by an organised collective and there are no leaders, fratricidal organisations, institutions, or bureaucracies that have sought to claim and control the debate. Occupancy of the public realm has been anarchic, organic, spontaneous, and uncoordinated. And like all effective groups in fusion the participants have had an impact largely because of their energy, diversity, and pursuit of varied and different arguments. This debate has accomplished much, unsettling those who enjoy the privilege of seeing without being seen, elevating the blight of sectarianism and bigotry into public debate, and impacting the policies of the Scottish Executive and Scottish Government. MacMillan and those who have taken up his case have succeeded in securing a degree of liberation from alterity and seriality.

For Sartre scarcity, defined in both relative and absolute terms, proved to be an active progenitor of colonial projects. The expansion of the metropolitan core could only occur if the resources of the peripheral colony were plundered. Because there existed a historical geography of natural resources so too there existed a historical geography of scarcity. Curiously however, Sartre rooted all resistances to colonial exploitation in the sphere of the cultural rather than the economic. It is not because they are losing battles over the allocation of scarce resources that colonies rise; it is because in so losing these battles colonial populations are taxed culturally and psychologically. When these interiorisations of inferiority and alterity become sufficiently entrenched the seeds of resistance begin. It is only when alienation becomes intolerable that anti-colonialism is possible. For Sartre then the economic may trigger colonial expansion but the cultural ultimately determines and seals the fate of such accumulation by dispossession. There are cultural consequences to colonial annexation and economic consequences to culture-led resistance. But the causal arrow is reversed through time.

One reading of the Scotland's secret shame debate is that this debate has been birthed by the potential re-routing of a scarce resource, public funds for Catholic schools, and to the erosion of denominational education. Anticipating a potential loss of this prized resource under a new Scottish parliament, for some feared as a Scottish Stormont of sorts, the Irish Catholic community has betrayed an elevated and disproportionate sense of being victimised. The virulence of Irish Catholic protestation over lingering practices of sectarianism, discrimination, and bigotry in contemporary Scotland is indeed irrational and culture led. This might constitute a form of paranoia but only in so far as there are no ambitions at any level in Scotland to withdraw support for faith-based schooling. This psychological sense of being under attack and being besieged and out flanked by a new Scottish political elite has proven to be the key threat that has animated a public reaction. And it is having results. Thus far the Scottish Nationalist Party has distanced itself from any policy which appears to question the rights of those who cherish Catholic schooling for their children. In a way then, the Sartrean dance between the economic and the cultural proves to be informative.

Whilst appreciating the merits of this proposition, I offer the idea of abundance as a catalyst of fusion as an alternative point of departure for any reading of the surging rebirth of Irish Catholic critique of anti Irish Catholicism in Scotland in the past decade. Arguably, it has been because of growing Irish Catholic success and confidence in the socio-economic sphere, the rise of a new educated Irish Catholic middle class, and not cultural alienation, paranoia, and intimidation, that the Irish Catholic community has rediscovered its sense of difference. Integration has been a progenitor of alterity. Arguably, the socio-economic trials of forebears were weathered so as to deliver a degree of economic strength and freedom. For some, seriality, or the keeping of one's head down so as to accumulate capital in a low profile way, has been lived without terminal existential and psychic costs because a pragmatic and practical intergenerational project has been pursued. A specific attitude towards cultural seriality has facilitated success in the battle for scarce resources and it is from a position of strength and cultural confidence and not alienation and dejection that equal rights to the city are now being reclaimed. My reworking of Sartre then draws attention to the extent to which influential speaking positions become more possible only when battles over scarcity are partially won and not when they are decisively lost. We need to reflect upon processes of fusion which stem from immigrant advancement, socio-economic integration and advancement as well as processes of fusion which are triggered by socio-economic marginality and dispossession. Increasingly Sartre's sequencing of the imbrication of the 'cultural' and the 'economic' maps only in complex ways onto the workings of anti-Irish Catholic sentiment and pro-Irish Catholic reaction in Scotland's past.

The Irish Catholic community in Scotland and the Sartrean Group in Fusion

Sartre's drift from Marxism to Existential Marxism eventually led him to concede that specific and concrete anti-colonial movements could not be regarded as merely instances of a more universal struggle to replace capitalism with a socialist utopia. Each anti-colonial movement emerged in a historically unique way and germinated into a historically exceptional social, cultural, economic, and political formation. For Sartre anti-colonial movements announced the arrival of newness into the world and this newness had no particular meaning and could not be rendered especially intelligible in terms of the unfolding of history. Instead of path dependent historical processes marching over space towards a set destination, space was now to be approached as a fundamental generative force, constituting a more open and unpredictable temporality. Sartre was interested in the work these emergent forms performed, their lapses, encrustation, praxis, and metamorphoses. A Sartrean topology would approach the Irish Catholic adventure in Scotland with a view to scrutinising the kinds of historically novel cultural secretions which this adventure has birthed. A Sartrean inquiry into the meaning of the Irish Catholic encounter with Scotland in history would foreground the role of this community as a progenitor of a particular and unique series of anti-colonial cultural formations.

But for Sartre, processes of fusion which announce resistance to the sensation of being seen and objectified by the colonial panopticon often themselves secrete social and cultural movements which are predicated upon potent and virulent national identities. These movements and identities solidify and become a source of inertia. It is for this reason that Sartre was suspicious of racial, ethnic and national identities as a call to action and called for those who contest the colonial look to renounce and annul markers of ethnicity, race, and nationality, as soon as they become the end in themselves rather than the means to an end. This is especially pertinent as some critics charge the Irish Catholic community in Scotland with an excessive and obsessive preoccupation with Irish concerns, an elevated and disproportionate sense of grievance, paranoia and patriotism, and an unhealthy and debilitating devotion to forebears and ancestry. And there can be no doubt that the history of the Irish Catholic community in Scotland has been marked by lapses into seriality and mutations into metastatic encrustations; it has been affected by endless flights into bad faith and sporadic metamorphoses into regressive tribalism.

But this book has also shown that at the core of this history has been a community with a disposition towards liquefying seriality and entering the historical stage as an advocate for the discriminated, the underdog and the marginalised. My claim is that there exists a steady state or equilibrium to which the Irish Catholic community has repeatedly returned no matter what social, political, cultural, and economic offshoots it has spawned. Of course over the past two centuries this community has oscillated between masses, spontaneity and tribe but arguably it has always returned to a default position which is best characterised as a disposition to court nausea or a state of primitive fusion. The Irish Catholic community has shown itself able take stock of its story and Scotland without dwelling or revelling or remaining stuck in it; it has demonstrated a capacity to recognise that whilst its story is special and valuable it is not one that should be committed to freeze frame for posterity. I call this *progressive tribalism*; the idea that all cosmopolitanisms are situated; to be cosmopolitan one needs to be cosmopolitan from somewhere. Although ceaselessly emerging, I use the concepts multiple belongings and identities, anti-colonialism and the political rainbow, Catholic *aggiornamento*, and the class conscious drag, to capture the workings of this progressive tribalism today.

Multiple belongings

Living in a former heartland of the British empire, amongst some indigenes who continue to feel the need to venerate Britain's imperial past and colonial subjugation of Ireland, it is assumed by some that Irish Catholics have found great difficulty in bonding with Scottish society. Scotland remains little more than an inhospitable borderzone. Estrangement, alienation and existential insecurity persist as more powerful emotions than inclusion, attachment and belonging. The sensation of being seen or frozen through objectification leads to bad faith and serial behaviours, serial feelings, and serial attitudes. But it is clear that to think of the Irish Catholic community in Scotland as outsiders and exiles, serving their purgatory in Scotland and longing for the day when they return to Ireland, is fundamentally misconstrued. Whilst it would be wrong to underestimate the difficulties Irish Catholics have experienced in securing an emotional attachment to Scotland, it would be equally erroneous to ignore the complex roots which they have now planted in Scotland. The metaphor of a jarring between two tribes cannot survive serious scrutiny.

I propose that the Irish Catholic community has interlaced with Scottish society in at least five different ways. Firstly, for many Britain's fractious relationship with Ireland has indeed carried over into the present day in mutant forms, soiled the settlement experience of the Irish Catholic community, and mitigated against assimilation. Alterity has sponsored a culture of resentment and birthed a steely defiance. Secondly, others recognise themselves to be simply different from the Scots but assume that this difference does not make both communities incommensurable. Alterity is experienced as benign. Thirdly, coexistence has bracketed the question of difference: difference has been suspended as part of the practice of everyday life and everyday life has been productive of new ways of thinking about the other. Alterity has been necessarily effaced in everyday practices. Fourthly, yet others recognise that some Scottish constituencies have proven welcoming to Irish Catholics, that the Scots and the Irish have a shared history and close affinity and that communion has always been a powerful antidote to marginalisation. Cultural proximity trumps alterity. Finally, changes in both Ireland and Scotland and the emergence of a new youthful cosmopolitan Scottish community have meant that any differences which have existed in the past have now being forgotten and transcended. Amnesia has erased alterity.

Because they have become laced into Scotland's diaspora space in a variety of ways, the Irish Catholic community betrays a variety of senses of attachment to Scotland. In the oral history testimonies at least six senses of belonging could be detected: 'Irish', 'Irish Scot', 'Irish and Scottish', 'illegitimate' or 'neither Irish nor Scottish', 'Scottish with an Irish heritage', and 'Scottish with a suppressed Irish blood line'. For the 'Irish', the category Irish Catholic in Scotland has literal meaning and captures more or less the totality of their national identity. For the 'Irish Scot', the category defines the cultural stock from which one has derived, but one's sense of identity is derivative of this category and not subsumed by it. Concern is with the way in which the category has become Scottified. Those who see themselves as both Irish and Scottish seem capable of aligning the category Irish Catholic with narratives of the Scottish nation, largely through the shared Celtic heritage. The category defines who they are and this identity is not compromised by being in Scotland but redefined and perhaps even fortified by being situated as part of a family of categories and network of categorical kin relations. Those who see themselves as neither Irish or Scottish approach the category Irish Catholic as mutating when sent into diaspora. It is a category that is not equivalent to Irish Catholic in Ireland and not commensurable with Presbyterian Scotland. The category takes on a nomadic and disorientating character. Those who see themselves as Scottish but with an Irish heritage approach the category Irish Catholic as integral to who they are and part of a claiming of a new form of Scottishness. The category has vibrancy in Scotland in so far as the Irish story is part of a reconstitution of the Scottish story and the formation of a more inclusive sense of Scottishness. Finally, there are some diasporic families who, for a variety of rational or irrational, justifiable or inauthentic, happenstance and strategic reasons, have sought to deny their Irish roots and pronounce themselves essentialised Scots. For these 'lace curtain Irish' the category Irish Catholic in Scotland is a stain to be sanitised from the family tree.

The political rainbow

Whilst some participants had definite views about Irish history and in particular about the political situation in Northern Ireland, it was widely acknowledged that the wisest course of action was to keep one's beliefs to oneself. Of course there exists a basic incommensurability in the starting assumptions held by Loyalist and Unionist supporters in Scotland and those cherished by some members of the Irish Catholic community. If the British presence in Ireland and more particularly in Northern Ireland is viewed as legitimate and if the present Protestant majority in Northern Ireland have the right to insist that the democratic will of the majority is adhered to, then Nationalists and Republicans are to be viewed as little more than terrorists and career criminals and support for them is tantamount to condoning murder. If being Irish was in itself a reason to feel exposed, then being publicly supportive of nationalist and republican causes was to open oneself up to an even greater degree of vulnerability. Many participants noted therefore that whilst Irish politics was frequently discussed behind closed doors and with family members and selected friends, they were particularly wary about airing their political views in public and would often shy away from potentially confrontational situations.

Nevertheless, historically, the Irish Catholic diaspora has played an active and at times key role in the rise and fall of Irish nationalist and republican social, economic, cultural, and political movements in Ireland itself. This support has taken the form of one or other of leadership and organisation, volunteering, moral and political solidarity, fundraising for nationalist movements, the provision of armaments and explosives, and the dissemination of political propaganda. It is unsurprising then that stories of British colonial subjugation of Ireland and tales of heroic rebellion and struggle continue to figure prominently in the lexicon of communities throughout the Irish diaspora, and the Irish community in Scotland is no exception. Activists, advocates, and agitators who feel courageous enough to speak out in solidarity with the Irish Catholic cause today recognise that in so doing they are potentially courting hostility from Unionist and Loyalist groups and from the State. But whilst for some, to act is intolerable, for others not to act is too alienating to countenance. Processes of seriality always threaten to envelop such actors but instead of being cowed these processes only prove to be a catalyst for new actions of fusion and the totalisation of individual resistances.

Groups in fusion remain fertile precisely when they are allowed to totalise in an anarchic way, guided by a range of third parties which themselves have only transitory and fleeting existence. In spite of sharing broadly similar views on the Irish question, it is evident that activists have translated their views so as to inform different kinds of domestic political projects in Scotland. Once planted into Scotland's diaspora space, Irish nationalism and republicanism it would seem, has germinated into a variety of different political agendas. In the case of the activists examined in this book, six areas of domestic political activity would appear to have resulted; socialist politics and trade union activity, Scottish nationalism and pan Celticism, anti-sectarianism, anti-racism and community politics, the rights of Irish organisations to express themselves culturally in the area of marching, intra-state reforms of penal and welfare policy and social work practice, and socialist Scottish nationalism. In this regard at least, the Irish Catholic community in Scotland embodies precisely that kind of fluid and emerging Group in Fusion which Sartre so cherishes. The politics of anti-imperialism has taken hold in Scotland only to blossom into a thousand flowers. The fact that historical ties with the Labour movement and Labour Party are now being contested and that some within the Irish Catholic community are investing their political futures in the Scottish Nationalist Party demonstrates a degree of openness and becoming that establishes that processes of fusion, totalisation, and creolisation remain alive and lively.

Catholic aggiornamento

Sartre paid little attention to the everyday lifestyles of those burdened by a serialised existence, alterity, bitter estrangement, and fundamental alienation. It is clear that it is with respect to cultural differences, and in particular the question of the acceptance of Roman Catholicism in Scotland, that the most acute and wounding encounters with difference are often felt. An important project would be to examine the behavioural consequences of those who endure seriality across an extended time period, perhaps even a lifetime. The importance of substance abuse as a form of relief, and in particular the significance of Ireland's colonial history to the problems of alcoholism among Irish migrants living in the United Kingdom, has attracted some interest within the psychiatric community and would merit further scrutiny. Of course alcoholism has a set of complex genetic, psychological, cultural, social, and economic causes, and cannot be reduced to an outworking of living a serial existence. But it would seem obvious that the existential dramas encountered in living out a life in an environment that is other and whose otherness carries assumptions of inferiority must play a role in creating and maintaining a desire for inoculation and anaestheticisation.

But of course cultural alterity has also been an important catalyst for processes of fusion. The Catholic Church has proven an interesting vehicle for the gathering of processes of fusion. Of course some regard the Catholic Church itself, especially in its hierarchical and patriarchal guises, as a source of seriality. The Catholic Church in Scotland is a classic example of a Group in Fusion which runs the risk itself of becoming a force of conservatism and even for some in extreme cases a crippling monstrosity: an organisation which has fossilised and rendered inert the Irish Catholic community. The initial strength of the Catholic Church among the immigrant community has steadily sponsored a drift towards the formation of a Group in Metastases, a succumbing to an organisation which has ossified into a huge centralised bureaucracy and authoritarian regime. If not colonised by Britain the Irish have been colonised by Rome. But others might regard the Catholic Church as an important third party which has channelled processes of fusion which have originated in other spheres responsibly and to good effect; the Brother Walfrid story. The Catholic Church has defended the interests of the Irish Catholic community in a hostile environment, served as an advocate for this community and fed and clothed immigrants, and provided a fora for the plight of an immigrant population to be debated and progressed. As a minority Church it has served more to liberate and inspire than to enslave and debilitate.

In any event both secularism and ecumencism have changed the terms in which the Catholic Church operates and arguably fortified its capacity to promote fusion. Secularism is always an uneven and ongoing process and many display complex relations with the Catholic Church rather than rejecting it *tout court*. It remains an open question as to whether the Catholic Church will continue to ignite the passion of the Irish Catholic community in future as it did in yesteryear; perhaps we are witnessing a new moment in which the Church is redefining its role within the community rather than departing from it. Perhaps the critical question will be the extent to which the Catholic Church can invent a future for itself in which it formulates and evangelises progressive social and cultural agendas, builds and fortifies purposeful social movements in defence of the poor and exploited, widens and enriches public debate and democratic politics, and nurtures a stronger sense of global responsibility and care. For it to do so it may need to reform its structures so that it is based on its origins and oriented to the present rather than its medieval past, works on the basis of partnership and community and not patriarchal and hierarchical expressions of power; is ecumenical and inclusive and not fundamentalist and exclusive; and embraces multi-culturalism and cosmopolitanism and does not succumb itself to metrocentric arrogance.

Ecumenical bridge provides a necessary foundation for processes of fusion to come to fruition and for a common sense of humanity to emerge out of sectarian division and hatred. But there is a clear difference in the formal work done by officially constituted ecumenical bodies and the informal ecumenical synergies which occur routinely and informally in everyday life. The former tends to be marked by a cagey exercise in shadow boxing and a bracketing of real discussion about differences and their capacity to be transcended. Christian churches might unite in fusion but they do so always from a series of different bases and often without a commitment to work to dismantle the institutional fortress from which they speak. The latter in contrast is dominated by the productive role of everyday life in the generation of new meanings. Of course the philosophy of everyday life has attracted much attention recently. In place of the formal *strategies* adopted for overcoming differences here more attention would be given to the importance of many small *tactics*, encounters which replace difference with a common humanity, even if only for a short period. Perhaps an appropriate way to think of the two is to approach formal and official ecumenical bridge building as a way of releasing processes of fusion, whilst treating the organic processes of fusion which occur in everyday life as itself a prerequisite for grass roots ecumenical bridge building.

Class conscious drag

It is not true to say that anti-Irish Catholic bullying and discrimination took place in every workplace in Scotland or even in most or many. But it is the case that some members of the Irish Catholic community suffered measurable mental and physical intimidation. The oral testimonies provide a vivid and dramatic insight into how seriality was lived out by at least some young Irish Catholic men and women venturing out into the labour market for the first time. Lost innocence is clearly the primary casualty in this experience. Of course many young men found that putting one's head down and trying to survive was the only way to live through the workplaces they were thrust into. I refer to this as strategic seriality. They and their family needed the money for mere survival. There was little point in worrying parents and so young men and women had to shoulder the burden of miserable and intimidating workplaces themselves. Nevertheless, it is striking to note that seriality was occasionally punctured by those within indigenous Scotland who might be expected to be less empathetic. Often the lost common humanity which was witnessed in ritualised abuse became so great that people with wisdom and insight realised that they could not stand back and do nothing. It was men of real Christianity and standing within the Orange Order and the Masonic Lodges that sometimes reached out a hand of comfort and who helped those who suffered most. Those moments of communion, when people see a little light in an otherwise black tunnel, are the seeds of fusion. From these moments great things can happen.

How is immigrant advancement and the upward socio-economic drift of the Irish Catholic community in Scotland to be viewed? On one level it perhaps underscores the fact that anti Irish Catholic sentiment in Scotland, to the extent it existed and exists, has not been pervasive enough to retard socio-economic improvement. It might have slowed down the pace of socio-economic assimilation but it has not blocked or stunted it *per se*. We might conclude then that class has not been as strong a marker of alterity as other badges of difference. To the extent that the Irish Catholic community has secured occupational progress, captured a share of the economy of the west of Scotland, and now resides in the more affluent suburbs as well as the poorer peripheral housing estates in the city, it is perhaps true to conclude that lack of control over the economy and the labour market has not been a particularly decisive source of alterity for the Irish Catholic community. Its psychic costs notwithstanding, strategic seriality has borne fruit.

It is interesting then to ask whether economic advancement has been used to enhance processes of fusion or whether it has merely constituted a new form of seriality. There are instances, especially surrounding defensive ethnic and racialised practices, where there is evidence of groups in metastases forming in regard to the control of economic resources and the distribution of items of collective consumption. These groups in metastases threaten to become a new source of incarceration for some members of the Irish Catholic community, who jealously defend and claim their share of the resource cake, fearful of other groups prising this share away. An immigrant group which itself looked for empathy and support from the indigenous population and perhaps rightly complained when such assistance was lacking or withheld, now finds some of its own members and kin calling for a rationing of assistance and withdrawal of support to other immigrant groups. Lost in debates about the worthy and the unworthy immigrant, and the morality and meritocracy of different systems and methods of distributing welfare support, is the simple fact that the once oppressed is itself showing signs of being an able oppressor. Resource allocation models threaten to drive a wedge between the Irish Catholic community and other immigrant groups when in fact both ought to see each other's humanity more keenly. This duplicity and contradiction is not lost on some migrants who lament the degenerative and racialised attitudes of some of their friends and family.

But overall, it would seem that the Irish Catholic community betrays a greater class consciousness than one might expect given their occupational profile and socio-economic status. This might be referred to as the Irish Catholic 'drag' effect.

The Irish Catholic community occupies an ambivalent attitude to success within the capitalist economy. Like all other groups, but perhaps with a greater degree of urgency, they valorise socio-economic development. There is a fierce pride underpinning success as specified by capitalist status hierarchies. On the other hand their pride is grounded; it is success tempered with a profound and emotion-filled respect for those left behind and for the poverty and sacrifices made by their forebears. In some respects socio-economic success has resourced a marginalised group. Better armed with economic, cultural, and educational capital the Irish Catholic community clearly occupy a less vulnerable position within Scottish society than they once did. It is more able to speak out against injustices, both in Ireland and Scotland, without fearing economic ruination for doing so. It can be more resourceful now in its advocacy work and promotion of the causes of the Irish Catholic community in Scotland. This combination of socio-economic progress and class consciousness drag has produced a community well placed to practice progressive tribalism.

This book then recognises that there is certainly merit in charting, celebrating, explaining, clarifying, critiquing, and developing the category Irish Catholic in Scotland, especially when it has shown tendencies to ossify into oppressive metastatic forms. But when considered in its totality I conclude that the category Irish Catholic in Scotland is a fluid, emerging, and open one, comprising a variety of meanings and used by a variety of groups with different claims to national identity, competing political passions, varying and self-critical cultural investments, and complex class status and class consciousness. Sartre became interested in historically grounded insights on potential pathways to revolutionary praxis and came close to renouncing dogmatic, prefabricated models of social change, which ultimately imprisoned freedom. His focus was upon a species of socialism that was centred on the freedom of the human person and not the tyrannical encrustations of a fossilised 'Party'. Arguably, the Irish Catholic community in Scotland stands as a potentially historically novel and progressive social and cultural force. The Irish Catholic community defines itself as culturally distinctive in ways which perhaps equate to Sartre's interest in novel, creolised, hybridised, and emancipatory cultural and political formations.

Conclusion

It is undoubtedly time to dust the debris of fifty years or more of neglect and partial, selective, and at times outright misunderstanding and misappropriation, to consider anew what Sartre might bequeath to Postcolonial Studies today and to critics of the colonial present. I offer this book as a potential contribution to Sartrean scholarship more widely and to the fortification of a renewed interest in Sartre's theory of colonialism. I introduce to Sartrean scholarship such supplementary concepts as 'liberating nausea'. 'the embryonic circular dialectic', 'colonialism's double look', 'the diasporic vaccine', 'mandatory Manicheanism', 'integration as a progenitor of alterity', 'strategic seriality', 'progressive tribalism', 'multiple belongings', the 'political rainbow', 'Catholic *aggiornamento*', and the 'class consciousness drag'. Of course in no sense am I claiming that the Irish Catholic adventure in Scotland is an ideal typical model of Sartre's theory of practical ensembles nor is it an exemplar of the fruits of Sartre's political prescriptions. This case is unique and specific. My deployment of Sartre has been firmly against the backdrop of a wariness of tendencies to over invest in metropolitan illusions, and at times delusions and hallucinations. The dialogue which this chapter has constructed between Sartrean topology and the topographical mappings of Irish Catholic biographies is necessarily situated, partial, brittle, and at best only suggestive. Until established otherwise my addition of new concepts to the Sartrean lexicon remains pertinent only to this specific case study. But it is my contention that this case study holds fascinating insights which the Sartrean scholar and activist might find instructive, revealing, and encouraging. I submit that the Irish Catholic adventure in Scotland can instruct as well as be instructed by the much anticipated Sartrean revival.

References

Newspaper and media citations have not been included in this list of references as the full citation has been incorporated into the main body of the text.

Abbotts J, Williams R, Ford G, Hunt K and West P. 1997 Morbidity and Irish Catholic descent in Britain: an ethnic and religious minority 150 years on *Social Science and Medicine* 45 3–14

Abbotts J, Williams R and Smith GD. 1998 Mortality in men of Irish heritage in the West of Scotland *Public Health* 112 229–32

Abbotts J, Williams R and Smith GD. 1999 Association of medical, physiological, behavioural and socio-economic factors with elevated mortality in men of Irish heritage in the West of Scotland *Journal of Health Medicine* 21 46–54

Abbotts J, Williams R and Ford G. 2001 Morbidity and Irish Catholic descent in Britain: relating health disadvantage to socio-economic position *Social Science and Medicine*, 52 999–1005

Akenson DH 1992 The historiography of the Irish in the United States. In O'Sullivan P, editor *The Irish worldwide, history, heritage and identity volume 2: The Irish in the new communities* London: Leicester University Press 99–127

Akenson DH 1993 *The Irish Diaspora: a primer* P.D. Meany: Toronto

Aron R 1975 *History and the dialectic of violence: An analysis of Sartre's critique de la raison dialectique* Oxford: Blackwell

Aronson R 1987 *Sartre's second critique* Chicago: The University of Chicago Press

Aronson R 2004 *Camus and Sartre: The story of a friendship and the quarrel that ended it* Chicago: University of Chicago Press

Aspinwall B 1996 A long journey: the Irish in Scotland' In O'Sullivan P (editor) *The Irish world wide: history heritage and identity Volume 5: Religion and identity* London: Leicester University Press 146–82

Aspinwall B 2008 Catholic realities and pastoral strategies: Another look at the historiography of Scottish Catholicism, 1878–1920 *The Innes Review* 59 77–112

Badiou A 2007 The event in Deluze *Parhesia* 2 37–44

Battu H (2005) *Is there an Earnings Penalty to being Catholic in Scotland*, www.scotecon.net,University of Aberdeen

Blunt A and Wills J 2000 *Dissident geographies: An introduction to radical ideas and practice* Harlow: Prentice Hall

Blunt A and McEwan C (editors) 2002 *Postcolonial geographies* London: Continuum

Boyce DG 1982 (reprinted 1993) *Nationalism in Ireland* London: Routledge

Boyle M. 2001a Towards a (Re)theorisation of the historical geography of nationalism in diasporas: The Irish Diaspora as an exemplar *International Journal of Population Geography* 7 429–46

Boyle M 2001b Edifying the rebellious Gael In Harvey DC, Jones RH, McInroy N and Milligan C (editors) *Celtic Geographies: Old Culture, New Times* London: Routledge 173–91

Boyle M 2005 Sartre's circular dialectic and the empires of abstract space: a history of space and place in Ballymun, Dublin *Annals of the Association of American Geographers* 95 181–20

Boyle R and Lynch P 1998 *Out of the ghetto? The Catholic community in modern Scotland* Edinburgh: John Donald Press

Bradley JM 1996 Abstruse and insecure? Irish immigrant identity in modern Scotland *Social Identities* 2 293–310

Bradley J 2004 *Celtic Minded: Essays on religion, politics, society, identity – and football* Glasgow: Thirsty Books

Bradley JM 2006 One Scotland, Many Cultures *Irish Studies Review* 14 189–205

Bradley JM 2008 *Celtic Minded 2: Essays on identity* Glasgow: Argyll

Bradley JM 2009 *Celtic Minded 3* Glasgow: Argyll

Brah A 1996 *Cartographies of Diaspora: Contesting Identities* London: Routledge

Bruce S 1999 Social divisions and the social impact of Catholic schools *Scottish Affairs* 29 1–8

Bruce S 2003 Catholic Schools in Scotland: a rejoinder to Conroy *Oxford Review of Education* 29 269–77

Bruce S, Glendinning T, Paterson I, and Rosie M. 2004 *Sectarianism in Scotland* Edinburgh: Edinburgh University Press

Bruce S, Glendinning T, Paterson I, and Rosie M. 2005 Religious discrimination in Scotland: Fact or myth? *Ethnic and Racial Studies* 28 151–68

Burawoy M 2005 American Sociological Association Presidential address: For public sociology *American Sociological Review* 70 4–28

Burdsey D. and Chappell R 2001 'And if you know your history ...' An examination of the formation of football clubs in Scotland and their role in the construction of social identity *Sport in History* 21 94–106

Busch TW 1999 *Circulating being – From embodiement to incorporation: essays in late existentialism* New York: Fordham University Press

Buttimer A 1993 *Geography and the human spirit* Baltimore: Johns Hopkins University Press

Carter E and Hirschkop K (editors) 1996 Cultural Memory: Special Issue *New Formations* 30

Catalano JS 1986 *A commentary on Jean Paul Sartre's critique of dialectical reason Vol 1: Theory of practical ensembles* Chicago: University of Chicago Press

Chakrabarty D 2007 *Provincialising Europe: Postcolonial thought and historical difference* (new edition) London: Verso

Chiodi P 1976 *Sartre and Marxism* London: The Harvester Press

Church of Scotland 2002 *The demon in our Society: Sectarianism in Scotland* Edinburgh: Church of Scotland

Clayton T 2002 Politics and nationalism in Scotland: a Clydeside case study of identity construction *Political Geography* 21 813–43

Clayton T 2005 'Diasporic Otherness': racism, sectarianism and 'national exteriority' in modern Scotland *Social and Cultural Geography* 6 99–116

Cohen WB 2003 The Algerian war and the revision of France's overseas mission. *French Colonial History* 4 227–39

Conroy JC 2001 A very Scottish Affair – Catholic education and the state *Oxford Review of Education,* 27 543–58

Conroy JC 2003 'Yet I Live Here ...' A reply to Bruce on Catholic education in Scotland *Oxford Review of Education,* 29 403–12

Conway B 2010 New directions in the Sociology of collective memory and commemoration *Sociology Compass* 4 442–53

Cooper F 2005 *Colonialism in Question: Theory, Knowledge, History* Berkeley: University of California Press

Craib I 1976 *Existentialism and sociology: A study of Jean Paul Sartre* Cambridge: Cambridge University Press

Davidson J 2003 *Phobic Geographies: The phenomenology of spatiality and identity* Aldershot: Ashgate

Davis NZ and Starn R 1989 Special Issue: Introduction *Representations* 26 1–6

Delaney E 2007 *The Irish in post war Britain* Oxford: Oxford University Press

Deuchar R and Holligan CP 2010 Gangs, sectarianism and social capital: A qualitative study of young people in Scotland *Sociology* 4413–30

Devine TM *Irish immigrants and Scottish society in the nineteenth and twentieth centuries* Edinburgh: John Donald

Devine TM 2000 *Scotland's shame? Bigotry and sectarianism in modern Scotland.* Edinburgh: Mainstream Publishing

Esplin R and Walker G 2007 *It's Rangers for me* Ayrshire: Fort Publishing Limited

Esplin R and Walker G 2010 *Rangers: Triumphs, troubles, traditions* Ayrshire: Fort Publishing Limited

Fatouros AA 1965 Sartre on colonialism *World Politics* 17 703–19

Finn GPT and Guilianotti R (editors) 2000 *Football culture: Local contests, global visions* London: Frank Cass Publishers

Finn GPT 1999 Scottish myopia and global prejudices *Sport in Society* 2 54–99

Finn G, Uygun F, and Johnston A 2009 *Sectarianism and the Workplace* Glasgow: STUC

Flint J 2008 Governing sectarianism in Scotland *Scottish Affairs* 63 107–24

Flynn TR 1997 *Sartre and Foucault: Toward an existentialist theory of history Vol 1* Chicago: The University of Chicago Press

Foster J, Houston M and Madigan C 2010 Irish immigrants in Scotland's shipyards and coalfields: employment relations, sectarianism and class formation *Historical Research,* 84: no. doi: 10.1111/j.1468-2281.2010.00554.x

Fox NF 2003 *The new Sartre* London: Continuum

Gallagher T 1987 *Glasgow, the uneasy peace: Religious tension in modern Scotland* Manchester: Manchester University Press

Gerassi J 1989 *Jean Paul Sartre: Hated conscience of his century Vol 1 – Protestant or Protestor?* Chicago: University of Chicago Press

Gray B 2000 Gendering the Irish diaspora: Questions of enrichment, hybridization and return *Women's Studies International Forum* 23 167–85

Gray B 2004 *Women and the Irish diaspora* London: Routledge

Haddour A 2005 Sartre and Fanon: On negritude and political participation *Sartre Studies International* 11 286–301

Halbwachs M 1992 *On collective memory* Chicago: The University of Chicago Press

Handley JE 1943 *The Irish in Scotland* Cork: Cork University Press

Hartmann K 1981 Sartre's theory of practical ensembles in Schilpp PA (editor) *The philosophy of Jean Paul Sartre* Illinois: Open Court 631–60

Harvey D 1989 *The condition of postmodernity* Oxford: Blackwell

Hickman M 1999 Alternative historiographies of the Irish in Britain: a critique of the segregation/assimilation model In Swift R and Gilley S (editors) *The Irish in Victorian Britain: the local dimension* Dublin: Four Courts Press 236–53

Hickman M 2000 'Binary opposites' or 'unique neighbours'? The Irish in multi-ethnic Britain *The political quarterly* 71 50–58.

Hickman M, Morgan S, Walter B and Bradley J 2005 The limitations of whiteness and the boundaries of Englishness: second generation Irish identifications and positionings in multi-ethnic Britain *Ethnicities*, 5 160–82

Holligan CP and Deuchar R 2009 Territorialities in Scotland: perceptions of young people in Glasgow *Journal of Youth Studies* 12 731–46

Holligan C and Raab G 2010 *Inter-sectarian couples in the 2001 census* Research working paper 7 Edinburgh: General Register Office

Hutchinson J 1987 *The dynamics of cultural nationalism: The Gaelic revival and the creation of the Irish nation state* London: Allen and Unwin

Jameson F 1961 *Sartre: the origins of a style* New Haven: Yale University Press

Kearns G 2009 *Geopolitics and empire: The legacy of Halford Mackinder* Oxford: Oxford University Press

Kelly, E. (2003) Challenging Sectarianism in Scotland: The Prism of Racism *Social Affairs*, 42(Winter 2003), 32–56

Kelly M 1999 Towards a heuristic method: Sartre and Lefebvre *Sartre Studies International* 5 1–15

Kenefick W 1997 Irish Dockers and trade unionism on Clydeside *Irish Studies Review*, 5 22–9

Kobayashi A 1989 in Kobayashi A and Mackenzie S (editors) A Critique of Dialectical Landscape *Remaking Human Geography* London: Unwin Hyman 164–83

Kobayashi A 2004 Geography, spatiality, and racialisation: The contribution of Edward Said *Arab World Geographer* 7 79–90

Lattas A 1996 Introduction: Mnemonic regimes and strategies of subversion. *Oceania, 66* 257–65

Lawler JP 1976 *The existentialist Marxism of Jean Paul Sartre* Amsterdam: BR Gruner Publishing Co

Lowe WJ 1989 *The Irish in mid-Victorian Lancashire: The shaping of a working class community* New York: Peter Lang

Lummis T 1988 *Listening to History: The authenticity of oral evidence* New Jersey: Barnes and Noble

Mac An Ghaill M 2001 British critical theorists: The production of the conceptual invisibility of the Irish diaspora *Social Identities* 7 179–201

Majumdar MA 2007 *Postcoloniality: The French dimension* London: Berghahn Books

Massey D 2005 *For space* London: Sage

Merleau-Ponty M 1955 *Les Aventures de la Dialectique* Paris: Gallimard

Middleton D and Edwards D (editors) 1990 *Collective remembering* London: Sage

Mignola WD 1995 *The darker side of the Renaissance: Literacy, territoriality, & colonization* Michigan: University of Michigan Press

Miller KA 1988 *Emigrants and exiles: Ireland and the Irish exodus to North America* Oxford: Oxford University Press

Minca C 2003. Critical peripheries *Environment and Planning D: Society and Space* 21 160–68

Mitchell MJ 1998 The Irish in the west of Scotland 1797–1848: trade unions, strikes and *political movements* Edinburgh: John Donald

Mitchell MJ 2009 *New perspectives on the Irish in Scotland* Edinburgh: John Donald

Mullen K, Williams R and Hunt K 2000 Irish descent, religion and food consumption in the west of Scotland *Appetite* 34 47–54

McAspurren L 2005 *Religious discrimination & sectarianism in Scotland: A brief review of evidence (2002–2004)* Edinburgh: Scottish Executive Social Research

McBride T 2006a Irishness in Glasgow, 1863–70 *Immigrants and Minorities* 24 1–21

McBride T 2006b John Ferguson, Michael Davitt and Henry George-Land for the People *Irish Studies Review* 14 421–30

McBride T 2007 *The experience of Irish Migrants to Glasgow, Scotland 1863–1891: A new way of being Irish* London: Mellen Press

McBride T 2008 History Politics and Cultural Studies *Irish Studies Review* 16 77–112

McBride T 2010 The secular and the radical in Irish associational culture of Mid-Victorian Glasgow *Immigrants and Minorities* 28 31–4

McBride WL 1981 Sartre and Marxism in Schilpp PA (editor) *The philosophy of Jean Paul Sartre* Illinois: Open Court 605–30

McEwan C 2008 *Postcolonialism and development* London: Routledge

McFarland EW 2003 *John Ferguson, 1836–1906: Irish issues in Scottish politics* East Linton: Tuckwell Press

McKinney SJ 2007 *Catholic schools in Scotland: Mapping the contemporary debate and their continued existence in the 21st century.* Unpublished Ph.D. thesis Glasgow: University of Glasgow

McKinney SJ 2008 Catholic schools in Scotland and divisiveness *Journal of Beliefs and Values,* 29 173–84

McMenemy D, Poulter A, and O'Loan S 2005 A robust methodology for investigating Old-Firm related sectarianism online *International Journal of Web Based Communities* 1 488–503

McMenemy D and Poulter A 2005 An identity of two halves? *Irish Studies Review* 13 139–50

Nash C 2004 Postcolonial geographies: spatial narratives of inequality and interconnection in Cloke P, Crang P and Goodwin M (editors) *Envisioning human geographies* London: Arnold 187–216

Nash C 2008 *Of Irish descent: Origin stories, genealogy, and the politics of belonging* New York: Syracuse University Press

Neal F 1988 *Sectarian violence: The Liverpool experience 1819–1914* Manchester: Manchester University Press

Nora P 1999 *Rethinking France: Les lieux de memoire, Volume 1: The state* Chicago: University of Chicago Press

Nora P 2006 *Rethinking France: Les lieux de memoire, Volume 2: Space* Chicago: University of Chicago Press

Nora P 2009 *Rethinking France: les lieux de memoire, Volume 3: Legacies* Chicago: University of Chicago Press

Nora P 2010 *Rethinking France: les lieux de memoire, Volume 4: Histories and memories* Chicago: University of Chicago Press

O'Cathain MS 2007 *Irish Republicanism in Scotland 1858–1916: Fenians in exile* Dublin: Irish Academic Press

Paolucci G 2007 Sartre's humanism and the Cuban revolution *Theory and Society* 36 245–63

Paterson I 2002 Sectarianism and municipal housing allocation in Glasgow *Scottish Affairs* 39 39–53

Paterson L 2000 The social class of Catholics in Scotland *Journal of the Royal Statistical Society* 163 363–79

Paterson L and Iannelli C 2006 Religion, social mobility and education in Scotland *The British Journal of Sociology* 57 353–77

Perk R and Thomson A 2006 *The oral history reader* New York: Routledge

Peet D 1998 *Modern Geographical Thought* London: Blackwell

Pickles J 2005 'New cartographies' and the decolonisation of European Geographies *Area* 37 355–64

Pollard J, Nina L, McEwan C, and Stenning A 2009 Economic Geography under postcolonial scrutiny *Transactions of the Institute of British Geographers* Ns. 34 137–42

Poster M 1975 *Existential Marxism in post war France: From Sartre to Althusser* Princeton: Princeton University Press

Priest S 2001 *Jean-Paul Sartre: basic writings* London: Routledge

Reid IA 2008 'An outsider in our midst': narratives of Neil Lennon, soccer & ethno-religious bigotry in the Scottish press *Soccer & Society* 9 64–80

Reilly P 2000 Kicking with the left foot: Being Catholic in Scotland in Devine TM 2000 *Scotland's shame? Bigotry and sectarianism in modern Scotland* Edinburgh: Mainstream Publishing 29–40

Richie DA 2003 *Doing an oral history: A practical guide* New York: Oxford University Press

Rosie M 2004 *The Sectarian Myth in Scotland: Of Bitter Memory and Bigotry* London: Palgrave MacMillan

Said E 1978 *Orientalism* New York: Vintage

Said E 2000 My encounter with Sartre *London Review of Books* June 1st 1–3

Samuel R 1994 *Theatres of memory. Volume 1: past and present in contemporary culture* London: Verso

Samuels MS 1978 Existentialism and human geography in Ley D and Samuels MS (editors) *Humanistic geography: Problems and prospects* Chicago: Marooufa Press 22–40

Samuels MS 1981 An existential geography in Harvey ME and Holly BP (editors) *Themes in geographic thought* London: Croom Helm 86–106

Santoni R 2003 *Sartre on violence: Curiously ambivalent* Penn: Penn State University Press

Sartre J-P 1938 *La Nausée* Paris: Gallimard

Sartre J-P 1943 *Being and Nothingness: an essay on phenomenological ontology* London: Routledge

Sartre J-P 1964 *The problem of method* London: Methuen

Sartre J-P 1969 *The Communists and Peace* New York: Hamilton

Sartre J-P 1974 *Between Existentialism and Marxism: Sartre on philosophy, politics, psychology, and the arts* London: Panthean Books

Sartre J-P 1976a *Critique of dialectical reason Vol 1: Theory of practical ensembles* London: New Left Books

Sartre J-P 1976b *Black Orpheus* London: French and European Publications Inc

Sartre J-P 1991 *Critique of dialectical reason Vol 2: The intelligibility of history* London: Verso

Sartre J-P 1987 *The Family Idiot: Gustave Flaubert, 1821–1857, Volumes 1–5.* Chicago: University of Chicago Press

Sartre J-P 2001 *Colonialism and neo-colonialism* Paris Routledge France

Scottish Executive 2005a *Analysis of religion in the 2001 census: summary report* Edinburgh: Scottish Executive

Scottish Executive 2005b *Record of the Summit on Sectarianism 14 February 2005* Edinburgh: Scottish Executive

Scottish Executive 2005c *A Nation of Opportunity, Not a State of Fear: A progress report to the Summit on Sectarianism* Edinburgh: Scottish Executive

Scottish Executive 2006a *Action Plan on Tackling Sectarianism in Scotland* Edinburgh: Scottish Executive

Scottish Executive 2006b *Calling Time on Sectarianism* Edinburgh: Scottish Executive

Scottish Executive 2006c *Sectarianism: Update on Action Plan on Tackling Sectarianism in Scotland* Edinburgh: Scottish Executive

Scottish Executive 2006d *Review of Marches and Parades In Scotland: Report of the Working Group on Marches and Parades* Edinburgh: Scottish Executive

Sidaway J 2000 Postcolonial geographies: an exploratory essay *Progress in human geography* 24 591–612

Smith J 1984 Labour tradition in Glasgow and Liverpool *History workshop journal* 17 32–54

Soja E 1989 *Postmodern Geographies: The reassertion of space in social theory* London: Verso

Spivak G-C 1981 French Feminism in an international frame *Yale French Studies* 62 154–84

Spivak G-C 1988 Can the Subaltern Speak? in Nelson C and Grossberg B (editors) *Marxism and the Interpretation of Culture* Urbana, IL: University of Illinois Press, 271–313

Stewart J 1998 *The debate between Sartre and Merleau-Ponty* Illinois: Northwestern University Press

Thelen D 1989a Memory and American history *The Journal of American History* 75 1117–29

Thelen D 1989b Remembering and discovering the Watergate tapes: Introduction *The Journal of American History* 75 1222–7

Thompson P 2000 *The voice of the past: Oral history* Oxford: Oxford University Press

Walker G 1991 The Protestant Irish in Scotland In Devine TM (editor) *Irish immigrants and Scottish society in the nineteenth and twentieth centuries* Edinburgh: John Donald 212–27

Walls P and Williams R 2003 Sectarianism at work: Accounts of employment discrimination against Irish Catholics in Scotland *Ethnic and Racial Studies* 26 632–61

Walls P and Williams R 2004 Accounting for Irish Catholic ill health in Scotland: a qualitative exploration of some links between religion, class and health *Sociology of Health and Illness* 26 527–56

Walls P and Williams R 2005 Religious discrimination in Scotland: A rebuttal of Bruce et al.'s claim that sectarianism is a myth *Ethnic and Racial Studies* 28 759–67

Walter B 2001 *Outsiders inside: Whiteness, place and Irish women* London: Routledge

Wehrs DR 2003 Sartre's legacy in Postcolonial theory; or Who's afraid of non-western historiography and cultural studies? *New Literary History* 34 761–89

Withers CWJ 2007 *Placing the enlightenment: Thinking Geographically about the Age of Reason* Chicago: University of Chicago Press

Young R 2001 Sartre: the African philosopher. Introduction to Sartre J-P 2001 *Colonialism and neo-colonialism* Paris Routledge France 1–18

Index

www.ingramcontent.com/pod-product-compliance
Ingram Content Group UK Ltd.
Pitfield, Milton Keynes, MK11 3LW, UK
UKHW020358010325
455677UK00021B/519